THE FOREIGN VOCABULARY OF THE QUR'ĀN

THE FOREIGN VOCABULARY OF THE QUR'ĀN

ARTHUR JEFFERY

GYAN

Published by

GYAN

Gyan Publishing House
5, Ansari Road
Daryaganj, New Delhi-110002
Phone: 011-47034999, 9811692060
E-mail: books@gyanbooks.com

Distribution Network
gyanbooks.com
India, USA, Canada, UK, Australia

ISBN: 978-93-6780-597-8 (PB)

First Published, 1938

2nd Impression 2024

Printed at: Gyan Press, Delhi.

THE FOREIGN VOCABULARY OF THE QUR'ĀN
Author: ARTHUR JEFFERY

THE FOREIGN VOCABULARY OF THE QUR'ĀN

THE FOREIGN VOCABULARY OF THE QUR'ĀN

By

ARTHUR JEFFERY, Ph.D.
Professor of Semitic Languages
School of Oriental Studies
Cairo

1938
Oriental Institute
Baroda

TO MY WIFE

FOREWORD

Little further advance can be made in our interpretation of the Qur'ān or of the life of Muḥammad, until an exhaustive study has been made of the vocabulary of the Qur'ān. It is interesting to note how recent work at Islamic origins, such as that done by the late Professor Horovitz and his pupils at Frankfurt, and in the books of Tor Andrae and Karl Ahrens, has tended to run to a discussion of vocabulary. The Qur'ān is the first Arabic book, for though there was earlier poetry, it was not written down till much later, and some doubts have been raised as to the genuineness of what did get written down. For the interpretation of this first Arabic book, we have been content until recently to turn to the classical commentaries, but the tendency of the commentators is to interpret the book in the light of the Arabic language of their own day, and with few exceptions their philological lucubrations are of more interest for the study of the development of Muslim thought about the Qur'ān, than they are for settling the meaning the words must have had for the Prophet and for those who listened to his utterances.

Some day, it is to be hoped, we shall have a Glossary to the Qur'ān comparable with the great *Wörterbücher* we have to the Old and New Testaments, in which all the resources of philology, epigraphy, and textual criticism will be utilized for a thorough investigation of the vocabulary of the Qur'ān. Meanwhile this present Essay attempts to make one small contribution to the subject by studying a number of the non-Arabic elements in the Qur'ānic vocabulary.

Emphasis has been placed in recent years on the too long forgotten fact that Arabia at the time of Muḥammad was not isolated from the rest of the world, as Muslim authors would have us believe. There was at that time, as indeed for long before, full and constant contact with the surrounding peoples of Syria, Persia, and Abyssinia, and through intercourse there was a natural interchange of vocabulary. Where the Arabs came in contact with higher religion and higher civilization, they borrowed religious and cultural terms. This fact was fully recognized by the earliest circle of Muslim exegetes, who show no hesitation in noting words as of Jewish, Christian, or Iranian origin. Later, under the influence of the great divines, especially of ash-Shāfi'ī, this was pushed into the background, and an orthodox doctrine was elaborated to the effect that the Qur'ān was a unique production of the Arabic language. The modern Muslim savant, indeed, is as a rule seriously distressed by any discussion of the foreign origin of words in the Qur'ān.

To the Western student the Jewish or Christian origin of many of the technical terms in the Qur'ān is obvious at the first glance, and a little investigation makes it possible to identify many others. These identifications have been made by many scholars whose work is scattered in many periodicals in many languages. The present Essay is an attempt to gather them up and present them in a form convenient for the study of interested scholars both in the East and the West.

The Essay was originally written in 1926, and in its original form was roughly four times the size of the present volume. It would have been ideal to have published it in that form, but the publishing costs of such a work with full discussion and illustrative quotation, would have been prohibitive. The essential thing was to place in the hands of students a list of these foreign words which are recognized as such by our modern scholarship, with an indication of their probable origin, and of the sources to which the student may turn for fuller discussion. Our own discussion has therefore been cut down to the minimum consistent with intelligibility. The same reason has made it necessary to omit the Appendix, which consisted of the Arabic text, edited from two MSS. in the Royal Library at Cairo, of as-Suyūṭī's *al-Muhadhdhab*, which is the original treatise at the basis of his chapter on the foreign words in the *Itqān* and of his tractate entitled *al-Mutawakkilī*.

In making a choice of such references to the old poets as remain, it was thought better to retain those used in the older works of reference which would be generally accessible to students, rather than make a display of learning by references to a host of more modern works dealing with the early poetry. In the case of references to Iranian sources, however, the author, for lack of library facilities, has been compelled to limit himself to the few texts, now somewhat antiquated, which were available to him in Cairo.

No one is more conscious than the author of the limitations of his philological equipment for the task. A work of this nature could have been adequately treated only by a Nöldeke, whose intimate acquaintance with the literatures of the Oriental languages involved, none of us in this generation can emulate. With all its limitations and imperfections, however, it is hoped that it may provide a foundation from which other and better equipped scholars may proceed in the important task of investigation of the Qur'ānic vocabulary.

For reasons of general convenience the verse numbering of the Qur'ān citations is throughout that of Flügel's edition, not the Kūfan verse numbering followed in the Egyptian standard text.

The thanks of the author, as of all students interested in Oriental research, are due in a special manner to the kindness and generosity of H.H. the Maharaja Gaekwad of Baroda, which have permitted the work to appear in the series published under his august patronage.

ARTHUR JEFFERY.

CAIRO.
December, 1937.

BIBLIOGRAPHY

Addai Sher. *Al-Alfāẓ al-fārisiyya al-mu'arraba.* Beirut, 1908.

Aghānī. *Kitāb al-Aghānī of Abū'l-Faraj al-Iṣfahānī*, 20 vols. Cairo, 1868.

Ahlwardt, W. *Diwans of the Six Ancient Arabic Poets.* London, 1870.

Ahrens, K. "Christliches im Qoran," in *ZDMG*, lxxxiv (1930), pp. 15–68 and 148–190.

—— *Muhammed als Religionsstifter.* Leipzig, 1935.

Andrae, Tor. *Der Ursprung des Islams und das Christentum.* Upsala, 1926.

al-Baiḍāwī. *Anwār at-Tanzīl*, 5 parts. Cairo, 1330.

al-Baghawī. *Ma'ālim at-Tanzīl.* Four vols, on margin of Tafsīr al-Khāzin. Cairo, 1332.

Barth, J. *Sprachwissenschaftliche Untersuchungen zum Semitischen.* Leipzig, 1907–1911.

—— *Etymologische Studien zum Semitischen.* Leipzig, 1893.

Bartholomae, C. *Altiranisches Worterbuch.* Strassburg, 1904.

Bell, R. *Origin of Islam in its Christian Environment.* London, 1926.

Brockelmann, C. *Grundriss der vergleichenden Grammatik der semitischen Sprachen*, 2 vols. Berlin, 1908–13.

Burhān-i Qāṭi'. *Persian Lexicon.* Calcutta, 1818.

Caetani, L. *Annali dell' Islam*, vols. i and ii. Milano, 1905, 1907.

Cheikho, L. *An-Naṣrānīya wa Ādābuhā bain 'Arab al-Jāhiliyya.* Beirut, 1912–1923.

Corpus Inscriptionum Semiticarum. Paris, 1881 ff.

Cook, S. A. *Glossary of the Aramaic Inscriptions.* Cambridge, 1898.

Cooke, G. A. *North Semitic Inscriptions.* Oxford, 1903.

Delitzsch, F. *Wo lag Paradies?* Leipzig, 1881.

—— *Assyrisches Handwörterbuch.* Leipzig, 1896.

De Vogué, M. *La Syrie centrale : Inscriptions sémitiques.* Paris, 1868.

Dillmann, A. *Lexicon Linguae Aethiopicae.* Lipsiae, 1865.

Dinkard. Pahlavi Text and Translation of the *Dinkard* by Peshotun D. B. Sanjana, vols. i–iv. Bombay, 1880.

Dozy, R. *Supplément aux Dictionnaires arabes*, 2 vols. Leide, 1881.

Dussaud, R. *Mission dans les régions désertiques de la Syrie moyenne.* Paris, 1903.

Dvořák, R. *Über die Fremdworter im Koran.* Wien, 1885.

—— *Ein Beitrag zur Frage uber die Fremdworter im Koran.* München, 1884.

Eickmann, W. *Die Angelologie und Dämonologie des Korans.* Leipzig, 1908.

Encyclopædia of Islam. Ed. Houtsma, etc. Leiden, 1913 ff.

Euting, J. *Nabatäische Inschriften aus Arabien.* Berlin, 1885.

—— *Sinàitische Inschriften.* Berlin, 1891.

Fihrist. *Ibn an-Nadīm's Kitāb al-Fihrist*, ed. Flügel. Leipzig, 1871.

Fischer, A. *Glossar to Brünnow's Arabische Chrestomathie.* Berlin, 1928.

Fleischer, H. *Kleinere Schriften gesammelt*, 3 vols. Leipzig, 1885–8.

Fraenkel, S. *De Vocabulis in antiquis Arabum carminibus et in Corano peregrinis.* Leiden, 1880.

—— *Die Aramäischen Fremdwörter im Arabischen.* Leiden, 1886.

—— "Miscellen zum Koran," in *ZDMG*, lvi, 71 ff.

Frahang. Glossary to the *Frahang i Pahlavik*, by H. F. J. Junker. Heidelberg, 1912.

Freytag, G. *Lexicon Arabico-Latinum*, 4 vols. Halle, 1837.

Geiger, A. *Was hat Mohammed aus dem Judenthume aufgenommen?* Bonn, 1833.

Gesenius-Buhl. *Hebräisches und aramäisches Handworterbuch über das A. T.* Leipzig, 1899.

Geyer, R. "Zwei Gedichte von al-A'sha," in *SBAW.* Wien, 1904 and 1921.

Glaser, E. *Die Abessinier in Arabien und Afrika.* Munchen, 1895.

—— *Altjemenische Nachrichten.* München, 1908.

—— *Skizze der Geschichte und Geographie Arabiens.* Berlin, 1890.

Goldziher, I. *Die Richtungen der islamischen Koranauslegung.* Leiden, 1920.
—— *Muhammedanische Studien*, 2 vols. Halle, 1888–1890.
—— "Linguistisches aus der Literatur der muhammedanischen Mystik," in *ZDMG*, xxvi (1872).
—— *Abhandlungen zur arabischen Philologie.* Leiden, 1896.
Grimme, H. "Über einige Klassen südarabischer Lehnworter im Qoran," in *ZA*, xxvi (1912).
—— *Mohammed*, 2 vols. Münster, 1892–5.
Grünbaum, M. Über schem hammephorasch und über sprachliche Nachbildungen," in *ZDMG*, xxxix (1885).
Guidi, I. *Della Sede primitiva dei popoli semitici.* 1879.
Harris, Z. S. "Glossary of Phœnician," in his *Grammar of the Phœnician Language.* Philadelphia, 1936.
Herzfeld, E. *Paikuli. Monument and Inscription.* Berlin, 1924.
Hess, J. J. *Die Entzifferung der thamüdischen Inschriften.* Freiburg, 1911.
Hirschfeld, H. *New Researches into the Composition and Exegesis of the Qoran.* London, 1902.
—— *Beiträge zur Erklärung des Ḳorān.* Leipzig, 1886.
—— *Jüdische Elemente im Koran.* Berlin, 1878.
—— "Essai sur l'histoire des Juifs de Medine," in *REJ*, vii and ix. 1883–5.
Hommel, F. *Die Namen der Saugethiere bei den südsemitischen Volkern.* Leipzig, 1879.
—— *Südarabische Chrestomathie.* München, 1893.
Horn, P. *Grundriss der neupersischen Etymologie.* Strassburg, 1893.
Horovitz, J. *Das koranische Paradies.* Jerusalem, 1923.
—— "Jewish Proper Names and Derivatives in the Koran," in the *Hebrew Union College Annual*, ii. Cincinnati, 1925.
—— *Koranische Untersuchungen.* Berlin, 1926.
Hübschmann, H. "Die semitischen Lehnworter im Altarmenischen," in *ZDMG*, xlvi.
—— *Armenische Grammatik.* Theil i, "Etymologie." Leipzig, 1897.
—— *Persische Studien.* Strassburg, 1895.
Hurgronje, C. Snouck. Review of Fraenkel's "Aramaische Fremdworter," in *WZKM*, i. 1887.
Ibn Hishām. *Sīrat an-Nabī*, ed. Wustenfeld. Gottingen, 1858–1860.
Ibn Qutaiba. *Adab al-Kātib*, ed. Grunert. Leiden, 1909.
Ibn Sa'd. *Tabaqāt*, ed. Sachau et aliis. Leiden, 1904 ff.
Ibn al-Athīr. *An-Nihāya*, 4 vols. Cairo, 1322.
Jacob, G. *Das Leben der vorislamischen Beduinen, nach den Quellen geschildert.* Berlin, 1895.
al-Jawālīqī. *Al-Mu'arrab*, ed. Sachau. Leipzig, 1867.
al-Jawharī. *As-Sihāh*, 2 vols. Cairo, 1296.
Kāmil. *The Kāmil of al-Mubarrad*, ed. W. Wright. Leipzig, 1864–1892.
al-Khafājī. *Shifā al-Ghalīl fī mā fī Kalām al-'Arab min ad-Dakhīl.* Cairo, 1325.
al-Kindī. *Risāla*, ed. Muir. London, 1880.
Krauss, S. *Griechische und lateinische Lehnwörter im Talmud, Midrasch und Targum*, vol. ii. Berlin, 1899.
von Kremer. *Geschichte der herrschenden Ideen des Islams.* Leipzig, 1868.
—— *Culturgeschichtliche Streifzuge auf dem Gebiete des Islams.* Leipzig, 1873.
Lagarde, P. de. *Gesammelte Abhandlungen.* Leipzig, 1866.
—— *Persische Studien.* Göttingen, 1884.
—— *Armenische Studien.* Göttingen, 1877.
—— *Mittheilungen*, iii. Göttingen, 1889.
—— *Übersicht über die Bildung der Nomina.* Göttingen, 1889.
Lammens, H. *L'Arabie occidentale avant l'Hégire.* Beirut, 1928.
—— *La Mecque à la veille de l'Hégire.* Beirut, 1924.
—— *Les Sanctuaires préislamites dans l'Arabie occidentale.* Beirut, 1926.

Lane, E. W. *Arabic English Lexicon*, 8 vols. London, 1863-1893.
Leszynsky, R. *Die Juden in Arabien zur Zeit Mohammeds*. Berlin, 1910.
Levy, J. *Chaldäisches Wörterbuch über die Targumim*, 2 vols. Leipzig, 1867.
—— *Neuhebräisches und chaldäisches Wörterbuch über die Talmudim und Midraschim*, 4 vols. 1876.
Lewy, H. *Die semitischen Fremdwörter im Griechischen*. Berlin, 1895.
Lidzbarski, M. *Ephemeris für semitische Epigraphik*, 3 vols. Giessen, 1902 ff.
—— *Handbuch der nordsemitischen Epigraphik*. Weimar, 1898.
—— *Das Johannesbuch der Mandäer*, 2 vols. Giessen, 1905–1915.
Lisān al-'Arab. *Arabic Lexicon of Ibn Manẓūr*, 20 vols. Cairo, 1308.
Littmann, E. *Semitic Inscriptions*. New York, 1904.
—— "Zur Entzifferung der thamudenischen Inschriften," *MVAG*. Berlin, 1904.
Low, I. *Aramäische Pflanzennamen*. Leipzig, 1881.
Margoliouth, D. S. *Schweich Lectures on Relations between Arabs and Israelites*. London, 1924.
Mingana, A. "Syriac Influence on the Style of the Ḳur'an," in *Rylands Bulletin*. 1927.
Montgomery, J. A. *Aramaic Incantation Texts from Nippur*. Philadelphia, 1913.
Mordtmann und Müller. *Sabaische Denkmäler*. Wien, 1883.
Mordtmann, J. H. *Beiträge zur minäischen Epigraphik*. Weimar, 1897.
—— *Himjarische Inschriften*. Berlin, 1893.
Muḥīt al-Muḥīṭ. *Arabic Lexicon of Bustānī*, 2 vols. Beirut, 1867–1870.
Muller, D. H. *Epigraphische Denkmäler aus Arabien*. Wien, 1889.
—— "Arabisch-aramaische Glossen," in *WZKM*, i (1887).
—— "Südarabische Studien," in *SBAW*, Wien, 1887.
—— *Südarabische Denkmäler*. Wien, 1899.
—— *Epigraphische Denkmaler aus Abessinien*. Wien, 1894.
Noldeke, Th. *Geschichte des Qorans*. Gottingen, 1860.
—— *Mandaische Grammatik*. Halle, 1875.
—— *Neue Beiträge zur semitischen Sprachwissenschaft*. Strassburg, 1910.
—— *Persische Studien*, 2 vols. 1888–1892.
—— *Geschichte der Perser und Araber zur Zeit der Sasaniden*. Leiden, 1879.
—— *Die Ghassanischen Fürsten aus dem Hause Ǧafnas*. Berlin, 1887.
—— "Hatte Muhammed christliche Lehrer?" in *ZDMG*, xii (1858).
Noldeke-Schwally. *Geschichte des Qorans*, 2nd ed. vol. i. Leipzig, 1909.
Nyberg, H. S. *Hilfsbuch des Pehlevi. Glossar*. Uppsala, 1931.
Opitz, K. *Die Medizin im Koran*. Stuttgart, 1906.
Oxford Hebrew Lexicon, ed. Brown, Driver, and Briggs. Oxford, 1907.
Pahlavi-Pazand Glossary, by Hoshangji Jamaspji Asa, revised by M. Haug. Bombay, 1870.
Payne-Smith, R. *Thesaurus Syriacus*, 2 vols. 1879–1901.
Pautz, O. *Muhammeds Lehre von der Offenbarung*. Leipzig, 1898.
Qāmūs. *The Qāmūs of al-Fairūzabādī*, 2 vols. Cairo, 1298.
Rāghib. *Al Mufradāt fī Gharīb al-Qur'ān, of Rāghib al-Iṣfahānī*. Cairo, 1324.
Reichelt, H. *Awestisches Elementarbuch*. Heidelberg, 1909.
—— *Avestan Reader*, with Glossary. Strassburg, 1911.
Reckendorf, H. *Die syntaktischen Verhältnisse des Arabischen*. Leiden, 1898.
Rhodakanakis, N. "Zur semitischen Sprachwissenschaft," in *WZKM*, xxv.
Rossini, Conti. *Chrestomathia Arabica Meridionalis Epigraphica*, with Glossarium. Roma, 1931.
Rothstein, G. *Die Dynastie der Lakhmiden in al-Hīra*. Berlin, 1899.
Rudolph, W. *Die Abhängigkeit des Qorans von Judenthum und Christenthum*. Stuttgart, 1922.
Ryckmans, G. *Les Noms propres sud-sémitiques*, i–iii. Louvain, 1934–5.
Sacco, G. *Le credenze religiose di Maometto*. Roma, 1922.
Sachau, E. *Ǧawaliqi's Almu'arrab mit Erläuterungen herausgegeben*. Leipzig, 1867.

Salemann, C. "Mittelpersisch," in Geiger und Kuhn's *Grundriss der iranischen Philologie*. Strassburg, 1895.

—— *Maniçhäische Studien*. St. Petersburg, 1908.

Šāyast-ne-Šāyast, ed. with Glossary by Jehangir C. Tavadia. Hamburg, 1930.

Schulthess, Fr. *Lexicon Syropalæstinum*. Berlin, 1903.

Schwally, Fr. *Idioticon des christlich-palästinischen Aramäisch*. Giessen, 1893.

—— "Lexicalische Studien," in *ZDMG*, liii (1899).

Shikand-Gūmānīk-Vijār—the Sanskrit-Pazend Text edited with Glossary by Jamasp Asa and E. W. West. Bombay, 1887.

Siddiqi, A. *Studien über die persischen Fremdwörter im klassischen Arabisch*. Göttingen, 1919.

as-Sijistānī. *Nuzhat al-Qulūb fī Gharīb al-Qur'ān*. Cairo. 1924.

Spiegel, Fr. *Eranische Altertumskunde*, 3 vols. Leipzig, 1871–8.

—— *Die altpersische Keilinschriften*. Leipzig, 1881.

Spitta, W. "Lücken in Ǧawaliqi's al-Mu'arrab," in *ZDMG*, xxxiii (1879).

Sprenger, A. *Das Leben und die Lehre des Mohammad*, 3 vols. Berlin, 1861–5.

as-Suyūṭī. *Al-Itqān fī 'Ulūm al-Qur'ān*. Calcutta, 1852–4.

—— *Al-Muzhir fī 'Ulūm al-Lugha*, 2 vols. Cairo, 1282.

—— *Al-Mutawakkilī*, ed. Wm. Y. Bell. Cairo, 1926.

Sycz, S. *Ursprung und Wiedergabe der biblischen Eigennamen im Qoran*. Frankfurt, 1903.

aṭ-Ṭabarī. *Annales*, ed. De Goeje et aliis, 15 vols. Leiden, 1879–1901.

—— *Tafsīr al-Qur'ān*, 30 vols. Cairo, 1321.

Tāj al-'Arūs. *Arabic Lexicon of as-Sayyid Murtada*, 10 vols. Cairo, 1307.

ath-Tha'ālibī. *Kitāb Fiqh al-Lugha wa Sirr al-'Arabīya*. Cairo, 1923.

Tisdall, W. St. C. *The Original Sources of the Qur'ān*. London, 1911.

Torrey, C. C. *The Commercial-theological Terms in the Koran*. Leiden, 1892.

—— *The Jewish Foundation of Islam*. New York, 1933.

Vollers, K. "Beiträge zur Kenntniss der lebenden arabischen Sprache," in *ZDMG*, l and li (1896–7).

Vullers, J. A. *Lexicon Persico-Latinum Etymologicum*, 2 vols. Bonn, 1855.

Wellhausen, J. *Reste arabischen Heidenthums*, 2nd ed. Berlin, 1897.

Wensinck, A. J. *Mohammed en de Joden te Medina*. Leiden, 1908.

West, E. W. *Glossary and Index of Pahlavi Texts*. Bombay, 1874.

Yāqūt. *Mu'jam al-Buldān*, ed. Wustenfeld, 6 vols. Leipzig, 1866–1870.

az-Zamakhsharī. *al-Kashshāf*, ed. Nassau Lees. Calcutta, 1856.

—— *Asās al-Balāgha*, 2 vols. Cairo, 1923.

Zimmern, H. *Akkadische Fremdwörter als Beweis für babylonischen Kultureinfluss*. Leipzig, 1917.

ABBREVIATIONS

Act. Or	*Acta Orientalia*, ediderunt Societates Orientales Batava, Danica, Norvegica. Lugd. Batav. 1923 ff.
AIW	*Altiranisches Wörterbuch.* (Bartholomae.)
AJSL	*American Journal of Semitic Languages.*
BA	*Lexicon Syriacum of Bar Ali.*
Bagh	*Al-Baghawī's Commentary on the Qur'ān.*
Baiḍ	*Al-Baiḍāwī's Commentary on the Qur'ān.*
BB	*Lexicon Syriacum of Bar Bahlul.*
BDB	Brown, Driver, and Briggs *Oxford Hebrew Lexicon.*
Beit. Ass	*Beiträge für Assyriologie.*
BGA	De Goeje's *Bibliotheca Geographorum Arabicorum.*
BQ	*Lexicon Persicum, Burhān-i Qāṭi'.* Calcutta, 1818.
CIS	*Corpus Inscriptionum Semiticarum.*
Div. Hudh	*The Divan of the Hudhailites.* Part i, ed. Kosegarten; part ii, ed. Wellhausen.
EI	*Encyclopædia of Islam.*
ERE	*Encyclopædia of Religion and Ethics.*
GA	Lagarde's *Gesammelte Abhandlungen.*
GGA	*Göttingische Gelehrte Anzeigen.*
HAA	*Handbuch der altarabischen Altertumskunde*, i. Kopenhagen, 1927.
JA	*Journal asiatique.*
Jal	*The Qur'ān Commentary of Jalālain.*
JAOS	*Journal of the American Oriental Society.*
JASB	*Journal of the Asiatic Society of Bengal.*
JE	*The Jewish Encyclopædia*
JRAS	*Journal of the Royal Asiatic Society.*
JThS	*Journal of Theological Studies.*
KU	Horovitz's *Koranische Untersuchungen.*
LA	The Arabic Lexicon *Lisān al-'Arab.*
MGWJ	*Monatsschrift für Geschichte und Wissenschaft des Judentums.*
MVAG	*Mittheilungen der vorderasiatischen Gesellschaft.*
MW	*The Moslem World.*
NSI	Cooke's *North Semitic Inscriptions.*
OLZ	*Orientalische Literaturzeitung.*
PPGl	*Pahlavi-Pazend Glossary.*
PSBA	*Proceedings of the Society for Biblical Archæology.*
PSm	Payne Smith's *Thesaurus Syriacus.*
REJ	*Revue des Études juives.*
RES	*Répertoire d'épigraphie sémitique.*
ROC	*Revue de l'orient chrétien.*
SBAW	*Sitzungsberichte der königl. Akad. d. Wissenschaft.* (Berlin or Wien.)
TA	The Arabic Lexicon *Tāj al-'Arūs.*
Ṭab	Aṭ-Ṭabarī's *Commentary on the Qur'ān.*
ThLZ	*Theologisches Literaturzeitung.*
TW	*Targumisches Wörterbuch*, ed. Levy.
WZKM	*Wiener Zeitschrift für Kunde des Morgenlandes.*
ZA	*Zeitschrift für Assyriologie.*
Zam	Az-Zamakhsharī's *Commentary on the Qur'ān.*
ZATW	*Zeitschrift für alttestamentliche Wissenschaft.*
ZDMG	*Zeitschrift der deutschen Morgenländischen Gesellschaft.*
ZS	*Zeitschrift für Semitistik.*

INTRODUCTION

One of the few distinct impressions gleaned from a first perusal of the bewildering confusion of the Qur'ān, is that of the amount of material therein which is borrowed from the great religions that were active in Arabia at the time when the Qur'ān was in process of formation. From the fact that Muḥammad was an Arab, brought up in the midst of Arabian paganism and practising its rites himself until well on into manhood,[1] one would naturally have expected to find that Islam had its roots deep down in this old Arabian paganism. It comes, therefore, as no little surprise, to find how little of the religious life of this Arabian paganism is reflected in the pages of the Qur'ān. The names of a few old deities [2]; odd details of certain pagan ceremonies connected with rites of sacrifice and pilgrimage [3]; a few deep-rooted superstitions connected with Jinn, etc., and some fragments of old folk-tales,[4] form practically all the traces one can discover therein of this ancient religion in the midst of whose devotees Muḥammad was born and bred. It may be true, as Rudolph insists,[5] that in many passages of the Qur'ān the Islamic varnish only thinly covers a heathen substratum, but even a cursory reading of the book makes it plain that Muḥammad drew his inspiration not from the religious life and experiences of his own land and his own people, but from the great monotheistic religions which were pressing down into Arabia in his day.[6] Most of the personages who move through the pages of the Qur'ān, viz. Ibrāhīm, Mūsā, Dāwūd, Sulaimān, Nūḥ, 'Īsā, are well-known Biblical characters. So also the place-names—Bābil, Rūm, Madyan, Sabā', and many of the commonest religious terms—Shaiṭān, Tawrah, Injīl, Sakīna, Firdaus, Jahannam, are equally familiar to all who know the Jewish and Christian Scriptures. So one is not surprised

[1] Convincing proof of this is found in the statement of the Prophet quoted in Yāqūt, *Mu'jam*, iii, 664, to the effect that on a certain occasion he sacrificed a ewe to 'Uzzā, which he excuses on the ground that at that time he was following the religion of his people.

[2] Sūra, liii, 19, 20; lxx, 22, 23.

[3] ii, 153; xxii, 28–30; v, 1–4; xxii, 37.

[4] Such as those of 'Ād and Thamūd.

[5] *Abhängigkeit*, 26, n. 9. His reference here is to Sūras cxiii, cxiv in particular, but the statement is true of many passages elsewhere.

[6] Nöldeke-Schwally, ii, 121; Buhl, *EI*, ii, 1066; Ahrens, *Muhammed als Religionsstifter*, 22 ff.

at the judgment of some of the earlier investigators, such as Marracci, *Prodromus*, i, 41: "Ita ut Alcoranus sit mixtura trium legum, seu religionum, Hebraicae, Christianae, et Israeliticae, additis paucis quisquillis, quae e cerebro suo Mahumetus extraxit."

Closer examination of the question reveals even further and more detailed correspondences than these which appear on the surface,[1] and forces on one the conviction that not only the greater part of the religious vocabulary, but also most of the cultural vocabulary of the Qur'ān is of non-Arabic origin. The investigation of the "Fremdwörter" of the Qur'ān thus becomes a question of primary importance for the study of the origins of Islām, for as Hirschfeld remarks: "One of the principal difficulties before us is . . . to ascertain whether an idea or expression was Muhammad's spiritual property or borrowed from elsewhere, how he learnt it and to what extent it was altered to suit his purposes."[2] By tracing these words back to their sources we are able to estimate to some extent the influences which were working upon Muḥammad at various periods in his Mission, and by studying these religious terms in their native literature contemporary with Muḥammad, we can sometimes understand more exactly what he himself means by the terms he uses in the Qur'ān.

Quite early in the history of Islām, Muslims themselves were confronted with the perplexing problem of these foreign words, for it presented itself immediately they were called upon to face the task of interpreting their Scripture. With the death of the Prophet and the cutting off of the fountain of revelation, came the necessity of collecting the scattered fragments of this Revelation and issuing them in book form.[3] Then as the Qur'ān thus collected became recognized as the ultimate source of both religion and law, there came the necessity of interpretation.[4] The primary source of such interpretation was the immediate circle of the Prophet's Companions, who were naturally

[1] *Vide* Rudolph, *Abhängigkeit des Qorans von Judenthum und Christenthum*, 1922, and Ahrens, *Christliches im Qoran*, 1930.

[2] *New Researches*, p. 4.

[3] The popular Muslim account of the collection is given in as-Suyūṭī, *Itq*, 135, and in many other well-known works, e.g. *Fihrist*, 24: Ya'qūbī, *Historia*, ii, 152; Ibn al-Athīr, *Chronicon* (ed. Tornberg), ii, 279; iii, 86. See also Noldeke-Schwally, ii, 11 ff., and the criticism in Caetani, *Annali*, vii, pp. 407–418.

[4] Goldziher, *Richtungen*, 55 ff.

supposed to know best what the Prophet meant in many of his revelations [1]; so the tendency grew in later days to trace back all explanations to this circle, with the result that we frequently find various conflicting opinions traced back through different chains of authorities to the same person.[2]

Now it is conceivable that there may have been correct tradition from the Prophet himself in many cases as to the interpretation of some of the strange words that meet us in the Qur'ān, but if so, it is evident that this tradition was soon lost,[3] for by the time the classical exegetes came to compile their works there was a bewildering entanglement of elaborate lines of conflicting tradition as to the meaning of these words, all emanating from the same small circle of the Prophet's immediate Companions. Numerous examples of this can be found on almost every page of the great Commentaries of aṭ-Ṭabarī, al-Baghawī, or ar-Rāzī, but a typical case may be cited here in illustration.

Thrice in the Qur'ān [4] we find mention of a people called Ṣābians, الصابؤن, who with the Jews and Christians (i.e. the اهل الكتاب), and the Magians, receive special recognition and favour. Yet as to the identity of these Ṣābians we find among the authorities the widest divergences. Thus aṭ-Ṭabarī, in commenting on ii, 59, tells us that some held that they were a community without a religion, others said they were a monotheistic sect but without a Book or a Prophet: others said they worshipped angels, and others that they were a community of the People of the Book who followed the *Zabūr* (زبور), as the Jews followed the *Taurah* and the Christians the *Injīl*. Later writers have a still greater variety of opinions about them, that they were star-worshippers, descendants of the people of Noah, or some sect midway between

[1] Quite early we find popular opinion claiming that only the Companions, or followers of Companions, were capable of giving correct interpretations of the difficulties of the Qur'ān.

[2] e.g. in commenting on الرقيم in xviii, 8, aṭ-Ṭabarī gives us lines of tradition all going back to Ibn 'Abbās to prove that *Raqīm* means a *village*, a *valley*, a *writing*, or a *mountain*. Thus we are forced to conclude either that Ibn 'Abbās is a very unsafe authority whose opinion on the meaning of important words varied considerably at different times, or that the lines of tradition are worthless.

[3] Lists of interpretations coming from the Prophet himself are given by some writers, e.g. as-Suyūṭī, *Itqān*, 918 ff. (and see Goldziher, *Richtungen*, 64), but such have little value.

[4] ii, 59; v, 73; xxii, 17.

Jews and Christians, or between Jews and Magians—and in all these cases the chains of tradition go back, of course, to the immediate circle of the Prophet. It would seem almost incredible that when the Qur'ān grants special privilege and protection to four communities as true believers, no exact tradition as to the identity of one of these communities should have survived till the time when the Traditionists and Exegetes began their work of compilation. The facts, however, are plain, and if so much uncertainty existed on so important a matter as the identity of a protected community, one can imagine how the case stands with regard to unimportant little details which are of profound interest to the philologist to-day, but which, in the early days of Islām, had no doctrinal or political significance to bring them prominently before the attention of the Muslim savants.

The traditional account of the development of Qur'ānic exegesis,[1] of which this problem of the foreign words forms a part, makes it begin with Ibn 'Abbās, a cousin of the Prophet, whom later writers consider to have been the greatest of all authorities on this subject.[2] He is called the ترجمان القرآن, the بحر or sea of Qur'ānic science, the حبر الامّة Rabbi of the Community, and many traditions give wonderful accounts of his vast erudition and infallible scholarship.[3] Modern scholarship, however, has not been able to endorse this judgment,[4] and looks with considerable suspicion on most traditions going back to Ibn 'Abbās. It would seem, however, that he had access to stores of information supplied by Jewish converts such as Ka'b b. Matī'[5] and Wahb b. Munabbih,[6] so that frequently, although his own interpretation of a word or verse may be of little value, the material he produces from these authorities with the phrase زعم كعب, etc., may be of the first importance. Tradition also credits Ibn 'Abbās with founding a

[1] as-Suyūṭī, *Itq*, 908 ff., gives an account of the earliest exegesis of the Qur'ān. Goldziher, *Richtungen*, chaps. i and ii.

[2] "Er gilt als Übermensch des tafsir," as Goldziher neatly expresses it, *Richtungen*, 65.

[3] See an-Nawawī, 351–4; Ibn Ḥajar's *Iṣāba*, ii, 802–813 (and *Kāmil*, 566–9, for examples of his authoritative explanation).

[4] Siddiqi, 12, 13, treats him with more deference than is merited. As illustrating the opinion of modern scholarship, we may note the judgment of three very different savants: Buhl, *EI*, i, 20; Noldeke, *Sketches*, p. 108; Sacco, *Credenze*, p. viii.

[5] Usually called Ka'b al-Aḥbār. See an-Nawawī, 523; Ibn Ḥajar, iii, 635–639; *EI*, ii, 582.

[6] See an-Nawawī, 619.

School of Qur'ānic Exegesis, and gives him several famous pupils, notable among whom were Mujāhid,[1] 'Ikrima,[2] Ibn Jubair,[3] 'Aṭā',[4] and Ibn Abī Rabāḥ.[5] It is probable that all these men had more or less contact with Ibn 'Abbās, but it is hardly correct to think of them as pupils of his in this science or as carrying on his tradition as a School in the way we speak of the pupils of the great Jewish Doctors. Any student of the Tafsīr will have noticed how much of the traditional exegesis is traced back to this group, much of it possibly quite correctly, and this is particularly true of the statements as to the foreign words in the Qur'ān,[6] so that al-Jawālīqī at the commencement of his *Mu'arrab*[7] can shield himself behind their authority from any accusation of unorthodoxy.

It is clear that in the earliest circle of exegetes it was fully recognized and frankly admitted that there were numerous foreign words in the Qur'ān. Only a little later, however, when the dogma of the eternal nature of the Qur'ān was being elaborated, this was as strenuously denied, so that al-Jawālīqī can quote on the other side the statement of Abū 'Ubaida[8] as given by al-Ḥasan—" I heard Abū 'Ubaida say that whoever pretends that there is in the Qur'ān anything other than the Arabic tongue has made a serious charge against God, and he quoted the verse: 'Verily we have made it an Arabic Qur'ān.' "[9] The question is discussed by many Muslim writers, and is excellently summarized by as-Suyūṭī in the Introduction to his treatise *Al-Muhadhdhab*, and further in chap. xxxviii of his *Itqān* (Calcutta ed., pp. 314-326). The discussion is of sufficient interest to engage our attention here.

[1] Mujāhid b. Jabr died in A.D. 719 at the age of 83. See an-Nawawī, 540; adh-Dhahabī, i, 14.

[2] He was a Berber slave of Ibn 'Abbās and died about A.D. 723 at the age of 80. He is said to have travelled widely in Irāq, Khorasān, Egypt, and S. Arabia. See an-Nawawī, 431; Yāqūt, *Irshād*, v, 62 ff.; adh-Dhahabī, i, 14.

[3] Sa'īd Ibn Jubair died in A.D. 713 at the age of 49. See adh-Dhahabī, i, 11; an-Nawawī, 278.

[4] 'Aṭā' b. Yasār died in A.D. 712. See an-Nawawī, 424; adh-Dhahabī, i, 13.

[5] 'Atā' b. Abī Rabāh died in A.D. 733. See an-Nawawī, 422; adh-Dhahabī, i, 16.

[6] A glance at as-Suyūṭī's *Mutawakkilī* will serve to show how large a proportion of the foreign words he treats are traced back to the authority of one or other of the members of this circle.

[7] Ed. Sachau, p. 4, quoted also by al-Khafājī, 3. قال ابو عبيدة وروى عن ابن عباس ومجاهد وعكرمة وغيرهم فى احرف كثيرة انه من غير لسان العرب.

[8] Abū 'Ubaida Ma'mar b. al-Muthanna, the great Humanist of the reign of Harūn ar-Rashīd, who was of Judaeo-Persian origin and a student of the rare words in Arabic. See *Fihrist*, 53, 54; Ibn Khallikān, iii, 388; al-Anbārī, *Ṭabaqāt al-Udabā'*, 137; an-Nawawī, 748; Siddiqi, *Studien*, 29.

[9] as-Suyūṭī, *Itqān*, 315, gives the tradition a little differently.

It appears that in the Schools a majority of authorities were against the existence of foreign words in the Qur'ān. "The Imāms differ," says as-Suyūṭī (*Itq*, 314) "as to the occurrence of foreign words in the Qur'ān, but the majority, among whom are the Imām ash-Shāfi'ī,[1] and Ibn Jarīr,[2] and Abū 'Ubaida, and the Qāḍī Abū Bakr,[3] and Ibn Fāris,[4] are against their occurrence therein." The fundamental argument of these authorities is that the Qur'ān in many passages refers to itself as an Arabic Qur'ān,[5] and they lay particular stress on the passage xli, 44: وَلَوْ جَعَلْنَاهُ قُرْآنًا أَعْجَمِيًّا لَقَالُوا لَوْلَا فُصِّلَتْ آيَاتُهُ أَأَعْجَمِيٌّ وَعَرَبِيٌّ "Now had we made it a foreign Qur'ān they would have said—Why are its signs not made plain? Is it foreign and Arabic?"[6] The Qur'ān thus lays stress on the fact that this revelation has been sent down in a form which the Arabs will easily understand—لعلكم تعقلون[7]—and how,

[1] This is the great Jurist who died in A.D. 820. He seems to have been particularly vehement in his denial of the existence of non-Arabic elements in the Qur'ān, for as-Suyūṭī says فقد شدد الشافعي النكير على القائل بذلك (*Itq*, 315).

[2] This is aṭ-Ṭabarī, the well-known commentator, whose full name was Abū Ja'far Muhammad b. Jarīr aṭ-Ṭabarī (A.D. 838–923), whom as-Suyūṭī frequently quotes under the name Ibn Jarīr. The reference here is to his great Commentary in the Introduction to which he treats of this question of "Fremdworter".

[3] This is in all probability the Qāḍī Abū Bakr al-Bāqilānī whose book أعجاز القرآن as-Suyūṭī mentions among his sources for the compilation of the *Itqān*, cf. *Itq*, 14.

[4] Abū'l-Ḥusain Ahmad b. Fāris of Qazwīn, also very frequently quoted by as-Suyūṭī both in the *Itqān* and in the *Muzhir* as well as in his smaller works. See Yāqūt's *Irshād*, ii, 6, and for his works, *Fihrist*, 80; Ḥājjī Khalīfa, 770; and Flugel, *Die grammatischen Schulen der Araber* (Leipzig, 1862), p. 246.

[5] e.g. قرآنا عربيا xii, 2; xxxix, 29; xli, 2, 44; xlii, 5; xliii, 2; لسانا عربيا xvi, 105; xxvi, 195; xlvi, 11: حكما عربيا xiii, 37.

[6] Some points in this translation need a note. First, the لولا is usually rendered as "unless" and the sentence left an unfinished one. In Qur'ānic Arabic, however, لو seems to be used frequently as a simple interrogative (cf. Reckendorff, *Syntax*, p. 35; Nöldeke, *Neue Beiträge*, p. 21), and Ṭab. on this verse expressly takes it as meaning هل. As آيات properly means "signs", that rendering has been left here though this is one of the passages where it approaches very near its later sense of *verses*. The concluding words are capable of many interpretations, the usual being to contrast the clauses as, "Is it a foreign Qur'ān and they to whom it is sent Arabs?" or "Is it a foreign Qur'ān and he who speaks an Arab?"

[7] xliii, 2; xii, 2, etc.

they ask, could the Arabs have been expected to understand it, were it sent down in a non-Arabic tongue ? [1]

Others took a different line of argument, and claimed that the existence of foreign words in the Qur'ān would be a reflection on the sufficiency of Arabic as a medium for the divine revelation. The Qur'ān, said the theologians, is the final and most perfect of divine revelations, and Allah naturally chose to reveal the final revelation in the most perfect of all languages, so how can one pretend that Arabic was lacking in the necessary religious vocabulary, and that Allah had to borrow Nabataean or Persian or Syriac words to express His purpose ? as-Suyūṭī (*Itq*, 315) quotes Ibn Fāris as representative of this attitude. "Ibn Fāris said that if there is therein anything from a language other than Arabic that would raise a suspicion that Arabic was imperfect as compared with other tongues, so that it had to come in a language they did not know." If asked to account for the fact that the early authorities had great difficulty in explaining certain words which they were forced to conclude must be of foreign origin, a thing which would hardly have been likely were they ordinary Arabic words, the advocates of this view reply that the Arabic language is so rich and copious that it is practically beyond the powers of any ordinary mortal to encompass all its variety,[2] so it is no wonder if certain words were strange to the interpreters. In illustration of this they refer to a tradition that Ibn 'Abbās was uncertain about the meaning of the word فاطر until one day he overheard two desert Arabs quarrelling over a well, when suddenly one of them said انا فطرتها, and immediately its meaning became clear.[3] If further asked how the Prophet could have known all these words, they quote the dictum of

[1] Dvořák reminds us (*Fremdwörter*, 5) that Muḥammad himself used these words قرآنًا عربيًا to reply to the charge of his contemporaries that a foreigner instructed him (xvi, 105 ; xxv, 5 ; xliv, 13), his argument being—what he hears from this foreigner is a foreign tongue, whereas he himself understands only Arabic. Yet the Qur'ān is Arabic which they understand perfectly, so their charge is false, for how could they understand the Qur'ān if it were composed of what he learned from this foreigner ? This argument does not seem to have had much effect in convincing the Meccans to whom it was addressed (see Osborn, *Islam under the Arabs*, 20, 21), though later Muslim theologians regarded it as conclusive.

[2] So as-Suyūṭī, *Itq*, 315 : ولكن لغة العرب متسعة جدًا ولا يبعد ان تخفى على الاكابر الجلة.

[3] *Vide* Baiḍ, on vi, 14.

ash-Shāfi'ī, لا يحيط باللغة الا نبي "None but a Prophet thoroughly comprehends a language".[1]

The authority of the great philologers, however, carried much weight, and many were fain to admit that Ibn 'Abbās and his successors must have been right in stating that certain words were Abyssinian, or Persian, or Nabataean, and yet they were very unwilling to grant that Arabic was thus confessedly imperfect.[2] To meet the difficulty they came forward with the suggestion that these were odd cases of coincidence where Arabic and these other tongues happened to use the same word for the same thing, but which in the case of Arabic happened to be used for the first time in the Qur'ān. This, curiously enough, is the position taken by aṭ-Ṭabarī in his *Tafsīr*,[3] and is even seriously defended at the present day by the ultra-orthodox in spite of the overwhelming weight of the probabilities against such a series of coincidences, not to speak of the definite linguistic evidence of borrowing on the part of Arabic.

This line of argument was not one which was likely to commend itself to many of the more instructed Muslim savants, so we are not surprised to find others taking up a more likely-looking position and claiming that in cases where the two languages agree, it is the Abyssinian or Nabataean, or Syriac, or Persian which has borrowed from Arabic. Since Arabic is the most perfect and richest of all languages, they argued, it is much more likely that the surrounding peoples would have borrowed vocabulary from the Arabs than that the Arabs took over words from them. This, as-Suyūṭī tells us, was the

[1] The reference is to ash-Shāfi'ī's *Risāla* (Cairo, 1312), p. 13. See further on this point, Dvořák, *Fremdw.*, 10, with his references to Goldziher, *ZDMG*, xxvi, 768. There are several traditions as to Muhammad's great linguistic attainments, and he is said to have been particularly skilled in Ethiopic; cf. Goldziher, op. cit., 770. Perhaps the most curious of these traditions is that in *Kanz*, ii. 41, that the language of Ishmael was a lost tongue but that Gabriel came and instructed Muhammad therein.

[2] This jealousy for the perfection of their language is characteristically Oriental. An interesting example of it from a Syriac writer will be found in Budge's *Cave of Treasures*, 1928, p. 132.

[3] Cairo ed. of 1323, vol. i, pp. 6–9, on which see Loth in *ZDMG*, xxxv, 595. as-Suyūṭī, *Itq*, 315, summarized his view: "Said Ibn Jarīr—What is handed down from Ibn 'Abbās and others on the interpretation of words of the Qur'ān to the effect that they are Persian or Abyssinian or Nabataean, etc., only represents cases where there is coincidence among the languages, so that the Arabs, Persians, and Abyssinians happen to use the same word." There is an excellent example of this line of argument in as-Sijistānī, 111.

opinion of Shaidhala. "Said Abū'l-Ma'ālī 'Azīzī b. 'Abd al-Malik,[1] these words are found in the Arabic language for it is the widest of languages and the most copious in vocabulary, so it is possible that it was the first to use these words which others then adopted."[2]

The swing of the pendulum in the opposite direction is represented at its furthest extreme by those who say that the very fact of the Qur'ān being in Arabic is a proof that it is not a Divine Book, for had it been a heavenly revelation it would have come down in one of the Holy tongues, i.e. Hebrew or Syriac. Unfortunately, we know little about the supporters of this opinion, but the fact that aṭ-Ṭabarī considers it necessary to refute them would seem to show that they exercised no inconsiderable influence in certain circles. Such an extreme position, however, was never likely to gain general acceptance, and the popular view among such as were constrained to admit the conclusions of the philologers as to the existence of foreign words in the Qur'ān, was that this was not strange in view of the fact that the Qur'ān is the final revelation. The Qur'ān itself states that when a Prophet was sent to any people he preached in the language of that people so as to be understood by them. Thus, e.g. we read in xiv, 4, وَمَا أَرْسَلْنَا مِنْ رَسُولٍ إِلَّا بِلِسَانِ قَوْمِهِ لِيُبَيِّنَ لَهُمْ "and we have sent no Prophet save in the tongue of his own people that (his message) might be plain to them". So it is obvious that the Qur'ān, being sent to the Arab people, must be in Arabic, but since it sums up and completes all previous revelations, it is only to be expected that technical terms of Hebrew and Syriac or other origin which were used in previous revelations should be included in this final revelation. Moreover, as the Qur'ān is intended for all peoples, one should not be surprised to find in it something from all languages,[3] a

[1] i.e. Shaidhala, whom as-Suyūṭī frequently quotes among his authorities, *vide Itq*, 13; *Mutaw*, 45.

[2] *Itq*, 315.

[3] aṭ-Ṭabarī quotes in favour of this idea the savant Abū Maisara at-Tābi'ī al-Jalīl, whom as-Suyūṭī, *Itq*, 316, also quotes, adding that Sa'īd b. Jubair and Wahb. b. Munabbih were of the same opinion, and that Ibn an-Naqīb claimed that one of the خصائص of the Qur'ān distinguishing it above all other Scriptures, is that while it was revealed in the tongue of the people to whom it was first sent, it also contains much of the tongues of the three great Empires of Roum, Persia, and Abyssinia. Dvořák, *Fremdw*, 11, 12, points out that some Muslim writers have illustrated this point by taking the tradition of the seven احرف to refer to seven different languages from whose vocabulary something is used in the Qur'ān. Here, however, there is no question of "languages" but of different Arab dialects (cf. as-Suyūṭī, *Itq*, 110; Ibn al-Athīr, *Nihāya*, i, 250, 251), so this is really irrelevant to the discussion.

point which is sometimes emphasized by a reference to the claim that the Qur'ān contains all previous knowledge, and information about everything, which would not be true if it did not contain all languages.[1] Obviously all of all languages was not contained, but what was sweetest, most pleasant, and most suitable.[2]

The most sensible statement on this whole question, however, is that suggested by as-Suyūṭī, *Itq*, 316, and expounded by ath-Tha'ālibī[3] in his *Kitāb al-Jawāhir*, i, 17: "In my opinion the truth of the matter is this. The Qur'ān is in plain Arabic containing no word which is not Arabic or which cannot be understood without the help of some other language. For these (so-called foreign) words belonged to the (language of the) ancient Arabs, in whose tongue the Qur'ān was revealed, after they had had contact with other languages through commercial affairs and travel in Syria and Abyssinia, whereby the Arabs took over foreign words, altering some of them by dropping letters or lightening what was heavy in the foreign form. Then they used these words in their poetry and conversation so that they became like pure Arabic and were used in literature and thus occur in the Qur'ān. So if any Arab is ignorant about these words it is like his ignorance of the genuine elements of some other dialect, just as Ibn 'Abbās did not know the meaning of *Fāṭir*, etc. Thus the truth is that these words were foreign, but the Arabs made use of them and Arabicized them, so from this point of view they are Arabic.[4] As for aṭ-Ṭabarī's opinion that in these cases the two languages agree word for word, it is far-fetched, for one of them is the original and the other a derivative as a rule, though we do not absolutely rule out coincidence in a few exceptional cases."

If challenged as to how, on this view, the Qur'ān could be called قرآن عربى مبين "a plain Arabic Qur'ān", its defenders reply with as-Suyūṭī,[5] that the presence of a few foreign words therein no more makes it

[1] as-Suyūṭī, *Itq*, 316—an opinion which is quoted also by al-Khafājī, 3 and 4. See also *Itq*, 322.

[2] As as-Suyūṭī says: فاختير له من كل لغة اعذبها واخفّها واكثرها استعمالا للعرب.

[3] This is not the famous philologer whose *Fiqh al-Lugha* we shall have occasion to quote frequently in the course of our work, but a N. African exegete 'Abd ar-Raḥmān ath-Tha'ālibī, whose *Tafsīr* was published in four volumes at Algiers in 1905.

[4] So al-Jawālīqī, *Mu'arrab*, 5, says: ان هذه الحروف بغير لسان العرب فى الاصل ثم لفظت به العرب بالسنتها فعربته فصار عربيا بتعريبها اياه فهى عربية فى هذه الحال اعجمية الاصل, a sentiment which is echoed by al-Khafājī.

[5] *Itq*, 315.

non-Arabic than the presence of many Arabic words in a Persian ode makes the ode non-Persian. In any case the reference of عربی مبين is to the Qur'ān as a whole, and not to individual words in it. as-Suyūṭī even finds one authority [1] who considered that the presence in the Qur'ān of such words as استبرق and سندس for fine silk brocade, زنجبيل and مسك for precious spices, سرادق and اباريق, etc., for other articles of luxury and civilization, is a proof of the excellence of the Qur'ān, for the Qur'ān was to tell men of the best things and thus could not be bound down and limited by the rude civilization of the Arabs of the Jāhiliyya. Naturally the pre-Islamic Arabs had not words for many things belonging to the higher stage of civilization to which the Qur'ān was to lead them, and it was only natural that the Qur'ān should use the new words that were necessary to describe the new excellences, words which indeed were not unknown to many of the Arabs of the Jāhiliyya who had come into contact with the civilization of Persia and of Roum.

So as-Suyūṭī concludes with al-Jawālīqī and Ibn al-Jauzī that both parties to the quarrel are right.[2] The great philologers were right in claiming that there are foreign words in the Qur'ān, for in regard to origin (أصل) these words are Persian or Syrian or Abyssinian. But the Imām ash-Shāfi'ī and his followers are also right, for since these words have been adopted into the Arabic language and polished by the tongues of the Arabs, they are indeed Arabic.[3] So we can comfortably conclude—قد اختلطت هذه الحروف بكلام العرب فمن قال انها عربية فهو صادق ومن قال عجمية فصادق.

Turning now to the question of the languages from which these

[1] *Itq*, 316, 317.

[2] *Itq*, 318, and al-Jawālīqī, *Mu'arrab*, 5. The reference to Ibn al Jauzī is doubtless to his *Funūn al-Afnān*, which as-Suyūṭī often quotes, cf. *Itq*, 13, and *Mutaw*, 44.

[3] Note as-Suyūṭī's quotation on this point from Abū 'Ubaid al-Qāsim b. Sallām, a quotation which is also given with slight verbal alterations in *TA*, i, 9, as from Abū 'Ubaida.

borrowed words came, we find that as-Suyūṭī,[1] whose classification is the most complete that has come down to us, divides them in the *Mutawakkilī* into the following classes :—

(i) Words borrowed from Ethiopic (لسان الحبشة)

(ii) Words borrowed from Persian (اللغة الفارسية)

(iii) Words borrowed from Greek (اللغة الرومية)

(iv) Words borrowed from Indian (اللغة الهندية)

(v) Words borrowed from Syriac (اللغة السريانية)

(vi) Words borrowed from Hebrew (اللغة العبرانية)

(vii) Words borrowed from Nabataean (اللغة النبطية)

(viii) Words borrowed from Coptic (اللغة القبطية)

(ix) Words borrowed from Turkish (اللغة التركية)

(x) Words borrowed from Negro (اللغة الزنجية)

(xi) Words borrowed from Berber (اللغة البربرية)

It is obvious at the first glance that much of this is mere guesswork, and equally obvious that the philologers whom as-Suyūṭī quotes had frequently very little conception of the meaning of the linguistic terms they use. It is necessary, therefore, to inquire a little more closely into what may have been meant by these terms and what may have been the possibilities of Arabic having drawn on any of these languages for religious and cultural vocabulary.

(i) *Abyssinian.*—Philologically, Ethiopic, the ancient language of Abyssinia, is the most closely related to Arabic of all the Semitic tongues ; Ethiopic and Arabic, with the languages of the S. Arabian

[1] Sprenger's list, "Foreign Words Occurring in the Qoran," in *JASB*, xxi (1852), pp. 109–114, is taken from his MS. of as-Suyūṭī's *Al-Muhadhdhab*.

inscriptions, being grouped together as South Semitic as opposed to the North Semitic group. The modern Abyssinian languages, and particularly Amharic, have in some respects diverged very considerably from the ancient Ge'ez, but it was presumably this ancient language with which the Arabs were in contact in pre-Islamic days and during Muḥammad's lifetime. These contacts, as a matter of fact, were fairly close. For some time previous to the birth of Muḥammad the southern portion of Arabia had been under Abyssinian rule,[1] and tradition relates that Muḥammad was born in the Year of the Elephant, when Mecca was saved from the Abyssinian army which marched up under Abraha to destroy the city. It is practically certain that there were trade relations between Abyssinia and Arabia at a much earlier period than the Axumite occupation of Yemen,[2] and that friendly relations continued in spite of the Year of the Elephant is clear from the fact that Muḥammad is said to have sent his persecuted followers to seek refuge in Abyssinia,[3] and that the Meccan merchants employed a body of mercenary Abyssinian troops.[4]

That Muḥammad himself had personal contact with people who spoke لسان الحبشة seems to be indicated from the fact that tradition tells us that his first nurse was an Abyssinian woman, Umm Aiman,[5] that the man he chose as first Muezzin in Islam was Bilāl al-Ḥabashī, and the tradition already noted that the Prophet was particularly skilled in the Ethiopic language.[6]

Abyssinian slaves appear to have been not uncommon in Mecca after the rout of the famous army of the Elephant,[7] and it would not have been difficult for Muḥammad in his boyhood to have learned many words of religious significance from such sources.[8] It must

[1] aṭ Ṭabarī, *Annales*, i, 926 ff.; Ibn Hishām, 25 ff.; al-Mas'ūdī, *Murūj*, iii, 157, and see particularly Noldeke's *Sasaniden*, 186 ff.

[2] *EI*, i, 119, and Lammens, *La Mecque*, 281 ff.

[3] This was in A.D. 616, and is known as the First Hijra, cf. aṭ-Ṭabarī, *Annales*, i, 1181. Dvořák, *Fremdw*. 25, would derive some of the Ethiopic elements in the Qur'ān from the two Abyssinian migrations, but this is hardly likely.

[4] Lammens, "Les Ahābīsh," in *JA*, xie ser., vol. viii, 1916, p. 425 ff.

[5] Abū'l-Fidā, *Vita Mohammedis*, p. 2, an-Nawawī, 756.

[6] *Infra*, p. 8. al-Khafājī, 111, under سنه gives an example of the Prophet's use of Ethiopic.

[7] Azrakī, p. 97. See also Essay 1 in Lammens' *L'Arabie occidentale avant l'Hégire*, Beyrouth, 1928.

[8] Sprenger, *Moh. und der Koran*, p. 54, suggests that the mentor referred to in Sūra, xvi, 105, xxv, 5, 6, may have been an Abyssinian.

also be borne in mind that during the Axumite occupation of S. Arabia many Ethiopic words of cultural significance may have come into current use in Arabia through commercial and political intercourse.[1]

(ii) *Persian.*—The contacts between Arabia and the Sasanian Empire of Persia were very close in the period immediately preceding Islam. The Arab Kingdom centring in al-Ḥīra on the Euphrates had long been under Persian influence and was a prime centre for the diffusion of Iranian culture among the Arabs,[2] and in the titanic struggle between the Sasanian and Byzantine Empires, where al-Ḥīra had been set against the kingdom of Ghassān, other Arab tribes became involved and naturally came under the cultural influence of Persia.[3] The court of the Lakhmids at al-Ḥīra was in pre-Islamic times a famous centre of literary activity. The Christian poet 'Adī b. Zaid lived long at this court, as did the almost-Christian al-A'shā, and their poems are full of Persian words.[4] Other poets also, such as Ṭarafa and his uncle Mutalammis, Al-Ḥārith b. Ḥilliza, 'Amr b. Kulthūm, etc., had more or less connection with al-Ḥīra,[5] while in some accounts we find 'Abīd b. al-Abraṣ and others there. There is some evidence to suggest that it was from al-Ḥīra that the art of writing spread to the rest of the Arabian peninsula.[6] But not only along the Mesopotamian area was Persian influence felt. It was a Persian general and Persian influence which overthrew the Abyssinian suzerainty in S. Arabia during Muḥammad's lifetime,[7] and there is even a suspicion of Persian influence in Mecca itself. How far Persian cultural influence penetrated the peninsula we have little means of telling, but it will be remembered that one of Muḥammad's rivals was

[1] It has been noted by more than one scholar that the terms connected with seafaring and sea-borne trade seem to be greatly influenced by Ethiopic. Andrae, *Ursprung*, 15, speaking of this Axumite occupation says: "Mit den neuen Herrschern kamen aber sicher auch Geistliche heruber, und wir durfen annehmen, dass eine grosse Zahl der äthiopischen Lehnworter als Bezeichnung für kultische und religiöse Dinge, die uns im Koran begegnen, während dieser Periode ihren Weg in den arabischen Sprachschatz gefunden haben."

[2] Rothstein, *Die Dynastie der Lakhmiden in al-Ḥīra, passim*, and Siddiqi, 76.

[3] We even hear of Arabs in that region becoming Zoroastrians, *vide* note on اسبذى in Siddiqi, 79.

[4] Ibn Qutaiba, *Shi'r*, 136 f. Siddiqi, 82 ff., gives examples from other poets showing how great was the Persian influence on the poetry of that period.

[5] Nicholson, *Literary History*, p. 107, and Shanqīṭī's introduction to the *Mu'allaqāt*, Cairo, 1338.

[6] Rothstein, *Lakhmiden*, 27.

[7] aṭ-Ṭabarī, *Annales*, i, 948 ff.; Ibn Hishām, 41–6; Ḥamza, *Annales*, 139; and see Spiegel, *Eranische Altertumskunde*, iii, 454.

an-Naḍr b. al-Ḥārith, who frequently drew away the Prophet's audiences by his tales of Rustam and Isfandiyār.[1]

By فارسى the Muslim writers obviously mean the later Persian language which was known to them when Persia had long been an important part of the Islamic Empire, but the language which would have been known in Arabia in pre-Islamic times, the language with which Muḥammad himself may have come in contact, was Pahlavi,[2] the official language of the Sasanian Empire (A.D. 226–640).[3] This Pahlavi was a curious language whose written form was strangely compounded with Semitic elements, but which in its spoken form doubtless represented a more archaic form of the Persian we find in the later Muslim literature of Persia, though with a greater admixture of Semitic words.

The fact that the pre-Islamic and early Muslim contacts with Persia were with a people using Middle and not Modern Persian has frequently been forgotten by Oriental investigators into the foreign elements in Arabic. Thus Addai Sher on p. 4 of the Introduction to his study كتاب الالفاظ الفارسية المعربة, in detailing the changes which Persian words have undergone in passing into Arabic, complains that the Arabs frequently added a ج or a ق at the end of words, e.g. they wrote جوزينج or جوزينق for the Persian كوزينه, and قريج or قريق for the Persian كربه. In such cases, of course, the Arabic ج or ق represents the Pahlavi suffix و *k*, which in Modern Persian becomes ه after a short vowel, but is dropped after a long vowel,[4] as in فرشته beside Arm. Հրեշտակ from Phlv. [illegible]. A good example

[1] Ibn Hishām, 235, 236, and see Blochet in *RHR*, xl, 20 ff. Naḍr is supposed to be the person referred to in Sūra xxxi, 5.

[2] Or Middle Persian, as the philologists prefer to call it, see Salemann in Geiger and Kuhn's *Grundriss*, i, and Noldeke, "Zum Mittelpersischen," in *WZKM*, xvi, 1–12.

[3] Haug, "Essay on the Pahlavi Language," p. 33 in *PPGl*; Herzfeld, "Essay on Pahlavi," in *Paikuli*, pp. 52–73.

[4] *Vide* Haug, *Essay on Pahlavi*, p. 117, and Blochet in *Revue Sémitique*, iv, 267. "Note sur l'arabisation des mots persans."

of this occurs in the Qur'ān in the word استبرق, where the Persian word is استبره and the Arabic ق and Persian ه represent a Pahlavi ݢ which appears again very clearly in the Syriac ܐܣܛܒܪܓܐ and Armenian *ըստաւրակ*, which are borrowed from the same Pahlavi word.

It is unfortunate that the Middle Persian literature which has survived to our own time has survived only in late copies, but we have every reason to believe, as in the similar case of the Hebrew codices of the O.T., that the MSS. in our hands represent the genuine ancient books very faithfully. What is even more unfortunate is that so little of the Pahlavi literature has come down to us. It will be noticed in any treatment of the Persian element in early Arabic that there are many cases where there can be little doubt that we are dealing with words borrowed from an Iranian source, but where the only form which can be quoted in comparison is from Modern Persian, the older form from which the word would have been derived not having survived in the remnants of the Pahlavi literature which have come down to our day.[1]

as-Suyūṭī sometimes refers to Persian by the definite title فارسية and sometimes by the more indefinite أعجمية, which like عجمية he also frequently uses as meaning nothing more than *foreign*.[2] There is no ground, however, for thinking that any distinction of dialect is meant to be indicated by the varying use of these terms.

(iii) *Greek*.—as-Suyūṭī uses two terms for Greek in his discussion of the foreign words, viz. رومية and يونانية. Thus in discussing the word رقيم in *Itq*, 321, he tells us that Shaidhala said it was رومية, whereas on the same page in connection with the word سرى he quotes Shaidhala again as saying that the word was يونانية. Dvořák, *Fremdw*, 20, thinks that a distinction is being made here between ancient and medieval

[1] It is possible that a fuller acquaintance with Pahlavi would enable us to explain a number of strange terms in the Qur'ān for which at present we have no solution.

[2] See the discussion on the use of these terms in Dvořák, *Fremdw*, 20, 21.

Greek, and that when the word يونانية is used we are to understand the ancient Classical Greek, whereas in contradistinction to this رومية stands for Byzantine Greek. When, however, we come to examine the words which are said by as-Suyūṭī's authorities to be either رومية or يونانية we find that these authorities have no understanding whatever of the matter, and it seems in the last degree unlikely that any of them would have known the distinction between the two forms of Greek.[1]

Any direct contact with the Greek language at the time of Muḥammad or the period immediately preceding his birth, would necessarily have been with Byzantine Greek. At that time Byzantine influence was supreme in Syria and Palestine, and the Arab confederacy of Ghassān, which acted as a buffer state between the Byzantine Empire and the desert tribes, and was used as an offset to the Persian influence at al-Ḥīra, was a channel whereby Byzantine influence touched the Arabs at many points.[2] Intercourse with Constantinople was constant, and both the pre-Islamic poet Imrū'ul-Qais,[3] and the Ḥanīf 'Uthmān b. al-Ḥuwairith [4] are said to have visited the Byzantine court. Contact with Christian communities in Syria which used the Greek language was a channel for the introduction of Greek words, and some trade words may have come as a result of Greek commercial ventures along the Red Sea littoral,[5] as we learn from the *Periplus Maris Erythraei*,[6] that Arab captains and crews were employed in this trade.

Byzantine Greek as a spoken language was doubtless widely spread in Palestine and Syria at the time, and the presumption is that it would be not unfamiliar to many Arabs connected more or less closely

[1] But see Jāhiẓ, *Three Essays*, ed. Finkel, pp. 16, 17.

[2] Noldeke, *Ghassanischen Fursten*, p. 12 ff. Note also the Greek words occurring in the Nabataean inscriptions, e.g. אופרנס = εὐφόρνιος; אסרתגא = στρατηγός; סקלטיקא = συγκλητικός; הפרכיה = ἐπαρχεία, etc. (on all of which see Cook, *Glossary*), and the number of Greek words in the Palestinian Talmud (cf. S. Krauss, *Griechische und lateinische Lehnworter im Talmud*, Berlin, 1899).

[3] Rückert, *Amrilkais der Dichter und Konig*, 94 ff.; Shanqīṭī, p. 9; Nicholson, *Literary History*, 104.

[4] Ibn Hishām, 144; and see Caetani, *Annali*, i, p. 190.

[5] Thus there is reason to believe that the Ar. فلك is from ἐφόλκιον; cf. Vollers in *ZDMG*, li, 300, 325.

[6] In C. Müller, *Geogr. Graec. Min.*, i, 271.

with the Ghassânid confederacy. Epigraphical remains collected by de Vogüé [1] and others, show many bi-lingual inscriptions from N. Arabia in which one of the languages is Greek, so we cannot absolutely rule out the possibility that Greek words may have been borrowed directly into Arabic in the pre-Islamic period, as they undoubtedly were later,[2] but the Greek words in the Qur'ān seem nevertheless with few exceptions to have come into Arabic through Syriac.[3]

(iv) *Indian.*—It is somewhat difficult at times to decide what the philologers meant by اللغة الهندية. West Syrian ecclesiastical writers both in the pre-Islamic and early Islamic period commonly use the word ܗܢܕܘ for South Arabia and Ethiopia, and ܗܢܕܘܝܐ generally means *Ethiopian* even in the oldest literature.[4] Thus in the famous passage, Jer. xiii, 23, "Can the Ethiopian change his skin or the leopard change his spots," we find ܗܢܕܘܝܐ used to translate the Hebrew כושי (LXX Ἀιθίοψ),[5] and in the writings of Dionysius of Tell Maḥre,[6] and Michael the Syrian,[7] we find the S. Arabian and Abyssinian area called *India*.[8] It was not only the Syriac writers, however, who made this confusion. Epiphanius in the fourth century details the nine kingdoms of India,[9] and his mention among them of the *Homeritae* [10] and *Azumitae* [11] makes it obvious that he is referring to the Ethiopian Kingdom. Sozomen [12] and Socrates,[13] in their accounts of the mission of Frumentius to convert the people of this Kingdom, speak of them as τῶν Ἰνδῶν τῶν ἐνδοτέρω, and so the term passed to the Latin writers and from them to the geographers of the Middle Ages.[14] It is thus probable that in early Arabic اللغة الهندية referred to the language of S. Arabia.

[1] *La Syrie centrale*, 1868–1877.

[2] e.g. لغثيط = λογοθέτης the Chancellor of the Byzantine Court (cf. de Goeje, *Glossary*, p. 349); قندلفت = κανδηλάπτης from κανδήλα and ἅπτω (Dozy, *Supplément*, ii, 410); استيخارة = στιχάριον, a sacerdotal robe (Dozy, *Supplément*, i, 21).

[3] Dvořák, *Fremdw*, 25 agrees.

[4] *PSm*, sub voc.

[5] ܘܐܝܟ ܕܠܐ ܡܫܟܚ ܗܢܕܘܝܐ ܕܢܫܚܠܦ ܡܫܟܗ ܘܢܡܪܐ ܒܒܠܘܬܗ.

[6] In Assemani, *Bibl. Or.*, i, 359 ff.

[7] Ed. Chabot, ii, 183 ff.

[8] Mingana, *Rylands Library Bulletin*, x, 445, gives quotations from other less-known writers.

[9] Ed. Dindorf, iv, 179, 180, in the tractate *Libri de XII Gemmis*.

[10] i.e. the Ὁμηρῖται of *Haer*, lxvi, 83.

[11] i.e. the Ἀξωμῖται of *Haer*, lxvi, 83.

[12] *Hist. Eccl.*, ii, § 24.

[13] *Hist. Eccl.*, i, § 19. See also *Philostorgius*, ii, 6.

[14] See Yule's *Marco Polo* (ed. Cordier), ii, 431 ff., and Noldeke, *Sasaniden*, 222 n.

This S. Arabian language, or language group, as revealed to us from the inscriptions of the Minaean, Sabaean, Himyaritic, and other kingdoms, belongs to the S. Semitic group, and is closely related to Ethiopic, the classical language of Abyssinia. The latest inscriptions in the language date from A.D. 550, and the language would seem to have been supplanted by Arabic as a spoken language in those regions,[1] even before the time of Muḥammad, though the survival to the present day of the Mahri and Soqoṭri [2] dialects would seem to indicate that in odd corners this old language might have survived until quite a late period. With the break-up of the S. Arabian kingdom tribes of these peoples migrated to other areas of Arabia, so that at the commencement of the Islamic period we find them widely scattered over the peninsula.[3] Though when we meet them there they are using the N. Arabian dialects of the tribes among whom they dwelt,[4] there can be no doubt that words of S. Arabian origin could have found their way into Arabic from these scattered communities.

When we examine the words which the philologers class as *Indian*,[5] we find, however, that none of them are real S. Arabian words. They are merely words which the early authorities could not explain, and had to refer to some remote origin, and so for them الهند might quite well have meant the distant land of India, with which the Muslim conquests in the East had made them vaguely familiar.

(v) *Syriac.*—This is undoubtedly the most copious source of Qur'ānic borrowings. Syriac, which still survives to-day as a liturgical language and as the dialect of a few communities of Oriental Christians in Syria, Mesopotamia, and Persia, was at that time the spoken language of those Christian communities best known to the Arabs.[6] How widely Syriac was spoken at the time of Muḥammad

[1] Nicholson, *Literary History*, p. 6.

[2] Cf. D. H. Muller, *Die Mehri und Soqoṭri-Sprache*, Wien, 1902–5.

[3] *Vide* Blau, "Die Wanderung der sabäischen Völkerstämme," *ZDMG*, xxii (1868), p. 654 ff.

[4] This fact has been forgotten by Taha Ḥusein in his essay on the pre-Islamic poetry, where he argues against the genuineness of some of the old poetry on the ground that while the poet was of a South Arabian tribe his language is North Arabic, and not one of the South Arabian dialects.

[5] Cf. the list in as-Suyūṭī, *Mutaw*, 51, 52.

[6] For the purposes of this Essay, Syriac = Christian Aramaic, and thus includes the Christian-Palestinian dialect and the Aramaic dialect of the Christian population of N. Syria as well as the Classical Syriac dialect of Edessa, which is the one best known to us from the literature and commonly usurps to itself the title of Syriac.

in the area now known as Syria, is difficult to determine, but it seems fairly certain that while Greek was the dominant literary language in the region at that period the common people of native origin generally spoke Syriac. South of Syria, however, we find that the so-called Christian-Palestinian dialect was more or less in literary use down to the eleventh century,[1] while in the fifth and sixth centuries it was in such common use there and of such importance as to warrant a special translation of the Scriptures and Church manuals into the dialect.[2] It was in Mesopotamia, however, that Syriac was in widest use as a literary and as a colloquial language. It was from this area that Aramaic made such a profound impress on the Middle Persian language and literature,[3] and there can be no doubt that from the Syriac used by the Christian portion of the community of al-Ḥīra and the surrounding districts came the major portion of Syriac influence upon Arabic.

It will be remembered that it was in this area that one of the earliest forms of Arabic script, the Kūfic, was invented, based apparently on a modification of the Syriac script,[4] and it was from the same area that the system of vowel pointing in Arabic was developed from the old Nestorian system.[5] Here also in the court of the kings of al-Ḥīra, the Christian 'Ibādites laid the foundation of Arabic literature,[6] and it was in this area that Arab tribes such as Tamīm and Taghlib and Quḍā'a seem first to have come under Christian influence,[7] so that from here, along the trade routes, streams of Christian culture spread throughout Arabia.[8]

We are still in need of a critical discussion of the spread of Christianity in Arabia,[9] but one fact seems certain, namely that such Christianity as was known among the Arabs in pre-Islamic times was

[1] The date when the scribe Ābūd copied the Lectionary published by Erizzo, *Evangelarium Hierosolymitanum*, Verona, 1861.

[2] Noldeke, *ZDMG*, xxii, 525, gives this as the date of the version. Since about A.D. 700 (Schulthess, *Grammatik*, p. 7), the language has been superseded as a colloquial by Arabic, and there are Arabicisms to be met with in the MSS. which were written by Arabic-speaking monks, cf. Nöldeke, loc. cit., p. 523 n.

[3] See Haug in *PPGl*, and *Essays*, p. 81; and Salemann in Geiger and Kuhn's *Grundriss*, i, 250.

[4] Rothstein, *Lakhmiden*, 27; Moritz in *EI*, i, 383.

[5] Moritz in *EI*, i, 384.

[6] Nicholson, *Literary History*, 138.

[7] Cheikho, *Naṣrāniya*, see Index under these names.

[8] Nicholson, op. cit., 39.

[9] The discussion was begun by Wright, *Early Christianity in Arabia*, 1855, and continued, though in an uncritical way, by Cheikho in his *Naṣrāniya*. The latest and best discussion, though by no means complete, is in Andrae's *Ursprung*, 1926.

largely of the Syrian type, whether Jacobite or Nestorian. In the kingdom of Ghassān the dominant party appears to have been Monophysite,[1] though some, under Byzantine influence, became Melkite.[2] In al-Ḥīra also many important Christian families would seem to have been Monophysite, if we can believe the accounts of the mission of Simeon of Beth Arsham,[3] though the predominant party there was Nestorian.[4] The Christian community in S. Arabia at Najrān, which was perhaps the oldest Christian community in Arabia,[5] and whose persecution by the Jewish king Dhū Nawās is mentioned in the Qur'ān,[6] appears to have been a mixed community. There is no doubt that many of them were Nestorians,[7] while others as clearly were Monophysites more or less related to the Monophysite Church of Abyssinia.[8]

Vocabulary of Syriac origin was already coming into use in Arabia in pre-Islamic times. The court of al-Ḥīra was a rendezvous of the poets and litterateurs of the day. and many of the pre-Islamic poets, such as Imrū'ul-Qais, Mutalammis, and 'Adī b. Zaid, were Christians. Their poetry, naturally, was impregnated with Christian words and ideas, but even in the extant poetry of such non-Christians as an-Nābigha and al-A'shā,[9] who spent much time at al-Ḥīra, we find the same strong influences of Syrian Christianity.[10] The trade routes again were channels whereby Syriac vocabulary entered Arabic. The wine trade,[11] e.g., was largely in the hands of these Christians,[12] and so

[1] Nöldeke, *Ghassanischen Fursten*, pp. 20, 21. [2] Andrae, *Ursprung*, 31.

[3] See "Lives of the Eastern Saints", by John of Ephesus. in *Patr. Orient*, xvii, p. 140. These converts of Simeon are said to have been brought back to the orthodox faith by the preaching of Maraba (Labourt, *Le Christianisme dans l'Empire perse*, p. 191). Assemani, *Bibl. Or.*, iii, 2, 606, mentions Monophysite Bishops of al-Ḥīra.

[4] Andrae, *Ursprung*, 25; Lammens in *ROC*, ix, 32 ff.

[5] See the long account of them in Andrae, *Ursprung*, 7–24.

[6] Sūra, lxxxv, 4 ff. It is only fair, however, to state that Western scholars are not unanimous in accepting this as a reference to the persecution of Najrān, though the weight of probability is strongly in its favour.

[7] Cf. the "Histoire Nestorienne", in *Patr. Orient.*, v, 330 ff.

[8] Littmann, *Deutsche Aksum.-Expedition*, i, 50.

[9] There is a tradition that an-Nābigha was a Christian, on the strength of which Cheikho includes him among the Christian Arab poets, but Nicholson (*Literary History*, 123), rightly rejects the tradition as without authority. Al-A'shā also is frequently claimed as a Christian, and is included by Cheikho in his collection, but see Nicholson, p. 124.

[10] Wellhausen. *Reste*, 234; Lyall, *Ancient Arabian Poetry*, pp. 92 and 119: von Kremer in *SBAW*, Wien (1881), vol. xcviii, 555 ff.

[11] Jacob, *Altarabisches Beduinenleben*, 99, has an interesting note hereon, referring to *Aghānī*, viii, 79; cf. Wellhausen, *Reste*, 231.

[12] Though Jews also engaged in the trade, cf. Goldziher, *ZDMG*, xlvi, 185.

we find that most of the early Arabic terms in connection with this trade are of Syriac origin.[1]

There were slight differences in pronunciation between the Jacobites and the Nestorians, and Mingana notes that the vowelling of the proper names in the Qur'ān seems to follow the Nestorian pronunciation rather than the other,[2] though in many cases, as we shall see, the Qur'ānic forms approximate most closely to those found in the Christian-Palestinian dialect.

It is possible that certain of the Syriac words we find in the Qur'ān were introduced by Muḥammad himself. That he had personal contact with Christians of the Syrian Church is definitely stated in the Traditions. We read that he went in early life on trading journeys to Syria with the caravans of the Quraish,[3] and there is an account of how on one occasion he listened to a sermon by Quss, Bishop of Najrān,[4] at the festival of 'Ukāẓ near Mecca.[5] Earlier Christian writers suggested that his mentor was a monk named Sergius,[6] and the legends of Nestor and Baḥīra [7] at least show that there was an early recognition of the fact that Muḥammad was at one time in more or less close contact with Christians associated with the Syrian Church.[8]

[1] Rothstein, *Lakhmiden*, p. 26.

[2] *Syriac Influence*. 83. as-Suyūṭī once (*Itq*, 325) quotes a word as being from the Ḥaurānic dialect, by which he apparently means some dialect of Syriac.

[3] aṭ-Ṭabarī, *Annales*, i, 1123; Ibn Sa'd, I, i, 75 ff.; Ibn Hishām, 115 ff.; al-Mas'ūdī, *Murūj*, iv, 132, 152; Sprenger, *Mohammed und der Koran*, p. 6, sees in Sūra, xxxvii, 137, a recollection of his having passed the Dead Sea on one of these journeys.

[4] That he was Bishop of Najrān we learn from *LA*, viii, 58. From al-Baihāqī's *Mahāsin*, 351 ff., we would gather that he was rather an Arab soothsayer and fortune-teller.

[5] Jāhiẓ, *Bayān*, i, 119. *Khizāna*, i, 268. On Quss see Sprenger, *Leben*, i, 102 ff. and Andrae, *Ursprung*, 202 ff.

[6] Al-Kindi, *Risāla*, p. 76, and the Byzantine writers, e.g. ἦν δέ τις ψευδαββᾶς ὀνόματι Σέργιος, says George Phrantzes (ed. Niebuhr, p. 295). It is doubtful whether Sergius and Bahīra are different personages.

[7] aṭ-Ṭabarī, *Annales*, i, 1124; Ibn Sa'd, I, i, 76; al-Mas'ūdī, *Murūj*, iv, 153. On these legends see Hirschfeld, *New Researches*, 22 ff.; Gottheil, *ZA*, xiii, 189 ff.; Sprenger, *Leben*, i, 178 ff.; ii, 381 ff.; Caetani, *Annali*, i, 136, 169; Noldeke, *ZDMG*, xii, 699 ff.

[8] Nestor is obviously connected with Nestorianism (cf. ܢܣܛܘܪ) and Buḥaira or Baḥīra is the Syr. ܒܚܝܪܐ = ὁ ἐκλεκτός (Noldeke, *ZDMG*, xii, 704 n.), commonly used of monks (Nau, *Expansion nestorienne*, p. 215), though Hirschfeld, p. 23, argues that it is a Jewish word. Loth, *ZDMG*, xxxv, 620 ff., suggests that some of Muhammad's material may have come from one Ṣuhaib, a Greek from the region of Mosul. The question as to whether Muḥammad could have had a Scripture teacher has been discussed by the present writer in an essay in the volume, *From the Pyramids to Paul* (New York, 1935), pp. 95–118.

It goes without saying that not all the words which as-Suyūṭī's authorities class under the term السريانية are of Syriac origin. Goldziher has pointed out[1] that سرياني was frequently used by Muslim writers for anything ancient, time honoured, and consequently little understood, and he quotes a line from Ibn 'Abd Rabbihi, who in his *'Iqd al-Farīd*, speaking of a notoriously bad copyist, says: كان اذا نسخ الكتاب مرتين عاد سريانيا "if he copied a book twice 'twould be Syriac". Dvořák[2] also refers to a common Turkish phrase quoted by Vambéry: بو سريانيميدر بو بز اكليمه دق "Is it perhaps Syriac? We could not understand it," somewhat as we say, "It was all Greek to me." It is thus clear that سرياني in the writings of the Muslim exegetes may frequently have meant nothing more than that a word was of the old learned tongues and so more or less unintelligible to the ordinary person.

(vi) *Hebrew*.- We learn from the Muslim historians that Jews were prominent in the pre-Islamic community at Madīna,[3] and that there were in fact three considerable tribes of Jews in that area, the Banū Qainuqā', Banū Quraiẓa, and Banū Naḍīr,[4] who were proprietors of lands and plantations of palm trees, and who exercised no little influence on the Arabs around them.[5] There were also many Jewish tradesmen in the city who are said to have been particularly skilled as jewellers and armourers.[6] We learn also of communities at al-'Alā[7] (the ancient Dedan), Taima,[8] Khaibar,[9] and Fadak,[10] in North Arabia,

[1] *ZDMG*, xxvi, 774. [2] *Fremdwörter*, 22 n.

[3] Ibn Hishām, 351; aṭ-Ṭabarī, *Annales*, i, 1359 ff. For a discussion of their position and influence there, see Hirschfeld, *REJ*, vii, 167 ff.; Leszynsky, *Die Juden in Arabien*, 1910; and Wensinck, *De Joden te Medina*, Leiden, 1908.

[4] We learn also of a tribe Banū Hadal (or Handal or Bahdal), cf. Yāqūt *Mu'jam*, iv, 462, and see Hirschfeld, *REJ*, vii, 169 ff. The *Aghānī* also mentions other smaller tribes or families.

[5] *Aghānī*, xix, 94.

[6] Cf. Hirschfeld, op. cit.; Wellhausen, *Reste*, 230; Caetani, *Annali*, i, 386.

[7] Rudolph, *Abhängigkeit*, p. 1.

[8] Shammākh, *Divan*, ed. Shanqīṭi, p. 26; Yāqūt, *Mu'jam*, i, 907.

[9] Yāqūt, *Mu'jam*, ii, 504 ff.

[10] Yāqūt, *Mu'jam*, iii, 856, 857; Abū Dā'ūd, *Sunan*, xix, 26.

and doubtless they were known in many other areas from which, however, no evidence of their presence has survived. We have no evidence as to when they arrived in N. Arabia, but it was possibly at an early period.[1] Arabian legend places their first settlements there in the time of Moses and Aaron.[2] Acts ii, 11, would seem to indicate that there were settlements of them there at the commencement of the Christian era, and in the Mishna (Shabb. vi, 6)[3] we have fairly reliable evidence of early settlements in that area.[4] It has been frequently suggested that the destruction of Jerusalem in A.D. 70 drove many Jewish families to seek refuge in N. Arabia, and thus added to the importance of the communities already settled there.[5]

There were Jewish settlements also in S. Arabia.[6] Whether they were founded by Jews who had followed the spice road from N. Arabia,[7] or by traders who had crossed from Egypt or Abyssinia,[8] it is impossible now to say. Perhaps there were communities there from both these centres of trade. That they exercised no little religious influence there is indicated both by the Jewish imprint on many of the S. Arabian religious inscriptions,[9] and by the fact that we have very consistent tradition as to the conversion of one of the Himyarite kings to Judaism.[10] It was the persecution of the Christian communities by this proselyte Dhū Nawās, or Masrūq, which was said to have led to the Axumite invasion and occupation of S. Arabia.

The polemic of the Qur'ān itself is sufficient evidence of the importance of the Jews as a religious body in the community to which Muḥammad addressed his message. As, however, these Arabian Jews all bear Arab names, are organized in tribes on the Arab fashion, and, when we meet them in the literature, act and talk like genuine Arabs, some have thought that they were not real Jews but Arab

[1] Torrey, *Foundation*, 10 ff., argues for a considerable settlement of expatriated Jews in Taima as early as the sixth century B.C.

[2] *Aghānī*, xix, 94.

[3] i.e. fol. 65a.

[4] Notice also that there are numerous Arabic words and Arabisms in the Mishna, cf. Margoliouth, *Schweich Lectures*, p. 58.

[5] Caetani, *Annali*, i, 383; Leszynsky, *Die Juden in Arabien*, p. 6.

[6] *Aghānī*, xiii, 121.

[7] Rudolph, *Abhängigkeit*, p. 1; Wellhausen, *Reste*, 230.

[8] Caetani, *Studi*, i, 261.

[9] Margoliouth, op. cit., 67 ff., thinks there is some doubt about this, but see *MW*, xix, 13.

[10] Moberg, *Book of the Himyarites*, xlii ff.; Fell in *ZDMG*, xxxv, 1–74; Ibn Hishām, 20 ff.; aṭ Ṭabarī, *Annales*, i, 918 ff.; al-Mas'ūdī, *Murūj*, i, 129.

proselytes.[1] It is difficult, however, in face of the polemic of the Qur'ān, to think of them as other than Jews by race as well as religion, and their adoption of Arab customs may well be explained by the Jewish habit of assimilating themselves to the community in which they dwell.[2]

Whether these Jews had any great familiarity with Hebrew, however, is a different question. One would gather from the Qur'ān that they were far better acquainted with the Rabbinic writings than they were with the Scriptures, and when we find Muḥammad borrowing technical terms of Jewish origin they are generally of an Aramaic rather than a Hebrew form. It would seem from a passage in Ibn Hishām,[3] that they had a Beth ha-Midrash which Muḥammad visited on at least one occasion,[4] though we are left to conjecture what they studied there. Some accounts we have do not speak very highly of their intellectual acquirements.[5] On the whole, one would judge that much of Muḥammad's knowledge of Judaism was gained from the general stock of information about Jewish practice and versions of Jewish stories and legends that were current among the Arabs who had lived in contact with Jewish communities, for much of this material, as we shall see, can be found also in the old poetry.[6] Certainly some of his knowledge of Judaism came through Christian channels, as is demonstrated by the Christian form of many Old Testament

[1] Winckler, *MVAG*, vi, 222; Margoliouth, op. cit., 61. Hirschfeld, *New Researches*, p. 3, notes that the Arabs seem to have intermarried freely with them.

[2] The second essay in Lammen's *L'Arabie occidentale* contains much interesting material on the position of Jews in the Ḥijāz at the time of Muhammad, though he is inclined to emphasize their influence a little too strongly.

[3] p. 383 and Baiḍ, on Sūra, ii, 91. Abū Bakr also visited this Beth ha-Midrash, *vide* Ibn Hishām, 388. Pautz, *Offenbarung*, 39, translates the words بيت المدراس by *Synagogue*, but see Geiger, 13.

[4] There is also a Tradition that Muhammad used to listen to Jabr and Yasar, two Jewish smiths at Mecca, as they read together out of their Scriptures. *Vide* Margoliouth, *Mohammed*, 106.

[5] This is indeed suggested by the Qur'ān itself, Sūra, ii, 80, though we also gather from the Qur'ān that they had copies of their Scriptures and could write (ii, 73, 169). Ṭabarī, *Tafsīr*, xxi, 4, has a tradition that the Madinan Jews read the Torah in Hebrew and interpreted it in Arabic. (On their dialect, cf. Caetani, *Annali*, i, 386; Leszynsky, 22 ff.) As to what Scriptures we may reasonably suppose them to have possessed, see Hirschfeld, *New Researches*, 103.

[6] Torrey, *Foundations*, following Aug. Muller, assumes that these Arabian Jews spoke a Judaeo-Arabic dialect, and refers to this dialect all the curious forms found in the Qur'ān, e.g. زبور for מזמור, etc. The theory is interesting but hardly convincing. Even less convincing is the theory of Finkel, elaborated in an essay in *MW*, 1932, p. 169 ff., that the Jewish material in the Qur'ān comes from non-Talmudic, old Israelitish tradition.

names that occur in the Qur'ān.[1] It is probable that in the Qur'ān there is evidence that Muḥammad attempted to purchase information about the Scriptures from certain Jews of the city only to find later that they had deceived him,[2] and Geiger seems to suggest [3] that perhaps Muḥammad deliberately sought for and incorporated Jewish terminology into his revelation in order to win over the Jews before he made his final break with them.

as-Suyūṭī sometimes uses عبرية or عبرانية to denote Hebrew, and sometimes لغة اليهود, and once, in discussing لينة, he says that the word was بلسان يهود يثرب " in the tongue of the Madinan Jews ".[4] Dvořák, *Fremdw*, 19, would draw a distinction from as-Suyūṭī's use of these terms, taking عبرية and عبرانية to mean classical Hebrew, and لغة اليهود as the language of the Jews of later times, perhaps the dialectal Hebrew used in Arabia.[5] One is inclined to doubt, however, whether the Arab philologers had sufficient knowledge to make such a distinction between the earlier and later forms of Hebrew, and an examination of the words which as-Suyūṭī's authorities place in the two classes,[6] makes it perfectly clear that there is nothing more in this distinction than there is in his varying use of بالنبطية and بلغة النبط. Moreover, from *Muzhir*, i, 105, it would seem that the term عبرانية was used somewhat vaguely by the philologers.

(vii) *Nabataean*.—We find in as-Suyūṭī's lists quite a number of words which various authorities claim to be of Nabataean origin. The Nabataean kingdom, which from about the sixth century B.C. had stretched over the territory from the old Edomite kingdom in the

[1] See herein under اسمعيل, يونس, سليمان, الياس, etc. Mingana, *Syriac Influence*, 82, goes so far as to say that there is not a single Biblical name in the Qur'ān which is exclusively Hebrew in form.

[2] Sūra, ii, 74, 169.

[3] *Was hat Mohammed aus dem Judenthume aufgenommen*, p. 36.

[4] *Itq*, 324.

[5] Especially in view of the phrase : لغة يهود يثرب.

[6] *Vide Mutaw*, pp. 56–9.

south-east of Palestine as far north as Damascus,[1] was of Arab origin, and exercised no little influence on the Ḥaurān and N. Arabia, even after it was absorbed in the Roman *Provincia Arabia.* Its deities Allāt, Manūthu, and Hubalu, were reverenced even in Mecca,[2] and its period of power and prosperity was near enough to the period when we first come in contact with the pre-Islamic literature for the memory of it still to linger, much embellished with legendary details, in the poetic lore of the desert Arabs. We have a fair idea of the Nabataean language[3] from numerous inscriptions collected in N. Arabia,[4] but the Nemara inscription from the Ḥaurān, dated A.D. 328,[5] is in classical Arabic, though written in Nabataean characters, and shows that by that date the old Nabataean language had been supplanted by Arabic. When the philologers use the term نبطى, however, it does not necessarily refer to these Ναβαταῖοι of Petra and the Ḥaurān, for the Arabs used the word for many communities in Syria and Irāq, and as Nöldeke has shown,[6] the Muslim philologers really mean Aramaic when they speak of النبطية.

We have already discussed how Syriac words may have come into Arabic, and need say no more on the subject of the Christian Aramaic. If the Jews of Arabia were Jews by race, and not merely proselytes, we might expect that Jewish Aramaic would have been more commonly known among them than Hebrew,[7] and this is confirmed by the fact that, as we have already noticed, the Jewish words in the Qur'ān are more generally Aramaic in form than Hebrew. It is not necessary

[1] *ERE*, ix, 121, and Quatremère in *JA*. xv (1835, p. 5 ff.).

[2] אלת and מנותו are the اللات and مناة of Sūra, liii, 19, 20, and הבלו is the هبل who, as we learn from al-Mas'ūdī, *Murūj*, iv, 46, was the chief god of the Ka'ba.

[3] Nabataean was a dialect of West Aramaic, though full of Arabic words and idioms.

[4] Collections will be found in *CIS*, vol. ii; de Vogüé, *Inscriptions sémitiques*; and Euting, *Nabatäische Inschriften aus Arabien*, Berlin, 1885.

[5] Lidzbarski, *Ephemeris*, ii, 34.

[6] *ZDMG*, xxv, 122 ff. al-Mas'ūdī, *Murūj*, iii, 240, says that the country of Babel was occupied by the Nabataeans. Sometimes, however, نبطى is used just like سريانى to mean something in a language unintelligible to the Muslim savants, cf. the reference in Margoliouth's *Schweich Lectures*, p. 55 n., to *Iṣlah al-Mantiq*, p. 168.

[7] "The Jews in North Arabia and Syria read the Bible in Synagogues in the Hebrew original, but for domestic study they probably used Aramaic translations as did the Christians. Many Biblical words which occur in the Qur'an have evidently gone through an Aramaic channel."—Hirschfeld, *New Researches*, 32.

to assume that many of these words were borrowings of the Prophet himself, for in a city like Madīna, where Jewish influence was so strong and where there was apparently a keen interest in religious matters, it is probable that many such words would have been borrowed in pre-Islamic times, and as a matter of fact many such are to be found in the old poetry.[1]

It is not impossible, of course, that Aramaic words may have entered from sources which were neither Syriac nor Jewish, but it is doubtful if any words of the genuine Nabataean dialect are to be found in the Qur'ān. A glance at as-Suyūṭī's list of so-called Nabataean words[2] gives one the impression that the philologers used the term mainly as a cloak for their ignorance, نبطية being a good enough designation for any strange word whose origin they could not ascertain.[3]

(viii) *Coptic.*—as-Suyūṭī finds some six words which his authorities, Shaidhala, al-Wāsiṭī, and others, classed as Coptic loan words.[4] It hardly needs saying that none of them are Coptic, and indeed in the case of some of them one wonders why anyone ever thought of considering them other than Arabic. Coptic was the liturgical language of the Christian communities of Egypt at the time of Muḥammad, as indeed it has remained to the present day. How much more than a liturgical language it was is doubtful, though we have reason to believe that the cultural language, if not the language of everyday life in Egypt at that period, was Greek.[5] It is practically certain that Greek would have been the language of commerce, and we may well doubt whether any Coptic vocabulary would have entered Arabic along the trade routes.[6] It is a remarkable fact that the colloquial Arabic of Egypt which grew up after the Muslim conquest of the country, while it is full of Greek loan words contains but few words derived from Coptic.

That Muḥammad himself had at least one point of intimate contact

[1] The classical discussion of this element in Arabic vocabulary is Fraenkel's *Aramäische Fremdwörter im Arabischen*, Leiden, 1886.

[2] *Mutaw*, 59–62.

[3] So Dvořák, *Fremdw*, 21, 22.

[4] *Mutaw*, pp. 62–4.

[5] Burkitt, *JThS*, xxvii, 148 ff. suggests that Coptic was perhaps never much more than a liturgical language.

[6] Evidence of early contact with Mecca may be seen in the story of Coptic workmen having been employed in the rebuilding of the Ka'ba.

with Egyptian Christianity is evident from the fact that one of his concubines was Miriam, a Coptic slave girl,[1] who was the mother of his beloved son Ibrahīm, and the cause of no little scandal and flurry in the Prophet's domestic circle. It is possible that he learned a few Christian legends from Miriam, but if he learned along with them any new Christian terminology of Coptic origin, this has left no trace in the Qur'ān.

As we might expect, the Muslim philologers show no real acquaintance with the Coptic language, in spite of the fact that in discussing the word غساق as-Suyūṭī (*Itq*, 323) refers to a dialect of Coptic, viz. الطحاوية.[2] Dvořák, arguing from the fact that the philologers stated that الاولى meant الآخر in Coptic, and الآخر meant الاولى,[3] suggests that the Muslims simply made these statements in order to throw contempt on the Coptic community.[4] In any case it is clear that there is no philological justification whatever for their attribution of a Coptic origin to any Qur'ānic words.

(ix) *Turkish.* It goes without saying that no dialect of Turkish had any influence on Arabic until well on into the Islamic period. There is one word, however, which we find given as Turkish by quite an array of authorities including even al-Jawālīqī,[5] and Ibn Qutaiba,[6] viz. غساق, which occurs twice in the Qur'ān (xxxviii, 57, lxxviii, 25), and is said to mean the corruption which oozes from the bodies of the damned. The word غساق certainly can be found in the Turkish

[1] There is, of course, no certainty that Miriam was a Copt by race, and there are some grounds for thinking that she may have been an Abyssinian slave-girl living in Egypt before she was sent as a gift to Muhammad.

[2] طحا is a district of Upper Egypt, cf. Yāqūt, *Mu'jam*, iii, 516.

[3] *Itq*, 319; *Mutaw*, 63.

[4] *Fremdw*, 23, 24. Along with الاولى must be classed بطائن of lv, 54, which clearly means "inner linings", but which the same authorities, according to as-Suyūṭī, say means "exteriors" (ظواهر) in Coptic. It should be noted, however, that as-Suyūṭī also quotes authorities as claiming that وراء was Nabataean for امام, see *Itq*, 325; *Mutaw*, 61.

[5] *Mu'arrab*, 107 (cf. Khafājī, 142); as-Suyūṭī, *Itq*, 323; *Mutaw*, 64. Others, however, as we have seen, said it was Coptic.

[6] *Adab al-Kātib*, 527.

Lexicons, but is obviously a loan word from Arabic.[1] The only reason one can suggest for the common opinion that it was Turkish is that the word may in later times have come to be commonly used by the Turkish soldiery at the Muslim courts, so that the scholars, at a loss how to explain so curious a word, jumped to the conclusion that it must be Turkish, and this opinion was then, as usual, attributed to the circle of Ibn 'Abbās.

(x) *Negro.*—Two words, حصب meaning *fuel* and منسأة a *staff*, as-Suyūṭī tells us,[2] were considered by some authorities to be borrowings from the language of the woolly haired blacks الزنجية. This زنجية is the language of the زنوج, and the Lexicons inform us that الزنج is جيل من السودان,[3] so that زَنجى or زِنجى from زنج is like رومى from روم or فارسى from فرس. The only reason for the philologers classing Qur'ānic words as من الزنجية is that they were entirely at a loss to explain the words and so suggested an origin in some remote corner of the earth, which perhaps appealed to them as better than giving no origin at all.[4]

(xi) *Berber.*—Sometimes we find as-Suyūṭī quoting authority for words being بلغة البربر, and at other times for their being بلسان اهل المغرب or بلسان اهل الغرب, which mean the same thing.[5] By

[1] See Redhouse, *Turkish Lexicon*, sub voc.

[2] *Itq*, 320; *Mutaw*, 64. Other authorities, however, said that منسأة was Ethiopic (*Itq*, 325; *Mutaw*, 42).

[3] *LA*, iii, 114. The word is familiar to us from Zanzibar.

[4] "Es lässt sich nicht verkennen, dass wir es hier mit willkurlicher Verhullung und Verschönerung der Unwissenheit zu thun haben, die sich uberdies, indem sie eine weit abliegende Sprache als Ursprung eines Wortes hinstellt, moglicherweise auch den Schein der Gelehrsamkeit zu geben trachtet. Dies scheint mir der Fall bei den Wörtern zu sein, die auf die Sprache der Berbern, Neger, Afrikabewohner u.a. zuruckgeführt werden, Sprachen, die von unserem erweiterten Standpunkte der Wissenschaft wenig bekannt sind: umso weniger können wir eine Kenntniss derselben bei den Arabern voraussetzen, und noch weniger ihr Vorkommen im Koran erklären." Dvořák, *Fremdw*, 21.

[5] This is obvious from as-Suyūṭī's discussion of مهل, *vide Itq*, 325.

Berber, the philologers mean the Hamitic languages of N. Africa,[1] known to us at the present day from the Tamashek, Kabyli, and kindred dialects. The spread of Islam along N. Africa brought the Arabs into contact with these Berber tribes,[2] whose influence on Islam in that area was as profound as that of the Turks in Mesopotamia, but it is ridiculous to think that any elements of Berber vocabulary entered Arabic in the pre-Islamic or Qur'ānic period. One may doubt whether any of the Muslim philologers had any acquaintance with the Berber dialects,[3] and certainly the words quoted as Berber by as-Suyūṭī's authorities have no connection with any Hamitic tongue. Again all we can say is that these words were puzzles to the scholars of the day, and بلسان اهل المغرب or بلغة البربر at least sounded well as a cloak for their ignorance.

From the discussion thus far it has become obvious that we cannot rate very highly the work of the Muslim authorities who have dealt with this difficult and important subject.[4] Goldziher has well said that "to attempt to explain all that has been set forth (by these authorities) as Hebrew, Syriac, Nabataean, etc., from one's knowledge of these tongues would be undertaking a fruitless task. These, languages, like the people who spoke them, belong to a grey antiquity, and are merely general terms for anything mysterious, esoteric, and ununderstandable, and to which belongs everything of whose origin there is no certainty, but whose great age is obvious." [5] Occasionally one gets flashes of what looks like philological learning, as e.g. when we find aṭ-Ṭabarī in the Introduction to his *Tafsīr* (i, 6), quoting Ḥammād b. Salama on فرت من قسورة,[6] to the effect that the word for *lion* in

[1] See al-Mas'ūdī, *Murūj*, iii, 242, for the home of the Berbers.

[2] Once, in dealing with قنطار as-Suyūṭī (*Itq*, 323) refers to لسان اهل الافريقية, by which he probably means Berber.

[3] Their theories as to the origin of the Berbers are interesting. al-Mas'ūdī, *Murūj*, iii, 241, makes a curious confusion between the Philistines and the Phoenicians, for he tells us that the Berbers came from Palestine and settled in N. Africa, and that their kings were known as جالوت a dynastic name, the last bearer of which was the Jālūt who was killed by David.

[4] The philologers did much better in dealing with such foreign words outside the Qur'ān, i.e. with later borrowings of Islamic times. Some account of them and their methods will be found in Siddiqi, *Studien*, 14–64.

[5] *ZDMG*, xxvi, 766.

[6] lxxiv, 51. Ḥammād's line of Tradition as usual goes back to Ibn 'Abbās.

Arabic is أسد, in Persian شار, in Nabataean أريا, and in Ethiopic قسورة. An examination of the Lexicons, however, shows that there is nothing in Aramaic or Ethiopic even remotely resembling these words, though شار is somewhat like the Persian شير = Pahlavi ویط, *shêr* meaning *tiger* or *lion.*[1] Indeed, as a general rule, the philologers are at their best when dealing with Persian words, a fact which may perhaps be explained by the Persian origin of so many of these savants themselves.

All things considered, one is not surprised that they had so little success with the problems of the foreign words in the Qur'ān, or that they detected so few out of the relatively large number recognized by modern scholarship, for they had but the most meagre philological resources at their disposal. What is cause for surprise is that as-Suyūṭī is able to gather from the older authorities so many words whose Arabic origin to us is obvious, but which they regarded as foreign.

One group of these we may explain as Dvořák does,[2] as cases where the Arabic word is rare,[3] or occurs in a context where the usual meaning perhaps does not lie immediately on the surface, but where the word can be easily explained from related words or from the sense of the passage, and so comes to be regarded as a foreign word with that meaning. As examples we may take two words that are said to be the one Nabataean and the other Coptic.

(i) In xix, 24, we have the word تحت which as-Suyūṭī tells us [4] was considered by Abū'l-Qāsim in his *Lughāt al-Qur'ān*, and by al-Kirmānī in his *Al-'Ajā'ib*, to be a Nabataean word meaning بطن. The growth of this theory is fairly clear. The word occurs in a passage where Muḥammad is giving an account of the birth of Jesus, an account whose main features he had derived from some oral reproduction of the fables of the *Hist. Nativ. Mariae.* In the first place we note that the Qurrā' were not certain of the reading, for Baiḍ, *in loco*, tells us that some read فَنَادَاهَا مَنْ تَحْتَهَا while others read فَنَادَاهَا

[1] Cf. *PPGl*, 214; Horn, *Grundriss*, § 803. [2] *Fremdw*, 29.

[3] In the list of words of this class it will be noted that most are *hapax legomena* in the Qur'ān.

[4] *Itq*, 320; *Mutaw*, 63.

مِنْ تَحْتِهَا. Secondly, there was some difference of opinion among the exegetes as to whether the one who called was Gabriel, standing at the foot of the hill, or the babe Jesus. Now it seems clear that when they felt some difficulty over this تحت, certain of the exegetes who knew from Christian sources that the one who called was the babe, and who had probably heard of the legends of Jesus speaking to his mother before his birth,[1] assumed that تحت could not be taken here in its usual Arabic meaning of *beneath*, but must be a foreign word meaning بطن or *womb*. The guess of Nabataean, of course, has nothing to support it, for the Aramaic תחת like the Hebrew תחת, Syriac ܬܚܬ, and Ethiopic ታሕተ, has exactly the same meaning as the Arabic تحت.

(ii) In xii, 23, we read that Joseph's mistress says to him هيت لك. The word occurs only in this passage in the Qur'ān and is a rare expression even outside the Qur'ān, though, as has been pointed out by Barth,[2] there can be no question that it is genuine Arabic. It was so rare and unusual a word, however, that it was early taken by the exegetes as foreign [3] and explained as Coptic,[4] doubtless on the ground that the Egyptian lady would have spoken to her slave in the Egyptian tongue, and as the only Egyptian language known to the Muslim philologers was Coptic, this rare word was taken to be of Coptic origin.

Similarly سيّدها in xii, 25, which is explained as Coptic for زوجها,[5] was doubtless a case of the same sort, and likewise two other Coptic suggestions in the same Sūra, viz. مزجاة and بضاعة of xii, 88, both of

[1] See Tha'labī, *Qiṣaṣ al-Anbiyā'*, p. 269.

[2] *Sprachwiss. Untersuch*, i, 22, with reference to Ibn Ya'ish, i, 499, line 7. Cf. also Reckendorf, *Die syntaktischen Verhältnisse des Arabischen*, Leiden, 1898, p. 325; Wright, *Arabic Grammar*, i, 294 d.

[3] Siddiqi, *Studien*, 13.

[4] *Itq*, 325. Others thought it Aramaic (*Mutaw*, 54) or Ḥauranic (*Muzhir*, i, 130), or Hebrew (*Itq*, 325).

[5] *Itq*, 322, from Al-Wāsiṭī.

which are said to be Coptic for قليل,[1] though, of course, there is nothing in the Coptic vocabulary to justify this assertion, and the words are undoubtedly genuine Arabic.

In this group we may also class the following words collected by as-Suyūṭī from earlier authorities as foreign borrowings, but which are all obviously Arabic. عَبَّدْتَ in xxvi, 21, which is said to be Nabataean for قَتَّلْتَ,[2] also ابلعى in xi, 46, which some took to be Indian or Ethiopic for اشربى[3]; and اخلد of vii, 175, which was said to be Hebrew for مال[4]; and حصب of xxi, 98, said to be Zinjī for حطب[5]; also رَمْزًا in iii, 36, said to be a Hebrew word meaning تحريك الشفتين[6]; and رَهْوًا of xliv, 23, said to be of Nabataean or Syriac origin[7]; and شطر of ii, 139–145, which is claimed as Ethiopic[8]; and غاض in xi, 46; xiii, 9, also said to be Ethiopic[9]; also كُوِّرَ of xxxix, 7; lxxxi, 1, explained as the Persian for غور[10]; and لينة of lix, 5, said to be Hebrew[11]; and مناص of xxxviii, 2, said to be Nabataean or Coptic

[1] *Itq*, 324, and *Mutaw*, 63. There is apparently some confusion between the two on the part of the *Mutaw*, for in the *Muhadhdhab*, from which both the *Itqān* and the *Mutaw* draw, only مزجاة is given.

[2] *Itq*, 323, and see Dvořák, *Fremdw*, 29.

[3] *Itq*, 318; *Mutaw*, 39, 51. Ethiopic በለዐ (Heb. בָּלַע; Syr. ܒܠܥ; Aram. בְּלַע) will give a form አብለዐ, but the Qur'ānic ابلعى is doubtless a normal Arabic formation from بلع, cf. Rāghib, *Mufradāt*, 59.

[4] *Itq*, 318; *Mutaw*, 56.

[5] *Itq*, 320; *Mutaw*, 64; see also Fleischer, *Kl. Schr*, ii, 132.

[6] *Itq*, 321; *Mutaw*, 57.

[7] *Itq*, 321; *Mutaw*, 54, 61.

[8] *Itq*, 322; *Mutaw*, 37.

[9] *Itq*, 323; *Mutaw*, 45.

[10] *Itq*, 324; *Mutaw*, 46.

[11] *Itq*, 324; *Mutaw*, 59; and see Dvořák, *Fremdw*, 20.

for فرار[1]; and منسأة of xxxiv, 13,[2] and ناشئة of lxxiii, 6,[3] both of which are said to be derived from an Abyssinian source; also هَوْنًا of xxv, 64, claimed as Syriac or Hebrew[4]; and وزر of lxxv, 11, said to be Nabataean for الجبل والملجاء[5]; also يَحُور of lxxxiv, 14, explained by some as Ethiopic for يرجع,[6] and صهر of xxii, 21, said to be Berber for نضج[7]; also أصرى in iii, 75, which is said to be Nabataean for عهدى[8]; and أوّاه of ix, 115; xi, 77, which some took to be Abyssinian or Hebrew[9]; and اوّاب in xvii, 27, etc., which was also claimed as of Abyssinian origin[10]; and يصدون of xliii, 57, which some said meant يضجون in Ethiopic.[11]

Another group consists of rare words used in the Qur'ān, which may be Arabic or may not be. A word like قسورة in lxxiv, 51, is a puzzle at the present day, so that it is no wonder if it gave some trouble to the early exegetes. It is usually taken to mean *lion*, and as-Suyūṭī quotes authorities for its being an Abyssinian word.[12] There is no such word, however, in Ethiopic or any of the later Abyssinian dialects, the common Ethiopic words for *lion* being **አሰድ** = Ar. أسد, or **ዐንበሳ** (sometimes **አንበሳ**) = Ar. عنبس. Addai Sher, 126, suggests that the word is of Persian origin, but there seems no basis for this. So far as one can see there is nothing in any of the other languages

[1] *Itq*, 325; *Mutaw*, 63; the *Muhadhdhab* agrees with *Mutaw*.

[2] *Itq*, 325; *Mutaw*, 42, 64.

[3] *Itq*, 325; *Mutaw*, 43.

[4] *Itq*, 325; *Mutaw*, 53, 56.

[5] *Itq*, 325; *Mutaw*, 61.

[6] *Itq*, 325; *Mutaw*, 44, **ይሑር** from **ሖረ** is perhaps in mind here, or may be **ይሖር**.

[7] *Itq*, 326; *Mutaw*, 65.

[8] *Itq*, 319; *Mutaw*, 62.

[9] *Itq*, 319; *Mutaw*, 38, 57.

[10] *Itq*, 319; *Mutaw*, 42.

[11] *Itq*, 326; *Mutaw*, 44.

[12] *Itq*, 323; *Mutaw*, 43.

to help us out, and perhaps the simplest solution is to consider it as a formation from قسر, though the great variety of opinions on the word given by the early authorities makes its Arabic origin very doubtful. Very similar is مهل,[1] which is said to mean either *fused brass* or the *dregs of oil.*[2] as-Suyūṭī quotes early authorities for its being a Berber word,[3] which of course is absurd. Hebrew מָהוּל [4] and Aram. מְהַל, meaning to spoil wine by mixing water with it, may have some connection with the meaning عكر الزيت or دردى الزيت given by the Lexicons,[5] but it is difficult to derive the Qur'ānic مهل from this, and equally difficult to explain it as an Arabic word.[6]

Yet a third group consists of those few words where a little linguistic learning has led the Muslim philologers into sad error. For instance, the word إلّ which occurs only in ix, 8, apparently means *consanguinity, relationship*, and is a good Arabic word, yet we find as-Suyūṭī [7] telling us that Ibn Jinnī [8] said that many of the early authorities held that this إلّ was the name of God in Nabataean, the reference of course being to the common Semitic divine name *El.* Similarly منفطر of lxxiii, 18, which there is no reason for taking as other than a regular formation from فطر to *rend* or *cleave* (cf. Heb. פטר; Syr. ܦܛܪ), is said by some authorities to be Abyssinian,[9] on the ground, apparently, of some hazy connection in their minds between it and ፈጠረ. So also درّى of xxiv, 35, which Shaidhala and

[1] Sūra, xviii, 28; xliv, 45; lxx, 8.
[2] Jawharī, *Ṣiḥāḥ*, ii, 241; Rāghib, *Mufradāt*, 494.
[3] *Itq*, 325; *Mutaw*, 65.
[4] Used only in Is. i, 22.
[5] *LA*, xiv, 155.
[6] غسّاق of xxxviii, 57; lxxviii, 25 (cf. as-Suyūṭī, *Itq*, 323; *Mutaw*, 64), and طوى of xx, 12; lxxix, 16 (cf. as-Suyūṭī, *Itq*, 322; *Mutaw*, 57), are perhaps to be included along with these.
[7] *Itq*, 319; *Mutaw*, 61.
[8] The *Mutaw.* tells us that the reference is to his grammatical work *Al-Muhtasib.*
[9] *Itq*, 325; *Mutaw*, 43.

Abū'l-Qāsim said was of Abyssinian origin,[1] cannot be other than Arabic, the Eth. ድሪሪ providing a possibility of solution for philologers who found some difficulty in deriving دريّ from درّ *to flow abundantly.* With these we may perhaps class سَكَرٌ of xvi, 69, which was said to be Abyssinian for خلّ,[2] though Eth. ሰከር is from ሰክረ *to get drunk* (cognate with Heb. שכר; Syr. ܫܟܪ, and cf. Akk. *šikaru*, Gr. *σίκερα*), the difficulty apparently arising because the Arabic root سكر means *to fill a vessel.* Also حرم, a very common word, cognate with Heb. חרם, was by some taken to be Abyssinian,[3] doubtless because ሐረመ was commonly used in the technical sense of *to consecrate* or *dedicate* to God. Perhaps also أليم from ألِم *to suffer pain*, which some thought was a Zinjī word, and some Heb.,[4] should come under this head.

Perhaps a fourth class may be formed of a few words like طه and يس. These particular signs occur among the mystic letters of the Qur'ān, which Goossens takes with some probability as contractions for older names of the Sūras,[5] but which puzzled the exegetes, and are taken by them to be foreign words.[6] Similarly سينين of xcv, 2, is obviously only a variant of سيناء used for purposes of rhyme, but we learn from as-Suyūṭī that some authorities took it to be Abyssinian.[7]

As was to be expected, modern scholarship has detected many more words of foreign origin in the vocabulary of the Qur'ān than

[1] *Itq*, 320; *Mutaw*, 45.

[2] *Itq*, 321; *Mutaw*, 40.

[3] *Itq*, 320.

[4] *Itq*, 319; *Mutaw*, 58.

[5] In his article in *Der Islam*, xiii, 191 ff.

[6] For طه see as-Suyūṭī, *Itq*, 322; *Mutaw*, 40, 52, 61; and for يس *Itq*, 325; *Mutaw*, 42.

[7] *Itq*, 322; *Mutaw*, 44. As these authorities say it means *beautiful* in Eth. and ሠነየ does mean *to be beautiful*, we might perhaps class سينين in group three as a blunder due to uncritical knowledge of the cognate languages.

were ever noted by Muslim investigators. In the sixth century Arabia was surrounded on all sides by nations of a higher civilization, the Empires of Byzantium, Persia, and Abyssinia possessed most of her fertile territory, and mighty religious influences, both Jewish and Christian, were at work in the peninsula at the time when Muḥammad was born. In his young manhood Muḥammad was greatly impressed by this higher civilization and particularly by the religion of the great Empire of Roum, and there can be no serious doubt that his conception of his mission, as he first clearly outlined it for himself, was to provide for the Arabs the benefit of this religion and in some measure this civilization.[1] It was therefore natural that the Qur'ān should contain a large number of religious and cultural terms borrowed from these surrounding communities. This religion, as he insists over and over again in the Qur'ān, is something new to the Arabs : it was not likely, therefore, that native Arabic vocabulary would be adequate to express all its new ideas, so the obvious policy was to borrow and adapt the necessary technical terms.[2] Many of these terms, as a matter of fact, were there ready to his hand, having already come into use in Arabia in pre-Islamic times, partly through Arab tribes who had accepted Christianity, partly through commerce with Jews, Christians, and Persians, and partly through earlier inquirers interested in these religions. In fact it is very probable that if we knew more about those elusive personalities—Umayya b. Abī'ṣ-Ṣalt, Musailama, and the Ḥanīfs, we should find that there was in Arabia at that time a little circle of seekers after monotheism who were using a fairly definite vocabulary of religious terms of Jewish and Christian origin, and illustrating their preaching by a little group of stories partly of Judaeo-Christian, and partly Arabian origin. In the beginning Muḥammad but followed in their footsteps, but he grasped the political arm and became a figure in the world, while of the others we can now discern but the hazy outlines, though they so largely prepared the way for him.

It is clear also that Muḥammad set himself definitely to learn about things Jewish and Christian,[3] and thus undoubtedly himself

[1] Bell, *Origin*, 98, 99.

[2] "Thus the Qur'an appeared so foreign to everything with which Arabic thought was familiar, that the ordinary vernacular was inadequate to express all these new ideas," Hirschfeld, *New Researches*, p. 4.

[3] Hirschfeld, however, goes a little too far when he says, *New Researches*, 13, "Before entering on his first ministry, Muhammed had undergone what I should like to call a course of Biblical training."

imported new technical terms from these sources. It has been remarked not infrequently that the Prophet had a penchant for strange and mysterious sounding words,[1] and seemed to love to puzzle his audiences with these new terms,[2] though frequently he himself had not grasped correctly their meaning, as one sees in such cases as فرقان and سكينة. Sometimes he seems even to have invented words, such as غساق, تسنيم, and سلسبيل.[3]

The foreign elements in the Qur'ānic vocabulary are of three distinct kinds:—

(i) Words which are entirely non-Arabic, such as زنجبيل, استبرق, فردوس, نمارق, etc., which cannot by any linguistic juggling be reduced to developments from an Arabic root, or which though seemingly triliteral, e.g. جبت, have no verbal root in Arabic. These words were taken over as such from some non-Arabic source.

(ii) Words which are Semitic and whose triliteral root may be found in Arabic, but which nevertheless in the Qur'ān are used not in the Arabic sense of the root, but in a sense which developed in one of the other languages. Such words as بارك, درس, صوامع, فاطر are illustrations. Words of this class when once naturalized in Arabic may and do develop nominal and verbal forms in a truly Arabic manner, and thus frequently disguise the fact that originally they were borrowings from outside.

(iii) Words which are genuinely Arabic and commonly used in the Arabic language, but which as used in the Qur'ān have been coloured in their meaning by the use of the cognate languages. For instance, نور meaning *light* is a common enough Arabic word, but when

[1] Hirschfeld, op. cit., 5; Dvořák, *Fremdw*, 17, who says: "In solchen Fällen haben wir dann nichts anderes anzunehmen, als das Streben Muhammed's, durch die seinen Landsleuten mehr oder weniger unverständlichen Ausdrucke sich selbst den Schein der Gelehrsamkeit zu geben und zu imponiren, vielleicht auch die Absicht, mystisch und undeutlich zu sein"; Bell, *Origin*, 51.

[2] Cf. Sūra, ci, 1, 2, 6, 7; lxxiv, 27; lxxxvi, 1, 2, etc.

[3] Nöldeke, *Sketches*, 38.

used with the meaning of *religion* as in ix, 32—"But God determineth to perfect His religion though the unbelievers abhor it," it is undoubtedly under the influence of the Syr. use of ܕܝܢܐ. So روح used in a theological sense has been influenced by ܪܘܚܐ,[1] and in particular روح القدس is obviously the Syriac ܪܘܚܐ ܕܩܘܕܫܐ.[2] So أمّ in the sense of *metropolis* in vi, 92, etc., was doubtless influenced by the Syr. ܐܡܐ,[3] and نفس when used as a technical religious term may have come under the influence of the Christian use of ܢܦܫܐ.[4] Sometimes there is no doubt of the Qur'ānic word being a translation of some technical term in one of the cognate languages. A clear instance is that of كلمة used of Jesus in iv, 169, etc., where it is obviously a translation of the Syr. ܡܠܬܐ of Jno. i, 1, etc.,[5] which like the Eth. ቃል and the Copt. ϣⲁϫⲉ represents the Gk. λόγος. Similarly رسول is doubtless a translation of the Syr. ܫܠܝܚܐ = ἀπόστολος, and يوم and ساعة in eschatological passages translate the ἡμέρα and ὥρα of the Judaeo-Christian eschatological writings.[6] Casanova [7] claims that علم in such passages as ii, 140, 114; iii, 17, 54, 59, etc., has a technical meaning associated with كتاب and is opposed to the word جاهلية,[8] and is thus meant as a translation of γνῶσις,[9] and so of Christian or Gnostic origin. So one might go on enumerating words of undoubtedly

[1] Cf. the Mandaean רוחא in Lidzbarski's *Mandäische Liturgien*, Berlin, 1920.

[2] Mingana, *Syriac Influence*, 85; Pautz, *Offenbarung*, 36; Fraenkel, *Vocab*, 24.

[3] Mingana, op. cit., 88; Horovitz, *KU*, 141, though אם is used in precisely the same sense on Phoenician coins.

[4] Mingana, op. cit., 85.

[5] Margoliouth, *ERE*, x, 540.

[6] Doubtless through the Syr. ܝܘܡܐ and ܫܥܬܐ.

[7] *Mohammed et la fin du monde*, 88 ff.

[8] Which Wellhausen, *Reste*, 71, n. 1, considered to be a translation of ἄγνοια as in Acts xvii, 30. See also, Casanova, 90; Gerock, *Christologie*, 104; Noldeke-Schwally, i, 242, n. 10. Lidzbarski, *ZS*, i, 94, suggested Gnostic influence here.

[9] Again probably through the Syr. ܝܕܥܬܐ.

Arabic origin, but which as used in the Qur'ān have been influenced more or less by the vocabulary of the religions which were so strongly influencing Arabia just before Muḥammad's day and which made such a profound impress on his own teachings. As these, however, can hardly be called foreign words, only in the rarest instances are they included in the following lists.

Philological questions as to the changes which foreign words undergo in coming into Arabic, need not be discussed here, as such discussion has already been given for Aramaic words by Fraenkel in the Introduction to his *Aramäische Fremdwörter*, and for Iranian words by Siddiqi, *Studien*, 19 ff., 65 ff. On the broader question of demonstration of borrowing, the writer feels that the form of demonstration demanded by certain modern writers is really uncalled for and unnecessary. The English musical terms *piano*, *cantata*, *soprano*, *adagio*, *fortissimo*, *contralto*, *arpeggio*, etc., are obviously borrowed from the Italian, and there is no need of an elaborate demonstration of cultural contact with dates and names and historical connections, to prove that these words, though English, are of Italian origin. Similarly such Arabic words as استبرق ; زنجبيل ; مِسْك ; جناح are on the very surface obvious borrowings from Middle Persian, and the philological argument for their foreign origin is perfectly valid on its own ground, without elaborate proof of cultural contact, etc., in each individual case.

THE FOREIGN WORDS

أَبٌّ (*abb*).

lxxx, 31.

Herbage.

It occurs only in an early Meccan passage describing the good things God has caused to grow on the earth by sending down rain. The early authorities in Islam were puzzled by the word as is evident from the discussion by Ṭab. on the verse, and the uncertainty evidenced by Zam. and Baiḍ. in their comments, an uncertainty which is shared by the Lexicons (cf. *LA*, i, 199; Ibn al-Athīr, *Nihāya*, i, 10), and particularly by the instructive story given in Bagh, vii, 175. as-Suyūṭī, *Itq*, 318, quotes Shaidhala as authority for its being a foreign word meaning *grass* in the language of اهل الغرب, by which, as we gather from the *Mutaw*, 65, he means the Berber tongue.

There can be little doubt that it is the Aram. איבא (= אנבה of Dan. iv, 9, where the Dagesh forte is resolved into Nūn). The איבא of the Targums is the equivalent of Heb. אב from אבב *to be green* (cf. Cant. vi, 11; Job viii, 12). Fraenkel, *Vocab*, 24, thought that the Arabic word was a direct borrowing from the Targumic איבא, but the probabilities seem in favour of its coming rather from Syr. ܐܒܐ, meaning *quicquid terra producit* (Mingana, *Syriac Influence*, 88). It was probably an early borrowing from the Mesopotamian area.[1]

أَبَابِيل (*abābīl*).

cv, 3.

In the description of the rout of the Army of the Elephant we read—وَأَرْسَلَ عَلَيْهِمْ طَيْرًا أَبَابِيلَ where ابابيل is said to mean *flocks*—حزائق Zam., or جماعات Bagh. and to be the plu. of ابالة, which Khafājī, *Shifā*, 31, lists as a foreign word whether spelled ابالة or ابّالة or ايبالة. The long account in *LA*, xiii, 5, makes it clear that the philologers knew not what to make of the word.

[1] Cf. Zimmern, *Akkadische Fremdwörter*, p. 55.

Burton, *Pilgrimage*, ii, 175, quotes a Major Price as suggesting that the word has nothing to do with the birds but is another calamity in addition, the name being derived from ابيلة a *vesicle*. Sprengel indeed as early as 1794 (see Opitz, *Die Medizin im Koran*, p. 76), had suggested a connection of the word with smallpox, deriving it from اب = *father* and ابيل = *lamentation*, and stating that the Persians use the word ابيلة for smallpox. This theory has some support in the tradition that it was smallpox which destroyed Abraha's army,[1] but it is difficult to see how the word could be of Pers. origin for it occurs in Pers. only as a borrowing from Arabic, and doubtless from this passage.

Carra de Vaux, *Penseurs*, iii, 398, has a suggestion that it is of Persian origin, and would take the طيرا ابابيل as a mistaken reading for تير بابيل = *babylonian arrows*, which caused the destruction of the army. The suggestion is ingenious, but hardly convincing, as we seem to know nothing elsewhere of these تير بابيل.

Apparently the word occurs nowhere in the early literature outside the Qur'ān, unless we admit the genuineness of Umayya's line—

حول شيطانهم ابابيل * ربيون شدّوا سَنَوَّراً مدسورا (Frag. 4, l. 3, in Schulthess' ed.), where it also means *crowds*. If it is to be taken as an Arabic word it may possibly be a case of توكيد الاتباع, especially in view of the expression quoted from al-Akhfash جاءت ابلك ابابيل. The probability, however, seems in favour of its being of foreign origin, as Cheikho, *Naṣrāniya*, 471, notes, though its origin is so far unknown.

إِبْرَاهِيمُ (*Ibrāhīm*).

Occurs some 69 times, cf. ii, 118; iii, 30; xlii, 11, etc.
Abraham.

[1] See Sprenger, *Life*, 35.

It is always used of the Biblical Patriarch and thus is ultimately derived from Heb. אַבְרָהָם. If the name had come direct from the Heb. we should have expected the form أَبْرَهَام, and as a matter of fact the Muslim philologers themselves recognized that the Qur'ānic form was not satisfactory, for we hear of attempts to alter the form,[1] and an-Nawawī, *Tahdhīb*, 126, gives variant forms ابرهام ; ابراهيم ; ابرهم ; ابرهَم and ابراهُم. Moreover we learn from as-Suyūṭī, *Muzhir*, i, 138, and al-Jawālīqī, 8, that some early authorities recognized it as a foreign borrowing, al-Mārwardī, indeed, informing us that in Syriac it means اب رحيم (Nawawī, 127), which is not far from the Rabbinic derivations.

The form ابراهيم cannot be evidenced earlier than the Qur'ān, for the verses of Umayya (ed. Schulthess, xxix, 9), in which it occurs, are not genuine, and Horovitz, *KU*, 86, 87, rightly doubts the authenticity of the occurrences of the name in the *Usd al-Ghāba* and such works. The form would thus seem to be due to Muḥammad himself, but the immediate source is not easy to determine. The common Syr. form is ܐܒܪܳܗܳܡ which is obviously the source of both the Eth. አብርሃም and the Arm. Աբրահամ.[2] A marginal reading in Luke i, 55, in the *Palestinian Syriac Lectionary of the Gospels* reads ܐܒܪܗܝܡ, but Schulthess, *Lex*, 2, rightly takes this as due to a scribe who was familiar with the Arabic.[3]

Lidzbarski, *Johannesbuch*, 73,[4] compares the Mandaean בראהים, which shortened form is also found as [ܐ]ܒܪܗܡ in the Christian Palestinian version of Luke xiii, 16 (Schulthess, *Lex*, 2), and may be compared with the برهام mentioned in Ibn Hishām, 352, l. 18, and the Braham b. Bunaj whom Horovitz, *KU*, 87, quotes from the Safā inscriptions. The final vowel, however, is missing here. Brockelmann,

[1] Sprenger, *Leben*, i, 66; Sycz, *Eigennamen*, 21; Margoliouth in *MW*, xv, 342.

[2] Hübschmann, *Arm. Gramm*, i, 290.

[3] The forms ܐܒܪܗܝܡ and ܐܒܪܗܝܡ found in Bar Hebraeus are also probably of Arabic origin.

[4] See also *Ephemeris*, ii, 44, n. 1.

Grundriss, i, 256, would derive ابراهيم from אברהם as شيطان from שטן, by assuming a dissimilation form in Aramaic, i.e. אברהים*. There is no trace of such a form, however, and Brockelmann's choice of شيطان as illustration is unfortunate as it appears to be a borrowed word and not original Arabic. The safest solution is that proposed by Rhodokanakis in ***WZKM***, xvii, 283, and supported by Margoliouth,[1] to the effect that it has been vocalized on the analogy of *Ismā'īl* and *Isrā'īl*.[2] The name was doubtless well enough known in Jewish circles in pre-Islamic Arabia,[3] and when Muḥammad got the form اسمعيل from Judaeo-Christian sources he formed ابراهيم on the same model.

إِبْرِيقٌ (*Ibrīq*).

lvi, 18.

A ewer, or water jug.

Only in the plu. form أَبَارِيقُ in an early Meccan description of Paradise. It was early recognized as a Persian loan-word (Siddiqi, 13), and is given by al-Kindī, *Risāla*, 85; ath-Tha'ālibī, *Fiqh*, 317; as-Suyūṭī[4] and al-Jawālīqī[5] in their lists of Persian borrowings, as well as by the Lexicons, *LA*, xi, 299; *TA*, vi, 286, though some attempted to explain it as a genuine Arabic word derived from برق.[6]

In modern Persian the word is آبريز meaning *urn* or *waterpot*.[7]

[1] *Schweich Lectures*, p. 12; see also Lidzbarski, *Johannesbuch*, 73; Fischer, *Glossar*, 163.

[2] He says: "Die Form ابرهيم durfte am ehesten aus ihrer Anlehnung an اسمعيل und der Ausgleichung mit demselben zu erklaren sein, nach dem bekannten kur'-anischen Prinzip, dass Personennamen, deren Träger in irgendwelchem zusammen-hange stehn, lautlich auf eine Form zu bringen strebt."

[3] Horovitz, *KU*, 92; *JPN*, 160.

[4] *Itq*, 318; *Mutaw*, 46; *Muzhir*, i, 136.

[5] The text of the *Mu'arrab* (Sachau's ed, p. 17) is defective here, giving the first إمّا, but not the second. Correcting it by the *Itq.* we read: إمّا أن يكون طريق الماء وإمّا صب الماء على هينة.

[6] Rāghib, *Mufradāt*, 43; and see Bagh. on the passage.

[7] Vullers, *Lex*, i, 8. and for further meanings see *BQ*, 4; Addai Sher, 6. ابريق also occurs in Pers. but only as a borrowing from Arabic.

It would be derived from آب *water* (= Phlv. [Pahlavi] $\bar{a}\beta$, i.e. OPers. *āpi*[1] = Av. [Avestan] or [Avestan]; Skt. आप *aqua*), and ريختن *to pour* (= Phlv. [Pahlavi] *rēχtăn* from an old Iranian root **raek* = linquere),[2] as was suggested by Castle[3] and generally accepted since his time. It was from the Phlv. form that the word was borrowed into Arabic, the shortening of the آ being regular.[4] The word occurs in the early poetry, in verses of 'Adī b. Zaid, 'Alqama, and Al-A'shā, and so was doubtless an early borrowing among the Arabs who were in contact with the court at al-Ḥīra.

إِبْلِيسُ (*Iblīs*).

ii, 32; vii, 10; xv, 31, 32; xvii, 63; xviii, 48; xx, 115; xxvi, 95; xxxiv, 19; xxxviii, 74, 75.

Iblis. ὁ διάβολος—the Devil par excellence.

The tendency among the Muslim authorities is to derive the name from بلس to *despair*, he being so called because God caused him to despair of all good—so Rāghib, *Mufradāt*, 59, and Ṭab. on ii, 32. The more acute philologers, however, recognized the impossibility of this (an-Nawawī, 138), and Zam. on xix, 57, says—ابليس اعجمىّ وليس من الابلاس كما يزعمون. al-Jawālīqī, *Mu'arrab*, 17, also justly argues against an Arabic derivation.

That the word is a corruption of the Gk. διάβολος has been recognized by the majority of Western scholars.[5] In the LXX διάβολος represents the Heb. שטן in Zech. iii, but in the N.T. ὁ διάβολος is

[1] In the Behistun inscription, see Spiegel, *Die altpersischen Keilinschriften*, p. 205.

[2] West, *Glossary*, 136; Bartholomae, *AIW*, 1479; and see Horn, *Grundriss*, 141; Šāyast, *Glossary*, p. 164; Shikand, *Glossary*, 265.

[3] *Lexicon Heptaglotton*, p. 23. See Vullers, op. cit.: Lagarde, *GA*, 7; Horn, *Grundriss*, 141; but note Vollers, *ZDMG*, l, 627.

[4] Siddiqi, 69. On the ground of this change from *a* to *i*, Grimme, *ZA*, xxvi, 164, looks for S. Arabian influence, but there is nothing in favour of this.

[5] Geiger, 100; von Kremer, *Ideen*, 226 n.; Fraenkel, *Vocab*, 24; Sprenger, *Leben*, ii, 242; Wensinck, *EI*, ii, 351; Rudolph, *Abhängigkeit*, 35; Vollers, *ZDMG*, l, 620; Sacco, *Credenze*, 61. However, Pautz, *Offenbarung*, 69, n. 3, and Eickmann, *Angelologie*, 26, hold to an Arabic origin, though Sprenger, *Leben*, ii, 242, n. 1, had pointed out that words of this form are as a rule foreign.

more than "the adversary", and particularly in the ecclesiastical writers he becomes the chief of the hosts of evil. It is in this sense that ابليس appears in the Qur'ān, so we are doubly justified in looking for a Christian origin for the word.

One theory is that it came through the Syriac, the ܕ being taken as the genitive particle,[1] a phenomenon for which there are perhaps other examples, e.g. ܦܘܢܣ for διαφωνάς (*ZA*, xxiv, 51), قسطاس for δικαστής (*ZDMG*, l, 620), زنطارية for δυσεντερία (Geyer, *Zwei Gedichte*, i, 119 n.). The difficulty is that the normal translation of ὁ διάβολος is ܐܟܠܩܪܨܐ, the *accuser* or *calumniator*, both in the Peshitta (cf. Matt. iv) and in the ecclesiastical literature. There is a form ܕܝܒܘܠܘܣ, a transliteration of διάβολος, but *PSm*, 874, quotes this only as a dictionary word from *BB*. There is apparently no occurrence of the word in the old Arabic literature,[2] so it was possibly a word introduced by Muḥammad himself. If we could assume that some such form as ܕܝܒܘܠܘܣ was colloquially used among the Aramaic-speaking Christians with whom Muḥammad came in contact, the above explanation might hold, though one would have to assume that the ܕ had been dropped by his informants. The alternative is that it came into Arabic directly from the Greek, and was used by the Arabic-speaking Christians associated with the Byzantine Church.[3]

Grimme, *ZA*, xxvi, 164, suggested that it might have come from S. Arabia, perhaps influenced by the Eth. ዲያብሎስ. This, however, is apparently a rare word in Eth., the usual translation for διάβολος being ሰይጣን, though sometimes ጋኔን is used (James iv, 7; I Pet. v, 8, etc.). Moreover, even if there were anything in Grimme's theory that this was the form that crossed over into Arabia, his further supposition that the ዲያ was taken to be the S. Arabian 𐩹 = ذى is very far fetched.

[1] So Horovitz, *KU*, 87. Mingana, *Syriac Influence*, 89, thinks rather that it was the fault of some early scribe or copyist who mistook the initial *Dal* for an *Alif*.

[2] The verses in Ibn Hishām, 318 and 516, noted by Horovitz, are from the period of the Hijra and so doubtless influenced by Muhammad's usage. They would seem fatal, however, to Mingana's theory.

[3] Künstlinger, "Die Herkunft des Wortes *Iblīs* im Ḳurān," in *Rocznik Orjentalistyczny*, vi (1928), proposes the somewhat far-fetched theory that *Iblīs* is derived from the Jewish *Belial* by deliberate transformation.

أَجْرٌ (*Ajr*).

Of common occurrence.

Reward, wages.

Besides the noun and its plu. أُجُور there occur also the verbal forms أَجَرَ and إِستأجر.

The Muslim savants have no suspicion that the word is not pure Arabic, though as a matter of fact the verb أَجَرَ *to receive hire*, is obviously denominative.

Zimmern, *Akkad. Fremdw*, 47,[1] has pointed out that the ultimate origin of the root in this sense is the Akk. *agru*, *agarru*, *hired servant*. From this come on the one hand the Aram. אגירא : Syr. ܐܓܝܪܐ, a *hireling*, and thence the denominative verbs אֲגַר and ܐܓܪ, *to hire*, with corresponding nouns אגר and ܐܓܪܐ, *hire*; and on the other hand (apparently from a popular pronunciation **aggaru*) the Gk. ἄγγαρος, *a courier*.[2]

It would have been from the Aram. that the word passed into Arabic, probably at a very early period, and as the word is of much wider use in Syriac than in Jewish Aramaic,[3] we are probably right in considering it as a borrowing from Syriac.

أحبار (*Aḥbār*).

v, 48, 68; ix, 31, 34.

Plu. of حِبْرٌ or حَبْرٌ—a Jewish Doctor of the Law.

The Commentators knew that it was a technical Jewish title and quote as an example of its use Kaʻb al-Aḥbār,[4] the well-known convert

[1] Cf. also Jensen in *ZA*, vii, 214, 215.

[2] Even the latest edition of Liddell and Scott persists in repeating the statement in Stephanus' *Thesaurus*, that it is a borrowing from Persian. It is, of course, possible that the word may be found in the OPers. vocabulary, but if so it was a loan-word there from the Akkadian, and there can be little doubt that the Gk. ἄγγαρος with ἀγγαρεύειν and ἀγγαρεία came directly from the Akkadian, as indeed Ed. Meyer (*Geschichte des Alterthums*, iii, 67) had already recognized.

[3] For its occurrence in Aramaic incantations, see Montgomery, *Aramaic Incantation Texts from Nippur*, Glossary, p. 281; and for the Elephantine papyri see Cowley, *Aramaic Papyri*, p. 178 (No. 69, l. 12).

[4] The plu. form احبار is explained by a verse in Ibn Hishām, 659, where we learn of one whose full name was Kaʻb b. al-Ashraf Sayyid al-Aḥbār.

from Judaism. It was generally taken, however, as a genuine Arabic word derived from حَبَرَ, *to leave a scar* (as of a wound), the Divines being so called because of the deep impression their teaching makes on the lives of their students; so Rāghib, *Mufradāt*, 104.

Geiger, 49, 53, claims that it is derived from חָבֵר *teacher*, commonly used in the Rabbinic writings as a title of honour, e.g. Mish. Sanh. 60 b.—מה אהרן חבר אף בניו חברים, "as Aaron was a Doctor so were his sons Doctors." [1] Geiger's theory has been accepted by von Kremer, *Ideen*, 226 n., and Fraenkel, *Vocab*, 23, and is doubtless correct, though Grünbaum, *ZDMG*, xxxix, 582, thinks that in coming into Arabic it was not uninfluenced by the Ar. خبر, اخبر, خبير. Mingana, *Syriac Influence*, 87, suggests that the word is of Syriac origin (see also Cheikho, *Naṣrāniya*, 191), but this is unlikely. The word was evidently quite well known in pre-Islamic Arabia,[2] and thus known to Muḥammad from his contact with Jewish communities. It was borrowed in the form of the singular and given an Arabic plural.

آدَم (*Ādam*)

ii, 29–35; iii, 30, 52; v, 30; vii, 10, 18, 25–33, 171; xvii, 63, 72; xviii, 48; xix, 59; xx, 114–119; xxxvi, 60.

Adam.

It is used always as an individual name and never as the Heb. and Phon. אדם for *man* in general, though the use of بنو آدم in Sūra, vii, approaches this usage (Nöldeke-Schwally, i, 242). It is one of the few Biblical names which the early philologers such as al-Jawālīqī (*Mua'rrab*, 8) claimed as of Arabic origin. There are various theories as to the derivation of the name, which may be seen in Rāghib, *Mufradāt*, 12, and in the Commentaries, but all of them are quite hopeless. Some authorities recognized this and Zam. and Baiḍ., on ii, 29, admit that it is a foreign word—إسم أعجمى.

[1] Hirschfeld, *Beiträge*, 51, translates by "Schriftgelehrte" (cf. the N.T. γραμματεύς = Syr. ܣܵܦܪܵܐ), and takes it as opposed to the עם הארץ.

[2] It occurs in the old poetry, cf. Horovitz, *KU*, 63, and Ibn Hishām, 351, 354, uses the word familiarly as well known; cf. also Wensinck, *Joden te Madina*, 65; Horovitz, *JPN*, 197, 198.

The origin of course is the Heb. אדם, and there is no reason why the name should not have come directly from the Jews,[1] though there was a tradition that the word came from Syriac.[2] The name occurs in the Safaite inscriptions (Horovitz, *KU*, 85), and was known to the poet 'Adī b. Zaid, so it was doubtless familiar, along with the creation story, to Muḥammad's contemporaries.

إِدْرِيسُ (*Idrīs*)

xix, 57 ; xxi, 85.

Idrīs.

He is one of the Prophets casually mentioned in the Qur'ān, where all the information we have about him is (i) that he was a man of truth (xix, 57) ; (ii) that God raised him to a "place on high" رَفَعْنَاهُ مَكَانًا عَلِيًّا (xix, 58) ; and (iii) that being steadfast and patient he entered God's mercy (xxi, 85).

The Muslim authorities are agreed that he is اخنوخ, i.e. חֲנוֹךְ, the Biblical Enoch,[3] a theory derived not only from the facts enumerated above, but from the idea that his name ادريس is derived from درس *to study*—both Jewish and Christian legend attributing to Enoch the mastery of occult wisdom.[4] The fallacy of this derivation was, however, pointed out by some of the philologers, as Zam. on xix, 57, shows, and that the name was of foreign origin was recognized by al-Jawālīqī, *Mu'arrab*, 8 ; *Qāmūs*, i, 215 ; which makes it the more strange that some Western scholars such as Sprenger, *Leben*, ii, 336,[5] and Eickmann, *Angelologie*, 26, have considered it to be a pure Arabic word.

[1] Ibn Qutaiba, *Ma'ārif*, 180 (Eg. ed.) notes a variant reading إيدام which may represent a Jewish pronunciation.

[2] Sycz, *Eigennamen*, 18.

[3] Tha'labī, *Qiṣaṣ*, 34.

[4] חנך of course means *to instruct, to initiate* (cf. حنك) and may have suggested the connection with درس. For the derivation see Tha'labī, loc. cit. ; Ibn Qutaiba, *Ma'ārif*, 8. Finkel, *MW*, xxii, 181, derives it from Εὐδώρεσχος, the 7th antediluvian King of Berossus, but this is very far-fetched.

[5] He seems to base this on the occurrence of the name Abū Idrīs, but see Horovitz, *KU*, 88.

Nöldeke has pointed out, *ZA*, xvii, 83, that we have no evidence that Jews or Christians ever called Enoch by any name derived from דרש or ܕܪܫ, and though Geiger, 105, 106, thinks the equivalence of ورفعناه مكانا عليا of xix, 58, with the μετέθηκεν αὐτὸν ὁ Θεός of Heb. xi, 5, from the Midrash, sufficient to justify the identification, we may well doubt it. Casanova, *JA*, 1924, vol. ccv, p. 358 (so Torrey, *Foundation*, 72) suggested that the reference was to Ἔσδρας which through a form Ἔζρας became ادريس. Albright[1] imagines that it refers to Hermes-Poemandres, the name being derived from the final element in the Greek name Ποιμάνδρης, while Montgomery, *JQR*, xxv, 261, would derive it from Atraḫasis, the Babylonian Noah. None of these suggestions, however, comes as near as that put forward by Nöldeke in *ZA*, xvii, 84, that it is the Arabic form of Ἀνδρέας filtered through a Syriac medium.[2] In Syriac we find various forms of the name ܐܢܕܪܐܘܣ : ܐܢܕܪܐܘܣ : ܐܢܕܪܝܘܣ and ܐܢܕܪܝܣ, this latter being the form in Christian-Palestinian, and from this by the coalescing of the *n* and *d* we get the Ar. ادريس. Grimme, *ZA*, xxvi, 164, suggested a S. Arabian origin but there is no trace of the name in the inscriptions and the Eth. እንድርያስ has nothing in its favour.

أَرَآئِكُ (*Arā'ik*)

xviii, 30; xxxvi, 56; lxxvi, 13; lxxxiii, 23, 35.

Couches. Plu. of أَرِيكَةٌ.

We find the word only in passages descriptive of Paradise. The Muslim authorities as a rule take it as an Arabic word derived from ارك but their theories of its derivation are not very helpful, as may be seen from Rāghib, *Mufradāt*, 14, or the Lexicons *LA*, xii, 269; *TA*, vii,

[1] *Journal of Palestine Oriental Society*, ii, 197–8, and in *AJSL*. 1927, p. 235 n.

[2] Nöldeke's earlier suggestion in *ZDMG*, xii, 706, was that it might stand for Θεόδωρος, but in *ZA*, xvii, he refers it to the Πράξεις Ἀνδρέου and thinks the lifting him "to a place on high" may refer to the saint's crucifixion. R. Hartmann, in *ZA*, xxiv, 315, however, recognized this Andreas as the famous cook of Alexander the Great.

100. Some early philologers concluded that it was foreign, and as-Suyūṭī, *Itq*, 318, says that Ibn al-Jawzī gave it as an Abyssinian loan-word, and on p. 310 has the interesting statement—" Abū 'Ubaid related that Al-Ḥasan said—We used not to know the meaning of الارائك until we met a man from Yemen who told us that among them an اريكة was a pavilioh containing a bed."

Addai Sher, 9, says that it is the Pers. اورنك, by which he probably means اورنگ *throne* the colloquial form for اورند (Vullers, *Lex*, i, 141), but there does not seem to be anything in this. There is nothing in Eth. with which we can relate it, and the probabilities are that it is of Iranian origin, especially as we find it used in the verses of the old poets, e.g. al-A'shā, who were in contact with Iranian culture (cf. Horovitz, *Paradies*, 15).

إِرَمُ (*Iram*)

lxxxix, 6.
Iram: the city of the people of 'Ād.

The number of variant readings for this إرم in ارم ذات العماد suggests of itself that the word was a foreign one of which the exegetes could make nothing. The older theory among Western scholars was that it was אֲרָם [1] but the story is clearly S. Arabian, as appears from xlvi, 20, and as a matter of fact Hamdānī (ed. D. H. Müller, p. 126, 129) mentions two other Irams in S. Arabia, so that the name is doubtless S. Arabian.[2] The name is frequently mentioned in the early literature.[3]

آزر (*Āzar*)

vi, 74.
Āzar—the father of Abraham.

[1] Wetstein in his Appendix to Delitzsch's *Hiob*, 1876; Pautz, *Offenbarung*, 273; Sycz, *Eigennamen*, 54; O. Loth, *ZDMG*, xxxv, 628.
[2] D. H. Müller, *Südarabische Studien*, 134 ff.; *Burgen und Schlösser*, p. 418.
[3] See passages in Horovitz, *KU*, 89, 90.

The consensus of opinion among the exegetes is that آزر is the name of Abraham's father, and is اسم اعجمى. It was also well known, however, that the real name of Abraham's father was تارح or تارخ, e.g. aṭ-Ṭabarī, *Annales*, i, 252; an-Nawawī, 128; al-Jawālīqī, *Mu'arrab*, 21; *TA*, iii, 12, etc., obviously reproducing the תֶּרַח of Gen. xi, 26, etc. In order to escape the difficulty some took آزر to be the name of an idol—اسم صنم, or an abusive epithet applied by Abraham to his father.[1] They also have various theories as to the origin of the word, some taking it to be Hebrew (as-Suyūṭī, *Itq*, 318), some Syriac (Zam. on vi, 74), and some Persian (Bagh. on vi, 74). Their suggestions, however, are obviously guesses and do not help us at all.

The solution generally found in European works is that which was first set forth by Marracci in *Prodromus*, iv, 90, that the Talmudic name for Terah, by a metathesis became Ἄθαρ in Eusebius, and this gives the Arabic *Āzar*. This has been repeated over and over again from Ewald [2] and Sale down to the modern Ahmadiyya Commentators, and even Geiger 128, though he does not mention Marracci, argues that תרח = Θάρα (LXX, Θάῤῥα) by metathesis gives Ἄθαρ and thus آزر, while Dvořák, *Fremdwörter*, 38, goes even further in discussing the probability of Gk. θ being pronounced like z. The fact, however, is that Marracci simply misread Eusebius, who uses no such form as Ἄθαρ.[3]

Hyde in his *Historia Religionis veterum Persarum*, p. 62, suggested that Āzer was the heathen name of Abraham's father, who only became known as Terah after his conversion. This heathen name he would connect with the Av. 𐬁𐬙𐬀𐬭 *ātar* [4] (cf. Skt. अथर्वन्), Phlv. [illegible]

[1] *Vide* as-Suyūṭī, 318, and the Commentators. It should be noted that Zam. gives a number of variant readings for the word, showing that the earliest authorities were puzzled by it.

[2] *Geschichte Israels*, i, 483.

[3] The passage reads (*Hist. Eccl*, ed. Schwartz, I, iv, p. 14)—*μετὰ δὲ καὶ τοῦτον ἑτέρους, τῶν δὲ τοῦ Νῶε παίδων καὶ ἀπογόνων ἀτὰρ καὶ τὸν Ἀβραάμ, ὃν ἀρχηγὸν καὶ προπάτορα σφῶν αὐτῶν παῖδες Ἑβραίων αὐχοῦσι*, where the unusual *ἀτάρ* was apparently misread as *Ἄθαρ*. Cf. Pautz, *Offenbarung*, 242 n.

[4] Bartholomae, *AIW*, 312.

ātur,[1] Paz. *âdur*, and the Mod. Pers. آذر used as the name of the fire demon,[2] and in the Persian histories given as the name of Abraham's father. Hyde, however, has fallen into error in not noticing that the name پور آذر given to Abraham in the Persian writings[3] simply means "son of the fire", and has no reference to his father, but is derived from the Qur'ānic account of his experiences in Sūra, xxi.

B. Fisher in *Bibel und Talmud*, Leipzig, 1881, p. 85 n., suggested that Muḥammad or his informants had misunderstood the epithet הָאֶזְרָחִי (he who has sprung from the East) applied to Abraham in the Talmud (Baba Bathra 15a), and taking it to mean "Son of אזרח", gave his father's name as آزر.

The correct solution, however, would appear to be that given by Fraenkel in *ZDMG*, lvi, p. 72, and accepted by both Horovitz, *KU*, 85, 86, *JPN*, 157, and Sycz, *Eigennamen*, 37. In *WZKM*, iv, 338, Fraenkel suggested that both عازر and آزر go back to the Heb. אלעזר, and in *ZDMG*, lvi, 72, he argues convincingly that the Qur'ānic form is due to a confusion on Muḥammad's part of the details of the Abraham story as it came to him, so that instead of his father תֶּרַח he has given the name of Abraham's faithful servant אליעזר. Sycz's theory that it was a mistake between two passages אליעזר עבד אברהם and תרח אבי אברהם is a little too remote, but the confusion of names can be held as certain. The אל was probably taken as the article,[4] and on the question of vowel change Fraenkel compares the series פֶּלֶג فالغ ܦܠܓ. As there is a genuine Arabic name عيزار (Ṭab, *Annales*, i, 3384 ; Ibn Sa'd, vi, 214), Horovitz, *KU*, 86, thinks that Muḥammad may have been influenced by this in his formation of the name.

[1] Horn, *Grundriss*, 4 ; Shikand, *Glossary*, 226 ; Nyberg, *Glossar*, 25 ; Herzfeld, *Paikuli*, Glossary, 126 and 148.

[2] In Phlv, ܐܬܪܘ *Ātarō* is the Angel of Fire ; see West, *Glossary*, p. 7.

[3] Vullers, *Lex*, i, 380.

[4] As often, cf. examples in Geyer, *Zwei Gedichte*, i, 118 n.

أَسَاطِيرُ (*Asāṭīr*)

vi, 25; viii, 31; xvi, 26; xxiii, 85; xxv, 6; xxvii, 70; xlvi, 16; lxviii, 15; lxxxiii, 13.

Fables, idle tales.

We find the word only in the combination اساطير الاولين "tales of the ancients", which was the Meccan characterization of the stories brought them by Muḥammad. Sprenger, *Leben*, ii, 396 ff., thought that the reference was to a book of this title well known to Muḥammad's contemporaries, but this theory has been combated in Nöldeke-Schwally, i, 16 ff.,[1] and its impossibility becomes clear from a passage in Ibn Hishām, 235, where Naḍr b. al-Ḥārith is made to say—"By Allah, Muḥammad is no better a raconteur than I am. His stories are naught but tales of the ancients (اساطير الاولين) which he writes down just as I do."

The Muslim authorities take it as a form افاعيل from سَطَرَ *to write*, considering it as a plu. of اسطورة or اسطارة (Sijistānī, 10), or the plu. of a plu. (*LA*, vi, 28). The verb سَطَرَ, however, as Fraenkel has shown (*Fremdw*, 250), is a denominative from سَطْرٌ, and this itself is a borrowing from Aram. שטרא, ܣܛܪܐ (Nöldeke, *Qorans*, 13). It is possible but not probable that اساطير was formed from this borrowed سطر.

Sprenger, *Leben*, ii, 395,[2] suggested that in اساطير we have the Gk. ἱστορία, a suggestion also put forward by Fleischer in his review of Geiger (*Kleinere Schriften*, ii, 119), and which has been accepted by many later scholars.[3] The objections to it raised by Horovitz, *KU*, 70, are, however, insuperable. The word can hardly have come into Arabic directly from the Greek, and the Syr. ܐܣܛܘܪܝܐ occurs only

[1] See also Hirschfeld, *New Researches*, 22, 41 ff., on Sprenger's *Ṣuḥuf* theories.

[2] *Vide* also his remarks in *JASB*, xx, 119, and see Freytag, *Lexicon*, sub voc.

[3] Vollers, *ZDMG*, li, 312. See also Künstlinger in *OLZ*, 1936, 481 ff.

as a learned word (*PSm*, 298). The derivation from Syr. ܐܣܛܪܐ suggested by Nöldeke-Schwally, i, 16 n., is much more satisfactory. ܐܣܛܪܐ (cf. Aram. שְׁטָרָא) is the equivalent of the Gk. χειρόγραφον,[1] and is a word commonly used in a sense in which it can have come into Arabic. It was doubtless borrowed in this sense in the pre-Islamic period,[2] for in a verse of the Meccan poet 'Abdallah b. az-Ziba'rā, quoted in 'Ainī, iv, 140, we read الهى قصيًّا عن المجد الاساطير "the stories have averted Quṣay from glory".

In S. Arabian, as D. H. Müller points out (*WZKM*, i, 29) we have 𐩪𐩲𐩧𐩩 meaning an *inscription*, and 𐩪𐩲𐩧 is the usual verb for *scripsit* (Rossini, *Glossarium*, 194), so it is not impossible that there was S. Arabian influence on the form of the word. See further under سطر.

أَسْبَاط (*Asbāṭ*)

ii, 130, 134; iii, 78; iv, 161; vii, 160.

The Tribes. Plu. of سبط.

It occurs only in Madinan passages and always refers to the Children of Israel. In vii, 160, it is used normally of the Twelve Tribes, but in all the other passages the اسباط are spoken of as recipients of revelation, and one suspects that here Muḥammad is confusing the Jewish use of "the Twelve" for the Minor Prophets with that for the Twelve Tribes.[3]

The philologers derive it from سبط *a thistle*, their explanation thereof being interesting if not convincing (*LA*, ix, 182). Some, however, felt the difficulty, and Abū'l-Laith was constrained to admit that it was a Hebrew loan-word (as-Suyūṭī, *Itqān*, 318; *Mutaw*, 58). The ultimate source, of course, is the Heb. שבט, and Geiger 141, followed by many

[1] Cf. ܐܣܛܪܐ ܕܚܫܝܫܬܐ *cheirographum dubium*, as contrasted with ܐܣܛܪܐ ܡܫܪܪܐ *cheirographum validum*.

[2] So Mingana, *Syriac Influence*, 89.

[3] *Vide* Sprenger, *Leben*, ii, 276, who thinks Muḥammad took it to be a proper name, which, however, is unlikely in view of vii, 160 (Hirschfeld, *Beiträge*, 41).

later scholars[1] has argued for the direct borrowing from Hebrew. Fraenkel, however, noted the possibility of its having been borrowed through the Syr. ܦܘܠܚܐ = φυλή[2] and Mingana, *Syriac Influence*, 86, definitely claims it as a Syriac loan-word. It is impossible to decide, but in any case it was borrowed in the sing. and given an Arabic plural.

There does not seem to be any well-attested pre-Islamic example of the use of the word, for the case in Samau'al cannot be genuine, as Nöldeke shows (*ZA*, xxvii, 178), and that in Umayya, lv, 7, seems to depend on Sūra, lxxxix, 23. This confirms the idea that it was a late introduction probably by Muḥammad himself.

إِسْتَبْرَق (*Istabraq*)

xviii, 30; xliv, 53; lv, 54; lxxvi, 21.

Silk brocade.

Used only in early passages in description of the raiment of the faithful in Paradise. It is one of the few words that have been very generally recognized by the Muslim authorities as a Persian loan-word, cf. aḍ-Ḍaḥḥāk in as-Suyūṭī, *Itq*, 319; al-Aṣma'ī in as-Suyūṭī, *Muzhir*, i, 137; as-Sijistānī, 49; al-Jawharī, *Ṣiḥāḥ* sub voc.; al-Kindī, *Risāla*, 85; Ibn al-Athīr, *Nihāya*, i, 38. Some, indeed, took it as an Arabic word, attempting to derive it from برق (cf. Baiḍ. on lxxvi, 21), but their argument depends on a variant reading given by Ibn Muḥaiṣin which cannot be defended (Dvořák, *Fremdw*, 39, 40).

The philologers, however, were in some confusion as to the original Persian form. *LA*, xi, 285, quotes az-Zajjāj as stating it was from Pers. استقره, and *TA*, vi, 292, quotes Ibn Duraid to the effect that it is from Syr. استروه, neither of which forms exist. The *Qāmūs*, s.v. برق, however, rightly gives it as from استبره,[3] which al-Jawharī,

[1] Fraenkel, *Vocab*, 21; Pautz, *Offenbarung*, 124 n.; Hirschfeld, *Beiträge*, 41; Horovitz, *KU*, 90.

[2] Horovitz also notes this possibility. The Palestinian form ܦܘܒܛܐ quoted by Schwally, *Idioticon*, 92, which agrees closely with the Talmudic שׁוּבְטָא, is not so close to the Arabic.

[3] So *TA*, loc. cit., and al-Khafājī, in his supercommentary to Baiḍāwī, cf. also Addai Sher, 10.

Ṣiḥāḥ, says is from سطبر, meaning غليظ.[1] Pers. استبر, sometimes written اسطبر, as al-Jawharī gives it,[2] is a form of سِتَبر, meaning *big, thick, gross*, apparently from a root, استوار *firm, stable* (cf. Skt. स्थविर[3]; Av. [Avestan] *staura*[4]; Oss. *st'ur*[5]; and Arm. ստուար).[6] The Phlv. [Pahlavi] *staβr* = *thick* (Nyberg, *Glossar*, 206), is used of clothing in eschatological writings, e.g. *Arda Viraf*, xiv, 14, [Pahlavi] "and glorious and thick splendid clothing". Phlv. [Pahlavi], with the suffix ، gives the Mod. Pers. استبرك, which *BQ*, 994, defines as دیبای کنده وسطبر, and Vullers, *Lex*, i, 94, as *vestis serica crassior*.

From Mid.Pers. the word was borrowed into Armenian as բաստուրակ[7], and into Syr. as ܐܣܛܒܪܩܐ or ܐܣܛܒܪܘܩܐ.[8] Ibn Duraid, according to *TA*, vi, 292, quoted استبرق as a borrowing from Syr., but *PSm*, 294, gives the Syr. forms only as dictionary words from *BA* and *BB*, and there can be little doubt that the word passed directly into Arabic from the Middle Persian.[9] The Ar. ق represents the Phlv. suffix ،[10] which in Syr. normally became ܩܐ, as we see in such examples

[1] *BQ*, 492, defines it as كنده ولك ويك وغليظ. [2] Vullers, *Lex*, i, 97.

[3] Lagarde, *GA*, 13. स्थविर means *thick*, *compact*, *solid*, cf. Monier Williams, *Sanscrit Dictionary*, 1265.

[4] Bartholomae, *AIW*, 1592; Horn, *Grundriss*, p. 158; Hubschmann, *Persische Studien*, 74.

[5] For this Ossetian form see Hubschmann, *ZDMG*, xxxix, 93.

[6] Hübschmann, *Arm. Gramm*, i, 493. Cf. also Gk. σταυρός.

[7] Hubschmann, *Arm. Gramm*, i, 153. The form seems proof that the borrowing was from Pers. and not from Ar., though the passage in Moses Kalankatuaci, which Hubschmann quotes, refers to բաստուրակս և դղիպակս, a gift from the Caliph Mu'āwiya I. Cf. Stackelberg in *ZDMG*, xlviii, 490.

[8] Fraenkel, *Vocab*, 25, quotes this as ܐܣܛܒܪܩܐ, which is copied by Dvořák, *Fremdw*, 42, and Horovitz, *Paradies*, 16, but neither this form nor the ܐܣܛܒܪܓ quoted by Addai Sher, 10, is to be found in the Syriac Lexicons.

[9] Mingana, *Syriac Influence*, 88, however, claims that the borrowing was from Syr. into Arabic.

[10] The philologers had recognized, however, that Pers. ك did sometimes become ق in Ar. Cf. Sībawaih in Siddiqi, 21.

as Phlv. 𐭠𐭯𐭮𐭲𐭠𐭪 *avistāk* (= Pers. ابستا or افستا),[1] which in Syr. is ܐܦܣܛܐܩ, and in Ar. ابستاق (Ibn al-Athīr, *Nihāya*, i, 38).

إسحاق (*Isḥāq*).

ii, 127–134 ; iii, 78 ; iv, 161 ; vi, 84 ; xi, 74 ; xii, 6, 38 ; xiv, 41 ; xix, 50 ; xxi, 72 ; xxix, 26 ; xxxvii, 112, 113 ; xxxviii, 45.

Isaac.

The Biblical Patriarch, who is never mentioned save in connection with one or more of the other Patriarchs, and never in an early passage.

It was early recognized by the philologers that it was a foreign name, cf. Sībawaih in Siddiqi, 20, and *LA*, xii, 20 ; al-Jawālīqī, *Mu'arrab*, 9 ; as-Suyūṭī, *Muzhir*, i, 138 ; though it was not uncommon in some quarters to regard it as an Arabic word derived from سحق, for as-Suyūṭī, *Muzhir*, i, 140, goes out of his way to refute this. It was even known that it was Heb. (cf. ath-Tha'labī, *Qiṣaṣ*, 76), and indeed Sūra, xi, 74, seems to show acquaintance with the popular Hebrew derivation from צחק.

The Arabic form which lacks the initial י of the *O.T.* forms יצחק and ישחק would seem to point to a Christian origin,[2] cf. Gk. Ἰσαακ, Syr. ܐܝܣܚܩ or ܐܣܚܩ,[3] though it is true that in the Talmud we come across a מרי בר איסק (*Baba Mezi'a*, 39ᵇ), showing a form with initial vowel among the Babylonian Jews of the fourth century A.D.[4] The name اسحق must have been known before the Qur'ān, but no pre-Islamic instances of it seem to occur, for those quoted by Cheikho, *Naṣrāniya*, 229, 230, are rightly rejected by Horovitz, *KU*, 91.

إسرائيل (*Isrā'īl*).

Occurs some 43 times. Cf. ii, 38.

[1] West, *Glossary*, 13.

[2] Sprenger, *Leben*, ii, p. 336 ; Fraenkel, *ZA*, xv, 394 ; Horovitz, *JPN*, 155, and Mingana's note, *Syriac Influence*, 83. Torrey, *Foundation*, 49, however, takes this to be a characteristic of his assumed Judaeo-Arabic dialect.

[3] This is the Christian Palestinian form, cf. Schulthess, *Lex*, 14.

[4] Derenbourg in *REJ*, xviii, 127, suggests that יצחק may have been pronounced among the Arabian Jews as אסחק.

Usually it stands for the Children of Israel, but in iii, 87, and xix, 59, it is the name of the Patriarch otherwise called يعقوب.

Some of the exegetes endeavoured to derive it from سرى "to travel by night", because when Jacob fled from Esau he travelled by night (cf. aṭ-Ṭabarī, *Annales*, i, 359, and Ibn al-Athīr). It was very generally recognized as a foreign name, however (cf. al-Jawālīqī, 9; al-Khafājī, 11),[1] and is given as such by the Commentators Zam. and Baiḍ. on ii, 38.

Here also the absence of the initial י stands against a direct derivation from the Heb. יִשְׂרָאֵל, and points to a Christian origin, cf. Gk. Ἰσραήλ, Syr. ܐܝܣܪܝܠ; Eth. እስራኤል. The probabilities are in favour of a Syriac origin [2] especially in view of the Christian Palestinian forms ܐܝܣܪܐܝܠ; ܐܝܣܪܐܝܠ (Schulthess, *Lex*, 16). The name was doubtless well enough known to the people of Muḥammad's day and though no pre-Islamic example of its use in N. Arabia seems to have survived [3] ישראל occurs in S. Arabian inscriptions, cf. *CIS*, iv, 543, l. 1.

أُسِّسَ (*Ussis*).

ix, 109.
Founded.

The verbal form أَسَّسَ occurs in ix, 110. The verb is denominative from أُسٌّ, *a foundation*, which Fraenkel, *Fremdw*, 11, noted was an Aramaic borrowing, cf. Aram. אשׁיא *foundation*, and in the Christian Palestinian dialect the verb ܐܫܬ = ἐθεμελίωσε; ܡܐܫܬ = τεθεμελίωτο, and ܐܫܬܐ = θεμέλιον (Schwally, *Idioticon*, 7), so classical Syr. ܫܬܐ (and see Nöldeke, *Mand. Gramm*, 98, n. 2; Zimmern, *Akkad. Fremdw*, 31; Henning, *BSOS*, ix, 80).

[1] al-Khafājī notes the uncertainty as to the spelling of the word, اسرال and اسرايل being known besides اسرائيل.

[2] Mingana, *Syriac Influence*, 81; Horovitz, *KU*, 91. The *Qāmūs*, as a matter of fact, says that all forms ending in ئيل are سريانى, though Ṭab. on ii, 38, claims that ايل is Heb.

[3] All those given by Cheikho, *Naṣrānīya*, 230, are doubtless influenced by Qur'ānic usage.

أَسْلَمَ (*Aslama*).

Of frequent use, cf. ii, 106, 125.
To submit, to surrender.

With this must be taken الاسلام (iii, 17, 79, etc.), and the participial forms مُسْلِمٌ, etc.

The verb سَلِمَ is genuine Arabic, corresponding with Heb. שָׁלֵם, Phon. שלם *to be complete, sound*: Aram. שְׁלֵים, Syr. ܫܠܡ *to be complete, safe*: Akk. *šalāmu, to be complete, unharmed*. This primitive verb, however, does not occur in the Qur'ān. Form II, سَلَّمَ, is fairly common, but this is a denominative from سلام, and سلام as we shall see is a borrowed word.[1]

As used in the Qur'ān أَسْلَمَ is a technical religious term,[2] and there is even some development traceable in Muḥammad's use of it.[3] Such a phrase as مَنْ يُسْلِمْ وَجْهَهُ إِلَى ٱللّٰهِ in xxxi, 21,[4] seems to give the word in its simplest and original sense, and then اسلم لربّ العالمين (xl, 68; vi, 70; ii, 125), and اسلم لله or اسلم له (xxvii, 45; ii, 127; iii, 77; xxxix, 55), are a development from this. Later, however, the word comes practically to mean "to profess Islam", i.e. to accept the religion which Muḥammad is preaching, cf. xlviii, 16; xlix, 14, 17, etc. Now in pre-Islamic times أسلم is used in the primitive sense of "hand over", noted above. For instance, in a verse of Abū 'Azza in Ibn Hishām, 556, we read—لاتُسْلِمونى لايَحِلُّ اسلام "hand me not over for such betrayal is not lawful".[5] The Qur'ānic use is an

[1] On the development of meaning in S. Arabian 𐩪𐩡𐩣 see Rossini, *Glossarium*, 196.
[2] See Lyall, *JRAS*, 1903, p. 782.
[3] See Lidzbarski's article, "Salām und Islām," in *ZS*, i, 85 ff.
[4] Cf. also, ii, 106; iii, 18; iv, 124. On the probable genesis of this, see Margoliouth in *JRAS*, 1903, pp. 473, 474.
[5] For other examples, see Margoliouth's article, as above.

intelligible development from this sense, but the question remains whether this was a development within Arabic itself or an importation from without.

Margoliouth in *JRAS*, 1903, p. 467 ff., would favour a development within Arabic itself, perhaps started by Musailama; but as Lyall pointed out in the same Journal (p. 771 ff.), there are historical difficulties in the way of this. Lidzbarski, *ZS*, i, 86, would make it a denominative from سلام which he takes as a translation of σωτηρία, but Horovitz, *KU*, 55, rightly objects.

The truth seems to be that it was borrowed as a technical religious term from the older religions. Already in the O.Aram. inscriptions we find that שלם as used in proper names has acquired this technical religious significance,[1] as e.g. שלמלת, etc. The same sense is found in the Rabbinic writings (Horovitz, *KU*, 55), but it is particularly in Syriac that we find ܐܫܠܡ used precisely as in the Qur'ān, e.g. ܐܫܠܡ ܢܦܫܗ ܠܐܠܗܐ ܘܠܥܕܬܗ "he devoted himself to God and His Church", or ܐܫܠܡܘ ܠܗ ܢܦܫܗܘܢ,[2] and one feels confident in looking here for the origin of the Arabic word.

مُسْلِمٌ, of course, is a formation from this,[3] and was in use in pre-Islamic Arabia. الاسلام, however, would seem to have been formed by Muḥammad himself after he began to use the word.

إِسْمَعِيلُ (*Ismāʿīl*).

ii, 119–134; iii, 78; iv, 161; vi, 86; xiv, 41; xix, 55; xxi, 85; xxxviii, 48.

Ishmael.

The Muslim philologers early recognized that it was non-Arabic, as is clear from Zam. on xix, 55, and from its being treated as non-Arabic by al-Jawālīqī, *Muʿarrab*, 9; al-Khafājī, 10; as-Suyūṭī, *Muzhir*,

[1] Robertson Smith, *Religion of the Semites*, 79 ff.

[2] The example given by Horovitz, viz. ܐܫܠܡ ܢܦܫܗ ܠܡܫܝܚܐ ܡܪܢ ܗܘ, is curiously like اسلم لربّ العالمين.

[3] Sūra, li, 36; xxii, 77; and note Bagh, vii, 192, and Yaʿqūbī, *Hist*, i, 259, and its use in Safaite (Ryckmans, *Noms propres*, i, 239).

i, 138. Various forms of the name are given—اسماعيل ; اسمعين ; اسمعيل and اشمائيل, the ش in this last form, quoted from Sībawaih in *Muzhir*, i, 132, being significant.

A Christian origin for the word is evident from a comparison of the Gk. Ἰσμαήλ ; Syr. ܐܝܣܡܥܝܠ ; Eth. እስማኤል, with the Heb. יִשְׁמָעֵאל. A form derived from Heb. occurs in the inscriptions of both the S. and N. of the Peninsula.[1] In S. Arabia we find in a Himyaritic inscription 𐩺𐩪𐩣𐩲𐩱𐩡[2] = יסמעאל (cf. Eth. ይስማኤል), and in the Safaite inscriptions of N. Arabia we find a form יסמעל.[3] It is thus clear that the form with initial י was well enough known in Arabia before Muḥammad's day, but on the other hand, there seems to be no evidence that the form used in the Qur'ān was in use as a personal name among the Arabs in pre-Islamic times.[4] The fact that in the Qur'ān we find يوسف for יוסף and يعقوب for יעקב, but اسرائيل for ישראל and اسمعيل for יִשְׁמָעֵאל, just as in Syr. we find ܝܘܣܦ and ܝܥܩܘܒ, but ܐܝܣܪܝܠ and ܐܝܣܡܥܝܠ makes it reasonably certain that the Qur'ānic form came from a Syr. source,[5] and the form ܐܝܣܡܥܝܠ in the Christian Palestinian dialect removes any difficulty which might have been felt of س for ش.[6]

[1] D. H. Müller suggests that the name is an independent formation in S. Arabian (*WZKM*, iii, 225, being followed in this by Horovitz, *JPN*, 155, 156), but this is a little difficult.

[2] Hal, 193, 1; cf. *CIS*, iv, i, 55, with other references in Pilter's "Index of S. Arabian Proper Names", *PSBA*, 1917, p. 110, and Hartmann, *Arabische Frage*, 182, 226, 252–4. Derenbourg in his note on this inscription, *CIS*, iv, i, 56, takes it as a composite name in imitation of the Heb., but see Müller, *WZKM*, iii, 225; *ZDMG*, xxxvii, 13 ff.; Ryckmans, *Noms propres*, i, 239, and *RES*, i, No. 219.

[3] Dussaud, *Mission*, 221; Littmann, *Semitic Inscriptions*, 116, 117, 123; *Entzifferung der Safā-Inschriften*, 58; Lidzbarski, *Ephemeris*, ii, 44.

[4] The examples collected by Cheikho, *Naṣrāniya*, 230, cannot, as Horovitz, *KU*, 92, shows, be taken as evidence for the pre-Islamic use of the name. The form Ἐσμαήλος quoted by Horovitz from Waddington, from an inscription of A.D. 341, may be only a rendering of יסמאל.

[5] Margoliouth, *Schweich Lectures*, 12; Mingana, *Syriac Influence*, 82, and cf. Sprenger, *Leben*, ii, 336.

[6] Schulthess, *Lex*, 15, and cf. Horovitz, *KU*, 92; Rhodokanakis, *WZKM*, xvii, 283.

أَلْأَعْرَافُ (*Al-A'rāf*).

vii, 44, 46.

Al-A'rāf.

It is usually taken to mean the wall which separates Paradise from Hell. The philologers were at a loss to explain the word, the two favourite theories being (i) that it is the plu. of عرف used of the mane of a horse or the comb of a cock, and thus a metaphor for the highest part of anything (Zam, in loco: *LA*, xi, 146), or (ii) that it is from عرف *to know*, and so called because of the knowledge أصحاب الأعراف had of those in the Garden and those in the Fire.

Tor Andrae, *Ursprung*, 78, and Lidzbarski, *ZS*, ii, 182, claim that the word is Arabic, though translating an idea derived from one of the older religions.[1] There is difficulty with this, however, and perhaps a better solution is that proposed long ago by Ludolf,[2] viz. that it is the Eth. **አዕረፈ**. Horovitz, *Paradies*, 8, objects to this on the ground that Muḥammad does not use اعراف for the souls of the departed, but for the place where they, or at least some of them, dwell, which would be **ምዕራፍ**. It is by no means unlikely, however, that Muḥammad understood the verb **አዕረፈ**,[3] used of the blessed departed, as a place-name, for **አዕረፈ** and **ዕረፍት** seem much more commonly used in this sense than **ምዕራፍ**. It is even possible that اعراف is a corruption of **ምዕራፍ**. The introduction of the word would seem to be due to Muḥammad himself, for the occurrence of the word in Umayya, xlix, 14, is rightly suspected by Horovitz of being under Qur'ānic influence.

[1] Lidzbarski would take it as an attempt to translate the Mandaean מאמטאראתא = the *watch towers*, but this is rather remote.

[2] *Ad Historiam Æthiopicam Commentarius*, p. 207. He writes: "اعراف: Muhammedis Limbus, medius inter Paradisum et Infernum locus, receptaculum mediis generis hominum, qui tantundem boni ac mali in hoc mundo fecerunt. Id autem aliunde justius derivari nequit, quam a rad-Æthiopica **አዕረፈ** = *requievit*, quo verbo Æthiopes de pie defunctis utuntur."

[3] Praetorius, *Beit. Ass*, i, 23, however, takes **አዕረፈ** as a denom. from عَرَّة.

أَللّٰهُ (*Allāh*).

Of very frequent occurrence.

God.

One gathers from ar-Rāzī, *Mafātīḥ*, i, 84 (so Abū Ḥayyān, *Baḥr*, i, 15), that certain early Muslim authorities held that the word was of Syriac or Hebrew origin. The majority, however, claimed that it was pure Arabic, though they set forth various theories as to its derivation.[1] Some held that it has no derivation, being مُرْتَجَل : the Kūfans in general derived it from أَلْإِلَاهُ, while the Baṣrans derived it from أَللَّاهُ, taking لَاهٌ as a verbal noun from لِيهَ *to be high* or *to be veiled*. The suggested origins for إِلَاهٌ were even more varied, some taking it from أَلَهَ *to worship*, some from أَلِهَ *to be perplexed*, some from أَلِهَ إِلَى *to turn to for protection*, and others from وَلِهَ *to be perplexed*.

Western scholars are fairly unanimous that the source of the word must be found in one of the older religions. In the Semitic area אלה was a widely used word for deity, cf. Heb. אֱלֹהַּ ; Aram. אֱלָהּ ; Syr. ܐܠܗܐ ; Sab. 𐩱𐩡𐩠 ; and so Ar. إِلَٰهٌ is doubtless a genuine old Semitic form. The form اللّه, however, is different, and there can be little doubt that this, like the Mandaean אלאהא and the Pahlavi ideogram,[2] goes back to the Syr. ܐܠܗܐ (cf. Grünbaum, *ZDMG*, xxxix, 571 ; Sprenger, *Leben*, i, 287–9 ; Ahrens, *Muhammad*, 15 ; Rudolph, *Abhängigkeit*, 26 ; Bell, *Origin*, 54 ; Cheikho, *Naṣrāniya*, 159 ; Mingana, *Syriac Influence*, 86). The word, however, came into use in Arabian heathenism long before Muḥammad's time (Wellhausen, *Reste*, 217 ; Nielsen in *HAA*, i, 218 ff.). It occurs frequently in the N. Arabian inscriptions,[3] and also in those from S. Arabia, as, e.g.,

[1] They are discussed in detail by ar-Rāzī on pp. 81–4, of the first volume of his *Tafsīr*.

[2] Herzfeld, *Paikuli*, Glossary, 135.

[3] Cf. Littmann, *Entzifferung der thamudenischen Inschriften*, p. 63 ff. ; *Sem. Inscr*, p. 113 ff. ; and Ryckmans, *Noms propres*, i, 2 ; *RES*, iii, 441.

𐩲𐩣𐩬 𐩫𐩡 𐩱𐩡𐩱𐩡𐩩𐩣 "with all the Gods" (in Glaser, *Abessinien*, 50),[1] as well as in the pre-Islamic oath forms, such as that of Qais b. Khaṭīm given by Horovitz, *KU*, 140, and many in ash-Shanqīṭī's introduction to the *Mu'allaqāt*. It is possible that the expression الله تعالى is of S. Arabian origin, as the name 𐩩𐩲𐩡𐩺 occurs in a Qatabanian inscription.[2]

اللّٰهُمَّ (*Allahumma*).

iii, 25; v, 114; viii, 32; x, 10; xxxix, 47.

An invocatory name for God.

The form of the word was a great puzzle to the early grammarians [3]: the orthodox explanation being that it is a vocative form where the final م takes the place of an initial يا. The Kūfans took it as a contraction of يا الله امنا بخير (Baiḍ. on iii, 25), but their theory is ridiculed by Ibn Ya'īsh, i, 181. As a vocative it is said to be of the same class as هَلُمَّ *come along*. al-Khafājī, 20, however, recognizes it as a foreign word.

It is possible, as Margoliouth notes (*ERE*, vi, 248), that it is the Heb. אלהים which had become known to the Arabs through their contacts with Jewish tribes.[4]

إِلْيَاسُ (*Ilyās*).

vi, 85; xxxvii, 123, 130.

Elijah.

[1] Derenbourg in *JA*, viiie ser., xx, 157 ff., wants to find the word in the 𐩱𐩡𐩠𐩬 of a Minaean inscription, but this is usually taken as a reference to a tribal god الهان, *vide* Halévy, ibid, p. 325, 326.

[2] Rhodokanakis, "Die Inschriften an der Mauer von Koḥlân Timna'," in *SBAW*, Wien, 1924.

[3] Margoliouth, *ERE*, vi, 248.

[4] There is to be considered, however, the Phon. אלם = godhead (see references in Harris' *Glossary*, p. 77), which is evidence of a Semitic form with final *m*. Cf. Nielsen in *HAA*, i, 221, n. 2.

In xxxvii, 130, for the sake of rhyme, the form is إِلْيَاسِينَ.[1]

From al-Jawālīqī, *Mu'arrab*, 8, we learn that the philologers early recognized it as foreign, and it is given as such by as-Suyūṭī, *Muzhir*, i, 138; as-Sijistānī, 51; *LA*, vii, 303. The Heb. forms are אֵלִיָּה and אֵלִיָּהוּ, so it is obvious that the Arabic form must have been derived from a Christian source, as even Hirschfeld, *Beiträge*, 56, recognizes.[2] The Gk. Ἡλίας or Ἡλείας gives us the final *s*, but this also appears in Syr. ܐܠܝܐܣ beside the more usual ܐܠܝܐ (*PSm*, 203), and in the Eth. ኤልያስ.

The name was no uncommon one among Oriental Christians before Islam, and Ἡλίας occurs not infrequently in the Inscriptions.[3] We also find an الياس in the genealogy of the poet 'Adī b. Zaid given in *Aghānī*, ii, 18.[4] The likelihood is thus that it entered Arabic through the Syriac.

أَلْيَسَعُ (*Al-Yasa'*).

vi, 86; xxxviii, 48.

Elisha.

The word is usually treated as though it were يسع and the ال the definite article,[5] and then derived from يسع or وسع. Ṭab., on vi, 86, argues against this view, and in the Lexicons (e.g. al-Jawharī, *sub voc.*, *LA*, x, 296), and in al-Jawālīqī, 134 (cf. al-Khafājī, 215), it is given as a foreign borrowing, a fact which is also indicated by the variant spelling اللّيسع (*LA*, x, 296).

[1] Geiger, 190; Mingana, *Syriac Influence*, 83. Grimme, *ZA*, xxvi, 167, would see S. Arabian influence in the production of this longer form, but it is difficult to see much point to his suggestion.

[2] So Sprenger, *Leben*, ii, 335; Rudolph, *Abhängigkeit*, 47; Horovitz, *JPN*, 171.

[3] Lebas-Waddington, Nos. 2159, 2160, 2299, etc.

[4] Ibn Duraid, 20, would take this as a genuine Arabic word from يئس, with which Horovitz, *KU*, 99, is inclined to agree. In *LA*, vii, 303, however, where we find this same genealogy, we are expressly told الياس اسم اعجمىّ وقد سميت به العرب.

[5] Cf. Goldziher, *ZDMG*, xxiv, 208 n.

The Heb. אֱלִישָׁע is near enough to the Arabic to make a direct borrowing possible, but the probability is that it came from a Christian source (Horovitz, *KU*, 152). The Gk. forms are Ἐλίσα, Ἐλισάιε, and Ἐλισάιος; the Syr. ܐܠܝܫܥ; and the Eth. ኤልሳዕ; the probabilities being in favour of a Syriac origin.

أُمَّة (*Umma*).

Of frequent occurrence, e.g. ii, 122, 128; iii, 106, etc.

People, race.

Apparently a borrowing from the Jews.[1] Heb. אמה is a *tribe*, or *people*, and the אומה of the Rabbinic writings was widely used. As the word is apparently not a native Semitic word at all, but Akk. *ummatu*; Heb. אמה; Aram. אומא, אומתא; and Syr. ܐܘܡܬܐ, seem all to have been borrowed from the Sumerian,[2] we cannot deny the possibility, that the Ar. أُمَّة is a primitive borrowing from the same source. In any case it was an ancient borrowing, and if we can depend upon a reading בכש האמת, "at the people's cost" in a Safaite inscription,[3] we have evidence of its early use in N. Arabia.

أَمْر (*Amr*).

xvi, 2; xvii, 87; xxxii, 4; xl, 15; xlii, 52; lxv, 12; xcvii, 4.

Revelation.

In the two senses (i) *command* or *decree*, (ii) *matter*, *affair*, it is a genuine Arabic word, and commonly used in the Qur'ān.

In its use in connection with the Qur'ānic doctrine of revelation, however, it would seem to represent the Aram. מימרא (Rudolph, *Abhängigkeit*, 41; Horovitz, *JPN*, 188; Fischer, *Glossar*, Nachtrag to 8*b*; Ahrens, *Christliches*, 26; *Muḥammad*, 134). The whole conception seems to have been strongly influenced by the Christian Logos doctrine,[4] though the word would seem to have arisen from the Targumic use of מימרא.

[1] Horovitz, *KU*, 52; *JPN*, 190.

[2] Zimmern, *Akkad. Fremdw*, 46; Pedersen, *Israel*, 505.

[3] See Horovitz, *KU*, 52.

[4] Grimme, *System*, 50 ff.

أَمْشَاجٌ (*Amshāj*).

lxxvi, 2.

Plu. of مَشِيجٌ, *mingled*.

In this passage, " we created man from a mingled clot," it occurs as almost a technical physiological term. The Muslim savants take it as a normal formation from the verb مَشَجَ, but this may be a denominative from the noun.[1] Zimmern, *Akkad. Fremdw*, 40, suggests an ultimate origin in the Akk. *munziqu—clear wine*. This was borrowed on the one hand into Heb. מֶזֶג (beside מסך ; cf. Barth, *ES*, 33, 51) ; Aram. מְזִגָא ; Syr. ܡܙܓܐ ; and on the other into Egyptian *mṯk*, Coptic ⲙⲟⲩϫϭ.

From the Syr. ܡܙܓܐ arose the Arabic مزاج, and apparently مشاج was a parallel form borrowed at an early period, from which the other forms have developed.

آمَنَ (*Āmana*).

Of very frequent occurrence.

To believe.

The primitive verb أَمِنَ with its derivatives is pure Arabic. Form IV, however, آمَنَ with its derivatives, مُؤْمِنٌ, *a believer* ; and إِيمَان *believing*, *faith*, is a technical religious term which seems to have been borrowed from the older faiths, and intended to represent the Aram. הֵימַן ; Syr. ܗܝܡܢ ; Eth. አምነ.[2] The word actually borrowed would seem to have been the participle مُؤْمِن from Eth. ምእምን.[3]

[1] As in the case of مزاج, cf. Fraenkel, *Fremdw*, 172.

[2] These Aram. forms themselves, of course, are borrowed from the Heb. הֶאֱמִין (but see Lagarde, *Übersicht*, 121).

[3] See Horovitz, *KU*, 55 ; *JPN*, 191 ; Fischer, *Glossar*, Neue Nachlasse to 9*a*.

In lix, 23, مُؤْمِن meaning *faithful*,[1] and in lix, 9, إيمان meaning *certainty*, may be genuine Arabic (see Fischer, *Glossar*, 9*a*).

إِنْجِيلٌ (*Injīl*).

iii, 2, 43, 58; v, 50, 51, 70, 72, 110; vii, 156; ix, 112; xlviii, 29; lvii, 27.

Gospel.

It is used always of the Christian revelation, is particularly associated with Jesus, and occurs only in Madinan passages.[2]

Some of the early authorities tried to find an Arabic origin for it, making it a form إِفْعِيل from نجل, but this theory is rejected with some contempt by the commentators Zam. and Baiḍ. both on general grounds, and because of al-Ḥasan's reading أَنجيل, which clearly is not an Arabic form. So also the Lexicons *LA*, xiv, 171; *TA*, viii, 128; and al-Jawālīqī, 17 (al-Khafājī, 11), give it as a foreign word derived from either Hebrew or Syriac (cf. Ibn al-Athīr, *Nihāya*, iv, 136).

Obviously it is the Gk. ἐυαγγέλιον, and both Marracci[3] and Fraenkel[4] have thought that it came directly into Arabic from the Greek. The probabilities, however, are that it came into Arabic through one of the other Semitic tongues. The Hebrew origin suggested by some is too remote. It is true that in the Talmud we find עוון גלוון for אוונגליון,[5] but this is merely a transcription of ܐܘܢܓܠܝܘܢ, and the הגליונים וספרי המינים "the Gilyonim and books of the Minim", merely reproduces the Syr. ܓܠܝܘܢ. The suggestion of a Syr. source is much more hopeful. It is true that ܐܘܢܓܠܝܘܢ is only a transliteration of the Gk. ἐυαγγέλιον, but it was as commonly used as the pure Syr. ܣܒܪܬܐ, and may be assumed to have been in common use among the Christians with whom Muḥammad may have been in contact. Nöldeke has pointed out, however, that

[1] With which may be compared the Sab. 𐩱𐩣𐩬𐩬, *faithful*. Cf. Hommel, *Südarabische Chrest*, 121; Rossini, *Glossarium*, 106.

[2] vii, 156, is perhaps an exception, but though the Sūra is given as late Meccan, this verse seems to be Madinan.

[3] *Prodromus*, i, 5, "corrupta Graeca voce."

[4] *Vocab*, 24.

[5] Krauss, *Griechische und lateinische Lehnwörter im Talmud*, ii, 21.

the Manichaean forms انكليون of Persian origin,[1] and *anglion* of Turkish origin,[2] still have the Gk. -ιον ending, and had the Arabic, like these, been derived from the Syr. we might have expected it also to preserve the final ن. The shortened form, he points out (*Neue Beiträge*, 47), is to be found in the Eth. ወንጌል, where the long vowel is almost conclusive evidence of the Arabic word having come from Abyssinia.[3] Grimme, *ZA*, xxvi, 164, suggests that it may have entered Arabic from the Sabaean, but we have no inscriptional evidence to support this. It is possible that the word was current in this form in pre-Islamic days, though as Horovitz, *KU*, 71, points out, there is some doubt of the authenticity of the verses in which it is found.[4]

آيَة (*Āya*).

Of very frequent occurrence. Cf. ii, 37; iii, 9; xxxvi, 33.

A sign.

Later it comes to mean a *verse* of the Qur'ān, and then a *verse* of a book, but it is doubtful whether it ever means anything more than *sign* in the Qur'ān, though as Muḥammad comes to refer to his preaching as a *sign*, the word tends to the later meaning, as e.g. in iii, 5, etc. It is noteworthy that in spite of the frequency of its occurrence in the Qur'ān it occurs very seldom in the early Meccan passages.[5]

The struggles of the early Muslim philologers to explain the word are interestingly set forth in *LA*, xviii, 66 ff. The word has no root in Arabic, and is obviously, as von Kremer noted,[6] a borrowing from Syr. or Aram. The Heb. אות (cf. Phon. את), from a verb אוה, to *sign* or *mark*, was used quite generally, for signs of the weather (Gen. i, 14; ix, 12), for a military ensign (Numb. ii, 2), for a memorial sign

[1] Vullers, *Lex*, i, 136; Salemann, *Manichaeische Studien*, i, 50; *BQ*, 88, which latter knows that it is the name of the book of Jesus and the book of Mani— نام كتاب نصار است كه انجيل عيسى ونام كتاب مانى. It is curious that Bagh. on iii, 2, gives انقليون as an attempt to represent the Syriac original.

[2] In the phrase *uluγ anglion bitig*, cf. Le Coq, *SBAW*, Berlin, 1909, p. 1204.

[3] Cf. Fischer, *Islamica*, i, 372, n. 5.

[4] Cf. Cheikho, *Naṣrāniya*, 185.

[5] Not more than nine times in Sūras classed by Nöldeke as early Meccan, though many passages in these are certainly to be placed much later, and one may doubt whether the word occurs at all in really early passages.

[6] *Ideen*, 226 n.; see also Sprenger, *Leben*, ii, 419 n.; Cheikho, *Naṣrāniya*, 181; and Margoliouth, *ERE*, x, 539.

(Josh. iv, 6), and also in a technical religious sense both for the miracles which attest the Divine presence (Ex. viii, 19; Deut. iv, 34; Ps. lxxviii, 43), and for the signs or omens which accompany and testify to the work of the Prophets (1 Sam. x, 7, 9; Ex. iii, 12). In the Rabbinic writings אות is similarly used, though it there acquires the meaning of a letter of the alphabet, which meaning, indeed, is the only one the Lexicons know for the Aram. אתא.[1]

While it is not impossible that the Arabs may have got the word from the Jews, it is more probable that it came to them from the Syriac-speaking Christians.[2] The Syr. ܐܬܐ, while being used precisely as the Heb. אות, and translating σημεῖον both in the LXX and N.T., is also used in the sense of *argumentum, documentum* (*PSm*, 413), and thus approaches even more closely than אות the Qur'ānic use of the word.

The word occurs in the old poetry, e.g. in Imrū'ul-Qais, lxv, 1 (Ahlwardt, *Divans*, 160), and so was in use before the time of Muḥammad.

أَيُّوب (*Ayyūb*).

iv, 161; vi, 84; xxi, 83; xxxviii, 40.

Job.

It is the Biblical Job, and the word was recognized as foreign, e.g. al-Jawālīqī, *Mu'arrab*, 8. The exegetes take him to be a Greek, e.g. Zam. on xxi, 83—رومى and ath-Tha'labī, *Qiṣaṣ*, 106—رجل من روم.

The name would seem to have come into Arabic through a Christian channel, as even Hirschfeld, *Beiträge*, 56, admits. The Heb. אִיּוֹב appears in Gk. (LXX) as Ἰώβ, and Syr. as ܐܝܘܒ, which latter is obviously the origin of the Arabic form.[3] The name appears to have been used in Arabia in the pre-Islamic period. Hess would interpret the איב of an inscription copied by Huber (No. 521, 1, 48), as Aiyūb [4]; there is

[1] In Biblical Aramaic, however, אָת means a *sign* wrought by God; cf. Dan. iii, 33.

[2] Mingana, *Syriac Influence*, 86. Note also the Mand. אותא = *sign*.

[3] Rudolph, *Abhängigkeit*, 47.

[4] Hess, *Die Entzifferung der thamudischen Inschriften* (1911), p. 15, No. 77; Littmann, *Entzifferung*, 15; and see Halévy in *JA*, ser. vii, vol. x, p. 332.

an أيوب in the genealogy of 'Adī b. Zaid given in *Aghānī*, ii, 18, and another Christian of this name is mentioned by an-Nābigha.[1]

بَابٌ (*Bāb*).

Occurs some twenty-seven times, e.g. ii, 55; iv, 153.

A door or gate.

Fraenkel, *Fremdw*, 14, noted that it was an early loan word, and suggested that it came from the Aram. בָּבָא which is in very common use in the Rabbinic writings. D. H. Müller, however (*WZKM*, i, 23), on the ground that ܒܒܐ occurs very rarely in Syr. and that the root is entirely lacking in Heb., Eth., and Sab., suggested that it was an early borrowing from Mesopotamia (cf. Zimmern, *Akkad. Fremdw*, 30), and may have come directly into Arabic. It occurs commonly in the old poetry, which confirms the theory of early borrowing, and it is noteworthy that from some Mesopotamian source it passed into Middle Persian (*Frahang*, Glossary, p. 103; Herzfeld, *Paikuli*, Glossary, 151).

بَابِلُ (*Bābil*).

ii, 96.

Babylon.

This sole occurrence of the word is in connection with the story of Hārūt and Mārūt who teach men magic. It is a diptote in the Qur'ān but *LA*, xiii, 43, takes this to be not because it is a foreign name, but a fem. name of more than three radicals (cf. Yāqūt, *Mu'jam*, i, 447).[2]

It is, of course, from the Akk. *Bab-ilu* (Delitzsch, *Paradies*, 212), either through the Syr. ܒܒܠ or the Heb. בָּבֶל. The city was well known in Arabia in the pre-Islamic period, and the name occurs in the old poetry, e.g. Mufaḍḍaliyāt (ed. Lyall, p. 133, l. 13), and al-A'shā (Geyer, *Zwei Gedichte*, i, 58 = *Dīwān*, lv, 5), and Halévy would find the name in a Safaite inscription.[3] Horovitz, *KU*, 101, notes that Babylon was well known as a centre for the teaching of

[1] Ahlwardt, *Divans*, p. 4; cf. Horovitz, *KU*, 100; *JPN*, 158.
[2] Some, however, recognized it as a foreign name, cf. Abū Ḥayyān, *Baḥr*, i, 319.
[3] *JA*, sér. vii, vol. x, p. 380.

magic, a fact which we would also gather from the use of the word *Bavil* in the Manichaean Uigur fragments from Idiqut-Schahri.[1]

بَارَكَ (*Bāraka*).

vii, 52, 133; xvii, 1; xxi, 71, 81, etc.

To bless.

With this should be taken the forms بَرَكَاتٌ (vii, 94; xi, 50, 76), and مُبَارَكٌ (iii, 90; vi, 92, 156, etc.).

The primitive verb بَرَكَ, which is not used in the Qur'ān, means to *kneel*, used specially of the camel, so that أَبْرَكَ is the technical word for making a camel kneel. In this primitive sense it is common Semitic, so we find Heb. נברכה לפני יהוה "let us kneel before Jehovah"; Syr. ܒܪܟ ܥܠ ܒܘܪܟܘܗܝ "he knelt upon his knees"; Eth. ወአስተብረኩ ፡ ቅድሜሁ "and they bowed the knee before him". It was in the N. Semitic area, however, that the root seems to have developed the sense of to *bless*, and from thence it passed to the S. Semitic area. Thus we have Heb. בָּרַךְ, and Phon. ברך to *bless*; Aram. בְּרַךְ to *bless* or *praise*; Syr. ܒܪܟ to *bless* or *praise*; and in Palm. such phrases as בריך שמו לעלמא (de Vogüé, No. 94) "blessed be his name for evermore", and יברך (*ibid.*, No. 144) "may he bless". From this N. Semitic sense we find derived the Sab. 𐩨𐩧𐩫 (Rossini, *Glossarium*, 118), Eth. በረከ to *bless, celebrate the praises of*, and Ar. بارك as above. Note also the formations—Heb. ברכה; Aram. ברכא; Syr. ܒܘܪܟܬܐ, which also were taken over into S. Semitic, e.g. Eth. በረከት; Ar. بَرَكَةٌ.

بَرَأَ (*Bara'a*).

lvii, 22.

To create.

[1] Ed. Le Coq, *SBAW*, Berlin, 1908, pp. 400, 401; cf. also Salemann, *Manichaeische Studien*, i, 58.

Note also بَارِئ *creator* used of Allāh in ii, 51; lix, 24; and بَرِيَّة *creation* in xcviii, 5, 6. It will be noticed that the word is only used in very late Madinan passages, the Meccan words being فطر, فاطر and خلق خالق.

The Arabic root بَرِئَ is *to be freed from a defect*, i.e. to be sound or healthy (cf. Heb. בריא), and in a moral sense *to be pure*. In this sense it is used not infrequently in the Qur'ān, cf. vi, 19. In the sense of *create*, however, it is obviously borrowed from the older religions, for this is a characteristic N. Semitic development.[1] Akk. *barū* to *make* or *create*: Heb. בָּרָא to *shape* or *create*: Aram. בְּרָא, Syr. ܒܪܳܐ to *create*, of which the Arabic equivalent is بَرَى, used in the older language for fashioning an arrow or cutting a pen.[2] Similarly بَرِيَّة is not an Arabic development (as is evident from the difficulties the philologers had with it, cf. *LA*, i, 22), but was also taken over from the older religions, cf. Heb. בריאה a *thing created*: Aram. בריאה and ברייה. So بارئ is from the Aram. ברייא, בוריא; Syr. ܒܪܘܝܐ, ܒܳܪܝܐ, meaning *Creator*, and used particularly of God (Lidzbarski, *SBAW*, Berlin, 1916, p. 1218 n.).[3]

Macdonald, *EI*, i, 303, writing of بارئ suggests that the borrowing was from the Heb.,[4] but the correspondences are much closer with the Aram. (Nöldeke, *Neue Beiträge*, 49), and especially with the Syriac (Mingana, *Syriac Influence*, 88), so that the probabilities are in favour of its having been taken from the Christians of the North.

[1] Schwally, *ZDMG*, liii, 201.

[2] And cf. the S. Arabian 𐩨𐩧𐩱 to *found or build a temple*, cf. *ZDMG*, xxxvii, 413. Rossini, *Glossarium*, 117. In Phon. ברא is a sculptor; cf. Harris, *Glossary*, 91.

[3] Massignon, *Lexique technique*, 52, however, considers it as an Arabic word specialized in this meaning under Aramaic influence.

[4] So Ahrens, *ZDMG*, lxxxiv, 20.

بَرْزَخٌ (*Barzakh*).

xxiii, 102 ; xxv, 55 ; lv, 20.

A barrier or partition.

In xxv, 55, and lv, 20, it is the barrier between the two seas (بحرين) where the reference is probably to some cosmological myth. In xxiii, 102, it is used in an eschatological passage, and the exegetes do not know what the reference is, though as a glance at aṭ-Ṭabarī's Commentary will show, they were fertile in guesses.

That the word is not Arabic seems clear from the Lexicons, which venture no suggestions as to its verbal root, are unable to quote any examples of the use of the word from the old poetry, and obviously seek to interpret it from the material of the Qur'ān itself.

Addai Sher, 19, sought to explain it from the Pers. برزك *weeping* or *crying*, but this has little in its favour, and in any case suits only xxiii, 102. Vollers, *ZDMG*, l, 646, makes the much more plausible suggestion that برزخ is a by-form of فرسخ *parasang* from the Phlv. *frasang*, Mod.Pers. فرسنک, which preserves its form fairly well in Gk. παρασάγγης, but becomes Aram. פרסא or פרסה [1]; Syr. ܦܪܣܚܐ whence the Ar. فرسخ. The Phlv. *frasangan* of *PPGl*, 116, means a measure of land and of roads,[2] and could thus fit the sense *barrier* in all three passages.

بُرْهَانٌ (*Burhān*).

ii, 105 ; iv, 174 ; xii, 24 ; xxi, 24 ; xxiii, 117 ; xxvii, 65 ; xxviii, 32, 75.

An evident proof.

In all the passages save xii, 24, and xxviii, 32, it is used in the sense of a proof or demonstration of the truth of one's religious position. In these two cases, one from the story of Joseph and the other from that of Moses, the word refers to an evident miraculous sign from

[1] Levy, *Wörterbuch*, iv, 125 ; Telegdi, in *JA*, ccxxvi (1935), p. 252.

[2] See Horn, *Grundriss*, 182 ; Nyberg, *Glossar*, 73.

God for the demonstration of His presence and power to him who beheld it. It is thus clearly used in the Qur'ān as a technical religious term.[1]

It is generally taken as a form فعلان from بره, Form IV of which is said to mean *to prove*, but the straits to which the philologers are put to explain the word (cf. Rāghib, *Mufradāt*, 44; *LA*, xvii, 369), show us that we are dealing with a foreign word. Sprenger, *Leben*, i, 108 had noted this,[2] but he makes no attempt to discover its origin. Addai Sher, 21, suggested that it is from the Pers. بُرُوهَان meaning *clearly manifest*, or *well known* (cf. Vullers, *Lex.*, i, 352), but this is somewhat remote. The origin clearly is, as Nöldeke has shown (*Neue Beiträge*, 58),[3] in the Eth. ብርሃን, a common Abyssinian word,[4] being found also in Amharic, Tigré, and Tigriña, meaning *light, illumination*, from a root ብርህ cognate with Heb. בהר; Ar. بهر. It seems to have this original sense in iv, 174; xii, 24, and the sense of *proof* or *demonstration* is easily derived from this.

بُرُوج (*Burūj*).

iv, 80; xv, 16; xxv, 62; lxxxv, 1.

Towers.

The original meaning occurs in iv, 80, but in the other passages it means the signs of the Zodiac, according to the general consensus of the Commentators, cf. as-Sijistānī, 63.

The philologers took the word to be from بَرَجَ *to appear* (cf. Baiḍ. on iv, 80; *LA*, iii, 33), but there can be little doubt that بُرُوج represents the Gk. πύργος (Lat. *burgus*), used of the towers on a city wall, as e.g. in Homer *Od*, vi, 262—πόλιος ἣν περὶ πύργος ὑψηλός. The Lat. *burgus* (see Guidi, *Della Sede*, 579) is apparently the source

[1] Ahrens, *Christliches*, 22, makes a distinction between xii, 24; iv, 147; xxiii, 117, where it means "Licht, Erleuchtung", and the other passages where it means "Beweis".

[2] Also Massignon, *Lexique technique*, 52.

[3] Also ibid., p. 25.

[4] It is in frequent use even in the oldest monuments of the language.

of the Syr. ܦܘܪܓܐ[1] a *turret*, and perhaps of the Rabbinic בורגן, בורנין a *resting place* or *station* for travellers.[2] From this sense of *stations* for travellers it is an easy transition to *stations* of the heavenly bodies, i.e. the Zodiac. Syr. ܦܘܪܓܐ is indeed used for the Zodiac (*PSm*, 475), but this is late and probably under the influence of Arabic usage.

It is possible that the word occurs in the meaning of *tower* in a S. Arabian inscription (D. H. Müller in *ZDMG*, xxx, 688), but the reading is not certain.[3] Ibn Duraid, 229, also mentions it as occurring as a personal name in the pre-Islamic period. The probabilities are that it was a military word introduced by the Romans into Syria and N. Arabia,[4] whence it passed into the Aramaic dialects [5] and thence to Arabia. It would have been borrowed in the sing. form بُرْج from which an Arabic plural was then formed.

بَشَّرَ (*Bashshara*).

Of frequent occurrence, cf. ii, 23; iii, 20; iv, 137, etc.

To announce good news.

The primitive verb بَشَرَ *to peel off bark*, then *to remove the surface of a thing*, i.e. to *smooth*, is not found in the Qur'ān, though it occurs in the old literature. From this we find بَشَرٌ *skin* and thence *flesh*, as Syr. ܒܣܪܐ; Heb. בשר[6]; Akk. *bišru*, *blood-relation*, whence it is an easy transition to the meaning *man*, cf. Heb. בשר; Syr. ܒܪ ܒܣܪܐ (plu. ܒܢܝ ܒܣܪܐ = ἄνθρωποι). بَشَرٌ in this sense occurs frequently in the Qur'ān [7] and Ahrens, *Christliches*, 38, thinks it is of Aramaic origin.

[1] So Fraenkel, *Fremdw*, 235, against Freytag and Rodiger, who claim that it is a direct borrowing from πύργος.

[2] But see the discussion in Krauss, *Griechische Lehnwörter*, ii, 143.

[3] Muller in *WZKM*, i, 28.

[4] Vollers in *ZDMG*, li, 312.

[5] The Arm. բուրգն came probably through the Aramaic also. Cf. Hübschmann. *Arm. Gramm*, i, 393; Brockelmann in *ZDMG*, xlvii, 2.

[6] So Sab. 𐩨𐩦𐩧 and Eth. በሰረ, but these apparently developed late under Jewish or Christian influence.

[7] And note باشر *to go in unto a wife* (ii, 183, only), with Heb. בשר *membrum virile*; Syr. ܒܣܪܐ *per euphemismum de pudendis viri et foeminae*.

The wider use of the root in the Qur'ān, however, is in the sense of *to announce good tidings*. Thus we have the verb بَشَّرَ as above ; بُشْرَى *good news* (ii, 91 ; iii, 122 ; viii, 10, etc.) ; بَشِير (v, 22 ; vii, 188, etc.), and بُشُرٌ (vii, 55 ; xxv, 50, etc.), *the bringer of good tidings* : also مُبَشِّر (ii, 209, etc.) with much the same meaning ; أَبْشَرَ (xli, 30) *to receive pleasure from good tidings* : and مُسْتَبْشِر (lxxx, 39), *rejoicing*. This use, however, seems not to be original in Arabic but derived from the older religions. Thus Akk. *bussuru*, is *to bear a joyful message* : Heb. בשר both *to bear good tidings* and *to gladden with good tidings* : התבשר *to receive good tidings.*[1]

The S. Semitic use of the word seems to be entirely under the influence of this Jewish usage. In Eth. the various forms በሰረ *to bring a joyful message*, አብሰረ *to bring good tidings*, ተበሰረ *to be announced*, ብስራት *good news*, አብሳሪ *one who announces good tidings*, are all late and doubtless under the influence of the Bible. So the S. Arabian 𐩨𐩦𐩧𐩩 *to bring tidings* and 𐩨𐩦𐩧𐩩 *tidings* (cf. *ZDMG*, xxx, 672 ; *WZKM* (1896), p. 290 ; Rossini, *Glossarium*, 119), are to be considered of the same origin, especially when we remember that the use of 𐩨𐩦𐩧𐩩 is in the *Raḥmān* inscription. The Syr. ܣܒܪ has suffered metathesis, but in the Christian Palestinian dialect we find ܒܣܪ *to preach*, used just as بَشَّرَ in iii, 20 ; ix, 34, etc., and so ܒܣܘܪܐ = εὐαγγέλιον, where again the influence is undoubtedly Jewish.

The probabilities are that the word was an early borrowing and taken direct from the Jews, though in the sense of *to preach* the influence was probably Syriac.[2]

بَطَلَ (*Baṭala*).

Occurs some thirty-six times in various forms.

To be in vain, false.

[1] Also בְּשׂוֹרָה *tidings* = Ar. بشرى and بشارة, which latter, however, is not Qur'ānic. Cf. also now the Ras Shamra בשר *to bring good news*.

[2] As probably the Phlv. *basariā*, *PPGl*, 95.

The passages in which it occurs are relatively late, and it is clearly a technical religious term for the nothingness, vanity, and falseness of that which is opposed to God's حقّ. In particular it is used of idols, as in xvi, 74; xxix, 52, 67, etc., where it forcibly reminds us of the Hebrew use of אלילים and the τὰ μάταια of Acts xiv, 15.

Now as a matter of fact the Peshitta translates τὰ μάταια by ܣܪܝܩܬܐ, and, as Ahrens, *Christliches*, 38, points out, we seem to have here the origin of the Qur'ānic باطل, whence probably the other forms were derived. Cf. the Eth. ከንቱ, *vanum, inanem, irritum*.

بَعْل (*Ba'l*).

xxxvii, 125.

Baal.

The word occurs in the Elijah story and as a proper name undoubtedly came to Muḥammad from the same source as his الياس. As this would seem to be from the Syr. we may conclude that بعل is from the Syr. ܒܥܠ.[1] On the question of the word in general the authorities differ. Robertson Smith[2] argued that the word was a loan-word in Arabia, but Nöldeke (*ZDMG*, xl, 174), and Wellhausen (*Reste*, 146), claim that it is indigenous. It is worthy of note that as-Suyūṭī, *Itq*, 310, states that بعل meant ربّ in the dialects of Yemen and of Azd, and as such we find it in the S. Arabian inscriptions, e.g. Glaser, 1076, 2, XoƆX 1oП "Lord of Teri'at" (see further Rossini, *Glossarium*, 116; *RES*, i, Nos. 184, 185). In any case from the Nabataean and N. Arabian inscriptions[3] we learn that the word was known in this sense in Arabia long before Muḥammad's time.[4] Horovitz, *KU*, 101, thinks it came from Eth. (cf. Ahrens, *Christliches*, 38).

[1] So Horovitz, *KU*, 101, and see Rudolph, *Abhängigkeit*, 47 n.

[2] *Religion of the Semites* (2 ed.), 100 ff.; *Kinship*, 210.

[3] See Cook, *Glossary*, 32; Lidzbarski, *Handbuch*, 240, 241; Ryckmans, *Noms propres*, i, 8, 54; Nielsen in *HAA*, i, 241.

[4] In the Qur'ān itself (xi, 75) it occurs in the sense of *husband*.

بَعِيرٌ (*Ba'īr*).

xii, 65, 72.

A full-grown camel.

It occurs only in the Joseph story, and Dvořák, *Fremdw*, 18, is doubtless right in thinking that its use here is due to Muḥammad's sources. In the Joseph story of Gen. xlv, 17, the word used is בעיר, and in the Syr. ܒܥܝܪܐ, which means originally *cattle* in general, and then any beast of burden. It is easy to see how the word was specialized in Arabic to mean *camel* (Guidi, *Della Sede*, 583 ; Rossini, *Glossarium*, 116 ; Hommel in *HAA*, i, 82 n.), the usual beast of burden in that country, and as such it occurs in the old poetry. There seems no reason to doubt the conclusion of Dvořák, *Fremdw*, 46 (cf. Horovitz, *JPN*, 192), that Muḥammad's informant, hearing the word in the story as he got it from a Jewish or Christian source, passed the word on as though it had its specialized Arabic meaning of *camel*.

بِغَالٌ (*Bighāl*).

xvi, 8.

Mules. Plural of بَغْلٌ.

al-Khafājī, 44, shows that some of the Muslim philologers suspected that it was non-Arabic. The root is clearly not Arabic, and Hommel, *Säugethiere*, 113, noted it as a borrowing from Abyssinia, where the mule was as characteristic an animal as the camel is in Arabia. Fraenkel, *Fremdw*, 110, accepts this derivation, and Nöldeke, *Neue Beiträge*, 58, has established it. The word is common to all the Abyssinian dialects—cf. Eth. and Tigré በቅል ; Amharic በቅሎ and በቕሎ ; Tigrina በቅሊ. The غ for ق is not an isolated phenomenon, as Hommel illustrates.

بَلَدٌ (*Balad*).

ii, 120 ; iii, 196 ; vii, 55, 56, etc. Also بَلْدَةٌ—xxv, 51 ; xxvii, 93 ; xxxiv, 14, etc.

Country, region, territory.

The verb بلد in the sense of *to dwell in a region* is denominative, and Nöldeke recognized that بلد in the sense of a "place where one dwells" was a Semitic borrowing from the Lat. *palatium*: Gk. *παλάτιον*. This has been accepted by Fraenkel, *Fremdw*, 28, and Vollers, *ZDMG*, li, 312, and may be traced back to the military occupation of N. Arabia.

بَنَّاء (*Bannā'*).

xxxviii, 36.

A builder.

The verb بَنَى *to build* occurs in the Qur'ān along with certain formations therefrom, e.g. بِنَاء *ceiled roof*, and مَبْنِيّ, and it would seem on the surface that بَنَّاء is another such formation. Nöldeke, *Mand. Gramm*, 120, n., however, has a suggestion that it is a borrowing from Aramaic, whence on the other hand it passed into Middle Persian (cf. Herzfeld, *Paikuli*, Glossary, p. 156). Fraenkel, *Fremdw*, 255, is doubtful, but thinks that if it is a loan-word it comes from the Jewish בנאה rather than from the Syr. ܒܢܝܐ. Zimmern, *Akkad. Fremdw*, 26, considers them all as borrowed from Akk. *banū—to build*, though the S. Arabian 𐩨𐩬𐩺 and its derivatives might suggest that the root developed independently in S. Semitic (Rossini, *Glossarium*, 115).

بُنْيَان (*Bunyān*).

ix, 110, 111; xvi, 28; xviii, 20; xxxvii, 95; lxi, 4.

A building or construction.

Again it would seem, on the surface, that this word also is from بَنَى *to build*. Sprenger, *Leben*, i, 108, has noted that words of this form are un-Arabic, e.g. قُرْبَان, فُرْقَان, سلطان, سبحان, etc., and lead us to look for an Aram. origin. Fraenkel, *Fremdw*, 27, points out that we have in Aram. בִּנְיָן, בִּנְיָנָא beside בנייתא and בנאיתא, and in Syr. ܒܢܝܢܐ, meaning building. In Heb. also we find בִּנְיָן, but as Lagarde, *Übersicht*, 205, shows, this is a borrowing from Aram. بنيان occurs in the old poetry so it was doubtless an early borrowing from Aramaic.

بُهْتَان (*Buhtān*).

iv, 24, 112, 155 ; xxiv, 15 ; xxxiii, 58 ; lx, 12.

Slander, calumny.

Only in Madinan passages.

It is usually taken from بهت *to confound*, which occurs twice in the Qur'ān, viz. ii, 260 ; xxi, 41 (*LA*, ii, 316 ; Rāghib, *Mufradāt*, 63), though we learn from the Lexicons that some took it from بَهَأ. Sprenger, as we have mentioned above, pointed out the Aram. form of these words ending in ـان, and Fraenkel, *Vocab*, 22, saw that بُهْتَان was to be explained from the Aram. בהת, Syr. ܒܗܬ *to be or become ashamed*, whence בַּהֵית and ܒܰܗܶܬ *to make ashamed*, a root connected with the Heb. בוש : Sab. 𐩨𐩠𐩩[1] : Ar. بات. The borrowing was doubtless from the Syr., where we have the parallel forms ܒܗܬܬܢܐ, ܒܗܬܬܘܬܐ.[2]

بَهِيمَة (*Bahīma*).

v, 1 ; xxii, 29, 35.

Animal.

A very late word, occurring only in material from towards the very end of the Madina period, and used only in connection with legislation about lawful and unlawful meats. It is well known that

[1] Cf. 𐩣𐩨𐩠𐩩𐩥 *evil doer*, *ZDMG*, xxxvii, 375.

[2] *PSm*, 461. Wellhausen in *ZDMG*, lxvii, 633, also decides in favour of an Aram. origin for the word.

these food regulations were formed under Jewish influence,[1] so that it is significant that the word in the Jewish legislation (Lev. xi) is בהמה.

The root of the word is probably a form בהם which we find in Eth. ብህመ *to be dumb*, connected with Ar. ابهم and استبهم, both of which refer to incoherence or ambiguity of speech. The Lexicons, however, are troubled about the word (cf. *LA*, xiv, 323), and there is little doubt that it was a direct borrowing from the Jewish בהמה.[2]

بُورٌ (*Būr*).

xxv, 19 ; xlviii, 12.

Ignorant.

The phrase قَوْمٌ بُورٌ in these two passages was a complete puzzle to the Commentators. As we find a verb بَارَ *to perish* in xxxv, 11, 26, and the noun بَوَارٌ in xiv, 33, most of the early authorities endeavoured to explain بور from this and make it mean *destruction*, cf. Ṭab., Zam., Baiḍ., and Bagh. on the verses. There was some philological difficulty over this, however, which as-Suyūṭī, *Itq*, 311, endeavours to avoid by claiming that it is a dialectal form, meaning هلاك in the dialect of 'Umān, a theory which seems also to have been held by al-Akhfash (*LA*, v, 153).

Hirschfeld, *Beiträge*, 40, suggests that it is the Aram. בור and like أُمِّىٌّ (vii, 156, 158, etc.), is a translation of עם הארץ.[3] In the Rabbinic writings בור means a boorish, ignorant, and uncultured

[1] Rudolph, *Abhängigkeit*, 61 ; Horovitz, *JPN*, 193.

[2] Addai Sher, 30, suggests that it is from the Pers. بهمان, which is absurd.

[3] "Im Munde der Juden war עם הארץ zweifellos ausserordentlich gelaufig, nicht minder haufig wohl auch das aram. בור. Die Seltenheit des Ausdrucks im Korān trotz zahlreicher Gelegenheit ihn zu brauchen, zeigt aber, dass derselbe Muhammad nicht sehr gelaufig geworden ist, er wendet ofter das dasselbe besagende '*Ummij* an, welches, wie Geiger bereits gefunden hat, die eigentliche arabische Übertragung von '*Am hā'ārez* darstellt," cf. Geiger, 28.

person, e.g. Yoma, 37a, המהלך כנגד רבו הרי זה בוב "he who walks ahead of his teacher is a boor", or Pirqe Aboth, ii, 6— אין בור ירא חטא "No boorish fellow fears sin", and corresponds with the Aram. בורא used, e.g., in the Targums on Prov. xii, 1, or Lev. Rabba, § 18, where the uncultured are contrasted with the learned. Horovitz, *JPN*, 193, also holds to a Jewish origin.

Precisely similar in meaning, however, is the Syr. ܒܘܪܐ, as when Paul in 2 Cor. xi, 6, says ܒܘܪܐ ܐܢܐ ܒܡܠܬܗ, "uncultured am I in speech (but not in knowledge)"—ἰδιώτης τῷ λόγῳ, referring to his difficulties with the Greek tongue. So Ephraem uses ܒܘܪܐ ܘܗܕܝܘܛܐ, and Mingana, *Syriac Influence*, 93, thinks that the Qur'ānic بور is of Syr. rather than Jewish origin. It is really impossible to decide. The word occurs in the old poetry, e.g. Ḥassān (ed. Hirschfeld, xcvi, 2), and a verse in *LA*, v, 153, so it was apparently an early borrowing.

بِيَعٌ (*Biya'*).

xxii, 41.

Plu. of بِيعَةٌ a place of worship.

It was early recognized as a foreign word (as-Suyūṭī, *Itq*, 320; *Mutaw*, 46), and is said by al-Jawālīqī, *Mu'arrab*, 35, to be a borrowing from Persian. One is at a loss to know why al-Jawālīqī should think it was Persian, when it is so obviously the Syr. ܒܝܥܬܐ,[1] unless perhaps we may suggest that he knew of Syrian churches in Persian territory called by this name and jumped to the conclusion that it was a Persian word. Syr. ܒܝܥܬܐ is originally an *egg* (cf. Ar. بيض; Heb. ביצה; Aram. ביעה), and then was used metaphorically for the top of a rounded arch—ܒܝܥܬܐ ܕܩܡܩܡܗ ܕܩܘܒܬܐ, and so for the domed buildings used for worship.

The word was well known in pre-Islamic times, being found in the S. Arabian inscriptions,[2] and occurring not infrequently in the old

[1] This has been generally recognized, cf. Sprenger, *Leben*, iii, 310, n.1; Fraenkel, *Vocab*, 24; *Fremdw*, 274; Rudolph, *Abhängigkeit*, 7; Cheikho, *Naṣrāniya*, 201.

[2] 𐩨𐩺𐩲 in the Abraha inscription, *CIS*, iv, No. 541, ll. 66 and 117.

poetry (e.g. *Diwan Hudh.*, ed. Kosegarten, 3, l. 5), and may be assumed to have entered Arabic from the Mesopotamian area. It is interesting that the traditional exegesis of the Qur'ān seems to favour the word in xxii, 41, being referred to معبد النصارى, though some thought it meant كنيسة اليهود, cf. Zam., Baiḍ., Ṭab., on the passage, and *TA*, v, 285; as-Sijistānī, 65.

تَابَ (*Tāba*).

Occurs very frequently.

To repent towards God.

Besides the verb تاب should be noted تَوْبٌ and تَوْبَةٌ *repentance*, and تَوَّابٌ *the relenting*, used as a title of Allah.

The word is undoubtedly a borrowing from the Aramaic (cf. Halévy in *JA*, ser. vii, vol. x, p. 423), for the Semitic root which appears in Heb. as שׁוּב, is in S. Semitic found as Sab. ΠΦ8; Ar. ثاب and only normally appears with initial ת in Aram. תּוּב; Syr. ܬܳܒ. The Ar. ثاب, particularly in the derived sense of *recompense*, is used not infrequently in the Qur'ān, cf. iii, 139; iv, 133; xviii, 42, etc.

Fraenkel, *Vocab*, 22, noted that the word was Aram.[1] but did not inquire further as to its Jewish or Christian origin. The balance of probability seems in favour of Hirschfeld's suggestion, *Beiträge*, 39, that it is of Jewish origin,[2] though in face of Syr. ܬܳܒ and ܬܳܝܒܳܐ *penitent* (ὁ μετανοῶν), ܬܝܳܒܽܘܬܳܐ *penitence*, one cannot absolutely rule out the possibility of a Christian origin. Horovitz, *JPN*, 186 lists it among those words of whose origin, whether Jewish or Christian, it is impossible to decide.

[1] So *Fremdw*, 83; *PSm*, 4399; Massignon, *Lexique technique*, 52; Fischer, *Glossar*, 18.

[2] See also Pautz, *Offenbarung*, 157, n. 4.

تَابُوتٌ (*Tābūt*).

ii, 249; xx, 39.

An ark, or chest.

In ii, 249, تابوت means the Ark of the Covenant of the time of Samuel and Saul, the Heb. ארון, and in xx, 39, the Ark of papyrus, the תבה גמא, in which the infant Moses was committed to the water.

The Muslim authorities invariably treat it as an Arabic word, though they were hopelessly at sea as to its derivation, some deriving it from تاب (*LA*, i, 227; *TA*, i, 161); some from تبت (*LA*, ii, 322; *Siḥāḥ*, sub voc.); others from تبه (Ibn Sīda in *TA*, ix, 381), while 'Ukbarī, *Imlā'*, 69, frankly says—لا يعرف له اشتقاق.

The ultimate origin, of course, is Egyptian *ḏbꜣ.t*, whence came the Heb. תבה, which is used for Noah's ark in Gen. vi, 14; ix, 18 (Gk. κιβωτός), and the ark of papyrus in which Moses was hidden (Gk. θίβη).[1] In the Mishna תיבה is used for the Ark of the Covenant, especially in the phrase "coming before the Ark" for prayer, cf. Mishna Berak, v, 4, עבר לפני התיבה, and on this ground Geiger, 44, would derive تابوت from the Aram. תיבותא, which is consistently used in the Targums and Rabbinic literature for תבה. Geiger has been followed by most later writers,[2] but Fraenkel, *Vocab*, 24, pointed out that the correspondence is even closer with the Eth. ታቦት, and Nöldeke, *Neue Beiträge*, 49, agrees, although he admits the possibility of a derivation from the Aramaic.[3] A strong point in favour of the Abyssinian origin is the fact that not only is ታቦት used to translate κιβωτός in Gen. vi, 14, etc. (cf. Jub. v, 21), but is also the usual word

[1] Zimmern, *Akkad. Fremdw*, 45, disputes this Egyptian origin and suggests a connection with the Akkadian word *tēbītu*, but see Yahuda, *Language of the Pentateuch*, p. 114, n. 2.

[2] Von Kremer, *Ideen*, 226 n.; Sprenger, *Leben*, ii, 257 n.; Fleischer, *Kleinere Schriften*, i, 176 n.; Hubschmann, *ZDMG*, xlvi, 260. The Arm. թափուտ (Hübschmann, *Arm. Gramm*, i, 153) is from the Pers. تابوت, but this is itself a direct borrowing from Arabic. Geiger had been preceded in this suggestion by de Sacy in *JA*, 1829, p. 178.

[3] So Fischer, *Glossar*, 17.

for the Ark of the Covenant (cf. Ex. xxv, 10), and is still used in the Abyssinian Church for the box containing the sacred books and vessels.[1]

تُبَّع (*Tubba'*).

xliv, 36; l, 13.

Title of the Kings of the Himyarites.

The philologers would derive the word from تَبِعَ *to follow*, and explain the title as meaning that each king followed his predecessor, cf. Bagh. on xliv, 36.

Fraenkel, *Vocab*, 25, connected it with the Eth. ተብዐ *strong, manly*, and Nöldeke in Lidzbarski's *Ephemeris*, ii, 124, supports the connection. The word itself, however, is clearly S. Arabian, and occurs in the inscriptions in the compound names 1ሕoΠX, oΠXΨ1ሕ, Π)ሐoΠX, etc. Hartmann in *ZA*, xiv, 331–7, would explain it from oXΠ = בתע, but this seems very unlikely,[2] and everything is in favour of the other derivation. The word was apparently well known in pre-Islamic Arabia, for it occurs not infrequently in the old poetry.[3]

تَتْبِير (*Tatbīr*).

xvii, 7; xxv, 41.

Utter destruction.

It is the verbal noun from تَبَّرَ, an intensive of تَبَرَ *to break* or *destroy*, other forms from which are found in vii, 135, مُتَبَّر; and lxxi, 29, تَبَارًا. as-Suyūṭī, *Itq*, 320, tells us that some early authorities thought that it was Nabataean. By Nabataean he means Aramaic, and we do find Aram. תְּבַר: Syr. ܬܒܰܪ, *to break*, which are the equivalents of Heb. שבר; Akk. *šabāru*; Sab.)Π8[4]; Ar. ثبر;

[1] Dufton, *Narrative of a Journey through Abyssinia*, London, 1867, p. 88.

[2] Lidzbarski, *Ephemeris*, i, 224, says: "Ich halte diese Erklarung fur moglich, nicht wie Hartmann und Mordtmann für gesichert." See also, Glaser, *Altjemenische Studien*, i, 3; Rossini, *Glossarium*, 256; Ryckmans, *Noms propres*, i, 319.

[3] See Horovitz, *KU*, 102, 103.

[4] See Mordtmann, *Himjar. Inschr*, 74; D. H. Muller, *Hof. Mus*, i, l. 26; Rossini, *Glossarium*, 258.

Eth. ሰበረ. This is fairly clear evidence that Ar. تبر is a secondary formation and in all probability from the Aram. as Fraenkel, *Vocab*, 25, noted (so Ahrens, *Christliches*, 27).

تِجَارَةٌ (*Tijāra*).

ii, 15, 282 ; iv, 33 ; ix, 24 ; xxiv, 37 ; xxxv, 26 ; lxi, 10 ; lxii, 11.
Merchandise.

It will be noticed that the word occurs only in late passages. In three passages (ii, 15 ; iv, 33 ; xxiv, 37) it bears the sense of *trafficking* rather than *merchandise* or the substance of traffic, and this latter is perhaps a derived sense. The word تاجر *merchant* does not occur in the Qur'ān, nor any derived verbal form.

There can be no doubt that the word came from the Aram. Fraenkel, *Fremdw*, 182, thinks that تجارة was formed from the verb تجر which is a denominative from تاجر, the form which he thinks was originally borrowed from Aram. In view, however, of the Aram. תַּגָּארָא ; Syr. ܬܐܓܘܪܬܐ, both of which have the meaning *mercatura*, there would seem no reason for refusing to derive the Ar. تجارة directly. In fact, as Fraenkel's discussion shows (p. 181), there is some difficulty in deriving تاجر, a participial form, from Aram. תַּגָּרָא ; Syr. ܬܰܓܳܪܳܐ, and Nöldeke had to suggest a dialectal form תָּגְרָא to ease the difficulty. If, however, the original form in Ar. were تجارة from תַּגָּארָא, and the verb تجر a denominative from this, it is easy to see how تاجر a *merchant*, i.e. " one who traffics ", would be formed as a participle from this verb.

That the borrowing was from the Aram. is clear from the fact that the original word was the Akk. *tamkāru* or *tamgāru*,[1] whence comes the Armen. Թանկար or Թանգար,[2] so that in the Aram. תַּגָּרָא

[1] Zimmern, *Akkad. Fremdw*, 16. [2] Hübschmann, *Arm. Gramm*, i, 303.

the doubled ג represents an original נ, which we find still unassimilated in the Mand. תנגארא. The word was well known in Arabia in pre-Islamic days, as is clear from the fact that we find both תגרא meaning *merchant* and תגרתא meaning *commerce* in the N. Arabian inscriptions,[1] while تاجر occurs commonly enough in the old poetry, particularly in connection with the wine trade.[2]

تَجَلَّى (*Tajallā*).

vii, 139; xcii, 2.
To appear in glory.

The simple verb جَلَا *to make clear*, is cognate with Heb. גלה *to uncover*; Aram. גלא; Syr. ܓܠܐ *to reveal*; and Eth. ገለየ *to manifest, explain*; and Form II, جَلَّى *to reveal, to manifest* occurs in vii, 186; xci, 3. The form تَجَلَّى, however, which is used once of God revealing Himself to Moses at Mt. Sinai, and once of the brightness of oncoming day, seems to have been formed under the influence of Syr. ܐܬܓܠܝ, which, as Mingana, *Syriac Influence*, 86, points out, had become specialized in this sense, and may have been known in religious circles at Mecca and Madina in this technical sense. It is at least suggestive that *LA*, xviii, 163, uses only Ḥadīth in explanation of the word.

تَسْنِيمٌ (*Tasnīm*).

lxxxiii, 27.
Tasnim—name of a fountain in Paradise.

The exegetes derive the word from سَنَّمَ to *raise*, Form II of سَنِمَ *to be high*, and the fountain is said to be called تسنيم because the water is carried from it to the highest apartment of the Pavilion, cf. Zam. on the passage, and Ṭab. quoting Mujāhid and Al-Kalbī; also *LA*,

[1] de Vogüé, *Syrie Centrale*, No. 4; Cook, *Glossary*, 119.
[2] Fraenkel, *Fremdw*, 158, 182; D. H. Müller, in *WZKM*, i, 27; and note *LA*, v, 156, with a verse from Al-A'shā.

xv, 199. It is obvious, however, that this is merely an attempt to explain a word that was strange to the exegetes, and which lent itself to explanation as a form تفعيل from سنم. There is no occurrence of the word earlier than the Qur'ān, and apparently nothing in the literature of the surrounding peoples from which we can derive it, so Nöldeke is doubtless right when in his *Sketches*, 38, he takes the word to be an invention of Muḥammad himself.

تَفْسِيرٌ (*Tafsīr*).

xxv, 35.

An explanation or interpretation.

The exegetes naturally take it as the verbal noun from فَسَّرَ *to explain*, Form II of فَسَرَ *to discover something hidden*. Fraenkel, *Fremdw*, 286, however, thinks that in this technical sense فَسَّرَ is a borrowing from the Syr. ܦܫܩ *to expound, make clear*, which is very commonly used in early Syriac texts in the sense of interpretation of Scripture. This sense of *to solve, to interpret* from the Aram. פְּשַׁר : Syr. ܦܫܰܪ *to dissolve*, seems a peculiar development of meaning in Aram., and Heb. פֵּשֶׁר is a loan-word from Aram. פִּשְׁרָא, so that Ar. فَسَّرَ is doubtless of the same origin,[1] and تَفَسَّرَ and تَفْسِيرٌ were later formed from this borrowed verb.

Halévy, *JA*, viie ser., vol. x, p. 412, thinks that he finds the word אפסר *interpreter* in the Safaite inscriptions, which, if correct, would point to the pre-Islamic use of the root in this sense in N. Arabia.

تَنُّورٌ (*Tannūr*).

xi, 42; xxiii, 27.

Oven.

It was early recognized by the philologers as a word of foreign origin. al-Aṣma'ī, according to as-Suyūṭī, *Muzhir*, i, 135, classed it as a

[1] Zimmern, *Akkad. Fremdw*, 68, however, would derive the Aram. forms from Akk. *pašāru*. See also Horovitz, *JPN*, 218.

Persian loan-word, which was also the opinion of Ibn Duraid, as we learn from al-Jawālīqī, *Mu'arrab*, 36.[1] ath-Tha'ālibī, *Fiqh*, 317, gives it in his list of words that are common to both Persian and Arabic, and Ibn Qutaiba, *Adab al-Kātib*, 528, quotes Ibn 'Abbās as saying that it was one of those words which are common to all languages.[2] Some, however, argued for its being an Arabic word from نار or نور, as the *Muḥīṭ*, sub voc., explains it—"It is said to be Arabic from نور or نار and that its original form was تنوور on the measure تفعول, then the و was given *hamza* because of the weight of the *ḍamma* on it, and then the *hamza* was suppressed and replaced by another ن, so that it became تنّور." This was not looked on with favour by the philologers, however, for we read in *TA*, iii, 70, "As for the statements about تنّور being from نار or نور and that the ت is an augment, it is all wrong, and Ibn 'Uṣfūr pointed this out clearly in his book *Al-Mumatti'* as others have done." This judgment of the philologers is vindicated by the fact that فعّول is not a genuine Arabic form at all.[3]

The Commentators differ among themselves as to the meaning of the word, some taking it to mean the "surface of the earth", or "the highest part of the earth", or "morning light", or "oven" (cf. Ṭab. on xi, 42). That the word does mean *oven* is evident from its use in the old poetry, e.g. Ḥamāsa, 792.

اقرص تصلّى ظهره نبطية بتنورها حتى يطير له قشر

"Is it a loaf which a Nabataean woman bakes in her oven till the crust rises,"

or a verse in *Aghānī*, iii, 16, l. 7. The Lexicons agree that this is the original meaning, cf. Jawharī, sub voc., and *LA*, v, 162.

Fraenkel, *Fremdw*, 26, suggested that the word came into Arabic

[1] al-Jawālīqī is the source of as-Suyūṭī, *Itq*, 320; *Mutaw*, 46; and al-Khafājī, 52.
[2] So al-Laith in *LA*, v, 163, and see the comment of Abū Manṣūr thereon.
[3] Roncevalles in *Al-Machriq*, xv, 949, and see *LA*, v, 163.

from the Aram.[1] In the O.T. תַּנּוּר occurs frequently for *furnace* or *oven*, i.e. the Gk. *κλίβανος*, and the form in the Aram. Targums is תַּנּוּרָא, corresponding with the Syr. ܬܢܘܪܐ of the Peshitta and ecclesiastical writings (*PSm*, 4473). It also occurs as *tinūru* in Akkadian,[2] a form which Dvořák takes to be a borrowing from the Heb. תנור, but without much likelihood.[3] Closely connected with this is another set of words, Aram. אתונא; Syr. ܐܬܘܢܐ; Eth. እቶን; Ar. أتون, with which group D. H. Müller would associate the Akk. *u-dun-tum*. With it again is to be connected yet another set of words—Aram. תננא; Syr. ܬܢܢܐ *smoke*; Eth. ተን = *ἀτμίς vapour*, and Mand. תאנא *furnace*.

As the root תנר is not original in any Semitic language, we may turn to the theory of Perisan origin suggested by the Muslim philologers. Fraenkel, indeed, though he claims that the Ar. تنّور is a borrowing from the Aram., yet thinks that the Aram. word itself is of Iranian origin.[4] In Avestic we find the word 𐬙𐬀𐬥𐬏𐬭𐬀 *tanūra* (cf. *Vendidad*, viii, 254), and in Phlv. it is [Pahlavi script] meaning *baking oven*.[5] The word, however, is no more Iranian than it is Semitic, and as Dvořák and Hurgronje point out, the Iranian scholars treat it as a loan-word from Semitic.[6] Now the word occurs also in Armenian, cf. *թոնիր oven*, and *թոնրատուն a bakery*, where Hübschmann takes it as a borrowing from Iranian,[7] and Lagarde as a borrowing from Semitic.[8]

The truth would seem to be that it is a word belonging to the

[1] The *Muḥīṭ*, sub voc., says that some authorities considered it as of Hebrew or Syriac origin, but he does not mention these, and as he explains it as due to the combination of تن and نار or نور, one may suspect that he is merely copying from the old American translation of Gesenius' Hebrew Lexicon. Guidi, *Della Sede*, 597, noted its foreign origin.

[2] Zimmern, *Akkad. Fremdw*, 32.

[3] *Zeitschrift fur Keilschriftforschung*, i, 119 ff. D. H. Müller, *WZKM*, i, 23, is nearer the mark, however, in suggesting that תנור is a borrowing from Mesopotamia from an older form *tannūra*.

[4] *Fremdw*, 26, cf. also Noldeke, *Sasaniden*, 165.

[5] West, *Glossary*, 121.

[6] Dvořák, op. cit.; Hurgronje, *WZKM*, i, 73. Cf. Bartholomae, *AIW*, 638; Haug, *Parsis*, 5; Justi, *Handbuch der Zend-Sprache*, 1864, p. 132; Spiegel, *ZDMG*, ix, 191.

[7] *Arm. Gramm*, i, 155.

[8] *Zur Urgeschichte der Armenier*, 1854, p. 813, and *Armenische Studien*, 1877, No. 863.

pre-Semitic and pre-Indo-European population of the area which has been taken over into both groups in its original form and with its original meaning.[1] If this is so then there is no reason why the Arabs might not have obtained the word from this primitive source, and not through the Aramaic.

تَوَّابٌ (*Tawwāb*).

ii, 35, 51, 122, 155; iv, 20, 67; ix, 105, 119; xxiv, 10; xlix, 12; cx, 3.

The Relenting one.

One of the names of God, used only of Him in the Qur'ān and only in Madinan passages.

The Muslim authorities take it as a formation from تاب. We have already seen, however, that تاب is a borrowed religious term used by Muḥammad in a technical sense, and Lidzbarski in *SBAW*, Berlin 1916, p. 1218, argues that توّاب instead of being a regular Arabic formation from the already borrowed تاب, is itself a distinct borrowing from the Aram. The Akk. *taiaru*, he says,[2] was borrowed into Aram., e.g. into Palmyrene, and the Mand. תאיאבא is but a rendering of the same word. Halévy, *JA*, viie ser., vol. x, p. 423, would recognize the word in תוב of a Safaite inscription, and if this is correct there would be clear evidence of its use in N. Arabia in pre-Islamic times.

تَوْرَاةٌ (*Taurāh*).

iii, 2, 43, 44, 58, 87; v, 47–50, 70. 72, 110; vii, 156; ix, 112; xlviii, 29; lxi, 6; lxii, 5.

The Torah.

[1] It may be noted that the word occurs also in Turkish تنور; Turki, *tanur*; Afghan, *tanārah*. See also Henning in *BSOS*, ix, 88.

[2] Lidzbarski admits that Delitzsch, *Assyrisches Handwörterbuch*, 703*a*, and Zimmern, *Akkadisches Fremdworter*, 66, had earlier shown the connection between *taiaru* and توّاب.

It is used as a general term for the Jewish Scriptures,[1] but particularly as associated with Moses, and in a few passages (iii, 44, 87; lxi, 6, etc.) it seems to have the definite sense of ὁ νόμος. With the possible exception of vii, 156, it occurs only in Madinan passages.

Clearly it represents the Heb. תורה, and was recognized by some of the early authorities to be a Hebrew word, as we learn from az-Zajjāj in *TA*, x, 389; and Bagh. on iii, 2. Some, however, desired to make it an Arabic word derived from ورى, a view which Zam. on iii, 2, scouts, though it is argued at length in *LA*, xx, 268, and accepted without question by Rāghib, *Mufradāt*, 542. Western scholars from the time of Marracci, *Prodromus*, i, 5, have recognized it as a borrowing direct from the Heb.,[2] and there is no need to discuss the possible Aram. origin mentioned by Fraenkel, *Vocab*, 23.[3] The word was doubtless well known in Arabia before Muḥammad's time. cf. Ibn Hishām, 659.

تِين (*Tīn*).

xcv, 1.

Fig.

That the word has no verbal root and was a primitive borrowing was noted by Guidi, *Della Sede*, 599, with whom Fraenkel, *Fremdw*. 148, agrees. The borrowing was probably from the Aram. In Heb. we have תְּאֵנָה, and in Phon. תין which appears to have been vowelled תִּין,[4] but the Aram. תינא, Syr. ܬܐܢܐ, which occur beside the forms תינתא and Syr. ܬܐܢܬܐ (usually contracted to ܬܐܬܐ, then ܬܬܐ,

[1] Hirschfeld, *Beitrage*, 65, would go further. He says: "Der Begriff Torā ist im Koran bekanntlich moglichst weit zu fassen, so dass auch Mischnah Talmud. Midrasch und Gebetbuch darunter zu verstehen sind." Geiger, 46, on the other hand, would limit the meaning of the word to the Pentateuch. It should be remembered, however, that both in Jewish and Christian circles the "Law" frequently stood for the whole O.T. (Cf. תורה in Sanh., 91*b*, and the N.T. use of ὁ νόμος in Jno. x, 34; 1 Cor. xiv, 21. Cf. 2 Esdras, xix, 21, and *Mekilta*, Beshallah, 9 (ed. Friedmann, p. 34*b*).

[2] So de Sacy, *JA*, 1829, p. 175; Geiger, 45; von Kremer, *Ideen*, 226 n.; Pautz, *Offenbarung*, 120, n. 1; Hirschfeld, *Beiträge*, 65; Horovitz, *KU*, 71; *JPN*, 194; Margoliouth, *ERE*, x, 540.

[3] Fischer, *Glossar*, 18*a*, however, suggests that it may be a mixed form from the Heb. תורה and Aram. אוריתא; cf. also Ahrens, *ZDMG*, lxxxiv, 20, and Torrey, *Foundation*, 51.

[4] D. H. Muller, *WZKM*, i, 26, and see Lagarde's discussion in *GGA*, for 1881.

cf. Akk. *tittu*),[1] give us the form we need, and which may also be the origin of the Iranian form found in Phlv. [Pahlavi], which Haug, *PPGl*, 217, takes to be a mispronunciation of [Pahlavi] *tīn* = ficus. The word occurs in the old poetry and was doubtless well known in pre-Islamic Arabia (cf. Laufer, *Sino-Iranica*, 411).

جَابِيَةٌ (*Jābia*).

xxxiv, 12.

A cistern.

It occurs in the Qur'ān in the Solomon story, in the plu. form جَوَابٌ, which is modified from جَوَابِى used of the "deep dishes like cisterns"—جفان كالجواب, which the Jinn made for Solomon.

Fraenkel in *Beit. Ass*, iii, 74, 75, points out that it is from the Syr. ܓܘܒܐ a *cistern* or any collection of water. The ج for ق is not without parallels, as Fraenkel shows, cf. جاثليق for ܩܬܘܠܝܩܐ.[2]

That the word was known in pre-Islamic Arabia is clear from a verse of al-A'shā in *Kāmil*, 4, 14.

جَالُوتُ (*Jālūt*).

ii, 250-2.

Goliath.

There was very general agreement among the Muslim authorities that the name was not Arabic, even Rāghib, *Mufradāt*, 94, agreeing that ذلك أعجمى لا اصل له فى العربية; cf. also al-Jawālīqī, *Mu'arrab*, 46; *LA*, ii, 325; *TA*, i, 535.

Clearly جالوت is an attempt to reproduce the Heb. גָּלְיַת of the O.T. narrative, of which the Qur'ānic story is obviously a garbled

[1] From *tiitu, see Zimmern, *Akkad. Fremdw*, 55.

[2] Fraenkel, *Fremdw*, 275; referring to Noldeke, *Mand. Gramm*, 38, n. 2; Hoffmann in *ZDMG*, xxxii, 748, and cf. *Ḥamāsa*, 244 (جمسوس and قمسوس).

version.[1] Hirschfeld, *New Researches*, 13, suggested that the Qur'ānic form is due to Muḥammad's informant having misread the גלית of his MS. as גלות, which of course it was very easy to do, and vowelling it גָּלוּת gave Muḥammad his جالوت. This is very ingenious, and has in its favour the fact that the Goliath story occurs only in the late Madina period when Muḥammad was beginning to pick up more and more detailed information from the Jews. It is difficult, however, to think that any Jewish informant skilled enough to read the Heb. text would not have known the Biblical story well enough to have avoided such a mistake, unless indeed he deliberately misled Muḥammad.

Like the Aram. גלותא (Syr. ܓܠܘܬܐ),[2] the word גלות means an *exile*, and in the Talmud (e.g. Sukkah, 31*a*), the Exilarch is called ריש גלותא, so Horovitz, *KU*, 106, suggests that this גלות, which must have been commonly used among the Jews of Arabia, may have become confused in Muḥammad's mind with the גלית of the Biblical story, and so have given rise to جالوت. In any case we are safe in attributing the introduction of the name to Muḥammad himself, for no trace of it can be found in pre-Islamic days.[3]

جُبّ (*Jubb*).

xii, 10, 15.

A well, or cistern.

The word is usually taken as a derivation from جَبَّ to *cut off*, though exactly how it is to be derived from this root is not clear. Rāghib, *Mufradāt*, 82, gives an alternative explanation, that it is so called because dug out of the جبوب, i.e. rough ground.

It is used only in the Joseph story, where in the O.T. we have

[1] Geiger, 182; Sycz, *Eigennamen*, 44.

[2] Which indeed was borrowed into Armenian. Cf. գաղութ (Hubschmann, *Arm. Gramm*, i, 301).

[3] It occurs in a verse of the Jewish poet as-Samau'al, but Nöldeke, *ZA*, xxvii, 178, shows that the verse in question is post-Islamic and under Qur'ānic influence.

בור, but the Targums read גבא or גובא, and the Peshitta has ܓܘܒܐ. The origin would thus be Aramaic and probably it was an early borrowing.[1] There is a Minaean 𐩴𐩥𐩨 but the meaning is uncertain (Rossini, *Glossarium*, 121).

جِبْت (*Jibt*).

iv, 54.

Jibt.

It occurs only along with the Ethiopic word طاغوت in the sentence "they believe in Jibt and Ṭāghūt". The exegetes knew not what to make of it, and from their works we can gather a score of theories as to its meaning, whether idol—صنم, or priest—كاهن, or sorcerer ساحر, or sorcery—سحر, or Satan, or what not. It was generally agreed that it was an Arabic word, Baiḍ., e.g., claiming that it was a dialectal form of جبس, a theory that was taken up by Rāghib, *Mufradāt*, 83, and others.[2] Some of the philologers, however, admitted that it was a foreign word (cf. Jawharī, sub voc., *LA*, ii, 325),[3] and from as-Suyūṭī, *Itq*, 320, we learn that some of them even knew that it was Ethiopic.

Margoliouth in *ERE*, vi, 249, suggested that it was the γλυπτά of the LXX from γλύφω *to carve* or *engrave*, which is used to translate פסל in Lev. xxvi, 1. This assumes that its meaning is very much the same as Ṭāghūt, i.e. *idol*, and this has the weight of evidence from the Commentators in its favour. It is a little difficult, however, to see how the Greek word could come directly into Arabic without having left any trace in Syriac. It is more likely that as-Suyūṭī's authorities were right for once, and that it is an Abyssinian word.

[1] Bräunlich, *Islamica*, i, 327, notes that it is a borrowed term. Cf. also Zimmern, *Akkadische Fremdworter*, 44. It is also the origin of the Arm. գուբ; cf. Hubschmann, i, 302.

[2] جبس itself is a foreign word according to al-Khafājī, 58. Vollers, *ZDMG*, li, 296, says it is from γύψος.

[3] Jawharī's clinching argument is that ج and ت do not occur as the first and last radicals of any genuine Arabic word.

This has been recognized by Dvořák, *Fremdw*, 50, and by Nöldeke, *Neue Beiträge*, 48, who shows that አምላክ፡ ገብት = θεὸς πρόσφατος, and in ገብት we have the form we need.

جِبْرِيلُ (*Jibrīl*).

ii, 91, 92 ; lxvi, 4.

Gabriel.

Always as the Angel of Revelation, and by name only in Madinan passages. (There is possibly a reference to his name גבריאל = " mighty one of God ", in liii, 5, " one mighty in power.")

There was considerable uncertainty among the early authorities as to the spelling of the name, for we find جِبْرِيلُ ; جَبْرَئِيلُ ; جَبْرَائِلُ ; جَبْرَئِلُ ; جَبْرَيِيلُ ; جَبْرَائِيلُ ; جَبْرَئِلّ ; جَبْرِيلُ ; جَبْرَاَلّ, and even جَبْرِينُ and جِبْرِينُ.[1] as-Suyūṭī, *Muzhir*, i, 140, notes that these variants point to its non-Arabic origin,[2] and this was admitted by some of the philologers, cf. Ṭab. on ii, 91 ; al-Jawālīqī, 144, and al-Khafājī, 60.

The ultimate origin, of course, is the Heb. גבריאל, and in Dan. viii, 16 ; ix, 21, Gabriel is one of the high angels and the agent of Revelation, just as he is in the Qur'ān. There is, however, the possibility that the Gabriel of the Qur'ān is of Christian rather than Jewish origin, and the form ܓܒܪܝܠ which is found in the Christian Palestinian dialect,[3] gives us the closest approximation to the usual Arabic form.

There is some question how well the name was known in Arabia before Muḥammad's time. Gabriel was known and honoured among the Mandaeans,[4] and this may have been a pre-Islamic element in their faith. The name occurs also in verses of poets contemporary with Islam, but seems there to have been influenced by Qur'ānic

[1] *Vide* al-Jawālīqī, *Mu'arrab*, 50, and Baiḍ. and Zam. on ii, 91.

[2] See also Ibn Qutaiba, *Adab al-Kātib*, 78.

[3] Schulthess, *Lex*, 34.

[4] Brandt, *Mandaer*, 17, 25 ; Lidzbarski, *Johannesbuch*, xxvi. It is interesting to note that *Gabrāīl* occurs in a Persian Manichaean fragment from Turfan ; cf. F. Müller, *SBAW*, Berlin, 1904, p. 351, Salemann, *Manichaeische Studien*, i, 63.

usage. Cheikho, *Naṣrāniya*, 235, gives an instance of a personal name containing the word, but Horovitz, *KU*, 107, rightly insists on the incorrectness of this.[1] Muḥammad seems to have been able to assume in his Madinan audience some familiarity with the name, and the probabilities are that it came to him in its Syr. form.

جَبِين (*Jabīn*).

xxxvii, 103.

The temple, or side of forehead.

The sole occurrence of the word is in the story of Abraham preparing to sacrifice his son, when he laid him down on his forehead. The exegetes got the meaning right, but neither they nor the Lexicons have any satisfactory explanation of the origin of the word from a root جبن.

Barth has suggested an Aramaic origin. גביניא means *brow* or *eyebrow*, and is fairly common in the Rabbinic writings. Similarly ܓܒܝܢܐ is *eyebrow* and a commonly used word. From either of these it may have been an early borrowing into Arabic.

جِزْيَة (*Jizya*).

ix, 29.

Tribute.

The word is used in a technical sense in this passage which is late Madinan, and looks very much like an interpolation in the Qur'ān reflecting later usage.

In later Islam جزية was the technical term for the poll-tax imposed on the Dhimmis, i.e. members of protected communities (cf. as-Sijistānī, 101). It is usually derived from جزى, and said to be so called because it is a compensation in place of the shedding of their blood (so Rāghib, *Mufradāt*, 91; *LA*, xviii, 159). It is, however, the Syr. ܓܙܝܬܐ, a

[1] Ṭulaiḥa, one of Muhammad's rival Prophets, claimed support from Gabriel (Ṭab, *Annales*, i, 1890, Beladhorī, 96), but this may have been in imitation of Muhammad, though the weight of evidence seems to point to his having come forward quite independently as a preacher of higher religion.

capitation or poll-tax, which though not a word of very common use (*PSm*, 695, 696), was nevertheless borrowed in this sense into Persian as گزیت, as Nöldeke, *Sasaniden*, 241, n., points out.[1]

On the ground of a word 𐩩𐩱𐩹𐩢 in a Minaean text (Glaser, 284, 3) which may mean *tribute*, Grimme, *ZA*, xxvi, 161, would take جزية as a borrowing from S. Arabia, but in the uncertainty of the correct interpretation of this text, it seems better at present to content ourselves with Fraenkel, *Fremdw*, 283, in holding to an Aramaic origin.[2]

جلابيب (*Jalābīb*).

xxxiii, 59.

Wrappers. Plu. of جلباب, a large outer covering worn by women.

It is as an article of women's attire that it is mentioned in the Qur'ān, though the Lexicons differ considerably as to the exact meaning (cf. *LA*, i, 265).

The difficulty of deriving the word from جلب is of course obvious, and Nöldeke, *Neue Beiträge*, 53, recognized it as the Eth. ገልባብ, from ገልበበ *to cover* or *cloak*, which is quite common in the oldest texts. It was apparently an early borrowing, for it occurs in the early poetry, e.g. *Div. Hudh*, xc, 12.

جناح (*Junāḥ*).

v, 94; xxxiii, 5, 51, etc.; some twenty-five times.

Sin, wrong, crime.

A favourite Madina word, occuring only in late passages. The favourite phrase is لا جناح على, and it is used as a technical term in Muḥammad's religious legislation.[3]

The Lexicons give no satisfactory explanation of the word, though

[1] Vullers, *Lex*, ii, 999.
[2] Cf. Schwally, *Idioticon*, 17.
[3] Horovitz, *KU*, 62, n.

they apparently treat it as a genuine Arabic formation. As Hübschmann showed in 1895 in his *Persische Studien*, 162, 212, it is the Pers. گناه ,[1] through the Pazend *gunāh* (Shikand, *Glossary*, 247) from Phlv. ورس *vināṡ*,[2] a *crime* or *sin* (as is obvious from the Arm. վնաս = ἁμάρτημα in the old Bible translation),[3] and the fact that *venāh* still occurs in one of the Persian dialects as a direct descendant from the Phlv. ورس,[4] which is related to Skt. विनाश *vinaça* and is quite a good Indo-European word. In Phlv. the word is used technically just as in the Qur'ān, and we find such combinations as سرورس *avināṡ* = sinless (*PPGl*, 77); ورس‌وںدلں *vināṡkārīh* = sinfulness, iniquity (West, *Glossary*, 248); and ورس‌ودل *vināṡkār* = a criminal, sinner (*PPGl*, 225).[5]

The word was borrowed in the pre-Islamic period and occurs in the old poetry, e.g. in the Mu'allaqa of al-Ḥārith, 70, etc., and was doubtless adopted directly into Arabic from the spoken Persian of the period, for the word is not found in Syriac.

جَنَّة (*Janna*).

Of very frequent occurrence. Cf. ii, 23, 33, 76, etc.

Garden.

It is used in the Qur'ān both of an earthly garden (liii, 16; xxxiv, 14; ii, 267, etc.), and particularly as a name for the abode of the Blessed (lxix, 22; lxxxviii, 10, etc.).

In the general sense of *garden*, derived from a more primitive meaning, *enclosure*, the word may be a genuine Arabic inheritance from primitive Semitic stock, for the word is widespread in the

[1] Vollers hesitatingly accepts this in *ZDMG*, l, 639 (but see p. 612, where he quotes it as an instance of sound change), and it is given as a Persian borrowing by Addai Sher, 45.

[2] Hubschmann, *Persische Studien*, 159, and Haug in *PPGl*, 225. Cf. West, *Glossary*, 247, Nyberg, *Glossar*, 243.

[3] Hübschmann, *Arm. Gramm*, i, 248.

[4] Horn, *Grundriss*, 208. Kurdish *gunāh* cannot be quoted in illustration as it is a borrowing from Mod. Persian.

[5] The Pazend has similar combinations, e.g. *gunâhî*, sinfulness; *gunâhkâr*, sinful, mischievous; *gunâhkârî*, culpability; *gunâh-sâmânihâ*, proportionate to the sin; *ham-gunâh* (cf. Phlv. همورس) accomplice (Shikand, *Glossary*, 247).

Semitic area, e.g. Akk. *gannatu* [1]; Heb. גַּנָּה; Aram. גַּנָּא, גַּנְתָא; Syr. ܓܢܬܐ; Phon. אגנן [2]; Eth. ገነት, though perhaps it was a peculiar N. Semitic development, for Nöldeke, *Neue Beiträge*, 42, would derive both the Ar. جنّة and Eth. ገነት from a N. Semitic source.[3] (See also Fischer, *Glossar*, 22*b*, and Ahrens, *Christliches*, 27.)

In any case in the meaning of Paradise it is certainly a borrowing from the Aram. and in all probability from the Syr.[4] where we find it specialized in this sense. This Christian origin was vaguely felt by some of the Muslim philologers, for as-Suyūṭī, *Mutaw*, 51, says that Ibn Jubair stated that جنة عدن was Greek, and in the *Itqān* he says that when Ka'b was asked about it he said that جنّة in Syriac meant *vines* and *grapes*. The word in the sense of *garden* occurs frequently in the old poetry, but in the sense of Paradise only in verses which have been influenced by the Qur'ān, as Horovitz, *Paradies*, 7, shows. In this technical sense it would thus have been adopted by Muḥammad from his Jewish or Christian environment (Horovitz, *JPN*, 196, 197).

جُنْد (*Jund*).

Some twenty-nine times in various forms. Cf. ii, 250; ix, 26, etc. Host, army, troop, force.

The word has no verbal root in Arabic, the verbs جَنَّدَ *to levy troops*, and تَجَنَّدَ *to be enlisted*, being obviously denominative, as indeed is evident from the treatment of the word in the Lexicons (cf. *LA*, iv, 106).

[1] Zimmern, *Akkad. Fremdw*, 40.

[2] Perhaps also גן; see Harris, *Glossary*, 94, and the Ras Shamra, גן.

[3] D. H. Müller, however, in *WZKM*, i, 26, opposes the idea that in the general sense of *garden* it is an Aram. borrowing, as Fraenkel like Noldeke holds. He points to the وادى الجنات mentioned by Hamadānī, 76, l. 16, and the place مصلح الجنات, as proving the existence of the word in S. Arabia. These, however, may be merely translations of older names.

[4] Fraenkel, *Fremdw*, 148; Mingana, *Syriac Influence*, 85. Horovitz, *Paradies*, 7, however, makes a strong plea for a Jewish origin on the ground that גן עדן is commoner for Paradise in the Rabbinic writings than in Syriac.

It is clearly an Iranian borrowing through Aram. as Fraenkel, *Vocab*, 13, notes, on the authority of Lagarde, *GA*, 24.[1] Phlv. گوند *gund*, meaning an *army* or *troop*,[2] is related to Skt. वृन्द *vṛinda*,[3] and was borrowed on the one hand into Arm. գունդ *army*,[4] and Kurdish جوند *village*, and on the other into Aram. where we find the גונדא of the Baby. Talmud, the Mand. גונדא (Nöldeke, *Mand. Gramm.* 75), and, with suppression of the weak *n*, in Syr. ܓܘܕܐ. The word may possibly have come into Arabic directly from the Iranian, but the probabilities are that it was through Aramaic.[5] In any case it was an early borrowing, for the word is found in the old poetry, e.g. in al-Aʿshā (Geyer, *Zwei Gedichte*, i, 24 = *Dīwān*, i, 56) and ʿAlqama.

جَهَنَّم (*Jahannam*).

Occurs some seventy-seven times. Cf. ii, 202.

Hell.

The fact that it was indeclinable as used in the Qur'ān early put the philologers on the track of it as a foreign word (al-Jawālīqī, *Muʿarrab*, 47, 48; *LA*, xiv, 378; Baid. on ii, 202; al-Khafājī, 59). Many of these early authorities gave it as a Persian loan-word (e.g. Jawharī, *Ṣiḥāḥ*; Rāghib, *Mufradāt*, 101), doubtless arguing from the fact that فردوس was Persian, but others knew it was a Hebrew word (cf. as-Suyūṭī, *Itq*, 320; Ibn al-Athīr, *Nihāya*, i, 223).

The earlier European opinion was that it was from the Heb. גֵּיהִנֹּם which in the Talmud becomes גֵּהִנָּם[6] (Buxtorf's *Lexicon*, 206) and is popularly used for Hell. De Sacy in *JA*, 1829, p. 175, suggested

[1] Lagarde, as a matter of fact, takes this suggestion back as far as Saint-Martin, *Mémoires*, i, 28.

[2] Dinkard, iii, Glossary, p. 6; Nyberg, Glossar, 86.

[3] Horn, *Grundriss*, 179, on the authority of Nöldeke. Hubschmann, *Persische Studien*, 83, however, thinks this unlikely.

[4] Lagarde, *GA*, 24; Hubschmann, *Arm. Gramm*, i, 130, and cf. Hubschmann, *Persische Studien*, 83.

[5] Sprenger, *Leben*, ii, 358, n.; Vollers, *ZDMG*, l. 611. We find גנדא and גונדא on incantation bowls as associated with the hosts of evil spirits; cf. Montgomery, *Aramaic Incantation Texts from Nippur*, Glossary, p. 285.

[6] Could this be the origin of the كِهنَّام quoted by the philologers as the Hebrew form?

this, and it has been championed by Geiger, 48, who argues that though the absence of the medial *h* in Gk. γεέννα might not dispose of a Christian origin, since this does appear in the Syr. ܓܗܢܐ and in the Arm. գեհեն derived therefrom,[1] yet the absence of the final *m* is conclusive, as this is lacking in both Greek and Syriac but appears in the Hebrew. Geiger has been followed by most later writers,[2] but it should be noted that his objections do not apply to the Eth. ገሀነም (sometimes ገሃነም), which is phonologically nearer the Arabic and a more likely source, as Nöldeke, *Neue Beiträge*, 47, has pointed out.[3]

The word apparently does not occur in the early poetry,[4] and was thus probably one of the words which Muḥammad learned from contact direct or indirect with Abyssinians.

جُودِى (*Jūdī*).

xi, 46.

The name of the mountain where the Ark rested.

The Commentators know that it is the name of a mountain in Mesopotamia near Mosul, and in this they are following Judaeo-Christian tradition. As early as the Targums we find that the apobaterion of Noah was Mt. Judi, i.e. the Gordyene mountains in Mesopotamia, which Onkelos calls קרדו and Jonathan b. ʿUzziel קרדון, the Peshitta agreeing with Onkelos.

This קרדו = Syr. ܩܪܕܘ = Arm. կորդուք—(sometimes כרדו, ܟܪܕܘ) is supposed to be the province of Kurdistan,[5] and a mountain to the S.W. of Lake Van is identified with the mount on which Noah's ark rested.[6] It is the τὰ Γορδυαῖα ὄρη of Ptolemy v, 12 (ed. C. Müller, i, 935), and according to the Talmud, *Baba bathra*, 91 a, Abraham was

[1] Hübschmann, *Arm. Gramm*, i, 290.

[2] Von Kremer, *Ideen*, 226 n.; Rodwell, *Koran*, 189 n.; Sycz, *Eigennamen*, 16; Margoliouth, *ERE*, x, 540; Sacco, *Credenze*, 158.

[3] ገሀነም, of course, is a borrowing from the Heb. (Nöldeke, op. cit., 34). Nöldeke's suggestion of an Eth. origin for جهنّم has been accepted by Pautz, *Offenbarung*, 217; Rudolph, *Abhängigkeit*, 34; Fischer, *Glossar*, 23.

[4] The verse in *Ḥamāsa*, 816, has doubtless been influenced by the Qur'ān.

[5] On the Arm. Korduk, see Hübschmann, *Arm. Gramm*, i, 519.

[6] Neubauer, *Geographie du Talmud*, 378 ff. It is now known as Jūdī Dagh. There is a description of the shrine there in Gertrude Bell's *Amurath to Amurath*, 1911, pp. 292–5.

imprisoned there seven years. This tradition that Qardu and not Ararat was the resting place of the ark is a very old Mesopotamian tradition and doubtless goes back to some ancient Babylonian story.[1] The Jewish tradition passed on to the Christians,[2] and from them to the Mandaeans and Arabs.[3]

Mingana, *Syriac Influence*, 97, thinks that Muḥammad got his name جودى from a misunderstanding of the name ܩܪܕܘ as he heard it in the story from Syrian Christians. Nöldeke, however, in the *Kiepert Festschrift*, p. 77, makes the much more interesting suggestion that in the Qur'ānic name we have a confusion between the Mesopotamian קרדו, ܩܪܕܘ and the Arabian جبل الجودى in the territory of Ṭa'ī mentioned by Yāqūt, ii, 270, and celebrated in a verse of Abū Ṣa'tara al-Baulānī in the *Ḥamāsa* (ed. Freytag, p. 564). It would seem that Muḥammad imagined that the people of Noah like those of 'Ād and Thamūd were dwellers in Arabia, and Mt. Jūdī being the highest peak in the neighbourhood would naturally be confused with the Qardes of the Judaeo-Christian story.

حَبْل (*Ḥabl*).

iii, 98, 108 ; xx, 69 ; xxvi, 43 ; l, 15 ; cxi, 5.

Rope, cord.

The original meaning of *cord* occurs in cxi, 5, " a cord of palm fibre," and in the Aaron story in xx, 69 ; xxvi, 43 ; all of which are Meccan passages. In l, 15, it is used figuratively of a *vein* in the neck, and in the Madinan Sūra, iii, the " cord of God ", " cord of men ", apparently means a compact.

Zimmern, *Akkad. Fremdw*, 15 (cf. also his *Babylonische Busspsalmen*, 93 n.), declares that the Akk. *ḫbl* is the source of the Heb. חֶבֶל ; Aram. חבלא ; Syr. ܚܒܠܐ, and that this Aram. form is the source of both the Arabic حبل and the Eth. ሐብል.

[1] Streck, *EI*, i, 1059 ; *ZA*, xv, 272 ff. Berossus says it landed πρὸς τῷ ὄρει τῶν Κορδυαίων.

[2] Various traditions in Fabricius, *Cod. Pseud. Vet. Test*, ii, 61 ff. ; and the Christian tradition in Nöldeke's article " Kardu und Kurden " in *Festschrift Kiepert*, 1898, p. 73.

[3] Yāqūt, *Mu'jam*, ii, 144 ; Mas'ūdī, *Murūj*, i, 74 ; Ibn Baṭūṭa, ii, 139 ; Qazwīnī, i, 157.

While there may be some doubt about the ultimate derivation from Akkadian (see *BDB*, 286), the Arabic verb حبل is obviously denominative "to snare a wild beast with a halter", and we may accept its derivation from the Aram. as certain.[1]

The Syr. ܚܒܠܐ seems to have been the origin of the Arm. հաղբք,[2] and we may suspect that the Arabic word came from the same source. In any case it must have been an early borrowing as it occurs in the old poetry.

حِزْبٌ (*Ḥizb*).

v, 61; xi. 20; xiii, 36; xviii, 11; xix, 38; xxiii, 55; xxx, 31; xxxiii, 20, 22; xxxv, 6; xxxviii, 10, 12; xl, 5 31; xliii, 65; lviii, 20, 22.

A party or sect.

The philologers derive it from a verbal root حزب but this primitively had quite a different meaning, and the sense of *divide into parties*, or حَزَّبَ *to form a party*, are clearly denominative.

The word is doubtless to be explained with Nöldeke, *Neue Beiträge*, 59, n., from the Eth. ሕዝብ plu. አሕዛብ [3] meaning *people, class, tribe* which in the Ethiopic Bible translates λαός; φυλαί; δῆμος and also αἵρεσις, as in ሕዝብ : ሰዱቃውያን or ሕዝብ : ፈሪሳውያን for the parties of the Sadducees and the Pharisees, which closely parallels the Qur'ānic usage. Nöldeke thinks it probable that the word was first made prominent by the Qur'ān, though from the way Muḥammad makes use of it one would judge that its meaning was not altogether unfamiliar to his hearers. As a matter of fact we find the word in the S. Arabian inscriptions, as e.g. in Glaser 424, 14 𐩹𐩧𐩺𐩵𐩬 𐩥𐩱𐩢𐩸𐩨 𐩢𐩨𐩦𐩩 "of Raidan and the folks of Ḥabashat",[4]

[1] The word occurs, however, in the Thamudic inscriptions; cf. Ryckmans, *Noms propres*, i, 87.

[2] Hübschmann, *Arm. Gramm*, i, 308, and cf. Fr. Muller in *WZKM*, vii, 381.

[3] That we have the same form in Amharic, Tigré, and Tigriña seems clear evidence that the word is native Abyssinian and not a borrowing.

[4] Glaser, *Die Abessinier im Arabien und Afrika*, München, 1895, p. 122. Nöldeke, op. cit., 60, n., would derive both the Ar. حزب and Eth. ሕዝብ from an old S. Semitic form. Cf. Rossini, *Glossarium*, 146, 147.

so that it is more likely that it came into use among the Northern Arabs from this area than that Muḥammad got it from Abyssinians.[1]

حَصَدَ (*Ḥaṣada*).

xii, 47—also حَصَادَهُ (vi, 142); حَصِيدٌ (xi, 102; l, 9); حَصِيدًا (x, 25; xxi, 15).

To reap.

The regular meaning of حَصَدَ is *to twist*, and in this sense it occurs in the old poetry, as in an-Nābigha, vii, 32 (Ahlwardt, *Divans*, p. 11) and Ṭarafa, *Mu'allaqa*, 38. The sense of *to reap*, however, is denominative from حَصَادَهُ, which is a borrowing from ܚܨܕܐ (Fraenkel, *Fremdw*, 132, 133), and the Ar. equivalent of the Aram. חצד. Syr. ܚܨܕ is خضد *to cut*, which is further illustrated by the S. Arabian [illegible], the name of the harvest month.[2]

حصاد is used not infrequently in the old poetry, and was probably an early borrowing first used among the Arabs who settled down on the borderlands to an agricultural life.

حِصْن (*Hiṣn*).

lix, 2.

A fortress.

It is only the plu. حُصُون that is found in the Qur'ān, though the denominative verb حَصَّنَ occurs participially in v. 14 of the same Sūra. The passages are late and refer to the Jews of Naḍīr near Madina.

The verb is clearly denominative though the philologers try to

[1] Horovitz, *KU*, 19, thinks it is a genuine Arabic word, though in its technical sense in the Qur'ān perhaps influenced by the Ethiopic.

[2] D. H. Müller, *WZKM*, i, 25; Rossini, *Glossarium*, 155.

derive it from a more primitive حصن *to be inaccessible* (*LA*, xvi, 275), and Guidi, *Della Sede*, 579, had seen that حِصْن was borrowed from the Syr. ܚܣܢܐ. Fraenkel, *Fremdw*, 235, 236, agrees with this on two grounds, firstly on the general ground that such things as fortresses are not likely to have been indigenous developments among the Arabs, and as a matter of fact all the place names compounded with حصن which Yāqūt collects in his *Mu'jam* are in Syria: secondly on philological grounds, for حِصْن *fortress* is not from a root *to be inaccessible* but from one *to be strong*, which we find in Heb. חָסַן; Aram. חֲסַן; Syr. ܚܣܢ,[1] of which the Arabic equivalent is خَسُنَ *to be hard, rough*. In the Targums חיסנא is *a store* or *warehouse*, but in the Syr. ܚܣܢܐ is properly a *fortress*. The word is frequently used in the old poetry and must have been an early borrowing.

حِطَّةٌ (*Ḥiṭṭa*).

ii, 55; vii, 161.

Forgiveness.

Both passages are late and were a puzzle to the exegetes as we see from Baiḍawī's comment on them. The exegetes are in general agreed that the meaning is *forgiveness*, and many of the early authorities admitted that it was a foreign word. *TA*, v, 119, quotes al-Farrā as taking it to be Nabataean, and as-Suyūṭī's authorities take it to be Hebrew (*Itq*, 320, compared with *Mutaw*, 58).

As early as 1829 de Sacy in *JA*, iv, 179, pointed out that it was the Heb. חטא, with which Geiger, 18, and Hirschfeld, *Beiträge*, 54 ff.; *New Researches*, 107, agree, though Dvořák, *Fremdw*, 55, suggests the Syr. ܚܛܛܐ as a possibility, and Leszynsky, *Juden in Arabien*, 32, a derivation from חטה. Horovitz, *JPN*, 198, points out that though it is clearly a foreign word, none of these suggested derivations is quite satisfactory, and the source of the word is still a puzzle.

[1] And perhaps the Eth. ሐነጸ to build.

حِكْمَة (*Ḥikma*).

Occurs some nineteen times, cf. ii, 123, 146; v, 110.

Wisdom.

It is clearly a technical word in the Qur'ān, being used in its original sense only in ii, 272, but applied to Luqmān (xxxi, 11), to David (ii, 252; xxxviii, 19), to the Prophet's teaching (xvi, 126; liv, 5), to the Qur'ān (ii, 231; iv, 113; xxxiii, 34; lxii, 2), and used synonymously with "revealed book" (iii, 43, 75, 158; iv, 57; v, 110; xvii, 41; xliii, 63). In connection with it should be noted also حكيم with its comparative احكم.

The root חכם is of wide use in Semitic, but the sense of *wisdom* appears to be a N. Semitic development,[1] while the S. Semitic use of the word is more in connection with the sense of *govern*. Thus in N. Semitic we find Akk. *ḫakamu* = *know*; Heb. חָכָם; Aram. חֲכַם; Syr. ܚܟܡ *to be wise*,[2] and חכמה *wisdom* in the Zenjirli inscription. Thus حكمة and حكيم[3] seem undoubtedly to have been formed under Aram. influence.[4] With حكمة compare Heb. חָכְמָה; Aram. חָכְמְתָא; Syr. ܚܟܡܬܐ, and the Zenjirli חכמה; and with حكيم compare Aram. חכים; Syr. ܚܟܝܡܐ, which as Horovitz, *KU*, 72, notes, is common in the earliest Aramaic period. It is possible that the word came into use from S. Arabia, for we find 𐩢𐩫𐩣 in a Qatabanian inscription published by Derenbourg,[5] and which Nielsen takes to be an epithet of the moon-god.

حَنَان (*Ḥanān*).

xix, 14.

Grace.

[1] But see Zimmern, *Akkad. Fremdw*, 29.

[2] So חכם in the Ras Shamra tablets.

[3] We already have חכם in Safaite, and the name 'Αχιμ. See Wuthnow, *Menschennamen*, 31, and Ryckmans, *Noms propres*, i, 91.

[4] Horovitz, *KU*, 72, rightly adds that حُكْم = حكمة is similarly under Aram. influence.

[5] "Nouveaux textes yéménites inédits," in *Rev. Ass*, 1902, p. 117 ff., and see Nielsen in *ZDMG*, lxvi, 592.

This sole occurrence of the word is in a passage descriptive of John the Baptist. Sprenger, *Leben*, i, 125,[1] noted that the word was probably of foreign origin, and Mingana, *Syriac Influence*, 88, claims that it is the Syr. ܚܢܢܐ.

The primitive verb حَنَّ does not occur in the Qur'ān. It may be compared with Sab. 𐩢𐩬 used in proper names,[2] Heb. חָנַן *to be gracious*, and Syr. ܚܢ, Aram. חֲנַן with the same meaning. It is to be noted, however, that the sense of *grace* is the one that has been most highly developed in N. Semitic, e.g. Akk. *annu* = *grace, favour*; Heb. and Phon. חֵן; Aram. חנא and חינא; Syr. ܚܢܢܐ, and this ܚܢܢܐ is used in the Peshitta text of Lk. i, 58, in the account of the birth of John the Baptist.

Halévy, *JA*, viie ser., x, 356, finds חנאל—*grace de Dieu* in a Safaite inscription, which if correct would be evidence of the early use of the word in N. Arabia.

حَنِيف (*Ḥanīf*).

ii, 129; iii, 60, 89; iv, 124; vi, 79, 162; x, 105; xvi, 121, 124; xxii, 32; xxx, 29; xcviii, 4.

A Ḥanīf.

The passages in which the word occurs are all late Meccan or Madinan, so the word was apparently a technical term which Muḥammad learned at a relatively late period in his public career. Its exact meaning, however, is somewhat difficult to determine.[3] Of the twelve cases, where the word is used, eight have reference to the faith of Abraham, and in nine of them there is an added phrase explaining that to be a Ḥanīf means not being a polytheist, this explanatory phrase apparently showing that Muḥammad felt he was using a word which needed explanation in order to be rightly understood by his hearers.

The close connection of the word with the مِلّة ابراهيم is important, for we know that when Muḥammad changed his attitude

[1] See also i, 581, and ii, 184, n.

[2] D. H. Muller, *Epigraphische Denkmäler aus Arabien*, 40, gives 𐩢𐩬 𐩩𐩢𐩡𐩡𐩺𐩩 which he translates "die Liebe des Frommen", and compares with Heb. חניאל and Phon. חנמלקרת. Cf. Rossini, *Glossarium*, 150.

[3] See Lyall, *JRAS*, 1903, p. 781.

to the Jews he began to preach a new doctrine about Abraham,[1] and to claim that while Moses was the Prophet of the Jews and Jesus the Prophet of the Christians, he himself went back to an earlier revelation which was recognized by both Jews and Christians, the ملّة ابراهيم, which he was republishing to the Arabs. Now all our حنيف passages belong to this second period. Muḥammad is bidden set his face towards religion as a Ḥanīf (x, 105 ; xxx, 29). He says to his contemporaries, " As for me, my Lord has guided me to a straight path, a right religion, the faith of Abraham, a Ḥanīf" (vi, 162). " They say—Become a Jew or a Christian. Say—nay rather be of the religion of Abraham, a Ḥanīf" (ii, 129); " Who hath a better religion than he who resigns himself to God, does what is good, and follows the faith of Abraham as a Ḥanīf" (iv, 124). He calls on the Arabs to " be Ḥanīfs to God " (xxii, 32), and explains his own position by representing Allah as saying to him—" Then we told thee by revelation to follow the ملّة ابراهيم a Ḥanīf" (xvi, 124). The distinction between Ḥanīfism and Judaism and Christianity which is noted in ii, 129, is very clearly drawn in iii, 60, " Abraham was neither a Jew nor a Christian but a resigned Ḥanīf—حنيفًا مُسلمًا," and this latter phrase taken along with the من اسلم وجهه لله of iv, 124, was probably connected in Muḥammad's mind with what he meant by إسلام, and has given the cue to the use and interpretation of the word in the later days of Islam.

The Lexicons are quite at a loss what to make of the word. They naturally endeavour to derive it from حنف to *incline* or *decline*. حَنَفٌ is said to be a natural contortedness of the feet,[2] and so حنف is used of anything that inclines away from the proper standard.

[1] Hurgronje, *Het Mekkaansche Feest*, Leiden, 1880, p. 29 ff. ; Rudolph, Abhängigkeit, 48. Torrey's arguments against this in his *Foundation*, 88 ff., do not seem to me convincing.

[2] Jawharī and *Qāmūs*, sub voc. ; *LA*, x, 402.

As one can also think of inclining from a crooked standard to the straight, so حنيف was supposed to be one who turned from the false religions to the true.[1] It is obvious that these suggestions are of little help in our problem.[2]

The word occurs not infrequently in the poetry of the early years of Islam.[3] All these passages are set forth and examined by Horovitz, *KU*, 56 ff., and many of them by Margoliouth, *JRAS*, 1903, p. 480 ff., the result being that it seems generally to mean *Muslim* and in the odd occurrences which may be pre-Islamic to mean *heathen*.[4] In any case in none of these passages is it associated with Abraham, and there is so much uncertainty as to whether any of them can be considered pre-Islamic that they are of very little help towards settling the meaning of the word for us. It is unfortunate also that we are equally unable to glean any information as to the primitive meaning of the word from the well-known stories of the Ḥanīfs who were earlier contemporaries of Muḥammad, for while we may agree with Lyall, *JRAS*, 1903, p. 744, that these were all actual historical personages, yet the tradition about them that has come down to us has been so obviously worked over in Islamic times, that so far from their stories helping to explain the Qur'ān, the Qur'ān is necessary to explain them.[5]

We are driven back then to an examination of the word itself. Bell, *Origin*, 58, would take it as a genuine Arabic word from حنف *to decline, turn from*, and thus agrees with the general orthodox theory.[6] We have already noted the difficulty of this, however, and as a matter of fact some of the Muslim authorities knew that as used in the Qur'ān it was a foreign word, as we learn from Mas'ūdī's *Tanbīh*,[7] where it is given as Syriac.

[1] *LA*, x, 403; Rāghib, *Mufradāt*, 133.

[2] Margoliouth, *JRAS*, 1903, p. 477. "These suggestions are clearly too fanciful to deserve serious consideration."

[3] The name 𐩢𐩬𐩰 in Sabaean and in the Safaite inscriptions (Ryckmans, *Noms propres*, i, 96) as well as the tribal name حنيفة ought perhaps to be taken into account.

[4] Noldeke, *ZDMG*, xli, 721; de Goeje, *Bibl. Geogr. Arab*, viii, Glossary, p. xviii. Wellhausen, *Reste*, 239, thought that it meant a Christian ascetic, and in this he is followed by Noldeke-Schwally, i, 8, but see Rudolph, *Abhängigkeit*, 70.

[5] Kuenen, *Hibbert Lectures*, 1882, p. 20. On these Ḥanīfs see especially Caetani, *Annali*, i, 183 ff., and Sprenger, *Leben*, i, 43–7, 67–92, 110–137.

[6] So apparently Macdonald, *MW*, vi, 308, who takes it to mean *heretic*, and see Schulthess in *Nöldeke Festschrift*, p. 86.

[7] Ed. de Goeje in *BGA*, viii, p. 91—وهذه كلمة سريانية عربت.

Winckler, *Arabisch-Semitisch-Orientalisch*, p. 79 (i.e. *MVAG*, vi, 229), suggested that it was an Ethiopic borrowing, and Grimme, *Mohammed*, 1904, p. 48, wants to link the Ḥanīfs on to some S. Arabian cult. The Eth. ሐናፊ, however, is quite a late word meaning *heathen*,[1] and can hardly have been the source of the Arabic.[2] Nor is there any serious ground for taking the word as a borrowing from Heb. חָנֵף *profane*, as Deutsch suggested (*Literary Remains*, 93), and as has been more recently defended by Hirschfeld.[3]

The probabilities are that it is the Syr. ܚܢܦܐ, as was pointed out by Nöldeke.[4] This word was commonly used with the meaning of *heathen*, and might well have been known to the pre-Islamic Arabs as a term used by the Christians for those who were neither Jews nor of their own faith, and this meaning would suit the possible pre-Islamic passages where we find the word used. Moreover, as Margoliouth has noticed, in using the word of Abraham, Muḥammad would be following a favourite topic of Christian apologists, who argued from Rom. iv, 10–12, that Abraham's faith was counted for righteousness in his heathen days before there was any Judaism.[5] (See Ahrens, *Christliches*, 28, and Nielsen in *HAA*, i, 250.)

حَوَارِيُّونَ (*Ḥawārīyūn*).

iii, 45; v, 111, 112; lxi, 14.

Disciples.

It is used only of the disciples of Jesus and only in late Madinan passages.

as-Suyūṭī, *Itq*, 320, includes it in his list of foreign words, but in this he is quite exceptional.[6] He says, "Ibn Abī Ḥātim quoted from aḍ-Ḍaḥḥāk that *Ḥawārīyūn* means washermen in Nabataean."[7]

[1] Dillmann, *Lex*, 605.

[2] Nöldeke, *Neue Beiträge*, 35.

[3] *Beiträge*, 43 ff. *New Researches*, 26; cf. also Pautz, *Offenbarung*, 14.

[4] *Neue Beiträge*, 30. It has been accepted as such by Andrae, *Ursprung*, 40; Ahrens, *Muhammed*, 15, and Mingana, *Syriac Influence*, 97.

[5] *JRAS*, 1903, p. 478. Margoliouth also notes that there may have been further influence from the prophecy that Abraham should be the father of many nations, as this word is sometimes rendered by ܚܢܦܐ. From ܚܢܦܐ was formed حنفاء, and then the sing. حنيف formed from this.

[6] Also *Mutaw*, 59, and given by al-Khafājī in his supercommentary to Baiḍ. on iii, 45.

[7] al-Alūsī, iii, 155, quotes the Nab. form as هُوَّارِى.

Most of the Muslim authorities take it as a genuine Arabic word either from حَوَرَ (i.e. حَارَ : يَحُورُ) *to return*, or from حَوِرَ *to be glistening white*. From the first derivation they get the meaning *disciples* by saying that a disciple means a helper, and so حوارى means one to whom one turns for help (cf. ath-Thaʿlabī, *Qiṣaṣ*, 273). The other, however, is the more popular explanation, and the disciples are said to have been called حواريون because they were fullers whose profession was to clean clothes, or because they wore white clothing, or because of the purity of their inward life (cf. Baiḍ. on iii, 45; *TA*, iii, 161; *LA*, v, 299). It was probably in this connection that there grew up the idea that the word was Aramaic, for חֲוַר like Syr. ܚܘܰܪ means *to become white*, both in a material and a spiritual sense.

There can be no reasonable doubt, however, that the word is a borrowing from Abyssinia. The Eth. ሐዋርያ is the usual Eth. translation of ἀπόστολος (cf. Mk. vi, 30). It is used for *messenger* as early as the Aksum inscription (Nöldeke, *Neue Beiträge*, 48), and as early as Ludolf it was recognized as the origin of the Arabic word.[1] Dvořák, *Fremdw*, 64, thinks that it was one of the words that was learned by Muḥammad from the emigrants who returned from Abyssinia, but it is very possible that the word was current in Arabia before his day, for its occurs in a verse of aḍ-Ḍābi' b. al-Ḥārith (*Aṣmaiyāt*, ed. Ahlwardt, p. 57) referring to the disciples of Christ.

حُوبٌ (*Ḥūb*).

iv, 2.

Crime, sin.

The passage is a late Madinan one referring to the devouring of the property of orphans.

It is generally taken as meaning إِثْم and derived from حاب (Rāghib, *Mufradāt*, 133). as-Suyūṭī, however, *Itq*, 320,[2] says that some

[1] So Fraenkel, *Vocab*, 24; Wellhausen, *Reste*, 232; Pautz, *Offenbarung*, 255, n.; Dvořák, *Fremdw*, 58; Wensinck, *EI*, ii, 292; Cheikho, *Naṣrāniya*, 189; Horovitz, *KU*, 108; Vollers, *ZDMG*, li, 293; Sacco, *Credenze*, 42.

[2] The tradition is given at greater length and more exactly in *Mutaw*, 38.

early authorities took it to be an Abyssinian word meaning *sin*. That the word is foreign is doubtless correct, but the Abyssinian origin has nothing in its favour, though in the S. Arabian inscriptions we find 𐩢𐩥𐩨, *peccatum, debitum* (Rossini, *Glossarium*, 146).

The common Semitic root חוב is *to be guilty*. In Heb. the verb occurs once in Dan. i, 10, and the noun חוב *debt* occurs in Ez. xviii, 7. Aram. חָיַב ; Syr. ܚܒ, *to be defeated, to be guilty* are of much more common use, as are their nominal forms חוֹבָא, ܚܘܒܐ. The Arabic equivalent of these forms, however, is خاب *to fail, to be disappointed* (*BDB*, 295), and حَوب or حُوب, as Bevan notes,[1] is to be taken as a loan-word from Aramaic, and the verb حَاب as a denominative. The probabilities are in favour of the borrowing being from Syriac rather than from Jewish Aram.,[2] for ܚܘܒܐ, especially in the plu., is used precisely in the Qur'ānic sense (*PSm*, 1214).

حُورٌ (*Ḥūr*).

xliv, 54 ; lii, 20 ; lv, 72 ; lvi, 22.

The Houries, or Maidens of Paradise.

Except in lv, 72, it is used always in the phrase حُور عِين. The occurrences are all in early Sūras describing the delights of Paradise, where the حور عين are the beauteous maidens whom the faithful will have as spouses in the next life.

The Grammarians are agreed that حور is a plu. of حوراء and derived from حَوِرَ, a form of حار, and would thus mean "the white ones". عِين is a plu. of أَعْيَن meaning "wide eyed" (*LA*, xvii, 177). It thus becomes possible to take حور عين as two adjectives used as nouns meaning "white skinned, large eyed damsels". The

[1] *Daniel*, 62 n.

[2] Mingana, *Syriac Influence*, 86.

Lexicons insist that the peculiar sense of حَوَرٌ is that it means the contrast of the black and white in the eye, particularly in the eye of a gazelle or a cow (cf. *LA*, v, 298; and *TA*, iii, 160). Some, however, insist equally on the whiteness of the body being the reference of the word, e g. al-Azharī in *TA*, "a woman is not called حوراء unless along with the whiteness of the eye there is whiteness of body." One gathers from the discussion of the Lexicographers that they were somewhat uncertain as to the actual meaning of the word, and in fact both *LA*. and *TA*. quote the statement of so great an authority as al-Aṣma'ī that he did not know what was the meaning of حور as connected with the eye.

The Commentators give us no help with the word as they merely set forth the same material as we find in the Lexicons. They prefer the meaning which refers it to the eye as more suited to the Qur'ānic passages, and their general opinion is well summarized in as-Sijistānī, 117.

Fortunately, the use of the word can be illustrated from the old poetry, for it was apparently in quite common use in pre-Islamic Arabia. Thus in 'Abīd b. al-Abraṣ, vii, 24 (ed. Lyall) we find the verse—

واوانس مثل الدمى حور العيون قد استبينا

"And maidens like ivory statues,[1] white of eyes, did we capture" and again in 'Adī b. Zaid.

هَيَّج الداء فى فؤادك حورٌ ناعماتٌ بجانب الملطاط

"They have touched your heart, these tender white maidens, beside the river bank."

and so in a verse of Qa'nab in the *Mukhtārāt*, viii, 7, we read—

وفى الخدور لوان الدار جامعة حور اوانس فى اصواتها غنن

"And in the women's chamber when the house is full, are white maidens with charming voices."

In all these cases we are dealing with human women, and except in the verse of 'Abīd the word حور could quite well mean white-

[1] So in al-A'shā we find حور كامثال الدمى, cf. Geyer, *Zwei Gedichte*, i, 196 = *Dīwān*, xxxiii, 11.

skinned, and even in the verse of 'Abīd, the comparison with ivory statues would seem to lend point to al-Azharī's statement that it is only used of the eyes when connected with whiteness of the skin.

Western scholars are in general agreed that the conception of the Houries of Paradise is one borrowed from outside sources, and the prevalent opinion is that the borrowing was from Persia. Sale suggested this in his *Preliminary Discourse*, but his reference to the *Sadder Bundahishn* was rather unfortunate, as Dozy pointed out,[1] owing to the lateness of this work. Berthels, however, in his article "Die paradiesischen Jungfrauen im Islam", in *Islamica*, i, 263 ff., has argued convincingly that though Sale's *Ḥūrān-i-Bihisht* may not be called in as evidence, yet the characteristic features of the حور of the Qur'ānic Paradise closely correspond with Zoroastrian teaching about the Daena. The question, however, is whether the name حور is of Iranian origin. Berthels thinks not.[2] Haug, however, suggested its equivalence with the Zoroastrian [illegible] *hūmat*, good thought (cf. Av. [illegible]; Skt. सुमत); [illegible] *hūχt*, good speech (cf. Av. [illegible]; Skt. सूक्त), and [illegible] *hūvarsht*, good deed (cf. Av. [illegible]),[3] but the equivalences are difficult, and as Horovitz, *Paradies*, 13, points out, they in no way fit in with the pre-Islamic use of حور. Tisdall, *Sources*, 237 ff., claims that حور is connected with the modern Pers. خور *sun* from Phlv. [illegible] *χvar*[4] and Av. [illegible] *havarə*,[5] but this comes no nearer to explaining the Qur'ānic word.

It is much more likely that the word comes from the Phlv. [illegible] *hurūst*, meaning *beautiful*, and used in the Pahlavi books of the beauteous damsels of Paradise, e.g. in *Arda Virāf*, iv, 18, and in

[1] *Het Islamisme*, 3 ed., 1880, p. 101.

[2] "Das Wort *Ḥūr* durfen wir naturlich ebensowenig in den iranischen Sprachen suchen."

[3] The three words occur together in Pand-nāmak, xx, 12, 13. Cf. Nyberg, *Glossar*, 109, 110.

[4] Horn, *Grundriss*, pp. 111, 112; *Shikand*, Glossary, 255.

[5] Bartholomae, *AIW*, 1847; Reichelt, *Awestisches Elementarbuch*, 512; cf. Skt. स्वर्.

Hādōχt Nask, ii, 23,[1] where we have the picture of a graceful damsel, white-armed, strong, with dazzling face and prominent breasts. Now [illegible] is a good Iranian word, the equivalent of Av. [illegible] *hūraoδa*,[2] and though these Pahlavi works are late the conceptions in them are early and there can be no question of borrowing from the Semitic.

To this Iranian conception we may now add the influence of the Aram. חור. Sprenger was doubtless right in his conjecture [3] that the root حور *to be white* came to the Arabs from Aramaic. The Heb. חוּר occurs in Is. xxix, 22, in the sense of becoming pale through shame, and Syr. ܚܘܪܐ is commonly used to translate λευκός, and is thus used for the white garments of the Saints in Rev. iii, 4. Carra de Vaux,[4] indeed, has suggested that Muḥammad's picture of the youths and maidens of Paradise was due to a misunderstanding of the angels in Christian miniatures or mosaics representing Paradise. This may or may not be so, but it does seem certain that the word حور in its sense of whiteness, and used of fair-skinned damsels, came into use among the Northern Arabs as a borrowing from the Christian communities, and then Muḥammad, under the influence of the Iranian [illegible], used it of the maidens of Paradise.

خَاتَم (*Khātam*).

xxxiii, 40.

A seal.

The passage is late Madinan and the word is used in the technical phrase خاتم النبيين.

On the surface it would seem to be a genuine derivative from خَتَمَ *to seal*, but as Fraenkel, *Vocab*, 17, points out, a form فَاعَل is

[1] See also *Minokhird*, ii, 125–139, for the idea.

[2] Bartholomae, *AIW*, 1836.

[3] *Leben*, ii, 222. He thinks it may have come to the Arabs from the Nabataeans.

[4] Art. "Djanna" in *EI*, i, 1015.

not regular in Arabic, and the verb itself, as a matter of fact, is denominative.[1] The verb occurs in the Qur'ān in vi, 46 ; xlv, 22, and the derivative خِتَام, which Jawharī says is the same as خاتم, is used in lxxxiii, 26. All these forms are in all probability derived from the Aram. as Nöldeke had already noted.[2]

Hirschfeld, *Beiträge*, 71, claimed that the word was of Jewish origin, quoting the Heb. חותם *seal* ; Syr. ܚܬܡܐ. In his *New Researches*, 23, he quotes Haggai ii, 23, a verse referring to Zerubbabel, which shows that the idea of a man being a seal was not foreign to Jewish circles, beside which Horovitz, *KU*, 53, appositely cites 1 Cor. ix, 2, "ye are the seal of my Apostleship"—σφραγίς μου τῆς ἀποστολῆς, where the Peshitta reads ܚܬܡܐ. The Targumic חתימה and Christian Palestinian ܚܬܝܡܘܬܐ,[3] meaning *obsignatio*, *finis*, *conclusio*, *clausula*, give us even closer approximation to the sense of the word as used in the Qur'ān.

In the general sense of *seal* it must have been an early borrowing, for already in Imru'ul-Qais, xxxii, 4 (Ahlwardt, *Divans*, p. 136), we find the plu. خواتم used, and in the S. Arabian inscriptions we have 𐩭𐩩𐩣 (Rossini, *Glossarium*, 158).

خُبْز (*Khubz*).

xii, 36.

Bread.

It occurs only in the baker's dream in the Joseph story.

The word is from the Eth. as Nöldeke, *Neue Beiträge*, 56, has noted, pointing out that bread is an uncommon luxury to the Arabs, but literally the staff of life among the Abyssinians, and therefore a word much more likely to have been borrowed by the Arabs than from them. ኀበዘ is *to bake* in general, and to bake bread in particular, ኀባዚ is a *baker*, as e.g. in the Joseph story, and ኅብስት is *bread*, the ዘ being modified to ሰ before ት, and was probably earlier *ኅብዝት,

[1] Fraenkel, *Fremdw*, 252. The variant forms of the word given in the *Ṣiḥāḥ* and in *LA*, xv, 53, also suggest that the word is foreign.

[2] *Mand. Gramm*, 112 ; see also Pallis, *Mandaean Studies*, 153.

[3] Schwally, *Idioticon*, 36. It translates ἐπισφραγίσμα, Land, *Anecdota*, iv, 181, l. 20. Cf. Schulthess, *Lex*, 71. Used of sealing magically, it occurs in the incantation texts, see Montgomery, *Aramaic Incantation Texts from Nippur*, Glossary, pp. 289, 290.

as is indicated by the common Tigré word ሕብዝት used for a popular kind of bread. It was probably an early borrowing into Arabic, for the root has become well naturalized and many forms have been built from it.

خَرْدَل (*Khardal*).

xxi, 48; xxxi, 15.

A mustard seed.

Both passages are reminiscent of the ὡς κόκκον σινάπεως of Matt. xvii, 20, etc.

The Muslim authorities take it as an Arabic word, though they are in some doubt as to whether it should be خَرْدَل or خَرْدَل. Fraenkel, *Fremdw*, 141, has shown, however, that the word is a borrowing from Aram. חרדל; Syr. ܚܪܕܠܐ. The probabilities are in favour of its being from the Syr. ܚܪܕܠܐ, which as a matter of fact translates σίναπι in the Peshitta text of Matt. xvii, 20, etc., and occurs also in Christian Palestinian.[1] The borrowing will have been early for the word is used in the old poems, e.g. *Divān Hudhail*, xcvii, 11.

خَزَانَة (*Khazāna*).

vi, 50; xi, 33; xii, 55; xv, 21; xvii, 102; xxxviii, 8; lii, 37; lxiii, 7.

Treasury, storehouse.

The verb خَزَنَ does not occur in the Qur'ān, but besides خزانة (which occurs, however, only in the plu. form خزائن), we find a form خَازِن "one who lays in store" in xv, 22; and خَزَنَة *keepers* in xxxix, 71, 73; xl, 52; lxvii, 8.

It is fairly obvious that خزن is a denominative verb, and the word has been recognized by many Western scholars as a foreign borrowing.[2] Its origin, however, is a little more difficult to determine. Hoffmann,

[1] Schulthess, *Lex*, 69.

[2] Fraenkel in *Beitr. Assy*, iii, 81; Vollers, *ZDMG*, l, 640; Horovitz, *Paradies*, 5 n.

ZDMG, xxxii, 760,[1] suggested that we should find its origin in the Pers. كَنْج. This كَنْج which *BQ* defines as زر وگوهری که در زمین دفن کنند, is cognate with Skt. गञ्ज (=कोश) a *treasury* or *jewel room*,[2] and has been borrowed through the Aram. גנזא; Syr. ܓܙܐ into Arabic as كَنز. It seems hardly likely that by another line of borrowing, through say Heb. גְּנָזִים[3] or Mand. גאזאנא,[4] it has come to form the Ar. خزانة.

Barth, *Etymol. Stud*, 51, makes the happier suggestion that it may be connected with the form that is behind the Heb. חֹסֶן *treasure*.

خَطِئَ (*Khaṭi'a*).

To do wrong, sin.

Several verbal and nominal forms from this root occur in the Qur'ān, e.g. خَطَأً *by mistake* (iv, 94); أَخْطَأَ *to be in error, to sin* (ii, 286; xxxiii, 5); خَاطِئ (xxviii, 7; lxix, 37); خِطْأً *sin, error* (xvii, 33); خَطِيئَة, plu. خطايا *sin, error* (ii, 55, 75; iv, 112, etc.); and خاطئة *habitual sinfulness* (lxix, 9; xcvi, 16).

The primitive meaning of the Semitic root was apparently *to miss*[5] as in Heb. חטא (cf. Prov. viii, 36, חטאי חמס נפשו "he who misses me wrongs himself"), and in the Eth. ኀጥአ *to fail to find*. The Hiphil form in Heb. is used of markmanship, and 𐩠𐩭𐩷𐩱 in S. Arabian seems to have the same meaning, as we may judge from two inscriptions given by Levy in *ZDMG*, xxiv, 195, 199 (cf. also Rossini, *Glossarium*, 155). It was from this sense of missing the mark that there developed the idea of *to sin*, which is the commonest use

[1] Cf. also his *Märtyrer*, 250.

[2] It is probably a loan-word in Skt. Lagarde, *GA*, 27, and *Arm. Stud*, § 453, thinks it is an old Median word.

[3] Cf. Esth, iii, 9; iv, 7, גנזי המלך.

[4] Fraenkel, *Beitr. Assy*, iii, 181, takes it to be from Aram.

[5] But see Zimmern, *Akkad. Fremdw*, 11.

of the verb in Heb. and the only meaning it has in Aram.[1] It was doubtless under Aram. influence that it gained a similar meaning in Eth.,[2] and there is little doubt that it came into Arabic as a technical term from the same source. It occurs very rarely in the old poetry,[3] though the casual way in which the term is used in the Qur'ān shows that it must have been well understood in Mecca and Madina.[4]

The Muslim authorities take خطيئة as a form فعيلة, but as Schwally notes (*ZDMG*, lii, 132), its form like that of the Eth. ኀጢአት [5] is proof conclusive that the borrowing of this form is direct from the Syr. ܚܛܝܬܐ, and doubtless the other Arabic forms are due to influence from the same source.[6]

خَلَاق (*Khalāq*).

ii, 96, 196 ; iii, 71 ; ix, 70.

A portion or share.

As a technical term for the portion of good allotted man by God this term occurs only in Madinan passages. In Sūra ix, it refers to man's portion in this world, and in Sūras ii and iii to man's portion in the life to come, the two latter passages indeed, as Margoliouth, *MW*, xviii, 78, notes, being practically a quotation from the Talmud (cf. Sanh, 90*a*, אין להם חלק לעולם).

It seems clear that it is a technical term of non-Arabic origin, for though the primitive sense of خَلَقَ is to *measure* (cf. Eth. ኈለቈ to *enumerate*), its normal sense in Qur'ānic usage is *to create*, and this Madinan use of خلاق in the sense of *portion* follows that of the older religions. Thus חלקה is a portion given by God, cf. Job xx, 29, and Aram. חולקא means a portion in both worlds (cf. *Baba Bathra*, 122*a*, and Buxtorf, *Lex*. 400). Syr. ܚܠܩܐ means rather *lot* or *fate*, i.e. μοῖρα as in ܚܠܩܐ ܕܡܘܬܐ = μοῖρα θανάτου,

[1] And now also in the Ras Shamra tablets.
[2] Pratorius, *Beitr. Ass*, i, 29.
[3] Examples occur in Abū'l-'Atāhiya (ed. 1888), p. 120, and in Qais b. ar-Ruqaiyāt, xviii, 3 (ed. Rhodokanakis, p. 129).
[4] But see Wensinck in *EI*, ii, 925.
[5] Nöldeke, *Neue Beiträge*, 36.
[6] Mingana, *Syriac Influence*, 86.

though in the Christ. Palest. dialect ܡܘܠܟܐ means *portion*, i.e. μέρος.[1]

It is noteworthy that the Lexicons, which define it as الحظ والنصيب من الخير والصلاح,[2] seem to interpret it from the Qur'ān, and the only verse they quote in illustration is from Ḥassān b. Thābit, which is certainly under Qur'ānic influence. Horovitz, *JPN*, 198 ff., thinks that the origin is Jewish, but Phon. חלק is also *to divide, apportion* (Harris, *Glossary*, 102), so that the word may have been used in the Syro-Palestinian area among other groups.

خَمْرٌ (*Khamr*).

ii, 216; v, 92, 93; xii, 36, 41; xlvii, 16.

Wine.

The word is very commonly used in the old poetry, but as Guidi saw,[3] it is not a native word, but one imported along with the article. The Ar. خَمَرَ means *to cover, to conceal*, and from this was formed خِمَار *a muffler*, the plu. of which, خُمُر, occurs in Sūra xxiv, 31. In the sense of *to give wine to*, it is denominative.[4]

Its origin was doubtless the Aram. חמרא = Syr. ܚܡܪܐ which is of very common use. The Heb. חֶמֶר is poetical (*BDB*, 330) and probably of Aram. origin.[5] It is also suggestive that many of the other forms from خمر are clearly of Aram. origin, e.g. ܚܡܝܪܐ *leaven*, gives خمير *ferment, leaven*, and Arm. խմոր *yeast*[6]; ܚܡܳܪܳܐ a *wineseller* is خمّار; ܚܡܪܢ is خمران, etc.

The probabilities are all in favour of the word having come into Arabic from a Christian source, for the wine trade was largely in the hands of Christians (*vide supra*, p. 21), and Jacob even suggests that

[1] Schulthess, *Lex*, 65, and cf. *Palestinian Lectionary of the Gospels*, p. 126.

[2] *LA*, xi, 380.

[3] *Della Sede*, 597, and note Bell, *Origin*, 145.

[4] Fraenkel, *Fremdw*, 161.

[5] We now have the word, however, in the Ras Shamra texts.

[6] Lagarde, *Arm. Stud*, § 991; Hübschmann, *ZDMG*, xlvi, 238, and *Arm. Gramm*, i, 305.

Christianity spread among the Arabs in some parts along the routes of the wine trade.[1] Most of the Arabic terms used in the wine trade seem to be of Syriac origin, and خَمْر itself is doubtless an early borrowing from the Syr. ܚܡܪܐ.

خِنْزِير (*Khinzīr*).

ii, 168; v, 4, 65; vi, 146; xvi, 116.

Pig, swine.

It occurs only in late passages and always in the list of prohibited foods, save in v, 65, where it refers to certain infidels whom God changed into apes and swine.

No explanation of the word from Arabic material is possible,[2] and Guidi, *Della Sede*, 587, was suspicious of the word. Fraenkel's examination of the word, *Fremdw*, 110, has confirmed the suspicion and indicated that it is in all probability a loan-word from Aramaic.[3] The dependence of the Qur'ānic food-regulations on Biblical material has been frequently noticed,[4] and in Lev. xi, 7, we find חזיר among the forbidden meats. In Aram. the word is חזירא and in Syr. ܚܙܝܪܐ, and only in S. Arabian do we find the form with *n*, e.g. Eth. ኀንዚር (also ሕንዘር or ሕንዚር, cf. Eth. Enoch, lxxxix, 10) meaning *wild boar* (though it is rare in Eth., the usual word being ሐራውያ), and Sab. 𐩭𐩬𐩸𐩧 (Ryckmans, *Noms propres*, i, 38).

It is possible of course that the Arabic word was derived from Eth., but the alternative forms in Eth. make one suspect that the borrowing was the other way, so it is safest to assume that the borrowing was from Aram. with a glide sound ن developed between the خ and ز [5] (Fraenkel, 111), which also appears in the חנזר of the Ras Shamra texts.

[1] *Beduinenleben*, 99. Fraenkel, *Fremdw*, 181, notes the curious fact that in early Arabic the commonest word for merchant, viz. تاجر, has the special significance of "wine merchant", on which D. H. Muller remarks, *WZKM*, i, 27: "sie zeigt dass die Civilization im Alterthum wie heute erst mit der Einfuhrung berauschender Getränke begonnen hat."

[2] *Vide* the suggestions of the Lexicographers in Lane, *Lex*, 732.

[3] But see Lagarde, *Ubersicht*, 113, and the Akk. *ḫumṣiru* (Zimmern, *Akkad. Fremdw*, 50).

[4] Cf. Rudolph, *Abhängigkeit*, 61, 62.

[5] That this inserted *n* was not infrequent in borrowed words is illustrated by Geyer, *Zwei Gedichte*, i, 118 n.

خَيْمَةٌ (*Khaima*).

lv, 72.

Tent; pavilion.

It is found only in the plu. خِيَامٌ in an early Meccan description of Paradise, where we are told that the Houries are مقصورات فى الخيام "kept close in pavilions".

The word is obviously not Arabic, and Fraenkel, *Fremdw*, 30, though admitting that he was not certain of its origin, suggested that it came to the Arabs from Abyssinia.[1] Eth. ኅይመት means *tentorium, tabernaculum* (Dillmann, *Lex*, 610), and translates both the Heb. אֹהֶל and Gk. σκηνή. Vollers, however, in *ZDMG*, l, 631, is not willing to accept this theory of Abyssinian derivation,[2] and thinks we must look to Persia or N. Africa for its origin. The Pers. خيمه, خيم and خيام, however, are direct borrowings from the Arabic[3] and not formations from the root خم meaning *curvature*.

We find the word not infrequently in the early poetry, and so it must have been an early borrowing, probably from the same source as the Eth. ኅይመት.

دَاوُدُ (*Dāwūd*).

ii, 252; iv, 161; v, 82; vi, 84; xvii, 57; xxi, 78, 79; xxvii, 15, 16; xxxiv, 10, 12; xxxviii, 16–29.

David.

In the Qur'ān he is mentioned both as King of Israel and also as a Prophet to whom was given the Zabūr زبور (Psalter).

[1] In S. Arabian we have 𐩭𐩺𐩣, which is said to mean *domus modesta* (Rossini, *Glossarium*, 155).

[2] "خيمة Zelt ist mir verdächtig, ohne dass ich mit Sicherheit die fremde Urform angeben kann. Die Erklarung schwankt in den Einzelheiten: ursprünglich primitivste Behausung scheint es allmänlich mit بيت Zelt gleichbedeutend geworden zu sein. Dass es durch äth. *ḫaimat* als echt semitisch erwiesen wird, kann ich Fränkel nicht zugeben, denn viele Entlehnungen sind auf den Süden beschränkt geblieben. Man muss an Persien oder Nordostafrika denken."

[3] Vullers, *Lex. Pers*, i, 776.

al-Jawālīqī, *Mu'arrab*, 67, recognized the name as foreign, and his statement is repeated in Rāghib, *Mufradāt*, 173; *LA*, iv, 147, etc. It was even recognized as a Hebrew name as we learn from Baiḍ. who, speaking of Ṭālūt, says, هو علم عبرى كداود, "it is a Hebrew proper name like David."

In two passages of the Qur'ān (xxi, 80; xxxiv, 10) we are told that he was an armourer, and as such he is frequently mentioned in the old poetry,[1] so the name obviously came to the Arabs from a community where these legends were circulating, though this may have been either Jewish or Christian. It was also used as a personal name among the Arabs in pre-Islamic days, for we hear of a Phylarch Dā'ūd al-Lathīq of the house of Ḍajā'ima of the tribe of Sāliḥ,[2] there appears to have been a contemporary of Muḥammad who fought at Badr, named ابو داود,[3] and possibly the name occurs in a Thamudic inscription.[4]

The form of the name presents a little difficulty, for the Heb. is דָּוִד or דָּוִיד, and the Christian forms follow this, e.g. Gk. Δαυείδ, Syr. ܕܘܝܕ or ܕܘܝܕ, Eth. ዳዊት. There is a Syr. form ܕܘܘܕ used by Bar Hebr., *Chron*, 325, but *PSm*, 801, is probably right in thinking that this was influenced by the Arabic. Horovitz, *KU*, 110, discusses the change in form from Dāwīd to Dā'ūd,[5] and on the whole it seems safest to conclude that it came to Arabic from some Aramaic source, though whether Jewish or Christian it is impossible to say.

دَرَسَ (*Darasa*).

iii, 73; vi, 105, 157; vii, 168; xxxiv, 43; lxviii, 37.

To study earnestly.

Always used in the Qur'ān of studying deeply into or searching the Scriptures, and the reference is always directly or indirectly to the Jews and Christians.[6] On this ground Geiger, 51, claimed that here

[1] *Vide* examples in Fraenkel, *Fremdw*, 242; Horovitz, *KU*, 109; *JPN*, 166, 167.
[2] Yāqūt, *Mu'jam*, iv, 70; and *vide* Noldeke, *Ghassanischen Fürsten*, p. 8.
[3] *Vide* Ibn Hishām, 505; Ibn Sa'd, iii, b, 74, and Wellhausen, *Wāqidī*, p. 88.
[4] Ryckmans, *Noms propres*, i, 65.
[5] *Vide* also Rhodokanakis in *WZKM*, xvii, 283.
[6] Taking v, 37, of Sūra lxviii to be late, as seems evident from the use of كتاب.

we have a technical word for the study of Scripture borrowed from the root דָּרַשׁ so widely used in this connection by the Jews.

Geiger's suggestion has had wide acceptance among Western scholars,[1] and it is curious that some of the Muslim philologers felt the difficulty, for as-Suyūṭī, *Itq*, 320, and in the *Muhadhdhab*, tells us that some considered it to be Heb., and in *Mutaw*, 56, he quotes others as holding it to be Syriac. Syr. ܕܪܫ does mean *to train, to instruct*, and Eth. ደረሰ *to interpret, comment upon*, whence ድርሳት and ድርሳን *commentary*, but neither of these is so likely an origin as the Jewish דרשׁ,[2] which, as Buxtorf, *Lex*, 297, shows, is the commonest word in the Rabbinic writings in connection with the exposition of Scripture, and which must have been commonly used among the Jewish communities of Arabia.[3]

دِرْهَم (*Dirham*).

xii, 20.

A dirham.

Only the plu. form دَرَاهِم is found in the Qur'ān, and only in the Joseph story.

It was commonly recognized by the philologers as a borrowed word. al-Jawālīqī, *Mu'arrab*, 66, notes it,[4] and ath-Tha'ālibī, *Fiqh*, 317, includes it in his list of words common to Persian and Arabic. There was some doubt as to the vowelling of the word, however, the authorities varying between دِرْهَم ; دِرْهِم and دِرْهَم or دِرْهَام (cf. *LA*, xv, 89).

The ultimate origin is the Gk. δραχμή,[5] which passed into Syr. as ܕܪܟܡܐ. Some, however, would derive δραχμή from a Semitic source. Boissacq suggests this, and Levy, *Fremdw*, 118, connects it

[1] Fraenkel, *Vocab*, 23; Fleischer, *Kleinere Schriften*, ii, 122; Sprenger, *Leben*, ii, 289; Hirschfeld, *Beiträge*, 51; *New Researches*, 28.

[2] Eth. ደረሰ and መድረስ are themselves derived from the Heb. Noldeke, *Neue Beiträge*, 38; Horovitz, *JPN*, 199.

[3] Rhodokanakis, *WZKM*, xvii, 285, thinks that in درس here we have a combination of דרשׁ and דרם. "Zur Radix درس ist nachzutragen, dass in ihr דרשׁ und דרם (v. Levy) zusammenfielen. Daher einerseits die Bedeutung *studieren* anderseits *arbeiten* abnutzen."

[4] So al-Khafājī, 83; *LA*, xv, 89.

[5] Fraenkel, *Vocab*, 13; *Fremdw*, 191.

with Heb. דרכמון (Phon. דרכמנם)[1] beside אדרכון, which is the Persian gold Daric, the Gk. δαρεικός, and the Cuneiform *da-ri-ku*, which appears in Syr. as ܕܪܟܡܘܢܐ. Liddell and Scott, however, are doubtless right in deriving it from δράσσομαι and meaning originally "as much as one can hold in the hand", then a measure of weight and lastly a coin. This δραχμή passed into Iranian first as a measure of weight and then as a coin. In Phlv. we find the ideograms دلم *dram* and دلسم *draχm* meaning a silver coin,[2] or sometimes *money* in general,[3] which is the origin of the Mod. Pers. درم and درهم and the Arm. դրամ,[4] and may be assumed as the source of the Ar. درهم also.[5]

It was doubtless an early borrowing from the Mesopotamian area, for it occurs in the old poetry, e.g. 'Antara xxi, 21 (Ahlwardt, *Divans*, p. 45).

دِهَاق (*Dihāq*).

lxxviii, 34.

Full.

It occurs only in an early Meccan passage descriptive of the delights of Paradise, where, besides an enclosed garden and full-bosomed virgins, the blessed are promised كَأْسًا دِهَاقًا.

The Commentators are agreed that it means *full* and there is considerable agreement that it is to be derived from دَهَقَ *to press*.

[1] Lidzbarski, *Handbuch*, 257; Harris, *Glossary*, 96; cf. also Aram. דרכום in Cook, *Glossary*, 41.

[2] *PPGl*, 105 and 110; Nyberg, *Glossar*, 58; *Šāyast*, Glossary, 160; Frahang, *Glossary*, 78. Haug thinks this of Babylonian origin, but Hubschmann rightly derives it from a form *drahm from δραχμή, and then compares Av. 𐬙𐬀𐬑𐬨𐬀 *taxma*, cf. *Arm. Gramm*, i, 145; *Pers. Stud*, 251.

[3] e.g. in the Dādistān-i-Dīnīk, cf. West, *Pahlavi Texts*, ii, 242.

[4] Hubschmann, *Arm. Gramm*, i, 145.

[5] Vullers, *Lex*, i, 832, 840; Vollers, *ZDMG*, li, 297, and Addai Sher, 62, though some statements of the latter need correction.

They are not very happy over the form, however, for كَأْس is fem. and we should expect دهاقة not دهاق. Exactly the same form, however, is found in a verse of Khidāsh b. Zuhair—

أتانا عامر يرجو قرانا فَأَتْرَعْنا له كاسا دهاقا

"There came to us 'Āmir desiring entertainment from us, so we filled for him a full cup."

so Sībawaih suggested that it should be taken not as an adj. to كاسا but as a verbal noun.[1]

There is ground, however, for thinking that the word is not Arabic at all.[2] Fraenkel, *Fremdw*, 282, would relate it to דחק, which we find in Heb. דָּחַק *to crowd, oppress, thrust*; Aram. דְּחַק; Syr. ܕܚܩ *to crowd, squeeze*, which is the Ar. دَحَقَ *to drive away, expel*. The change of ח to ה he would explain as Mesopotamian. Thus كاسا دهاقا would mean "a cup pressed out", referring to the wine pressed to fill the cup.

دِينٌ (*Dīn*).

Of very frequent occurrence. Cf. i, 3; ii, 257, etc.

Judgment, Religion, and in ix, 29, verbally "to make profession of faith".

In the Qur'ān we find also دَيْنٌ a *debt*, that which one owes (cf. iv, 12, 13; ii, 282), and مَدِينٌ for one who receives payment of a debt (xxxvii, 51; lvi, 85), besides the verb تَدَايَنَ "to become debtors to one another" (ii, 282). These, however, are later developments of the word within Arabic.

The Muslim authorities usually treat it as an Arabic word (cf.

[1] *Vide LA*, xi, 395, 396.

[2] Horovitz, *Paradies*, 11, says: "Auch die Herkunft von دهاق . . . ist unsicher."

Rāghib, *Mufradāt*, 175), and derive it from دَانَ "to do a thing as a habit", but this verb seems to be denominative from دِين in the sense of *obedience*, which, like مَدِينَة and دَيَّان (i.e. ܡܕܝܢܬܐ and ܕܝܢܐ), is a borrowing from the North, connected with Akk. *dānu*, Heb. דִּין; Syr. ܕܝܢ. There was a suspicion among the philologers, however, that it was a foreign word, for *LA*, xvii, 27, notes that some authorities admitted that it had no verbal root, and al-Khafājī, 90, and ath-Tha'ālibī, *Fiqh*, 317, include it in their lists of foreign words.

As a matter of fact we have here two separate words of different origin.[1] (i) In the sense of *religion* the word is a borrowing from Iranian. In Phlv. we find [Pahlavi] *dēn* meaning *religion*,[2] from which come [Pahlavi] *dēnāk* for religious law, [Pahlavi] *ham-dēn*, of the same religion,[3] and [Pahlavi] *dēnān*, used in the sense of "the religious", i.e. true believers. This Phlv. [Pahlavi] is derived from Av. 𐬛𐬀𐬉𐬥𐬁 *daēnā*, *religion*[4] (though this itself is probably derived from the Elamitish *dēn*),[5] and besides being the origin of the Mod. Pers. دین,[6] was borrowed into Arm. as դէն meaning *religion, faith* (and also *law*[7] in the sense of a "religious system", e.g. դէն մազդեզանց = [Pahlavi] the Mazdian religion or Law). (ii) In the sense of *Judgment* it is a borrowing from the Aramaic. Thus we find in common use the Rabbinic דִּינָא, Syr. ܕܝܢܐ, and Mand. דינא, all meaning *judgment* and, indeed, the judgment of the last day.[8]

From the Aramaic the word passed into S. Arabian 𐩵𐩺𐩬 and

[1] Noldeke in *ZDMG*, xxxvii, 534. See also Von Kremer, *Streifzüge*, p. vii, and Ahrens, *Christliches*, 28, 34.

[2] *PPGl*, 110; *Šāyast*, Glossary, 160, and the *dēn* of the Turfan Pahlavi; Salemann, *Manichaische Studien*, i, 67. For the borrowing cf. Nöldeke-Schwally, i, 20; Vollers, *ZDMG*, l. 641; Noldeke, *Mand. Gram*, 102.

[3] Cf. the Av. [Avestan] [Avestan], West, *Glossary*, 35.

[4] Bartholomae, *AIW*, 662; Horn, *Grundriss*, 133; cf. also the Pazend *edînî* = irreligion.

[5] But see Bartholomae, *AIW*, 665, and Zimmern, *Akkad. Fremdw*, 24, who derives it from Akk. *dē(ī)nu*.

[6] Addai Sher, 69, discusses its meaning. Curiously enough it is given by the Lexicons as a borrowing from Arabic, cf. Vullers, *Lex*, i, 956, but see Bartholomae, *AIW*, 665.

[7] Hubschmann, *Arm. Gramm*, i, 139.

[8] Montgomery, *Aramaic Incantation Texts from Nippur*, Glossary, p. 285.

Eth. ደይን with its verbal forms ደየነ and ተደየነ (and Amharic ዳኛ *judge*; Tigriña ደያኛ *judge*); into Iranian, where we find the Phlv. ideogram دینا *dēnā* = *judgment, decree*,[1] and also into Arabic.[2] As used in the Qur'ān it closely corresponds to Jewish use; in fact the constantly occurring يوم الدين so exactly corresponds with the Rabbinic יום דינא = יום הדין that on the surface it seems obviously a borrowing from Jewish sources. The fact, however, that in Syriac, besides ܕܝܢܐ meaning *judgment*, we have also a ܕܝܢ meaning *religion*, borrowed from the Iranian (Brockelmann, *Lexicon Syriacum*, 151*b*), giving us the same double usage as in Arabic, makes the probabilities seem in favour of the borrowing having been from a Christian source.[3] In any case it was an early borrowing for it is found not uncommonly in the early poetry.[4]

دِينَارٌ (*Dīnār*).

iii, 68.

A dīnār.

The name of a coin, the Lat. *denarius*, Gk. δηνάριον. The Muslim authorities knew that it was a loan-word and claim that it came from Persian, though they were not unanimous about it. al-Jawālīqī, *Mu'arrab*, 62, whose authority is accepted by as-Suyūṭī,[5] gives it as Arabicized from the Pers. دِنّار, but ath-Tha'ālibī, *Fiqh*, 317, places it among the words which have the same form in both Arabic and Persian. as-Suyūṭī, *Muzhir*, i, 139, places it among the words about which the philologers were in doubt, and Rāghib, *Mufradāt*, 171, while quoting the theory that it is of Pers. origin compounded from دين and آر,[6] yet gives his own opinion that it is from دِنّار and an Arabic word. Similarly the

[1] *Frahang*, Glossary, p. 79.

[2] Hirschfeld, *Beiträge*, 44; Noldeke, *Neue Beiträge*, 39; Fraenkel, *Vocab*, 22.

[3] Mingana, *Syriac Influence*, 85; Horovitz, *KU*, 62.

[4] See references in Horovitz, op. cit. Cheikho, *Naṣrāniya*, 171.

[5] *Itq*, 320; *Mutaw*, 46, *vide* also al-Khafājī, 86.

[6] *Vide* Vullers, *Lex*, i, 25 and 56. Dvořák, *Fremdw*, 66, points out that the late Greek explanations of the word take it to be from *din-ar*, i.e. δεκάχαλκον; cf. Steph., *Thesaurus*, ii, 1094: τὸ δεκάχαλκον οὕτως ἐκαλεῖτο δηνάριον, or the even more ridiculous τὸ τὰ δεινὰ ἄιρειν παρεχόμενον.

Lexicons differ. The *Qāmūs* says plainly that it is a foreign word like قراط and ديباج which the Arabs of old did not know and so borrowed from other peoples. *TA*, iii, 211, says that the authorities were uncertain—واختلفت في اصله, and Jawharī tries to explain it as an Arabic word.

The form دنّار seems an invention to explain the plu. دنانير, though it may be intended to represent the Phlv. 𐭣𐭩𐭭𐭠𐭫 *dēnār*, used for a gold coin in circulation in the Sasanian empire,[1] and which is the origin of the Pers. دينار. The Phlv. 𐭣𐭩𐭭𐭠𐭫, however, is not original, and the oft suggested connection with the Skt. दीनार, a gold coin or gold ornament, is hardly to the point, for this is itself derived from the Gk. δηνάριον,[2] and the Phlv. word was doubtless also borrowed directly from the Greek.

δηνάριον from the Lat. *denarius* was in common use in N.T. times, and occurs in the non-literary papyri.[3] The Greeks brought the word along with the coin to the Orient in their commercial dealings, and the word was borrowed not only into Middle Persian, but is found also in Arm. *դինար*,[4] in Aram. דינר, which occurs both in the Rabbinic writings (Levy, *Wörterbuch*, i, 399, 400) and in the Palmyrene inscriptions (De Vogüé, *Inscr*, vi, 3 = *NSI*, No. 115, p. 273),[5] and in Syr. ܕܝܢܪܐ. The *denarius aureus*, i.e. the δηνάριον χρυσοῦν, became known in the Orient as simply δηνάριον, and it was with the meaning of a gold coin that the word came into use in Arabic.[6]

Now as it was coins of Greek and not of Persian origin that first came into customary use in Arabia, we can dismiss the suggested Persian origin. Had the word come directly from Greek, however,

[1] *PPGl*, 110; *Karnāmak*, ii, 13; *Šāyast*, Glossary, 160.

[2] Monier Williams, *Sanskrit Dictionary*, 481.

[3] Kenyon, *Greek Papyri in the British Museum*, ii, 306: "The term *denarius* replaces that of *drachma* which was regularly in use before the time of Diocletian; the Neronian denarius reintroduced by Diocletian being reckoned as equivalent to the drachma and as $\frac{1}{6000}$ of a talent."

[4] Hübschmann, *Arm. Gramm*, i, 346. Brockelmann in *ZDMG*, xlvii, 11.

[5] The actual form is דינרין with the Aram. plu. ending.

[6] Zambaur in *EI*, i, 975, thinks that the shortened form of the name became current in Syria after the reform of the currency by Constantine I (A.D. 309–319).

we should expect the form دينارون, and the actual form دينار suggests an Aram. origin, as Fraenkel had noted.[1] It was from the Syr. ܕܝܢܪܐ that the Eth. ዲናር was derived,[2] and we may assume that the Arabic word was also taken from this source.[3] It was an early borrowing, as it occurs in the old poetry.

ذَكَّى (*Dhakkā*).

v, 4.

To make ceremonially clean.

Only once does this word occur, and then in a very late Madinan passage giving instruction about clean and unclean meats. Muslims are here forbidden to eat that which dieth of itself, blood, flesh of swine, that which has been offered to strange gods, anything strangled or gored or killed by an accident or by a beast of prey—" save what you have made ceremonially clean "—إِلَّا مَا ذَكَّيْتُمْ—the reference being, the Commentators tell us, to the giving of the death stroke in the orthodox fashion to such maimed or injured beasts.[4]

This whole passage is obviously under Jewish influence (cf. Lev. xi, 7 ; xvii, 10, 15, etc.), and Schulthess, *ZA*, xxvi, 151,[5] has suggested that the verb ذَكَّى here is a borrowing from the Jewish community. In Bibl. Heb. זכה (Pi) means " to make or keep clean or pure ",[6] but the Aram. דכי, דכא mean " to be ritually clean ", and the Pa. דַּכִּי is " to make ritually clean ", giving us precisely the form we need to explain the Arabic. The Syr. ܕܟܝ has the same meaning, but as the distinctions of clean and unclean meats meant little to the Christians, the probabilities are in favour of a Jewish origin.

[1] *Vocab*, 13 ; *Fremdw*, 191.

[2] Noldeke, *Neue Beiträge*, 41 ; but see p. 33, where he suggests a possible direct borrowing from the Greek.

[3] Mingana, *Syriac Influence*, 89.

[4] Wellhausen, *Reste*, 114, n. 4.

[5] " Wahrscheinlich ist aber dieses letzere ذكى irgendwie jüdischen Ursprungs."

[6] Note also Phon. זכא, Harris, *Glossary*, 99.

رَاعِنَا (*Rā'ina*).

ii, 98; iv, 48.

The reference is the same in both passages—" say not *rā'inā* but say *unẓurnā*." The Commentators tell us that the Jews in Arabia used to pronounce the word راعنا, meaning " look at us ", in such a way as to relate it with the root רַע *evil*, so Muḥammad urged his followers to use a different word انظرنا *behold us*, which did not lend itself to this disconcerting play on words.[1]

Hirschfeld, *Beiträge*, 64, thinks the reference is to ראהנא or ראנו occurring in connection with some Jewish prayer, but it is much more likely that the statement of the Commentators is correct and that as Geiger, 17, 18, noted,[2] it is a play on רע and ראה, and reflects the Prophet's annoyance at the mockery of the Jews.

رَبٌّ (*Rabb*).

Occurs very frequently, e.g. i, 1.

Lord, master.

The root רבב is common Semitic, probably meaning *to be thick*, as illustrated by Ar. رَبَّ *to increase*, رُبٌّ *thick juice*, the Rabbinic רְבָב *grease*, beside the Eth. ረበበ *to expand*, *extend*. The sense of *great*, however, which is so common in Heb. and Aram., and from which the meaning *Lord* has developed, does not occur in Ar. or in Eth. save as a borrowing.[3] This sense seems to have developed in the N. Semitic area, and Margoliouth, *ERE*, vi, 248, notes that رب meaning *Lord* or *Master* must have been borrowed from the Jews or Christians.

The borrowing was probably from Aram. for it was from an Aram. source that the word passed into Middle Persian, as witness the Phlv. ideogram رتد *rabā* meaning *great*, *venerable*, *splendid* (*PPGl*,

[1] as-Suyūṭī, *Itq*, 320, quoting Abū Na'īm's *Dalā'il an-Nubuwwa*. Cf. *Mutaw*, 59.
[2] *Vide* also Palmer, *Qoran*, i, 14; and Dvořák, *Fremdw*, 31; Horovitz, *JPN*, 204.
[3] It occurs, however, in Sab. ՈϽ, though this, like Eth. ረበ and ረበን, may be from the Aram. Torrey, *Foundation*, 52, claims that رب is purely Arabic.

190; *Frahang*, Glossary, 106), which occurs as early as the Sasanian inscriptions, where [illegible] is synonymous with the Pazend [illegible] *vazurg*.[1] We find רב very frequently in the Aramaic inscriptions, e.g. רב שוק "chief of the market", רב חילא "chief of the army", רב משריתא "camp master", etc.,[2] though its use in connection with deities is rarer,[3] names like רבאל meaning "El is great"[4] rather than "El is Lord". The special development of its use with God was in the Syriac of the Christian communities, and as Sprenger, *Leben*, i, 299, suggests, it was doubtless under Syr. influence that Muḥammad uses it as he does in the Qur'ān.[4] It was commonly used, however, both of human chieftains and of the deity in pre-Islamic days, as is evident from the old poetry, and from its use in the inscriptions (Ryckmans, *Noms propres*, i, 196; Rossini, *Glossarium*, 235).

رَبَّانِيّ (*Rabbānī*).

iii, 73; v, 48, 68.

Rabbi.

The passages are all late, and the reference is to Jewish teachers, as was recognized by the Commentators. Most of the Muslim authorities take it as an Arabic word, a derivative from رَبّ (cf. *TA*, i, 260; Rāghib, *Mufradāt*, 183; and Zam. on iii, 73). Some, however, knew that it was a foreign word, though they were doubtful whether its origin was Hebrew or Syriac.[5]

As it refers to Jewish teachers we naturally look for a Jewish origin, and Geiger, 51, would derive it from the Rabbinic רַבָּן, a later form of רבי used as a title of honour for distinguished teachers,[6]

[1] West, *Glossary*, 133; Herzfeld, *Paikuli*, Glossary, 240.

[2] See Cook, *Glossary*, under the various titles. So Phon. רב. Cf. Harris, *Glossary*, 145.

[3] Though in the S. Arabian inscriptions we find 𐩧𐩨𐩱𐩡. 𐩧𐩨𐩩𐩱𐩡𐩨, etc. (see Ryckmans, *Noms propres*, i, 248), and there is a similar use in the Ras Shamra tablets.

[4] Hirschfeld, *New Researches*, 30, however, argues that the dominant influence was Jewish. See also Horovitz, *JPN*, 199, 200.

[5] *Vide* al-Jawālīqī, *Mu'arrab*, 72; as-Suyūṭī, *Itq*, 320; *Muzhir*, i, 130; al-Khafājī, 94.

[6] Hirschfeld, *Beiträge*, 51 n., says: "Muhammad ermahnt die Rabbinen (rabbānī) sich nicht zu Herren ihrer Glaubensgenossen zu machen, sondern ihre Würde lediglich auf das Studium der Schrift zu beschränken, vgl. ix, 31." *Vide* also von Kremer, *Ideen*, 226 n.

so that there grew up the saying גדול מרבי רבן "greater than Rabbi is Rabbān". The difficulty in accepting رَبَّانِىّ as a direct derivative from רבן, however, is the final ى, which as Horovitz, *KU*, 63, admits, seems to point to a Christian origin. In Jno, xx, 16; Mk, x, 51, we find the form ῥαββουνεί (ὁ λέγεται Διδάσκαλε) or ῥαββωνεί, which seems to be formed from the Targumic רִבּוֹן,[1] and it was this form that came to be commonly used in the Christian communities of the East, viz. Syr. ܪܒܘܢܝ; Eth. ረቡኒ; Arm. ռաբբունի.[2] The Syr. ܪܒܘܢܝ was very widely used, and as Pautz, *Offenbarung*, 78, n. 4, notes, ܪܒܢ was commonly used for a *doctor* of learning, and the dim. ܪܒܘܢܝ was not uncommonly used as a title of reverence for priests and monks, so that we may conclude that the Qur'ānic word, as to its form, is probably of Syriac origin.[3]

رِبْح (*Ribḥ*).

ii, 15.

To be profitable.

A trading term which Barth, *Etymol. Stud*, 29 (but cf. Torrey, *Commercial Theological Terms*, p. 44), has equated with the Jewish ארווחה. It seems more likely, however, to have come from the Eth. ረብሐ *lucrari, lucrifacere*,[4] which is very commonly used and has many derivatives, e.g. ረባሒዊ *a business man*; ርብሕ *gain*; ርቡሕ *profit bearing*, etc., which are among the commonest trading terms. It is thus probably a trade term that came to the Arabs from Abyssinia, or may be from S. Arabia (cf. Ryckmans, *Noms propres*, i, 196; Rossini, *Glossarium*, 236).

رِبِّيُّونَ (*Ribbīyūn*).

iii, 140.

Myriads.

[1] Dalman, *Worte Jesu*, 267, and see his *Grammatik des jüd. paläst. Aramäisch*, p. 176.

[2] Hubschmann, *Arm. Gramm*, i, 376; *ZDMG*, xlvi, 251.

[3] Mingana, *Syriac Influence*, 85, agrees, but see Horovitz, *JPN*, 200.

[4] Fraenkel in *Beit. Ass*, iii, 74, says that Nöldeke suggested this derivation, but I cannot locate the reference.

The passage is a late Madinan one encouraging the Prophet in his difficulties.

as-Suyūṭī, *Itq*, 321, says that certain early authorities considered it a Syriac word, and this is probably correct. Syr. ܪܒܘܢ, the plu. of ܪܒܘ meaning *myriads*, translates both μυρίοι and μυριάδες of the LXX.[1]

•

رُجْز (*Rujz*).

lxxiv, 5.

Wrath.

The Sūra is an early one, and in this passage the Prophet is urged to magnify his Lord, purify his garments, and flee from the wrath to come—والرجز فاهجر.

It is usual to translate the word as *abomination* or *idolatry* and make it but another form of رِجْز, which occurs in ii, 56; vii, 131, etc. (cf. *LA*, vii, 219; Rāghib, *Mufradāt*, 186, and the Commentaries). There was some feeling of difficulty about the word, however, for Zam. thought the reading was wrong and wanted to read رِجْز, instead of رُجْز, and as-Suyūṭī, *Itq*, 311, would explain it as the form of رِجز in the dialect of Hudhail.

It seems probable, however, as Bell, *Origin*, 88, and Ahrens, *Muhammed*, 22, have suggested, that the word is the Syr. ܪܘܓܙܐ *wrath*, used of the "wrath to come", e.g. in Matt. iii, 7.[2] (Fischer, *Glossar*, 43, says Aram. רוּגְזָא.)

رَجِيم (*Rajīm*).

iii, 31; xv, 17, 34; xvi, 100; xxxviii, 78; lxxxi, 25.

Stoned, pelted, driven away by stones, execrated.

We find it used only of Satan and his minions, and it is said to

[1] Cf. also the Mandaean רובאן; Nöldeke, *Mand. Gramm*, 190.
[2] *Vide* also 1 Thess. i, 10, and Lagarde, *Analecta Syriaca*, p. 8, l. 19.

derive from the tradition that the demons seek to listen to the counsels of Heaven and are pelted away by the angels [1] (cf. Sūra lxvii, 5).

The Muslim authorities naturally take it as a pure Arabic word, a form فعيل from رَجَمَ, which is used several times in the Qur'ān. As a technical term associated with Satan, however, it would seem to be the Eth. ርጉም, and mean *cursed* or *execrated* rather than *stoned.* ረገመ means *to curse* or *execrate* and is used of the serpent in Gen. iii, 14, and of those who are delivered over to the fire prepared for the devil and his angels in Matt. xxv, 41. Rückert, in his notes to his translation of the Qur'ān (ed. A. Müller, p. 440),[2] had noted this connection with the Eth. and Nöldeke, *Neue Beiträge*, 25, 47, thinks that Muḥammad himself in introducing the Eth. word ሰይጣን = شيطان introduced also the epithet ርጉም, but not knowing the technical meaning of the word treated it as though from رجم = רגם. ܪܓܡ *to stone.*[3] (Cf. Ahrens, *Christliches*, 39.)

أَلرَّحْمٰن (*Ar-Raḥmān*).

Occurs some fifty-six times outside its place in the superscription of the Sūras.

The Merciful.

It occurs always as a title of God, almost as a personal name for God.[4]

Certain early authorities recognized the word as a borrowing from Hebrew. Mubarrad and Tha'lāb held this view, says as-Suyūṭī, *Itq*, 321 ; *Mutaw*, 58, and it is quoted from az-Zajjāj in *LA*, xv, 122.

The root רחם is common Semitic, and several Arabic forms are used in the Qur'ān, e.g. رَحِمَ ; رَحْمَةٌ ; رِحْمٌ ; رُحْمٌ ; رَحِيمٌ ; مَرْحَمَةٌ,

[1] There is, however, reason to believe that the epithet belongs to a much older stratum of Semitic belief in regard to demons, cf. Wellhausen, *Reste*, 111.

[2] See also Müller's statement in *ThLZ* for 1891, p. 348.

[3] Wellhausen, *Reste*, 232 ; Pautz, *Offenbarung*, 49 ; Margoliouth, *Chrestomathia Baidawiana*, 160. Praetorius, *ZDMG*, lxi, 620 ff., argues against this derivation, but unconvincingly. See also Van Vloten in the *Feestbundel aan de Goeje*, pp. 35, 42, who thinks that it was used in pre-Islamic Arabia in connection with pelting snakes.

[4] Sprenger, *Leben*, ii, 198.

but the form of رحمن is itself against its being genuine Arabic. Fraenkel, *Vocab*, 23, pointed out that רחמנא occurs in the Talmud as a name of God (e.g. אמר רחמנא "saith the all-merciful"), and as Hirschfeld, *Beiträge*, 38, notes, it is also so used in the Targums and in the Palmyrene inscriptions (cf. *NSI*, p. 300; *RES*, ii, 477). In the Christian-Palestinian dialect we find ܪܚܡܢ, which is the equivalent of the Targumic מרחמן and in Lk. vi, 36, translates οἰκτίρμων,[1] and in the S. Arabian inscriptions 𐩧𐩢𐩣𐩬𐩬 occurs several times [2] as a divine name.[3]

There can be little doubt that it was from S. Arabia that the word came into use in Arabic,[4] but as Nöldeke-Schwally, i, 113, points out, it is hardly likely to have originated there and we must look elsewhere for the origin.[5] Sprenger, *Leben*, ii, 198–210, in his discussion of the word, favours a Christian origin,[6] while Hirschfeld, *Beiträge*, 39, insists that it is of Jewish origin, and Rudolph, *Abhängigkeit*, 28, professes to be unable to decide between them.[7] The fact that the word occurs in the old poetry [8] and is known to have been in use in connection with the work of Muḥammad's rival Prophets, Musailama of Yamāma [9] and al-Aswad of Yemen,[10] would seem to point to a Christian rather than a Jewish origin, though the matter is uncertain.

رَحِيق (*Raḥīq*).

lxxxiii, 25.

Strong wine.

[1] Schwally, *Idioticon*, 88; Schulthess, *Lex*, 193, and see Wellhausen, *ZDMG*, lxvii, 630.

[2] Muller, *ZDMG*, xxx, 672; Osiander, *ZDMG*, x, 61; *CIS*, iv, No. 6; and particularly Fell in *ZDMG*, liv, 252, who gives a list of texts where it occurs.

[3] Halévy, *JA*, viiie sér, xx, 326, however, takes it as an adjective and not as a divine name. (Note also Ahrens, *Christliches*, 35; Ryckmans, *Noms propres*, i, 31.)

[4] Grimme, *ZA*, xxvi, 161; Bell, *Origin*, 52; Lidzbarski in *SBAW*, Berlin, 1916, p. 1218.

[5] Halévy, *REJ*, xxiii, in discussing the inscription, thinks that it is of purely pagan origin. See also Margoliouth, *Schweich Lectures*, 67 ff.

[6] So Pautz, *Offenbarung*, 171 n., and *vide* Fell, *ZDMG*, liv, 252. Mingana, *Syriac Influence*, 89.

[7] So Massignon, *Lexique*, 52. Sacco, *Credenze*, 18, apparently agrees with the Jewish theory. See also Horovitz, *JPN*, 201–3.

[8] *Div. Hudh.* (ed. Wellhausen), clxv, 6; *Mufaddaliyāt* (ed. Thorbecke), 34, l. 60; al-A'shā, *Dīwān*, lxvi, 8.

[9] aṭ-Ṭabarī, *Annales*, i, 1933–7. Ibn Hishām, 200.

[10] Beladhorī, 105, l. 6.

The passage is early Meccan describing the delights of Paradise.

The word is an unusual one and the Lexicons do not know quite what to make of it. They admit that it has no root in Arabic, and though they are agreed that it refers to some kind of wine, they are uncertain as to the exact meaning or even the exact spelling, i.e. whether it should be رَحِيق or رُحَاق (cf. *LA*, xi, 404).[1]

Ibn Sīda was doubtless not far from the mark when he said that it meant عتيق. That old, well matured wine was a favourite among the ancient Arabs, Fraenkel, *Fremdw*, 171, has illustrated by many examples from the old poetry, and I suspect that رحيق is the Syr. ܪܚܝܩ = Aram. רחיק *far, remote*,[2] which was borrowed as an ideogram into Phlv. as [Pahlavi] *old, antique* (*PPGl*, 192).

رزق (*Rizq*).

Of very frequent occurrence, cf. ii, 57 ; xx, 131.

Bounty.

It means anything granted to another from which he finds benefit, and in the Qur'ān refers particularly to the bounty of God, being used frequently as almost a technical religious term.

Besides the noun رزق we find in the Qur'ān the verb رَزَقَ (ii, 54, etc.), the part. رازق, he who provides (v, 114, etc.), and الرزّاق the Provider, one of the names of God. The verb, of course, is denominative and the other forms have developed from it.

It has long been recognized by Western scholarship that the word is a borrowing from Iranian through Aramaic. Phlv. [Pahlavi] *rōčik* means *daily bread*[3] (cf. Paz. *rōžī*) from [Pahlavi] *rōč, day*, the Mod.

[1] It occurs in the old poetry. Cf. Labīd (ed. Chalidi, p. 33) ; and D. H. Müller, *WZKM*, i, 27, notes its occurrence in the South Arabian inscriptions.

[2] But note the S. Arabian [South Arabian] *remotus*, and Eth. ርሑቅ (Rossini, *Glossarium*, 240).

[3] *Vide Shikand*, Glossary, p. 266.

Pers. روز, which is connected with Av. 𐬭𐬀𐬊𐬗𐬀𐬵 *raočah, light*,[1] O.Pers. *rauča, day*[2]; Skt. रोच *shining, radiant*. The Phlv. 𐭫𐭥𐭰𐭩𐭪 was borrowed into Arm. as ռոճիկ *daily provision*, and then *bread*,[3] and Syr. ܪܘܙܝܩܐ *daily ration*,[4] which translates τροφαί in 1 Macc. i, 35, and also *stipendium* (*ZDMG*, xl, 452). In Mod. Pers. by regular change of ك to ى we get روزى *daily need*, e.g. روزى خور "eating the daily bread".

It was from the Syr. that the word came into Arabic,[5] and thence was borrowed back into Pers. in Islamic times as رزق.[6] It was an early borrowing and occurs frequently in the old poetry.

رَقّ (*Raqq*).

lii, 3.

A volume, or scroll of parchment.

The Lexicons take the word from رَقّ *to be thin* (*LA*, xi, 414), which is plausible enough, but there can be little doubt that it is a foreign word borrowed from the Eth.,[7] where ረቅ means *parchment* (*charta pergamena, membrana*, Dillmann, *Lex*, 284), which translates μεμβράναι in 2 Tim. iv, 13. It was an early borrowing and occurs many times in the old poetry.

أَلرَّقِيم (*Ar-Raqīm*).

xviii, 8.

Ar-Raqīm is mentioned at the commencement of Muḥammad's version of the story of the Seven Sleepers. The Commentators present

[1] Bartholomae, *AIW*, 1489.

[2] Spiegel, *Die altpers. Keilinschriften*, 238.

[3] Hübschmann, *Arm. Gramm*, i, 234.

[4] Nöldeke, *ZDMG*, xxx, 768; Lagarde, *GA*, 81.

[5] So Lagarde, op. cit.; Ruckert, *ZDMG*, x, 279; Fraenkel, *Vocab*, 25; Pautz, *Offenbarung*, 164, n. 4; Siddiqi, *Studien*, 56.

[6] Lagarde, op. cit.; Vullers, *Lex*, ii, 28.

[7] Fraenkel, *Fremdw*, 246. ረቅ is from ረቀቀ *to be thin*; cf. רקק and ܪܩ, so that ረቂቅ corresponds to رقيق.

the widest divergences as to its meaning. Some take it as a place-name, whether of a village, a valley, or a mountain. Some think it was a document, a كتاب or a لوح. Others consider it the name of the dog who accompanied the Sleepers: others said it meant an inkhorn, and some, as Ibn Duraid, admitted that they did not know what it meant.

Their general opinion is that it is an Arabic word, a form فعيل from رقم, but some, says as-Suyūṭī, *Itq*, 321, said that it was Greek, meaning either *writing* or *inkhorn* in that tongue.

The probabilities are that it is a place-name, and represents ܪܩܡ ܕܓܝܐ, otherwise known as ܪܩܡ ܪܩܡ: ܓܐ ܕܓܝ, a place in the desert country of S. Palestine,[1] very much in the same district as the Muslim geographers place الرقيم.[2, 3]

رُمَّان (*Rummān*).

vi, 99, 142; lv, 68.

Pomegranate.

The generally accepted opinion among the Muslim authorities is that it is a form فُعلان from رمّ (cf. Rāghib, *Mufradāt*, 203), but some had considerable doubts about it as we see from *LA*, xv, 148; and Jawharī, sub voc.

Guidi, *Della Sede*, 582, noted it as a loan-word in Arabic, and Fraenkel, *Fremdw*, 142, suggested that it was derived from the Syr. ܪܘܡܢܐ, the Arabic form being built on the analogy of تُفَّاح. As the

[1] Cf. the Targumic רקם דגיעא.

[2] Ibn Athīr, *Chron*, xi, 259; Yāqūt, *Mu'jam*, ii, 804.

[3] Torrey in *Ajeb Nameh*, 457 ff., takes רקים to be a misreading of דקים and to refer to the Emperor Decius who is so prominent in the Oriental legends of the Seven Sleepers. Such a misreading looks easy enough in the Heb. characters, but is not so obvious in Syr. ܪܩܝܡ and ܕܩܝܘܣ, and as Horovitz, *KU*, 95, points out, it does not explain the article of the Arabic word. Horovitz also notes that names are carefully avoided in the Qur'ānic story save the place-name الكهف, which is at least a point in favour of Raqīm being also a place-name. (Torrey's remarks on Horovitz's objection will be found in *Foundation*, 46, 47.)

Eth. ሮማን and the Phlv. ideogram *rōramnā* or *romanā*,[1] are of Aram. origin we may assume the same for Ar. رمّان, but the ultimate origin of the word is still uncertain.[2] It occurs in Heb. as רמון, in Aram. רימונא and רומנא, as well as Mandaean רומאנא,[3] but appears to be non-Semitic.[4] Horovitz, *Paradies*, 9, thinks that if it is true that the pomegranate is a native of Socotra we may have to look in that direction for the origin of the word. It is, of course, possible that it is a pre-Semitic word taken over by the Semites. (See Laufer, *Sino-Iranica*, 285.)

رَوْضَةٌ (*Rauḍa*).

xxx, 14; xlii, 21.

A rich, well watered meadow; thence a luxurious garden. (*LA*, ix, 23.)

Both passages are late Meccan and refer to the blissful abode of the redeemed.

There can be little doubt that the word was borrowed as a noun into Arabic, and from it were then formed رَوَّض "to resort to a garden", راوض "to render a land verdant", أورض "to abound in gardens", etc. As some of these forms occur in the early literature the borrowing must have been an early one.

Vollers, *ZDMG*, l, 641, 642, noted that the word is originally Iranian, and he suggested that it was from the Iranian √ *rud*, meaning *to grow*.[5] The Av. *raod* means *to flow*,[6] from which comes

[1] *PPGl*, 198; *Frahang*, Glossar, p. 105; and Noldeke, *Neue Beiträge*, 42.

[2] Low, *Aramäische Pflanzennamen*, 310, says: "Etymologie dunkel," and see Zimmern, *Akkad. Fremdw*, 54.

[3] Noldeke, *Mand. Gramm*, 123; Lidzbarski, *Mandäische Liturgien*, p. 218.

[4] Hommel, *Aufsätze*, 97 ff.; *BDB*, 941, "a foreign word of doubtful origin"

[5] "روضة ist ohne Etymologie: zur Bedeutung ist hier nur daran zu erinnern, dass es in der Nomadensprache jeden grünen Fleck in oder Umgebung bezeichnet. Mit dem alten Sprachgebrauch deckt sich noch jetzt nach meiner Erfahrung genau die Sprache z.B. der Sinaibeduinen. . . . Ich glaube nicht fehl zu gehen, wenn ich, روضة, aus p. √ *rud* 'wachsen', erkläre."

[6] Bartholomae, *AIW*, 1495; Reichelt, *Awestisches Elementarbuch*, 493.

raoδah a *river*,[1] and *raoδa*, *growth* (cf. Skt. रोद, *rising, height*), also meaning *stature*.[2] From the same root comes Phlv. a *lake* or *riverbed*,[3] and the Pers. رُود commonly used for river, e.g. رود فرات the Euphrates. The Phlv. word is important, for the Lexicons tell us (cf. Tha'lab in *LA*, ix, 23) that water was an indispensable mark of a روضة. Thus the conclusion would seem to be that the Arabs learned the Phlv. [4] in the Mesopotamian area and used it for any well watered or irrigated land.

أَلرُّومُ (*Ar-Rūm*).

xxx, 1.

The Byzantine Empire.

It is the common name for the Byzantine Greeks, though also used in a wider sense for all the peoples connected or thought to be connected with the Eastern Roman Empire (cf. *TA*, viii, 320).

A considerable number of the early authorities took it as an Arabic word derived from رام *to desire eagerly*, the people being so called because of their eagerness to capture Constantinople (Yāqūt, *Mu'jam*, ii, 862). Some even gave them a Semitic genealogy—*LA*, xv, 150, and Yāqūt ii, 861. Others, however, recognized the word as foreign, as e.g. al-Jawālīqī, *Mu'arrab*, 73, who is the authority followed by as-Suyūṭī, *Itq*, 321.[5]

The ultimate origin, of course, is Lat. *Roma*, which in Gk. is Ῥώμη, which came into common use when ἡ Νεὰ Ῥώμη as distinguished from ἡ πρεσβυτέρα Ῥώμη became the name of Constantinople

[1] Horn, *Grundriss*, 139; Bartholomae, *AIW*, 1495. Cf. the O.Pers. *rauta* = *river* which is related to Gk. ῥύσις, ῥυτός.

[2] *PPGl*, 198.

[3] *PPGl*, 198, cf. Av. *urūd*, riverbed, from the root *raod* (Reichelt, *Avestan Reader*, 266), and Pazend *rôd*, Phlv. *a river* (*Shikand*, Glossary, 265).

[4] Addai Sher, 75, wants to derive روضة from Pers. رز, which seems to be wide of the mark.

[5] So *Mutaw*, 47, which classes it among the borrowings from Persian.

after it had become the capital of the Empire. Naturally the name travelled eastward, so that we find Syr. ܪܘܡܐ ; ܪܘܡܝܐ beside ܪܗܘܡܐ ; ܪܗܘܡܝܐ ; Arm. Հռոմ or Հռովմ [1] ; Eth. ሮም ; Phlv. *Arum* [2] ; Skt. रोम, and the *hrvm* of the Turfan texts.[3]

The word may have come directly from the Greek into Arabic through contacts with the Byzantine Empire such as we see among the Ghassānids, or it may be as Mingana, *Syriac Influence*, 98, thinks, that it came through the Syriac.[4] It is at any rate significant that רמי occurs not infrequently in the Safaite inscriptions, cf. Littmann, *Semitic Inscriptions*, 112 ff. ; Ryckmans, *Noms propres*, i, 315, 369, and also in the old poetry, cf. the *Mu'allaqa* of Ṭarafa, l. 23 (Horovitz, *KU*, 113), and is found in the Nemāra inscription (*RES*, i, No. 483).

زَادٌ (*Zād*).

ii, 193.

Provision for a journey.

In the same verse occurs the denominative verb تَزَوَّدَ, *to provide oneself for a journey*.

This may be genuine Arabic as the Muslim savants without exception claim. On the other hand, Zimmern, *Akkad. Fremdw*, 39, suggests that it may have had a Mesopotamian origin. There is an old Babylonian *zīdītu*, beside Akk. *ṣīdītu*, meaning the money and other provisions necessary for a journey, and from this in all probability came the Heb. צידה in the sense of provisions for a journey or a march, as in Gen. xlii, 25, etc. (see *BDB*, 845) ; and Aram. זודא ; Syr. ܙܘܕܐ ; Palm. זוד with the same meaning.

From some Aramaic form the word would then have passed into Arabic, probably at a quite early period, and then the verbal forms were built up on it in the ordinary way.

[1] Hübschmann, *Arm. Gramm*, i, 362.

[2] Dinkard, § 134, in the Bombay edition, p. 157, l. 8, of the Pahlavi text. See also Justi's Glossary to the *Bundahesh*, p. 62 ; *Shikand*, Glossary, 231 ; Herzfeld, *Paikuli*, Glossary, 194.

[3] Henning, *Manichaica*, ii, 70.

[4] *Vide* also Sprenger, *Leben*, iii, 332, n.

زَبَانِيَة (*Zabāniā*).

xcvi, 18.

The guardians of Hell.

They are said to be strong and mighty angels, and the name is usually derived from زَبَنَ *to push, thrust* (Bagh. on the passage). We see from Zam., however, that the philologers have some difficulty in explaining the form.

Vollers, *ZDMG*, li, 324, suggested a connection with Akk. *zibânîtu* meaning *balances*, and Addai Sher, 77, wants to derive it from Pers. زبانه *blaze, tongue of fire*, from Phlv. [Pahlavi word] *zūbān*, a tongue.[1] It seems, however, as Andrae, *Ursprung*, 154, points out, to be connected with the Syr. ܙܒܢܐ, the *ductores* who, as Ephraem Syrus tells us,[2] lead the departed souls to judgment.

زَبُور (*Zabūr*).

iv, 161 ; xvii, 57 ; xxi, 105.

The Psalter.

Always the Book of David, and xxi, 105, given as a quotation therefrom, is from Ps. xxxvii, 29.

The early authorities were not certain as to whether the word was to be read زَبُور or زُبُور, though they agree that it is from زَبَرَ *to transcribe* (Ṭab. on iv, 161; Rāghib, *Mufradāt*, 210; as-Sijistānī, 166 ; Jawharī, i, 324). The plu. زُبُر, as a matter of fact, is used in the Qur'ān of Scriptures in general (e.g. xxvi, 196 ; liv, 43, etc.), and once of the Books of Fate (liv, 52), so that there is on the surface some colour to the claim that زبور may be from زبر *to transcribe*.

It is obvious, however, that the word must somehow have arisen as a corruption of some Jewish or Christian word for the Psalter,

[1] West, *Glossary*, 150 and 50 ; *PPGl*, 130. Cf. Horn, *Grundriss*, 144.

[2] *Opera*, iii, 237, 244. Grimme, *Mohammed*, 1892, p. 19 n., thinks that some old name of a demon lies behind the word.

its form being doubtless influenced by the genuine Arabic زبر (Ahrens, *Christliches*, 29). Some have suggested that it is a corruption of זמרה a Psalm or chant,[1] used, e.g., in Ps. lxxxi, 3; xcviii, 5, the מ and ב being to some extent interchangeable in Arabic. Fraenkel, *Fremdwörter*, 248, however, thinks it more likely that it originated in a misunderstanding of מזמור, which occurs also in Syr. ܡܙܡܪܐ ; ܡܙܡܘܪܐ and Eth. መዝሙር.[2] Barth, *Etymol. Stud*, 26, suggested a connection between ספר and زبور,[3] but Schwally, *Idioticon*, 129, rightly rejects this solution.

When we remember the early use of ذبر beside زبر and the fairly frequent use of زبور in the early poetry in the general sense of a writing,[4] it seems simplest to think of some confusion made between derivatives from these roots and the מזמור or ܡܙܡܘܪܐ in use among Jews and Christians, so that even in pre-Islamic days زبور came to be used by a popular derivation for the Psalter.[5]

زُجَاجَةٌ (*Zujāja*).

xxiv, 35.

A glass vessel.

There was some uncertainty as to the vowelling of the word, whether زُجَاجَةٌ ; زَجَاجَةٌ or زِجَاجَةٌ. The philologers attempt to derive it from زَجَّ though they do not suggest how it can be explained from this root.[6] Fraenkel, *Fremdw*, 64, showed that it

[1] Hirschfeld, *Beiträge*, 61, supports a Jewish origin.

[2] See Horovitz, *JPN*. 205, 206.

[3] Cf. Fraenkel, in *Beitr. Ass*, iii, 74.

[4] *Vide* Imru'ul-Qais in Ahlwardt, *Divans*, 159, 160, an-Namrī in *Aghānī*, xii, 18, and other passages in Horovitz, *KU*, 69 ff., Cheikho, *Naṣrāniya*, 184, and *Al-Machriq*, xvi, 510.

[5] Cf. al-'Uqaili in *LA*, viii, 55, and the verses of the Jewish poet quoted by Hirschfeld. Margoliouth, *ERE*, x, 541, supports the solution suggested above, and *vide* Vollers, *ZDMG*, li, 293. Torrey, *Foundation*, 34, takes it to be an example of the Judæo-Arabic dialect spoken by the Jews of Arabia.

[6] *LA*, iii, 112.

has no verbal root in Arabic, and suggested that it is the Aram. זגוגיתא, Syr. ܙܓܘܓܝܬܐ meaning *glass* or *crystal*. The Syr. word is early and quite common, and it was probably when the Arabs came to use glass that they took over the word along with the article.

زُخْرُفٌ (*Zukhruf*).

vi, 112; x, 25; xvii, 95; xliii, 34.

Anything highly embellished.

As used in the Qur'ān it means ornamentation, though Ibn Sīda says that its primitive meaning was *gold*, and then any gilded decoration, and then decoration in general. There appears to be no occurrence of the word earlier than the Qur'ān, though it may well have been an early word.

It seems to be a deformation from the Syr. ܙܚܘܪܝܬܐ = Aramaic זחוריתא,[1] meaning a bright scarlet colour much used for adornment. It is used for the scarlet curtains of the Tabernacle in Ex. xxvi, 1, and for the χλαμὺς κοκκίνη of Matt. xxvii, 28. The interchange of פ and ח is not a great difficulty, cf. Praetorius, *Beit. Ass*, i, 43, and Barth in *ZDMG*, xli, 634.

زَرَابِيُّ (*Zarābī*).

lxxxviii, 16.

Rich carpets.

Plu. of زَرْبِيَّةٌ or زِرْبِيَّةٌ, occurring only in an early description of Paradise. The word occurs not infrequently in the early literature and the exegetes have a clear idea that it means fine wide carpets, but their explanations of the form are confused[2] (cf. Rāghib, *Mufradāt*, 211).

Fraenkel, *Fremdw*, 92, thought that it was from the Syr. ܙܪܒ *to check, stop*, though it is difficult to see how this can explain its meaning.

[1] Addai Sher, 77, would derive it from Pers. زيور *ornamentation*, but there seems nothing in favour of this.

[2] The fact would seem to be that زربية is a later formation, and that the form that was borrowed was زرابى, which as a matter of fact is the only form that occurs in the oldest texts.

He notes, however, that Geo. Hoffmann would derive it from the Pers. زیرپا *under the foot*,[1] which looks more likely, and which Horovitz, *Paradies*, 15, thinks possible, though if it is Persian it would seem more likely that it is connected with some formation from Phlv. [Pahlavi script] *zarrēn, golden* as in [Pahlavi script] *zarrēn-pēsīt* (West, *Glossary*, 148).[2] The most likely origin, however, is that suggested by Nöldeke, *Neue Beiträge*, 53, that it is from the Eth. ዘርቢት *carpet*. Nöldeke admits the possibility that the borrowing may have been the other way,[3] and one is inclined to derive both the Ar. and Eth. words from an Iranian source, but at present there is not sufficient evidence to decide what this source is.

زَكَرِيَّآءُ (*Zakariyyā'*).

iii, 32, 33; vi, 85; xix, 1, 7; xxi, 89.

Zachariah.

Always as the father of John the Baptist,[4] though in iii, 32, he is the elder who reared Mary from childhood, an idea dependent of course on *Protevangelion*, viii, 4.

There are variant spellings of the word, زكريا ; زكرياء and زكرى (Ṭab. on iii, 32), and the early authorities recognized the name as foreign, al-Jawālīqī, *Mu'arrab*, 77.[5] The probabilities seem to be that it came into Ar. from Syr. ܙܟܪܝܐ.[6] We find זאכריא in Mandaean,[7] but there seems reason to believe that this form, like Yaḥyā for Yoḥannā, has been influenced by Arabic (Brandt, *ERE*, viii, 380). The name apparently does not occur in the early literature,[8] though it must have been well known to Arabian Christians in pre-Islamic times.

[1] Vullers, *Lex*, ii, 168, 169.

[2] Addai Sher, 77, also argues for a Persian origin, but he wants to derive it from زرآب, meaning *yellow water*.

[3] So Fraenkel, op. cit.

[4] It is remotely possible that in the list of Prophets in vi, 85, it refers to someone else, but its close connection there with the name Yaḥyā would seem to indicate that the same Zachariah is meant as is mentioned in the other passages.

[5] So al-Khafājī, 99.

[6] Rhodokanakis, *WZKM*, xvii, 285; Horovitz, *KU*, 113; Mingana, *Syriac Influence*, 82.

[7] As in the *Liber Adami* (ed. Norberg), and *Ginza* (tr. Lidzbarski), 51, 213, 219.

[8] Horovitz rightly rejects the examples collected by Cheikho, 232.

زَكَى (*Zakā*).

Of frequent occurrence in many forms.

To be pure.

The three forms which particularly concern us are زَكَى (cf. xxiv, 21), زَكَّى (ii, 146; iv, 52; xci, 9), and تَزَكَّى (xx, 78; lxxxvii, 14).

The primitive meaning of the Arabic زكا is *to grow, to flourish, thrive*, as is recognized by the Lexicons (cf. *LA*, xix, 77; and Rāghib, *Mufradāt*, 212).[1] This is the meaning we find in the earliest texts, e.g. *Ḥamāsa*, 722, 11; Labīd (ed. Chalidi), etc., and with this we must connect the أزكى of ii, 232; xviii, 18, etc., as Nöldeke notes.[2] In this sense it is cognate with Akk. *zakū*, *to be free, immune*[3]; Aram. זכא to be victorious, Syr. ܙܟܐ, etc.

In the sense of *clean, pure*, however, i.e. زَكَى, زَكَّى, and تَزَكَّى, it is obviously a borrowing from the older religions.[4] Heb. זכא (like Phon. זכא) is to be clean or pure in the moral sense, and its forms parallel all the uses in the Qur'ān. So the related Aram. דכא, זכא, and זכי, Syr. ܕܟܐ, ܕܟܝ, and ܙܟܐ mean *to be clean* both in the physical and in the moral sense. The Arabic equivalent of these forms, of course, is ذكا *to be bright*, and so there can be little doubt that زكى used in its technical religious sense was borrowed from an Aramaic form. It is, of course, difficult to decide whether the origin is Jewish or Christian. Nöldeke, *Neue Beiträge*, 25, n.; Schulthess, *ZA*, xxvi, 152; and Torrey, *Foundation*, 141, favour a Jewish origin, but Andrae, *Ursprung*, 200, points to the close parallels between Muḥammad's use of the word and that which we find in contemporary

[1] And see Hurgronje, *Verspreide Geschriften*, ii, p. 11.

[2] *Neue Beiträge*, 25 n.

[3] Zimmern, *Akkad. Fremdw*, 25.

[4] Grimme, *Mohammed*, 1892, p. 15, tried to prove that تزكى for Muhammad meant "to pay legal alms" (Zakāt), but this is far fetched, as Hurgronje, *RHR*, xxx, 157 ff., pointed out. It is true, however, that in his later years Muhammad did associate justification before God with almsgiving (Bell, *Origin*, 80; see also Ahrens, *Christliches*, 21; Horovitz, *JPN*, 206 ff.).

Syriac literature,[1] so that there is ground for thinking that it came to him from Christian sources.

زَكَوٰة (*Zakāt*).

ii, 40, 77, 104, 172, 277 ; iv, 79, etc.

Legal Alms. Occurs only in Madinan passages.

Naturally the Muslim authorities explain this word from زكى, and tell us that an Alms is so called because it purifies the soul from meanness, or even because it purifies wealth itself (cf. Baiḍ. on ii, 40, etc.),[2] though some sought to derive it from the primitive meaning of *to increase* (see Rāghib, *Mufradāt*, 212, and the Lexicons).

Zakāt, however, is another of the technical religious terms taken over from the older faiths. Fraenkel, *Vocab*, 23, suggested that it was from the Aram. זכות. The primary sense of זכות, זכותא is *puritas, innocentia*, from which developed the secondary meaning of *meritum* as in the Targum on Ruth iv, 21, but it does not seem that זכותא, or its Syr. equivalent ܙܟܘܬܐ, ever meant *alms*, though this meaning could easily be derived from it. Fraenkel is inclined to believe that the Jews of Arabia had already given it this meaning before Islam—"sed fortasse Iudaei Arabici זכות sensu eleemosynarum adhibuerunt" (so Torrey, *Foundation*, 48, 141). Nöldeke, however (*Neue Beiträge*, 25), is inclined to believe that the specializing of the word for alms was due to Muḥammad himself.[3]

زَنجَبِيل (*Zanjabīl*).

lxxvi, 17.

Ginger.

[1] *Vide* also Bell, *Origin*, 51. It is possible that the Phlv. [illegible] *dakia* of *PPGl*, 104, may be from the same origin. *Frahang*, Glossary, p. 87.

[2] The origin of this idea, of course, is in the Qur'ān itself, cf. ix, 104.

[3] See also Bell, *Origin*, 80 ; Schulthess, in *ZA*, xxvi, 150, 151 ; Ahrens, *Muhammed*, 180 ; Von Kremer, *Streifzüge*, p. xi ; Horovitz, *JPN*, 206. Wensinck, *Joden*, 114, says : "Men zal misschien vragen of tot de Mekkaansche instellingen niet de zakat behoort. En men zou zich voor deze meening op talrijke Mekkaansche openbaringen kunnen beroepen waar van zakāt gesproken wordt. Men vergete echter niet, dat het woord zakāt زكوة, het Joodsche זכות, verdienste beteekent. Deze naam is door de Arabische Joden of door Mohammed uitsluitend op het geven van aalmoezen en daarna op de aalmoes zelf toegepast."

It occurs only in a passage descriptive of the delights of Paradise, where the exegetes differ as to whether Zanjabīl is the name of the well from which the drink of the Redeemed comes, or means the spice by which the drink is flavoured (*vide* Ṭab., Zam., and Baiḍ. on the passage and *LA*, xiii, 332).

There was fairly general agreement among the early authorities that it was a Persian word. ath-Tha'ālibī, *Fiqh*, 318, and al-Jawālīqī, *Mu'arrab*, 78, give it in their lists of Persian loan-words, and their authority is accepted by as-Suyūṭī, *Itq*, 321; *Mutaw*, 47; and al-Khafājī, 99.

The Mod. Pers. word for ginger is شنكليل (Vullers, *Lex*, ii, 472; cf. also ii, 148) from Phlv. *singaβēr*,[1] which is the source of the Arm. սնգրուէլ,[2] and the Syr. ܙܢܓܒܝܠ; Aram. זנגבילא.[3] The ultimate source seems to have been the Skt. शृङ्गवेर,[4] Pali *singivēra*, from which comes the Gk. ζιγγίβερις.[5] There can be little doubt that the word passed into Arabic from Syr. and was thence borrowed back into Persian in Islamic times.[6] It occurs in the early poetry [7] and so was evidently an early borrowing.

زَوْج (*Zawj*).

Occurs frequently in many forms, cf. ii, 33.

A pair, species, kind, sex, couple, companion, spouse.

It is a very early loan-word in Arabic from Gk. ζεῦγος through

[1] So Vullers, *Lex*, ii, 148, and cf. *Pahlavi Texts*, ed. Jamasp Asana, p. 31.

[2] Hubschmann, *Arm. Gramm*, i, 238.

[3] From which was then derived the form גִּנְגְּבְרָא, Levy, *Wörterbuch*, i, 345.

[4] Yule (*vide* Yule and Burnell, *Hobson Jobson*, ed. Cooke, 1903, p. 374) thought that the Skt. शृङ्गवेर was a made-up word, and that as the home of the plant is in the Malabar district, we should look for the origin of the word in the Malayalam ഇഞ്ചി *iñchi*, meaning *root* (cf. Tamil இஞ்சி *iñji*; Sinhalese ඉඟුරු *inguru*), but there is the equal probability that these are all derived from the Skt. शृङ्ग a *horn*. See, however, Laufer, *Sino-Iranica*, 545, 583.

[5] This then became γιγγίβερις and through the Lat. *gingiber* became the Middle English *gingevir* and our *ginger*. From ζιγγίβερις came the Syr. ܐܢܓܒܝܪ and other forms (Löw, *Aramäische Pflanzennamen*, p. 138).

[6] Fraenkel, *Vocab*, 11; Pautz, *Offenbarung*, 213; Horovitz, *Paradies*, 11; Addai Sher, 80.

[7] See Geyer, *Zwei Gedichte*, i, 57; ii, 83; Jacob, *Beduinenleben*, 258.

the Aram. The verbal forms زَوَّجَ, etc., with this meaning are clearly denominative, the primitive root زاج meaning "to sow discord between". In the Qur'ān we have many forms—زَوَّجَ *to marry, to couple with,* زَوْجٌ plu. ازواج *a wife* or *husband* (human); زَوْجٌ *kind, species*; زَوْجانِ *a pair*; زَوْجٌ *sex.*

No Muslim authority, as Fraenkel notes (*Fremdw*, 107), has any suspicion that the word is other than genuine Arabic, but no derivation of the word is possible from Semitic material, and there can be no reasonable doubt that its origin is to be found in ζεῦγος.[1] ζεῦγος is originally a *yoke* from ζεύγνυμι *to join, fasten*,[2] and then comes to mean a couple, so that κατὰ ζεῦγος or κατὰ ζεύγη meant *in pairs*, and thus ζεῦγος = *coniugium* was used for a married pair. From Greek it passed eastwards and in the Rabbinic writings we have זוג meaning both *pair* and *wife*,[3] and זוגא *pair, husband, companion*, besides the denominative זִוֵּג *to bind* or *pair*, and זִיווּג = ζύγωσις, זוגדס = ζεῦγος + δίς. So Syr. ܙܘܓܐ is *yoke*, and the very common ܒܪ ܙܘܓܐ = *yokefellow*, commonly used for husband or wife, with verbal forms built therefrom. It was from this Syr. that we get the Eth. ዘውግ (Nöldeke, *Neue Beiträge*, 44) and the Arm. զոյգ,[4] and it was probably from the same source that it passed into Arabic. One might expect that it would be an early borrowing, and as a matter of fact it occurs in the early poetry.[5]

زُورٌ (*Zūr*).

xxii, 31; xxv, 5, 72; lviii, 2.

Falsehood.

It is linked with idolatry in xxii, 31, but in the other passages is quite colourless.

[1] Fraenkel, op. cit, 106; Vollers, *ZDMG*, l, 622; li, 298; *PSm*, 1094.

[2] Cf. Lat. *iungere* and the Av. 𐬫𐬀𐬊𐬘 (Bartholomae, *AIW*, 1228; Reichelt, *Elementarbuch*, 477).

[3] See Meinhold's *Yoma* (1913), p. 29; Krauss, *Griechische Lehnworter*, ii, 240–242.

[4] Hübschmann, *Arm. Gramm*, i, 302; *ZDMG*, xlvi, 235.

[5] Cf. 'Antara, xxi, 31, in Ahlwardt's *Divans*, p. 46.

The usual theory of the philologers is that it is derived from زَوَّرَ though this is clearly a denominative, and that the authorities felt some difficulty with the word is clear from *LA*, v, 426.

Fraenkel, *Fremdw*, 273, suggested that it was from זור.[1] There is a Heb. word זרא *loathsome thing* from זור *to be loathsome*, but it seems hardly possible to derive the Arabic from this. It would seem rather to be of Iranian origin. Pers. زور is *lie, falsehood*, which Vullers, *Lex*, ii, 158, gives, it is true, as a loan-word from Arabic. He is certainly wrong, however, for not only does the word occur in Phlv. both simply as *zūr, a lie, falsehood, fiction*,[2] and in compounds as *zūr-gukāsīh* = *false evidence, perjury*,[3] and in the Pazend *zur, a lie*,[4] but also in the O.Pers. of the Behistun inscription (where we read (iv, 63–4) *naiy draujana āham, naiy zūrakara āham*, "I was no liar, nor was I an evil doer," and further (iv, 65) *naiy . . . zūra akunavam* "I did no wrong"),[5] and in the Av. *zūrōjata*.[6] From Middle Persian the word was borrowed into Arm., where we find զուր *false, wrong*,[7] which enters into several compounds, e.g. զրպարտն *caluminator*, զրկանք *injustice*, etc., so that it was probably directly from Middle Persian that it came into Arabic.

زَيْت (*Zait*).

xxiv, 35, also زَيْتُون; vi, 99, 142; xvi, 11; xxiv, 35; lxxx, 29; xcv, 1.

Olive oil. Olive tree.

[1] *Vide* also *Beit. Ass*, iii, 67, where he says: "Das Koranische زور habe ich in dringendem Verdacht aus der Fremde entlehnt zu sein. Schon die verschiedenartigen Erklarungen der Araber sind auffallend."

[2] e.g. *Gosht-i-Fryānō*, iii, 29.

[3] e.g. *Ardā Vīrāf*, lv, 6; xlv, 5.

[4] *Vide Shikand*, Glossary, p. 275; Salemann, *Manichaeische Studien*, i, 80.

[5] Spiegel in the Glossary to his *Altpersischen Keilinschriften*, p. 243, translates *zūra* by "Gewalt", but Hübschmann, *ZDMG*, xlvi, 329, rightly corrects him.

[6] Bartholomae, *AIW*, 1698; Horn, *Grundriss*, 149, § 674.

[7] Hubschmann, *Arm. Gram*, i, 151.

The word has no verbal root in Arabic, زَاتَ *to give oil* being obviously denominative, as was clear even to the native Lexicographers (*LA*, ii, 340, etc.).

Guidi, *Della Sede*, 600, had noted the word as a foreign borrowing, and Fraenkel, *Fremdw*, 147, points out that the olive was not indigenous among the Arabs.[1] We may suspect that the word belongs to the old pre-Semitic stratum of the population of the Syrian area. In Heb. זית means both *olive tree* and *olive*,[2] but Lagarde, *Mittheilungen*, iii, 215, showed that primitively it meant *oil*. In Aram. we have זיתא and Syr. ܙܝܬܐ, which (along with the Heb.) Gesenius tried unsuccessfully to derive from זהה *to be bright, fresh, luxuriant*. The word is also found in Coptic ϫωιτ beside ϫⲉⲉιⲧ and ϫⲟⲉιⲧ, where it is clearly a loan-word, and in Phlv. زیت[3] and Arm. ձէթ *oil*, ձիթենի *olive tree*, which are usually taken as borrowings from Aram.,[4] but which the presence of the word in Ossetian *zeti*, and Georgian ზეთი would at least suggest the possibility of being independent borrowings from the original population.[5]

The Arabic word may have come directly from this primitive source, but more likely it is from the Syr. ܙܝܬܐ, which also is the source of the Eth. ዘይት (Nöldeke, *Neue Beiträge*, 42).[6] It was an early borrowing in any case, for it occurs in the old poetry, e.g. *Divan Hudh*, lxxii, 6; *Aghānī*, viii, 49, etc.

سَاعَةٌ (*Sā'a*).

Of very frequent occurrence, cf. vi, 31; vii, 32; xii, 107, etc. Hour.

It is used in the Qur'ān both as an ordinary period of time—an hour (cf. xxx, 55; vii, 32; xvi, 63), but particularly of "the hour",

[1] He quotes Strabo, xvi, 781, whose evidence is rather for S. Arabia. Bekrī, *Mu'jam*, 425, however, says that the olive is found in Syria only, and we may note that in Sūra xxiii, 20, the tree on Mt. Sinai yields دهن not زيت.

[2] So Phon. זת (cf. Harris, *Glossary*, 99), and זת in the Ras Shamra texts.

[3] *PPGl*, 242.

[4] Hübschmann, *Arm. Gramm*, i, 309; *ZDMG*, xlvi, 243. Lagarde, *Mitth*, iii, 219, seemed to think that ձէթ was the origin of the Semitic forms (but see his *Arm. Stud*, No. 1347, and *Übersicht*, 219, n.).

[5] Laufer, *Sino-Iranica*, 411, however, still holds to a Semitic origin for all the forms.

[6] Eth. ዘይቶን, however, is from Ar. زيتون, cf. Nöldeke, op. cit.

the great Day of Judgment (liv, 46; xlii, 17; vi, 31, etc.). It occurs most commonly in late Meccan passages.

It is difficult to derive the word from the Ar. ساع "to let camels run freely in pasture", though it might conceivably be a development from a verbal meaning "to pass along", i.e. *to elapse*. The Lexicons, however (cf. *LA*, x, 33), seem to make no attempt to derive it from a verbal root.

The probabilities are that it is of Aram. origin. שעתא occurs in Bibl. Aram., and שעה, שעא and שעתא are common in the Targums and Rabbinical writings for both *a short time* [1] and *an hour*, both of which meanings are also found for the commonly used Syr. ܫܥܬܐ. In Syr. ܫܥܬܐ is very frequently used in eschatological passages for "the hour", cf. Mark xiii, 32; Jno. v, 28, etc.; and Ephraem (ed. Lamy) iii, 583, precisely as in the Qur'ānic eschatological passages. As the Eth. ሰዐት or ሰዓት, which is also used eschatologically, is a borrowing from the Syr. (Nöldeke, *Neue Beitr*, 44), we are fairly sure, as we have already noted (*supra*, p. 40), that as an eschatological term the Arabic has come from Syr., and the same is probably true of the word in its ordinary usage. It occurs in the early poetry, and so would have been an early borrowing.

أَلسَّامِرِيّ (*As-Sāmirī*).

xx, 87, 90, 96.

The Samaritan.

The Qur'ān gives this name to the man who made the golden calf for the Children of Israel.

Geiger 166 [2] thought that the word was due to a misunderstanding of the word סמאל, the Angel of Death who, according to the story in *Pirke Rabbi Eliezer*, xlv,[3] was hidden within the calf and lowed to deceive the Israelites. This, however, is rather remote, and there can be no doubt that the Muslim authorities are right in saying that it means "The Samaritan". The calf worship of the Samaritans may

[1] From the fact that the word can mean an extremely short period of time some have thought that its original meaning was "Augenblinck", "the blink of an eye", related to Akk. *še'u*, Heb. שָׁעָה *to gaze*.

[2] Followed by Tisdall, *Sources*, 113; but see Heller in *EI*, sub voc.

[3] In Friedlander's translation (London, 1916), p. 355.

have had something to do with the Qur'ānic story.[1] But as Fraenkel, *ZDMG*, lvi, 73, suggests, it is probably due to some Jewish Midrash in which later enmity towards the Samaritans led pious Jews to find all their calamities and lapses of faith due to Samaritan influence.[2]

A comparison of the Syr. ܫܡܪܝܐ with Heb. שֹׁמְרוֹנִי would suggest a Syr. origin for the Ar. سامرىّ, but as Horovitz, *KU*, 115, notes, there is a late Jewish שָׁמְרָאִי or שָׁמְרַיי which might quite well be the source of the Qur'ānic form.

سَاهِرَةٌ (*Sāhira*).

lxxix, 14.

The passage is an early one referring to the Last Day—" Lo there will be but a single blast, and behold they are بالساهرة," where the Commentators are divided in opinion as to whether Sāhira is one of the names of Hell—اسم جهنم, or a place in Syria which is to be the seat of the Last Judgment, or means the surface of the earth—وجه الارض. See Ṭab., Baiḍ. and Bagh. on the verse.

Sprenger, *Leben*, ii, 514, notes that " aus dem Arabischen lässt es sich nicht erklären ", and suggests that it is derived from the בית הסהר which as used in Gen. xxxix and xl means *prison*. There seems, however, to be no evidence that this סהר was ever connected with the abode of the wicked, and Schulthess, *Umayya*, 118, commenting on the verse of Umayya—عندنا صيد بحر وصيد ساهرة, " we are permitted hunting on sea and on dry land," would explain it from the Aram. סחרתא = Syr. ܣܚܪܬܐ[3] meaning *environs*. He points

[1] Cf. the עגל שמרון of Hos. viii, 5, 6.

[2] A confirmation of this is found in the words of v, 97, giving the punishment of the Sāmirī, where the " touch me not " doubtless refers to the ritual purifications of the Samaritans. Cf. Goldziher's article *La Revue Africaine*, No. 268, Alger, 1908. Halévy, *Revue Sémitique*, xvi, 419 ff., refers it to the cry of the lepers, but Horovitz, *KU*, 115, rightly insists that this is not sufficient to explain the verse.

[3] On which see his *Homonyme Wurzeln*, 41 ff.

out that ه = ח is not unknown in words that have come through Nabataean channels.[1]

It is not impossible, however, to take it as an ordinary Arabic word meaning *awake*.

سَبَأ (*Sabā'*).

xxvii, 22; xxxiv, 14.

Sabā'.

The name of a city in Yemen destroyed by a great inundation. We have fairly extensive evidence for the name of the city from non-Arabic sources. It is the ሰበአ of the S. Arabian inscriptions (*CIS*, ii, 375; Mordtmann, *Sab. Denkm*, 18; Glaser, *Zwei Inschriften*, 68; Rossini, *Glossarium*, 192; Ryckmans, *Noms propres*, i, 353), which occurs in the Cuneiform inscriptions as *Sab'a and Saba'*,[2] in Greek as Σαβά.[3] in Heb. שְׁבָא, from which are Syr. ܫܒܐ, Eth. ሳባ.

As the Qur'ānic statements about Sabā' are connected with the Solomon legend, it is possible that like the name *Suleimān*, it came to him from Christian sources, though we cannot absolutely deny its derivation from Rabbinic material (Horovitz, *KU*, 115; *JPN*, 157), and indeed the name may have come directly from S. Arabia.

سَبْت (*Sabt*).

ii, 61; iv, 50, 153; vii, 163; xvi, 125.

Sabbath.

(Sprenger and others would add to this سُبَات *rest* in xxv, 49; lxxviii, 9.)[4]

We find سَبْت only in relatively late passages and always of the Jewish Sabbath. The Muslim authorities treat it as genuine Arabic from سَبَتَ *to cut*, and explain it as so called because God cut off

[1] His examples are دهل = ܕܚܠ; دهق = דחק; and هرف = חרף.

[2] Delitzsch, *Paradies*, 303.

[3] Σαβά in LXX, but Σάβαται in Strabo.

[4] *Leben*, ii, 430; Grünbaum, *ZDMG*, xxxix, 584, but see Horovitz, *KU*, 96.

His work on the seventh day [1] (cf. Baiḍ. on ii, 61; and Mas'ūdī, *Murūj*, iii, 423).

There can be no doubt that the word came into Arabic from Aram.[2] and probably from the Jewish שַׁבְּתָא rather than from the Syr. ܫܒܬܐ. The verb سَبَتَ of vii, 163, is then denominative, as Fraenkel, *Vocab*, 21, has noted. It is doubtful if the word occurs in this meaning earlier than the Qur'ān.

سَبَّحَ (*Sabbaḥa*).

Of very frequent occurrence, cf. ii, 28, etc.

To praise.

Besides the verb we have سبحان *praise* [3]; تسبيح *act of praise*; مُسَبِّح *one who celebrates praise*, all obviously later formations from سَبَّحَ.

The primitive sense of the root is *to glide*, and in this sense we find سَبَحَ, سَبْحٌ, and سَابِح in the Qur'ān, so that some of the philologers endeavoured to derive سَبَّحَ from this (cf. Baiḍ. on ii, 28). It has been pointed out frequently, however, that the sense of *praise* is an Aram. development of the root. It occurs in Hebrew in this sense only as a late Aramaism (*BDB*, 986), and in S. Semitic only after contact with Aramaic speaking peoples.

שבח is found even in O.Aram.,[4] meaning *to laud*, *praise*, and has a wide use in Syriac. Fraenkel, *Vocab*, 20, and Hirschfeld, *Beiträge*, 45, are inclined to think that we must look for a Jewish source, but there is even more likelihood of its being Syr., for not only is ܫܒܚ widely used in the classical language, but we find ܫܘܒܚܢܐ = سبحان, and in

[1] It is curious that the Muslims object to deriving it from the sense of *to rest* (שבת) on the ground of Sūra l, 37. See Grünbaum, *ZDMG*, xxxix, 585.

[2] Geiger, 54; von Kremer, *Ideen*, 226 n.; Hirschfeld, *New Researches*, 104; Horovitz, *KU*, 96; *JPN*, 186; Fischer, *Glossar*, 52.

[3] Sprenger, *Leben*, i, 107 ff.

[4] Lidzbarski, *Handbuch*, 372; Cook, *Glossary*, 111.

the Christian Palestinian dialect ܠܫܒܚܐ = تسبيح.[1] It is clear that the word was known among the Arabs in pre-Islamic times, for we find ሰበሐ as a proper name in Sabaean (cf. Ryckmans, *Noms propres*, i, 146), so Horovitz, *JPN*, 186, lists it as one of those words which, while obviously a borrowing from the older religions, cannot be definitely assigned to a particular Jewish or Christian source.

سَبِيل (*Sabīl*).

Occurs frequently, cf. ii, 102.

A way, road—then metaphorically, a cause, or reason.

In the Qur'ān it is used both of a *road*, and in the technical religious sense of *The Way* (cf. Acts ix, 2), i.e. سبيل الله. The Muslim authorities take it as genuine Arabic, and Sprenger, *Leben*, ii, 66, agrees with them. It is somewhat difficult, however, to derive it from سبل, as even Rāghib, *Mufradāt*, 221, seems to feel, and the word is clearly a borrowing from the Syr. ܫܒܝܠܐ.[2] As a matter of fact Heb. שביל and Aram. שבילא mean both *road* or *way of life*, precisely as the Syr. ܫܒܝܠܐ, but it is the Syriac word which had the widest use and was borrowed into Arm. as շաւիղ,[3] and so is the more likely origin. It occurs in the old poetry, e.g. in Nābigha v, 18 (Ahlwardt, *Divans*, p. 6), and thus must have been an early borrowing.

سَجَدَ (*Sajada*).

Of very frequent occurrence. Cf. ii, 32.

To worship.

With the verbal forms must be taken سُجُود, e.g., ii, 119; xxii, 27, etc.

[1] Schwally, *Idioticon*, 91. See also Mingana, *Syriac Influence*, 86; Bell, *Origin*, 51, and Noldeke, *Neue Beiträge*, 36, who shows that the Eth. ሰብሐ is of the same origin.

[2] Schwally in *ZDMG*, liii, 197, says: "Bei der Annahme, dass سبيل 'Weg' echt arabisch ist, scheint es mir auffallend zu sein, dass unter den verschiedenen Synonymen gerade dieses dem Aramäischen und Hebraischen gleiche Wort für den religiösen Sprachgebrauch ausgesucht ist. Ich kann mir diese Erscheinung nur aus Entlehnung erklären."

[3] Hübschmann, *Arm. Gramm*, i, 313; *ZDMG*, xlvi, 246.

This root סגד is an Aram. formation. Even in O. Aram. it meant "prostration of reverence", as is evident from the סגידא of Sachau's Edessa inscription No. 3 (*ZDMG*, xxxvi, 158; cf. Dan. iii, 6). In later Aram. סְגֵד is to *bow down*, סגודא is *worship*, *adoration*, and בית סגידא an idol temple. Similarly Syr. ܣܓܶܕ, from a primitive meaning of "to salute reverentially" (cf. 2 Sam. ix, 6), comes to mean *to adore*, translating both σέβω and προσκυνέω, and giving ܣܶܓܕܬܳܐ and ܣܓܺܝܕܬܳܐ *adoration*, and ܣܳܓܽܘܕܳܐ a *worshipper*, etc.

It is from the Aram. that we get the Heb. סגד (Nöldeke, *ZDMG*, xli, 719) and the Eth ሰገደ (Nöldeke, *Neue Beiträge*, 36), and it was from Aram. that the word passed into Arabic,[1] probably at an early period, as we see from the *Mu'allaqa* of 'Amr b. Kulthūm, l. 112.

سِجِلّ (*Sijill*).

xxi, 104.

The meaning of Sigill in this eschatological passage was unknown to the early interpreters of the Qur'ān. Some took it to be the name of an Angel, or of the Prophet's amanuensis, but the majority are in favour of its meaning some kind of writing or writing material. (Ṭab. and Bagh. on the passage, and Rāghib, *Mufradāt*, 223.)

There was also some difference of opinion as to its origin, some like Bagh. taking it as an Arabic word derived from مساجلة, and others admitting that it was a foreign word, of Abyssinian or Persian origin.[2] It is, however, neither Persian[3] nor Abyssinian, but the Gk. σιγίλλον = Lat. *sigillum*, used in Byzantine Greek for an Imperial edict.[4] The word came into very general use in the eastern part of the Empire, so that we find Syr. ܣܝܓܝܠܠܘܢ (*PSm*, 2607)[5] meaning

[1] Nöldeke, op. cit.; Hirschfeld, *Beiträge*, 41; Schwally, *ZDMG*, lii, 134; Von Kremer, *Streifzüge*, p. ix, n.

[2] al-Jawālīqī, *Mu'arrab*, 87; al-Khafājī, 104; as-Suyūṭī, *Itq*, 321; *Mutaw*, 41. W. Y. Bell in his translation of the *Mutaw.* is quite wrong in taking the word رجل to mean *part, portion, blank paper*. It means *man* as is clear from *LA*, xiii, 347.

[3] Pers. سجل, meaning *syngrapha iudicis*, is a borrowing from the Arabic, Vullers, *Lex*, ii, 231.

[4] Vollers, *ZDMG*, l, 611; li, 314; Bell, *Origin*, 74; Vacca, *EI*, sub voc.; Fraenkel, *Vocab*, 17; *Fremdw*, 251.

[5] Nöldeke, *Neue Beiträge*, 27.

diploma, and Arm. սփգեղ meaning *seal.*[1] It may have come through Syriac to Arabic as Mingana, *Syriac Influence*, 90, claims, but the word appears not to occur in Arabic earlier than the Qur'ān, and may be one of the words picked up by Muḥammad himself as used among the people of N. Arabia in its Greek form. In any case, as Nöldeke insists,[2] it is clear that he quite misunderstood its real meaning.

سِجِّيل (*Sijjīl*).

xi, 84; xv, 74; cv, 4.

Lumps of baked clay.

The last of these passages refers to the destruction of the army of the Elephant, and the others to the destruction of Sodom and Gomorrah. In both cases the سجيل is something rained down from heaven, and as the latter event is referred to in Sūra li, 33, we get the equivalence of سجيل = طين, which gives the Commentators their cue for its interpretation.[3]

It was early recognized as a foreign word, and generally taken as of Persian origin,[4] Ṭab. going so far as to tell us وهو بالفارسية سنك وكل, which is a very fair representation of سَنْگ and گِل (Fraenkel, *Vocab*, 25; Siddiqi, *Studien*, 73). سَنْگ meaning *stone* is the Phlv. سنگ *sang* from Av. asan *asan*,[5] and گِل meaning *clay* the Phlv. gil *gīl*,[6] related to Arm. կաւ (Horn, *Grundriss*, 207).[7] From Middle

[1] Hübschmann, *Arm. Gramm*, i, 378.

[2] *Neue Beiträge*, 27.

[3] Others, however, would not admit this identification, and we learn from Ṭab. that some took it to mean the lowest heaven, others connected it with كتاب, and others made it a form فعيل from اسجل meaning ارسل. Finally, Baiḍ. tells us that some thought it a variant of سجين meaning *hell*.

[4] al-Jawālīqī, *Mu'arrab*, 81; Ibn Qutaiba, *Adab al-Kātib*, 527; al-Khafājī, 103; Rāghib, *Mufradāt*, 223; *Baiḍ* on xi, 84; as-Suyūṭī, *Itq*, 321; *Mutaw*, 35, and see Horovitz, *KU*, 11; Siddiqi, 8, n., 2.

[5] Bartholomae, *AIW*, 207.

[6] *PPGl*, 120.

[7] But see Hübschmann, *Arm. Gramm*, i, 172.

Persian it passed directly into Arabic. Grimme, *ZA*, xxvi, 164, 165, suggests S. Arabian influence, but there seems nothing to support this.

سِجِّين (*Sijjīn*).

lxxxiii, 7, 8.

The early authorities differed widely as to what the *Sijjīn* of this eschatological passage might be. It was generally agreed that it was a place, but some said it meant the lowest earth—الارض السابعة, or a name for hell, or a rock under which the records of men's deeds are kept, or a prison.[1] The Qur'ān itself seems to indicate that it means a document كتاب مرقوم, so as-Suyūṭī, *Mutaw*, 46,[2] tells us that some thought it was a Persian word meaning *clay* (tablet). Grimme, *ZA*, xxvi, 163, thinks that it refers to the material on which the records are written, and compares with the Eth. ጽንፕን or ጽንጉን meaning clay writing tablets. It is very probable, however, as Nöldeke, *Sketches*, 38, suggested long ago, that the word is simply an invention of Muḥammad himself. If this is so, then كتاب مرقوم is probably an explanatory gloss that has crept into the text.

سُحْت (*Suḥt*).

v, 46, 67, 68.

Unlawful.

The reference is to usury and to forbidden foods. It is clearly a technical term, and the passages, it will be noted, are of the latest Madinan group.

Sprenger, *Leben*, iii, 40, n., suggested that it was a technical term borrowed from the Jews, and there certainly is an interesting parallel from the Talmud, *Shabb*, 140*b*, where שחת is used in this technical sense. It is, however, the Syr. ܚܘܣܝܬܐ *depravity*, *corruption*, etc.,

[1] See Vacca, *EI*, sub voc., who suggests that it was this idea that the word was connected with سجن that gave rise to the theory that it was a place in the nethermost earth where the books were kept, rather than the books themselves.

[2] See also *Itq*, 321.

which gives us a nominal form from which سحت may have been derived.

سَحَرَ (*Saḥara*).

vii, 113, 129; xxiii, 91.

To enchant, bewitch, use sorcery.

Besides the verb there are used in the Qur'ān the nouns ساحر, plu. سَحَرَة and ساحرون, vii, 109, 110, etc., *sorcerer*; سحّار *a great magician*, xxvi, 36; سِحْر *enchantment, sorcery*, v, 110; vi, 7, etc.; مسحور *bewitched*, xvii, 50, 103, etc.; مُسَحَّر *bewitched*, xxvi, 153, 185.

The verb is denominative, formed either from the noun ساحر or سحر, which was the borrowed term.

It would seem that the word came to the Arabs from Mesopotamia, which was ever to them the home of sorcery and magic (see the Lexicons under بابل). Zimmern, therefore,[1] would derive it from the Akk. *sāḫiru, sorcerer, magician*. If this is so it may have been a very early borrowing direct from Mesopotamia, though a borrowing through the Aramaic is more probable.[2]

سِرَاجٌ (*Sirāj*).

xxv, 62; xxxiii, 45; lxxi, 15; lxxviii, 13.

A lamp or torch.

The Muslim authorities take it as pure Arabic, not realizing that the verb from which they derive it is denominative.

Fraenkel, *Vocab*, 7, pointed out that it was from Aram. שרגא = Syr. ܫܪܓܐ. These forms are, however, borrowed from the Pers. چراغ and in *Fremdw*, 95, he suggests that it probably came directly

[1] *Akkadische Fremdwörter*, 67.

[2] סחרא as used on the incantation bowls is significant; cf. Montgomery, *Aramaic Incantation Texts*, Glossary, 297.

into Arabic from an Iranian source, a theory also put forward by Sachau in his notes to the *Mu'arrab*, p. 21. This is of course possible, since the Arm. Ճրագ is from the Iranian, as also the Ossetian *ciraγ*,[1] but Syr. ܫܪܓܐ was a very commonly used word with many derivatives (*PSm*, 4325), and Vollers, *ZDMG*, l, 613, is doubtless right in deriving the Arabic word from the Syriac.

سُرَادِق (*Surādiq*).

xviii, 28.

An awning, tent cover.

The passage is eschatological, descriptive of the torments of the wicked, for whom is prepared a fire " whose awning shall enwrap them ". The exegetes got the general sense of the word from the passage, but were not very sure of its exact meaning as we see from Baiḍ's comment on the verse.

It was very generally recognized as a foreign word. Rāghib, *Mufradāt*, 229, notes that the form of the word is not Arabic, and al-Jawālīqī, *Mu'arrab*, 90, classes it as a Persian word,[2] though he is not very certain as to what was the original form. Some derived it from سرادر, meaning an *antechamber*, others from سراپرده *curtains*, others from سراطاق,[3] and yet others from سراچه.[4]

Pers. سراپرده is the form from which we must work. It is defined by Vullers as " velum magnum s. auleum, quod parietis loco circum tentorium expandunt ",[5] and is formed from پرده a *veil* or *curtain* (Vullers, i, 340), and an O.Pers. √*srāδa*,[6] from which came the

[1] Hübschmann, *Arm. Gramm*, i, 190. Addai Sher, 89, wants to derive the Pers. چراغ from the Syr., but this is putting things back to front. For the Pahlavi form see Salemann, *Manichaeische Studien*, i, 121 ; Telegdi, in *JA*, ccxxvi (1935), p. 255.

[2] So as-Suyūṭī, *Itq*, 321, and Siddiqi, *Studien*, 64.

[3] al-Khafājī, 105. On the form سرابرده see Noldeke, *Mand. Gramm*, xxxi, n. 3.

[4] Lagarde, *Übersicht*, 176 n.

[5] *Lex*, ii, 257.

[6] Hübschmann, *Persische Studien*, 199. Cf. the Phlv. [illegible] *srāïtan* and Pers. سرای, Horn, *Grundriss*, 161.

Arm. սրահ[1] and the Judæo-Persian סראה,[2] both meaning *forecourt* (αὐλή or στοά). From some Middle Persian formation from this √*srāδa* with the suffix ك was borrowed the Arm. սրահակ meaning *curtain*,[3] and the Mandaean סראדקא *roof of tent* or *awning*.[4] The word occurs in the old poetry, e.g. in Labīd (ed. Chalidi, p. 27), and was thus an early borrowing, but whether directly from Iranian or through Aram. it is impossible now to say.

سِرْبَال (*Sirbāl*).

xiv, 51; xvi, 83.

Garment.

From the use of the word in the old poetry, e.g. Imru'ul-Qais, lii, 14; 'Antara, xx, 18; *Ḥamāsa*, p. 349, it is clear that the word means a *shirt* and in particular a shirt of mail, and Rāghib, *Mufradāt*, 228, gives the Qur'ānic meaning as قميص من اى جنس.

Freytag, *Lex*, ii, 305, suggested that it was the Pers. شلوار which is taken to be the origin of سروال and then of سربال. Many authorities have favoured this view, but as Dozy, *Vêtements*, 202, points out, شلوار means *breeches* not *shirt* or *mantle*, and is formed from شل *femur* + وار (Vollers, *ZDMG*, l, 324). In Aram., however, we find סרבלא, which in the Rabbinic writings means *mantle*,[5] and gave rise to the verbal forms סִרְבֵּל and סַרְבֵּל "to enwrap in a mantle". This verbal form occurs in the old Arabic poetry, e.g. حتى تسربل بالدم in the *Mu'allaqa* of 'Antara, l. 73, and سربال may have been formed from this verbal

[1] Hubschmann, *Arm. Gramm*, i, 241, and see Lagarde, *Arm. Stud*, § 2071.

[2] Lagarde, *Persische Studien*, 72.

[3] Hubschmann, *Arm. Gramm*, i, 241.

[4] Noldeke, *Mand. Gramm*, xxxi; Lagarde, *Übersicht*, 176 n.; Fraenkel, *Fremdw*, 29. It may be argued, however, that the Mand. form is from Arabic.

[5] So סרבל in Dan. iii, 21, 27. *Vide* Andreas in the Glossary to Marti's *Grammatik d. bibl. aram. Sprache*, 1896, and the other suggestions discussed by S. A. Cook in the *Journal of Philology*, xxvi, 306 ff., in an article "The Articles of Dress in Dan. iii, 21".

form. Syr. ܦܪܙܠܐ, however, like Gk. σαράβαλλα, seems to have been used particularly for breeches.[1] All these, of course, are borrowings from Iranian, but the probabilities seem to be that the word was an early loan-word in Arabic from Aramaic.

سَرْد (*Sard*).

xxxiv, 10.

Chain armour, i.e. work of rings woven together.

It occurs only in a passage relating to David's skill as an armourer.

The Muslim authorities derive it from سَرَدَ to *stitch* or *sew* (cf. Rāghib, *Mufradāt*, 229), though it is curious that they know that *armourer* ought to be *Zarrād* rather than *Sarrād* (as-Sijistānī, 177). As a matter of fact سرد seems to be but a form of زرد, which, like مزرّد, was commonly used among the Arabs.[2] This زرد is a borrowing from Iranian sources as Fraenkel, *Vocab*, 13, noted.[3] Av. ܙܪܕ *zrāδa* (*AIW*, 1703) means a coat of mail, and becomes in Phlv. both ܙܪܗ *zrih*, whence Mod. Pers. زره and Arm. զրահք,[4] and also was borrowed into Syr. as ܙܪܕܐ.[5] The word was a pre-Islamic borrowing, possibly direct from Persia, or maybe through Syriac.

سَطَرَ (*Saṭara*).

يسطرون, lxviii, 1; مسطور, xvii, 60; xxxiii, 6; lii, 2; مستطر, liv, 53 [also the forms مصيطر, lxxxviii, 22; and مصيطرون, lii, 37].

To write, to inscribe.

They are all early passages save xxxiii, 6, and possibly all refer to the same thing, the writing in the Heavenly Scrolls.

1 Cf. Horn, *Grundriss*, § 789.
2 Ibn Duraid, 174.
3 See also his *Fremdw*, 241 ff.; and Telegdi in *JA*, ccxxvi (1935), p. 243.
4 Hubschmann, *Arm. Gramm*, i, 152; Jackson, *Researches in Manichaeism*, 1932, p. 66; Salemann, *Manichaeische Studien*, i, 80.
5 Nyberg, *Glossar*, 257; Horn, *Grundriss*, 146.

Nöldeke as early as 1860 [1] drew attention to the fact that the noun سطر seemed to be a borrowing from ܫܛܪܐ = שטרא,[2] so that the verb, as Fraenkel, *Fremdw*, 250, notes, would be denominative. The Aram. שטרא = ܫܛܪܐ means a *document*, and is from a root connected with Akk. *šaṭāru, to write*. It occurs as שטר in Nabataean and Palmyrene inscriptions,[3] and in the S. Arabian inscriptions we have 𐩪𐩷𐩧 *to write*, and 𐩱𐩪𐩷𐩧 *inscriptions*.[4] D. H. Müller, *WZKM*, i, 29, thinks that the Arabic may have been influenced both by the Aramaeans of the north, and the Sabaeans of the south, and as a matter of fact as-Suyūṭī, *Itq*, 311, tells us that Juwaibir in his comment on xvii, 60, quoted a tradition from Ibn ʻAbbās to the effect that مسطور was the word used in the Himyaritic dialect for مكتوب.[5] The presence of the Phlv. [Pahlavi] *stūrē*, as, e.g., in the phrase [Pahlavi] = in lines (*PPGl*, 205), makes us think, however, that it may have been Aramaic influence which brought the word to S. Arabia.[6] In any case the occurrence of the word in the early poetry shows that it was an early borrowing.

سِفْر (*Sifr*).

lxii, 5.

A large book.

It occurs only in the plu. اسفار in the proverb "like an ass beneath a load of books".

This sense of اسفار is quite unnatural in Arabic, and some of the early authorities quoted in as-Suyūṭī, *Itq*, 319,[7] noted that it was a borrowing from Nabataean or Syriac. It was apparently a word used among the Arabs for the Scriptures of Jews and Christians, for in

[1] *Geschichte des Qorans*, p. 13.
[2] Cf. Horovitz, *KU*, 70.
[3] Lidzbarski, *Handbuch*, 374.
[4] Lidzbarski, *Ephemeris*, ii, 381; Hommel, *Chrest*, 124; Muller, *Epigr. Denkm. aus Arabien*, lii, 2; liv, 2; Glaser, *Altjemenische Nachrichten*, 67 ff.; Rossini, *Glossarium*, 194.
[5] *Vide* Sprenger, *Leben*, ii, 395.
[6] Zimmern, *Akkad. Fremdw*, 29, takes the Arabic form as derived from Aramaic.
[7] *Mutaw*, 54, 59.

Bekrī, *Mu'jam*, 369, 18, we read of how aḍ-Ḍaḥḥāk entered a Christian monastery while the monk was reading سفرا من اسفارهم, and Ibn Duraid, 103, says that *Sifr* means " the volume of the Torah or the Injīl or what resembles them ".[1]

It is clearly a borrowing from Aramaic.[2] The common Heb. סֵפֶר appears in Aram. as סִפְרָא ; Syr. ܣܦܪܐ. From Aram. it passed on the one hand into Eth. as ሰፈረ and on the other into Arm. as *սափեր*. As the Arm. word seems to have come from Syr.,[3] we may suppose that it was from the same source that the Arabs got the word.

سَفَرَةٌ (*Safara*).

lxxx, 15.

Scribes ; plu. of سَافِرٌ (used of the heavenly scribes).

as-Suyūṭī, *Itq*, 321 (*Mutaw*, 60), tells us that some early authorities said it was a Nabataean word meaning قُرَّاء. Aram. סָפַר was a scribe or secretary who accompanied the Governor of a Province (Ezra iv, 8, etc.), and then came to mean γραμματεύς in general (cf. Ezra vii, 12, 21, and Cowley, *Aramaic Papyri*, Index, 301). So Syr. ܣܦܪܐ is both γραμματεύς and νομικός, and as Arabic terms connected with literary craft are commonly of Syriac origin we may suppose with Mingana[4] that this word is from Christian rather than from Jewish Aramaic, though the occurrence of Palm. ספרא[5] may point to an early borrowing in N. Arabia.

سفينة (*Safīna*).

xviii, 70, 78 ; xxix, 14.

A ship.

[1] See Goldziher in *ZDMG*, xxxii, 347 n.

[2] Fraenkel, *Fremdw*, 247 ; Schwally, *Idioticon*, 64. In Safaite ספר means an inscription ; cf. Littmann, *Semitic Inscriptions*, 113, 124, 127.

[3] Hübschmann, *Arm. Gramm*, i, 317, and see Müller, in *WZKM*, viii, 284.

[4] *Syriac Influence*, 85 ; Horovitz, *KU*, 68, n., is in doubt whether it is of Jewish or Syrian origin. As a matter of fact the heavenly scribes occur just as frequently in Jewish as in Christian books, so that a decision from the use of the word is impossible.

[5] *RES*, iii, No. 1739.

The reference in xviii is to the boat used by Moses and al-Khiḍr, and in xxix to Noah's ark.

The lexicographers fancifully derive it from سَفَنَ *to peel* or *pare* (cf. *LA*, xvii, 72). This, however, is denominative from سَفَنٌ an *adze*, which itself is not an Arabic word but the Pers. اِسْتَان which passed into Arabic through ܣܦܢܐ.[1] Guidi, *Della Sede*, 601, called attention to the fact that سفينة is a loan-word in Arabic, and the Semitic root is doubtless ספן *to cover in*, which we find in Akk. *sapannu* = *concealment*, Phon. מספנת a *roof*,[2] and Aram. סְפַן ; Heb. סָפַן *to cover*.

The form ספינה occurs in Heb. in the story of Jonah (Jonah i, 5),[3] and in the Talmud and Targums ספינא and ספינתא are commonly used. Even more commonly used are the Syr. ܣܦܝܢܐ ܣܦܝܢܬܐ, and as both the al-Khiḍr and Nūḥ stories of the Qur'ān seem to have developed under Christian influence we might suspect the word there to be a borrowing from Syriac. It occurs, however, in the old poetry, e.g. Imru'ul Qais xx, 4 (Ahlwardt, *Divans*, 128); *Div. Hudh*, xviii, 3, etc., so one cannot venture to say more than that it came from some Aram. source, as an early borrowing into Arabic.

سَكَر (*Sakar*).

xvi, 69.

Intoxicating drink.

With this should be associated all the other forms derived therefrom and connected with drunkenness, e.g. iv, 46; xv, 15, 72; xxii, 2. as-Suyūṭī, *Itq*, 321 (*Mutaw*, 40), tells us that some early authorities considered it an Ethiopic word. It is possible that the Eth. ሰከረ is the origin of the Arabic word, but the word is widely used in the Semitic languages, e.g. Akk. *šikaru* (cf. שֵׁכָר ; ܫܟܪ), *beer* [4]; and Heb. שֵׁכָר ; Aram. שִׁכְרָא ; Syr. ܫܟܪܐ *date wine*, and was borrowed into Egyptian,

[1] Vullers, *Lex*, i, 68; Fraenkel, *Fremdw*, 216, 217.
[2] Lidzbarski, *Handbuch*, 330; Harris, *Glossary*, 127.
[3] Cf. the ספינה and ספינתה of the Elephantine papyri (Cowley, *Aramaic Papyri*, No. 26).
[4] Zimmern, *Akkad. Fremdw*, 39.

e.g. *ṯkr*,[1] and Greek, e.g. *σίκερα*.[2] Thus while it may have come into Arabic from Syriac as most other wine terms did, on the other hand it may be a common derivation from early Semitic (Guidi, *Della Sede*, 603).

سَكَنَ (*Sakana*).

Of frequent occurrence.

To dwell.

Besides the simple verb we find اسكن, the participles ساكن and مسكون, and the nominal forms سَكَنٌ and مَسْكَنٌ.

Zimmern, *Akkad. Fremdw*, 30, thinks that the origin was Mesopotamian. The Akk. *šakānu* meant *to settle in a place* (*niederlegen, niedersetzen*), and was particularly used of dwelling somewhere. This, he thinks, was the origin on the one hand of the other Semitic forms, e.g. Heb. שָׁכַן; Phon. שכן; Syr. ܫܟܢ; and Ar. سَكَنَ, and, perhaps on the other hand, of the Gk. *σκηνή tent* (though in view of the evidence in Boissacq, 875, this is doubtful).

سِكِّينٌ (*Sikkīn*).

xii, 31.

A knife.

Nöldeke, *Mand. Gramm*, 125 n., had noted that it was a borrowed word, comparing it with Heb. שכין; Syr. ܣܟܝܢܐ, and Mand. סיכינא and סכינא.[3] The Heb. שכין is a loan-word from Aram. and the Aram. word is also the source of the Gk. *συκίνη*[4] and the Phlv. ideogram [illegible] *sakina*,[5] so that an Aram. origin of the Arabic word is fairly certain, though whether from Syr. or O.Aram. it is difficult to decide (cf. Guidi, *Della Sede*, 581).

[1] M. Muller, *Asien und Europa*, 1893, p. 102. Cf. Erman-Grapow, v, 410.

[2] Levy, *Fremdw*, 81, and Lagarde, *Mittheilungen*, ii, 357.

[3] Fraenkel, *Fremdw*, 84, says: "سكين ist seiner ganzen Bildung nach als Lehnwort deutlich, es hat ferner im Arabischen keine Ableitung und ausserdem ist die Lautverschiebungsregel darin gegenüber שכין deutlich verletzt."

[4] Levy, *Fremdw*, 176.

[5] *PPGl*, 201.

سَكِينَة (*Sakīna*).

ii, 249 ; ix, 26, 40 ; xlviii, 4, 18, 26.

The Shekinah.

The question of the Shekinah in the Qur'ān has been discussed at length by de Sacy [1] and by Goldziher,[2] and we need do no more here than briefly summarize the results.

The word occurs only in late Madinan passages and appears to have been a technical term learned by Muḥammad at a relatively late period. In ii, 249, it refers to the sign whereby the Israelites were to recognize Saul as their king, but in all the other passages it is some kind of assistance sent down to believers from Heaven.

Now there is a genuine Arabic word سكينة meaning *tranquillity*, from سَكَنَ *to rest, be quiet*, and the common theory of the exegetes is that this is the word used here. This, however, will hardly fit ii, 249,[3] and even in the other passages it is obvious that something more than merely tranquillity was meant, so that many thought it had the special meaning of نصر.[4] There was some doubt as to the vowelling of the word, for we find سِكِّينة, سَكِّينة, and سِكِينة beside the usual سَكِينة (*TA*, ix, 238; *LA*, xvii, 76). There can be little doubt, however, that we have here the Heb. שכינה,[5] though possibly through the Syr. ܫܟܝܢܬܐ.[6] Muḥammad would have learned the word from the People of the Book, and not quite understanding its significance, have associated it with the genuine Arabic word meaning *tranquillity*, and this gives us the curiously mixed sense of the word in the Qur'ān.

سَلَام (*Salām*).

Of very frequent occurrence, cf. iv, 96 ; v, 18 ; vi, 54, etc.

[1] *JA*, 1829, p. 177 ff. [2] *Abhandlungen*, i, 177–204, and *RHR*, xxviii, 1–13.

[3] So the Commentators admit that it means *tranquillity* in all passages save ii, 249.

[4] Cf. *LA*, xvii, 76.

[5] Geiger, 54 ; Weil, *Mohammed*, 181 ; Pautz, *Offenbarung*, 251 ; Horovitz, *JPN*, 208 ; von Kremer, *Ideen*, 226, n. ; Fraenkel, *Vocab*, 23 ; Joel, *EI*, sub voc. ; Grunbaum, *ZDMG*, xxxix, 581, 582.

[6] Nöldeke, *Neue Beiträge*, 24. It was doubtless through the Syr. that we get the Mand. שכינאתא. See Lidzbarski, *Mand. Liturgien* (1920), Register, s.v. ; Montgomery, *Aramaic Incantation Texts*, Glossary, p. 304.

Peace.

The denominative verbs سَلَّمَ and أَسْلَمَ with their derivatives are also used not uncommonly in the Qur'ān, though the primitive verb سَلِمَ does not occur therein.

The root is common Semitic, and is widely used in all the Semitic tongues. The sense of *peace*, however, seems to be a development peculiar to Heb. and Aram. and from thence to have passed into the S. Semitic languages. Heb. שָׁלוֹם is *soundness* then *peace* [1]; Aram. שְׁלָמָא *security*; Syr. ܫܠܡܐ *security, peace*. The Eth. ተሰለመ, however, is denominative,[2] so that ሰላም doubtless came from the older religions. Similarly 𐩪𐩡𐩣 [3] is to be taken as due to Northern influence, the 𐩪 like Eth. ሰ (instead of 𐩦 and ሠ), being parallel with the 𐩪 of the Safaite inscriptions.

In the Aram. area the word was widely used as a term of salutation, and in this sense we very frequently find שלם in the Nabataean and Sinaitic,[4] and סלם in the Safaite inscriptions.[5] From this area it doubtless came into Arabic [6] being used long before Islam, as Goldziher has shown (*ZDMG*, xlvi, 22 ff.). There can be little doubt that سَلَّمَ *to greet*, etc., is denominative from this, though Torrey, *Foundation*, would take the whole development as purely Arabic.

سِلْسِلَة (*Silsila*).

xl, 73; lxix, 32; lxxvi, 4.

Chain.

It is used only in connection with descriptions of the torments of hell, and may be a technical term in Muḥammad's eschatological vocabulary, borrowed in all probability from one of the Book religions.

In any case it cannot be easily explained from an Arabic root, and Guidi, *Della Sede*, 581, already suspected it as non-Arabic.

[1] So also the שלם of the Ras Shamra tablets.
[2] Dillmann, *Lex*, 322.
[3] Hommel, *Südarab. Chrest*, 124; Rossini, *Glossarium*, 196.
[4] For examples see Euting, *Nab. Inschr*, 19, 20; *Sin. Inschr*, 61 ff.
[5] Littmann, *Semitic Inscriptions*, pp. 131, 132, 134, etc.
[6] Nöldeke-Schwally, i, 33, n. See Künstlinger in *Rocznik Orjentalistyczny*, xi, 1–10.

Fraenkel, *Fremdw*, 290,[1] relates it to the Aram. שלשלתא; Syr. ܫܫܠܬܐ,[2] which is the origin of the Eth. ሰንሰለ (Nöldeke, *Neue Beiträge*, 42), and possibly of the late Heb. שַׁלְשֶׁלֶת.[3] The borrowing from Aram. would doubtless have been early, and it is possible that we find the word in Safaite (cf. Ryckmans, *Noms propres*, 151).

سُلْطَانٌ (*Sulṭān*).

Of very frequent occurrence, cf. iii, 144; iv, 93; vi, 81.

Power, authority. (ἐξουσία·)

The denominative verb سَلَّطَ *to give power over*, occurs in iv, 92; lix, 6.

The primitive verb سَلُطَ *to be hard* or *strong* occurs frequently in the old poetry [4] but not in the Qur'ān. It is cognate with Eth. ሠለጠ *to exercise strength*,[5] and with a group of N. Semitic words, but in N. Semitic the sense of the root has developed in general to mean *to domineer, have power over*, e.g. Akk. *šalāṭu*, *to have power* [6]: Heb. שָׁלַט *to domineer, be master of* [7]: Aram. שְׁלַט; Syr. ܫܠܛ *to have mastery over*. Under this Aram. influence the Eth. ሠለጠ later comes to mean *potestatem habere*.

The Muslim philologers were entirely at sea over the Qur'ānic سلطان, which they wish to derive from سليط (cf. *LA*, ix, 193), and Sprenger, *Leben*, i, 108, rightly took it as a borrowing from the Aram.[8] In Bibl. Aram. שָׁלְטָן occurs several times, with the meaning *sovereignty*, *dominion*, like the Rabbinic שולטנא and שולטנות. In the Nabataean inscriptions also we find שלטון *rule*, or *dominion* (cf. Lidzbarski, *Handbuch*, 376), but it is in Syriac that we find the

[1] See also p. 76 and Schwally, *Idioticon*, 94; Schulthess, *Lex*, 209.

[2] Zimmern, *Akkad. Fremdw*, 35, carries this itself back to Akk. *šaršarratu*.

[3] Also of the Arm. շղթայ, Hübschmann, *Arm. Gramm*, i, 314.

[4] A'shā in Geyer, *Zwei Gedichte*, i, 163; *Dīwān*, iv, 41; v, 60; *Aṣma'iyāt*, vi, 17.

[5] Cf. also ሰለጠ and Nöldeke's note *Neue Beiträge*, 39, n. 3.

[6] Zimmern, *Akkad. Fremdw*, 7.

[7] It is only a late word in Heb. and possibly a borrowing from Aramaic.

[8] So Nöldeke, *Neue Beiträge*, 39, n. 3; Wellhausen, *ZDMG*, lxvii, 633; Massignon, *Lexique technique*, 52.

word most widely used. In particular ܫܘܠܛܢܐ is used in precisely the same senses as سلطان is used in the Qur'ān, and it was doubtless from this source that both the Ar. سلطان and Eth. ሥልጣን were derived.[1]

سُلَّمٌ (*Sullam*).

vi, 35; lii, 38.

Ladder.

The word is clearly an Aram. borrowing, for it has no root in Arabic and can only be explained from Aram. סולמא, as Schwally has noticed (*ZDMG*, liii, 197). The word does not occur in Syriac, but its currency in N. Arabia is evidenced by a Palm. inscription—ועבד בסלמא דנה עמודין שבעא "and he has made along with this stairway seven columns" (De Vogüé, No. 11, line 3).[2] It would probably have been a fairly early borrowing, and as the word seems to be originally Akkadian,[3] one cannot lose sight of the possibility of the Arabic word having been an early borrowing from Mesopotamia.

سَلْوَى (*Salwā*).

ii, 54; vii, 160; xx, 82.

Quail.

The word is found only in connection with the story of the manna and quails sent as provision for the Children of Israel in their desert wanderings.

Some of the Muslim philologers endeavoured to derive it from سلا *to console* (cf. Zam. on ii, 54), but there can be no reasonable doubt that it is from the Heb. שְׂלָו through the Aram.[4] The Jewish Aram. סליו. שליו is little used, so all the probabilities are in favour of its

[1] Fischer, *Glossar*, 56, gives it from Aramaic.

[2] There is some doubt, however, as to whether the reading should be סלמא or צלמא, though in the facsimile it certainly looks like [Palm. letter] = ס and not [Palm. letter] = צ.

[3] See Schwally, *ZDMG*, liii, 197; Horovitz, *JPN*, 210.

[4] Horovitz, *KU*, 17, n. Lagarde, *Übersicht*, 190, n., however, curiously regards ܣܠܘܝ as borrowed from the Arabic.

having come through Syr. ܦܛܡܘܣ,[1] though it may have come from the Targums (Ahrens, *Christliches*, 25).

سُلَيْمَان (*Sulaimān*).

ii, 96; iv, 161; vi, 84; xxi, 78–81; xxvii, 15–45; xxxiv, 11; xxxviii, 29, 33.

Solomon.

All these references are to the Biblical Solomon, though the information about him in the Qur'ān is mostly derived from late legend.

The name was early recognized as a foreign borrowing into Arabic and is given as such by al-Jawālīqī, *Mu'arrab*, 85, though some were inclined to take it as genuine Arabic and a diminutive of سلمان from a root سلم (cf. *LA*, xv, 192). Lagarde, *Übersicht*, 86, thought the philologers were right in taking it as a diminutive from سلمان, quoting as parallel زُعَيْفِرَان from زَعْفَرَان, and Lidzbarski, *Johannesbuch*, 74, n. 1, agrees. The truth, however, seems to be that it is the Syr. ܫܠܝܡܘܢ, as Nöldeke has argued.[2] al-Jawālīqī, op. cit., said it was Heb., but Gk. Σαλώμων; Syr. ܫܠܝܡܘܢ; Eth. ሰሎሞን, beside Heb. שְׁלֹמֹה, are conclusive proof of Christian origin.

The name was well-known in the pre-Islamic period, both as the name of Israel's king, and as a personal name,[3] so it would have been quite familiar to Muḥammad's contemporaries.

سُنْبُل (*Sunbul*).

ii, 263; xii, 46, 47.

Ear of corn.

The double plu. سنابل and سنبلات suggests foreign borrowing.

[1] Fraenkel, *Vocab*, 24; Hirschfeld, *Beiträge*, 41; Mingana, *Syriac Influence*, 86.

[2] *ZDMG*, xv, 806; *ZA*, xxx, 158, and cf. Brockelmann, *Grundriss*, i, 256; Mingana, *Syriac Influence*, 82; Horovitz, *JPN*, 167–9.

[3] Horovitz, *KU*, 118, points out that we have evidence for it as a personal name only among the Madinan Jews. Cf. also Sprenger, *Leben*, ii, 335.

The usual theory is that it is derived from سبل (Rāghib, *Mufradāt*, 222, and the Lexicons), it not being realized that the verb اسبل *to put out ears*, is itself a denominative from سَبَلَة, سُبُولة, سَبُولة, which parallel Heb. שִׁבֹּלֶת ; Akk. *šubultu* ; Aram. שִׁבְּלְתָא ; Syr. ܫܒܠܬܐ (cf. Eth. ሰብል).

As a matter of fact سُنْبُل, سُنْبُلة, is an independent borrowing from the Aram. and may be compared with the Mand. שומבילתא (Nöldeke, *Mand. Gram.*, 19). The inserted *n* is not uncommon in loan-words in Arabic, as Geyer points out.[1] Cf. منجل from מַגָּל ; Syr. ܡܓܠܐ, or كَنَف from ܟܦܐ, or قُنْفُذ from קִפּוֹד, Syr. ܩܘܦܕܐ, or خنزير from חזיר, Syr. ܚܙܝܪܐ, etc.

سُنْدُس (*Sundus*).

xviii, 30 ; xliv, 53 ; lxxvi, 21.

Fine silk.

It occurs only in combination with استبرق in describing the elegant clothing of the inhabitants of Paradise, and thus may be suspected at once of being an Iranian word.

It was early recognized as a foreign borrowing, and is given as Persian by al-Kindī, *Risāla*, 85 ; ath-Tha'labī, *Fiqh*, 317; al-Jawālīqī, *Mu'arrab*, 79; al-Khafājī, 104; as-Suyūṭī, *Itq*, 322. Others, however, took it as Arabic, as the *Muḥīṭ* notes, and some, as we learn from *TA*, iv, 168, thought it was one of the cases where the two languages used the same word.

Freytag in his *Lexicon* gave it as *e persica lingua*, though Fraenkel, *Vocab*, 4, raised a doubt, for no such form as سندس occurs in Persian, ancient or modern.[2] Dvořák, *Fremdw*, 72, suggests that it is a corruption of the Pers. سَنْدُوقس, which like Syr. ܣܢܕܘܩܣ is derived from

[1] *Zwei Gedichte*, i, 118, n. [2] See now Henning in *BSOS*, ix, 87.

Gk. σάνδυξ,[1] a word used among the Lydians, so Strabo XI, xiv, 9, says, for fine, transparent, flesh-coloured women's garments of linen.

Fraenkel, *Fremdw*, 41, compares with the Gk. σινδών, the garment used in the Bacchic mysteries, and with this Vollers, *ZDMG*, li, 298, is inclined to agree, as also Zimmern, *Akkad. Fremdw*, 37. σινδών itself is derived from Akk. *sudinnu*, *sadinnu*, whence came the Heb. סָדִין ; Aram. סדינא. In any case it was an early borrowing as it occurs in the early poetry, e.g. in Mutalammis, xiv, 3, etc.

سِوَارٌ (*Siwār*).

Only in the plu. forms أَسْوِرَةٌ, xliii, 53, and أَسَاوِرُ, xviii, 30 ; xxii, 23 ; xxxv, 30 ; lxxvi, 21.

Bracelets.

The form اسورة occurs in the Pharaoh story, but اساور is found only in eschatological passages describing the adornment of the inhabitants of Paradise.

Zimmern, *Akkad. Fremdw*, 38, points out that the ultimate origin is the old Babylonian *šawiru*, *šewiru* meaning *ring* or *arm-bracelet*, whence was derived the Heb. שֵׁירָה and Aram. שֵׁירָא : Syr. ܫܝܪܐ *bracelet*. Zimmern would derive the Ar. سوار from the Aramaic.[2] The Syr. ܫܝܪܐ is a fairly common word, and is used to translate צמיד in Gen. xxiv, 22, etc., and חח in Ex. xxxv, 22, but from the form of the Arabic it would seem rather a direct borrowing from the Akk. at some early time, than a borrowing through the Aramaic.

Fraenkel, *Fremdw*, 56, thinks سوار is genuine Arabic, but the Muslim authorities were themselves in doubt about it, some of them giving it as of Persian origin (Lane, *Lex*, 1465). The borrowed form was certainly the سوار from which the plu. forms were developed.

سُورَةٌ (*Sūra*).

ii, 21 ; ix, 65, 87, 125, 128 ; x, 39 ; xi, 16 ; xxiv, 1 ; xlvii, 22.

Sūra.

[1] Vullers, *Lex*, ii, 331.

[2] So Meissner, in *GGA*, 1904, p. 756.

The passages in which it occurs are all late, and possibly all Madinan. It always means a portion of revelation, and thus was used by Muḥammad as a technical term.

The Muslim authorities are quite ignorant of the origin of the word.[1] Some took it as connected with سور, meaning a *town wall* (cf. Rāghib, *Mufradāt*, 248), others made it mean منزلة, an astronomical *statio* (cf. *Muḥīṭ*, sub voc.), while others, reading the word سؤرة, would derive it from أسأر *to leave over* (Rāghib, op. cit. ; cf. also *Itqān*, 121).

The older European opinion was that it was a Jewish word derived from שׁוּרָה, which is used in the Mishnah for *row, rank, file*. Buxtorf in his *Lexicon* suggested this equivalence, and it was accepted by Nöldeke in 1860 in his *Geschichte des Qorans*, p. 24; he has been followed by many later writers.[2] Lagarde, *Mittheilungen*, iii, 205, however, pointed out the difficulties of this theory, and thought that the origin of the word was to be found in Heb. שׂרה (which he would read in Is. xxviii, 25), and then, referring to Buxtorf's שרת הדין *lineae quas transsilire impune possumus*, he suggests that the meaning is κανών. שׂרה, however, is such a doubtful word that one cannot place much reliance on this derivation.

A further difficulty with Nöldeke's theory is that שׁורה seems not to be used in connection with Scripture, whereas the Qur'ānic سورة is exclusively so associated, a fact which has led Hirschfeld (*New Researches*, 2, n. 6) to think that the word is meant to represent the Jewish סדרה, the well-known technical term for the section marks in the Hebrew Scriptures. This is connected with his theory that فرقان is meant to represent the division marks called פרקים, which is certainly not the case, and though his suggestion that سورة

[1] Fraenkel, *Vocab*, 22—cuius derivationem Arabes ignorant.

[2] See also his *Neue Beiträge*, 26, and Fraenkel, *Vocab*, 22; *Fremdw*, 237, 238; Pautz, *Offenbarung*, 89; von Kremer, *Ideen*, 226; Vollers, *ZDMG*, li, 324; Klein, *Religion of Islam*, 3; Cheikho, *Naṣrāniya*, 182; Fischer, *Glossar*, 60*a*; Horovitz, *JPN*, 211; Ahrens, *Christliches*, 19.

is due to a misreading of סדרה as סורה is not without its subtlety, we cannot admit that it is very likely that Muḥammad learned such a technical term in the way he suggests.[1]

The most probable solution is that it is from the Syr. ܣܘܪܬܐ a *writing*,[2] a word which occurs in a sense very like our English *lines* (*PSm*, 2738), and thus is closely parallel to Muḥammad's use of قرآن and كتاب, both of which are likewise of Syriac origin.

سَوْطٌ (*Sawṭ*).

lxxxix, 12.

A scourge.

The Commentators in general interpret the word as *scourge*, though some (cf. Zam. *in loco*) [3] would take it to mean *calamities*, and others, in an endeavour to preserve it as an Arabic word from سَاطَ = خَلَطَ *to mix*, want to make it mean "mixing bowl", i.e. a vial of wrath like the φιάλη of Rev. xvi.

There can be no doubt that *scourge* is the right interpretation, and سَوط in this sense would seem to be a borrowing from Aramaic. In Heb. שוט is a scourge for horses and for men, and Aram. שוטא; Syr. ܫܘܛܐ have the same meaning, but are used also in connection with calamities sent by God as a scourge to the people.[4] From Aram. the word passed also into Eth. as ሰውጥ, plu. አስዋጥ = μάστιξ, *flagellum*, and though Mingana, *Syriac Influence*, 90, thinks the origin was Christian rather than Jewish, it is really impossible to decide. Horovitz, *JPN*, 211, favours an Ethiopic origin, while Torrey, *Foundation*, 51, thinks it is mixed Jewish Arabic.

[1] So Buhl in *EI*, sub voc., but his own suggestion of a derivation from سار *to mount up*, is no happier. See Kunstlinger in *BSOS*, vii, 599, 600.

[2] Bell, *Origin*, 52; the suggestion of derivation from ܣܒܪܬܐ *preaching* made by Margoliouth, *ERE*, x, 539, is not so near. Cf. Horovitz, *JPN*, 212.

[3] Cf. also Baiḍ. and Bagh. and *LA*, ix, 199.

[4] Barth, *Etymol. Stud*, 14, and *ZATW*, xxxiii, 306, wants to make it mean *flood*, but see Horovitz, *KU*, 13.

سُوق (*Sūq*).

xxv, 8, 22.

A street.

It occurs only in the plu. أسواق referring to the streets of the city.

In laṭer Arabic سوق normally means a *market place*, but in the Qur'ān it is used as the שוק of the O.T. and the Targums for *street*, in contradistinction to the Talmudic meaning of *broad place* or *market*.[1]

The philologers derive it from ساق *to drive along* (*LA*, xii, 33), but Fraenkel, *Fremdw*, 187, is doubtless right in thinking that it is a word taken over by the Arabs from more settled peoples.[2] The Aram. שוקא ; Syr. ܫܘܩܐ commonly mean ὅδος, as well as ἀγορά, and in a Palmyrene inscription (De Vogüé, xv, 5) we read והוא רב שוק, showing that the word was known in N. Arabia.

From some early Mesopotamian source[3] the word passed into Iranian, for we find the Phlv. ideogram ܫܘܩܐ *shōkā* meaning *market*, *public square*, or *forum*, whence comes the Judaeo-Persian סוך.[4] From Syriac it passed also into Arm. as շուկայ in the sense of *market*,[5] and it may have been from Christian Aramaic that the word came into Arabic.

سِيمَا (*Sīmā*).

ii, 274 ; vii, 44, 46 ; xlvii, 32 ; xlviii, 29 ; lv, 41.

Sign, mark, token.

A majority of the Muslim authorities take the word from سام, of which Form II سَوَّمَ means *to mark* or *brand* an animal, and Form V تَسَوَّمَ *to set a mark on*. These, however, are denominative and the

[1] Cooke, *NSI*, 280 ; Cowley, *Aramaic Papyri*, No. 5.

[2] But see Müller, *WZKM*, i, 27.

[3] In Akkadian inscriptions we find *sūqu*—a street ; cf. Zimmern, *Akkad. Fremdw*, 43.

[4] *PPGl*, 214 ; *Frahang*, Glossary, p. 82. It occurs in the Judaeo-Persian version of Jer. xvii, 1 ; see Horn, *Grundriss*, p. 84.

[5] Hübschmann, *ZDMG*, xlvi, 247 ; *Arm. Gramm*, i, 314.

primitive meaning of the root is *to pass along* (Rāghib, *Mufradāt*, 251). Some, however, as we learn from Baiḍ. on vii, 44, ventured to derive it from وسم *to brand.*

The Qur'ānic form is سيماء, but in the literature we find سيمة and سيميا with the same meaning,[1] and they seem all to be derivatives from Gk. *σῆμα*, a *sign, mark*, or *token*, especially one from heaven (Vollers, *ZDMG*, li, 298), i.e. the *σημεῖον* of the N.T. In the Peshitta *σημεῖον* is generally rendered by ܐܬܐ (i.e. Heb. אות ; Aram. אתא), but in the ecclesiastical literature we find a plu. ܣܝܡܝܐ which gives us exactly the form we need,[2] and it may well have been from some colloquial form of this, representing *σῆμα*, that the Arabic سيماء was derived.

سَيْنَاء (*Sainā'*).

xxiii, 20.

Mt. Sinai.

The usual Qur'ānic name for Sinai was طور (ii, 60, 87 ; iv, 153, etc.), and سيناء was quite generally recognized as a foreign borrowing. as-Suyūṭī, *Itq*, 322, says that it was considered to be Nabataean,[3] though some took it to be Syriac or Abyssinian,[4] and others claimed that it was genuine Arabic, a form فيعال from السناء meaning الارتفاع. It is curious that the exegetes were a little uncertain whether سيناء meant the mountain itself or the area in which the mountain was.[5]

[1] *Kāmil*, 14, 17. The *Muḥīṭ* would derive سيميا meaning *magic* from שֵׁם יה, but it is clearly *σημεῖα* through Syr. ܣܝܡܝܐ.

[2] *PSm*, 2613. It occurs also in the Christian-Palestinian dialect, cf. Schulthess, *Lex*, 135.

[3] So *Mutaw*, 59, and *Bagh.* on xxiii, 20, quoting al-Muqātil.

[4] *Bagh.* on xxiii, 20, quoting al-Kalbī and 'Ikrima.

[5] *Vide Bagh*, op. cit.—هو اسم المكان الذى فيه هذا الجبل, which may be a reflection of *ἐν τῷ ἐρήμῳ τοῦ ὄρους Σινᾶ*.

Either the Eth. ሲና [1] or the Christ.-Palast. ܣܝܢܐ representing the Gk. Σινᾶ would give us a nearer equivalence with سيناء than the Heb. סִינַי or the usual Syr. ܣܝܢܝ, but the Christ.-Palast. ܛܘܪ ܣܝܢܝ,[2] which is exactly the Ar. طور سيناء, makes the Syriac origin certain.[3]

The سينين of xcv, 2, is obviously a modification of سيناء for the sake of rhyme,[4] though some of the Muslim authorities want to make it an Abyssinian word (as-Suyūṭī, *Itq*, 322; *Mutaw*, 44), and both Geiger, 155, following d'Herbelot,[5] and Grimme, *ZA*, xxvi, 167, seek to find some independent origin for it.

شِرْك (*Shirk*).

Used very frequently, cf. xxxv, 38; xxxi, 12.

To associate anyone with God: to give God a partner.

In the Qur'ān the word has a technical sense with reference to what is opposed to Muḥammad's conception of monotheism. Thus we find أشرك, to give partners to God, i.e. to be a polytheist, مُشْرِك, one who gives God a partner, i.e. a polytheist, شُرَكاء, those to whom the polytheists render honour as partners with God, terms which, we may note, are not found in the earliest Sūras.

The root شَرِكَ is "to have the shoe strings broken", so شِراك means *sandal straps*, and أشرك is "to put leather thongs in sandals", with which we may compare Heb. שָׂרַךְ *to lay cross wise, to interweave*, Syr. ܣܪܟ to *braid*. From this the words شَرَكٌ a *net* and شَرِكَة a *partner*-

[1] Kunstlinger in *Rocznik Orjentalistyczny*, v (1927), pp. 59 ff., suggests that it is a descriptive adjective and not a proper name.

[2] Cf. the ܛܘܪ ܕܣܝܢܐ in one of the fragments edited by Schulthess, *ZDMG*, lvi, 257.

[3] Note the discussion in Geiger, 155, n., and Horovitz, *KU*, 123 ff.; *JPN*, 159.

[4] So Horovitz, *KU*, 123. He notes also that its vowelling represents the older spelling.

[5] See also Sycz, *Eigennamen*, 57, who, however, wrongly writes سنين for سينين.

ship, i.e. the interweaving of interests, are easily derived. In the technical sense of associating partners with God, however, the word seems to be a borrowing from S. Arabia. In an inscription published by Mordtmann and Müller in *WZKM*, x, 287, there occurs the line— 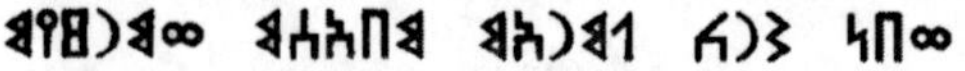 "and avoid giving a partner to a Lord who both bringeth disaster, and is the author of well being". Here 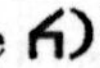 is used in the technical Qur'ānic sense of شرك [1] and there can be little doubt that the word came to Muḥammad, whether directly or indirectly, from some S. Arabian source.

شِعْرَى (*Shi'rā*).

liii, 50.

Sirius.

The Commentators know that it is the Dog Star, which was anciently worshipped among the Banū Khuzā'a (Bagh. and Zam. on the passage, and cf. *LA*, vi, 84).

The common explanation of the philologers is that it is from شعر and means "the hairy one", but there can be little doubt that it is derived from the Gk. Σείριος,[2] whose ρ, as Hess shows, is regularly rendered by Ar. ع. The word occurs in the old poetry [3] and was doubtless known to the Arabs long before Islam.

شَهْرٌ (*Shahr*).

ii, 181, 190, etc.; iv, 94; v, 2, 98; ix, 2, 5, 36; xxxiv, 11; etc.

Month.

[1] The editors of the inscription recognize this, and Margoliouth, *Schweich Lectures*, p. 68, says: "the Qur'ānic technicality *shirk*, the association of other beings with Allah, whose source had previously eluded us, is here traced to its home." Horovitz, *KU*, 60, 61, however, is not so certain and suggests Jewish influence connected with the Rabbinic use of שיתף.

[2] Hess, *ZS*, ii, 221, thinks we have formal proof of the foreign origin of the word in the fact that the Bedouin know only the name مرزم for this star. *LA*, ii, 116, and vi, 84, gives مرزم as a synomym for شعرى, and this word is found again in the Bishari *Mirdim*.

[3] See Hommel, *ZDMG*, xlv, 597, and Horovitz, *KU*, 119.

Besides the sing. we have both plu. forms أَشْهُر and شُهُور in the Qur'ān.

It occurs only in relatively late passages, mostly Madinan, and always in the sense of *month*, never with the earlier meaning *moon*.

The primitive sense of شَهَرَ is *to publish abroad*, and it was known to some of the early philologers that شَهْر meaning *month* was a borrowing, as we learn from as-Suyūṭī, *Itq*, 322, and al-Jawālīqī, *Mu'arrab*, 93. The borrowing was doubtless from Aram., where alone we find any development of the root in this sense. In O.Aram. שהר as the name of the moon-god occurs in the inscriptions of Nerab of the seventh century B.C.,[1] and in the proper name גרמאלשהרי we find it on an inscription from Sinai.[2] In the Targums סיהרא is the *moon*, and like the Syr. ܣܗܪܐ and the Aram. סהרא, is of quite common use. It was from the Aram. that the Eth. ሠሀር was derived, and in all probability the Arabic also, though the S. Arabian 𐩦𐩠𐩧 (Rossini, *Glossarium*, 247) may point to an early development in Arabic itself.

شُهَدَآءُ (*Shuhadā'*).

iv, 71 ; iii, 134 ; xxxix, 69 ; lvii, 18.

Witnesses.

Goldziher in his *Muhammedanische Studien*, ii, 387 ff., pointed out the connection of this with the Syr. ܣܗܕܐ, which in the Peshitta translates μάρτυρ.[3] The word itself is genuine Arabic, but its sense was influenced by the usage of the Christian communities of the time.

شَيْطَان (*Shaiṭān*).

Of frequent occurrence, cf. ii, 34, 271 ; iv, 85, etc.

It occurs (*a*) as a personal name for the Evil One—ὁ Σατανᾶς, cf. ii, 34 ; iv, 42, etc.

[1] Text in Lidzbarski, *Handbuch*, 445.
[2] Lidzbarski, op. cit., 252.
[3] *Vide* Horovitz, *KU*, 50 ; Schwally, *Idioticon*, 60.

(*b*) in the plu. شياطين, for the hosts of evil, cf. ii, 96; vi, 121, etc.

(*c*) metaphorically of evil leaders among men, cf. ii, 13; iii, 169; vi, 112, etc.

(*d*) perhaps sometimes merely for mischievous spirits, cf. vi, 70; xxi, 82; xxiii, 99.

The Muslim authorities were uncertain whether to derive the word from شَطَنَ *to be far from*, or from شاط *to burn with anger* (cf. Rāghib, *Mufradāt*, 261, and *LA*, xvii, 104; *TA*, ix, 253). The form فَيْعَال, however, is rather difficult. It is true, as the philologers state, that we do get forms like حيران *perplexed*, but this is from حار where the ن is no part of the root, and, like the هيمان, غيمان quoted as parallels in *LA*, is really a form فعلان not فيعال, and is a diptote whereas شيطان is a triptote. The real analogy would be with such forms as هيذار *babbler*, هيصار *mangled*, and هيذام *courageous*, quoted by Brockelmann, *Grundriss*, i, 344, but these are all rare adjectival forms and hardly parallel the Qur'ānic شيطان.

Now we learn from the Lexicons that Shaiṭān has the meaning of snake—حيّة له عُرْف (*LA*, xvii, 104, 105), and we find this meaning in the old poets, e.g. in a Rejez poet—

عنجرد تحلف حين احلف   كمثل شيطان الحماط أعرف

"A foul-tongued woman who swears when I swear, like the crested serpent from Al-Ḥamāt,"

and in a verse of Ṭarafa,

تلاعب متنى حضرميّ كانه   تعمّج شيطان بذى خروع قفر

"They (the reins) play on the back of the Ḥadramaut camel, like a snake's writhings in the desert where the Khirwa' grows."

Moreover, we find Shaiṭān used as a personal name in ancient

Arabia.[1] The *Aghānī*, xv, 53, mentions الشيطان بن بكر بن عوف among the ancestors of 'Alqama, and Ibn Duraid mentions a عاهان بن الشيطان (240, l. 4) and a شيطان بن الحارث (243, l. 3).[2] As a tribal name we find a sub-tribe of the Banū Kinda called بنو شيطان in *Aghānī*, xx, 97, and in Yāqūt, *Mu'jam*, iii, 356, we have mention of a branch of the Banū Tamīm of the same name. This use is probably totemistic in origin, for we find several totem clans among the ancient Arabs, such as the بنو حيّة who in the early years of Islam were the ruling caste of the Ṭayyi (*Aghānī*, xvi, 50, l. 7), the بنو افعى (Hamdānī, 91, l. 16), the بنو حنش a sub-tribe of Aus (Ibn Duraid, 260, 2), etc.[3] The serpent was apparently an old Semitic totem,[4] and as a tribal name associated with one of the many branches of the Snake totem. van Vloten and Goldziher take شيطان to be an old Arabic word.[5]

That the Arabs believed serpents to have some connection with supernatural powers, was pointed out by Nöldeke in the *Zeitschrift für Völkerpsychologie*, i, 412 ff., and van Vloten has shown that they were connected with demons and evil,[6] so that the use of the name شيطان for the Evil One could be taken as a development from this. The use of شيطان in the Qur'ān in the sense of mischievous spirits, where it is practically equivalent to Jinn, can be paralleled from the

[1] *Vide* Goldziher, *ZDMG*, xlv, 685, and *Abhandlungen*, i, 106; van Vloten in *Feestbundel aan de Goeje*, 37 ff.; Horovitz, *KU*, 120.

[2] So we find a شيطان بن مدلج of the tribe of Jushām (*TA*, iv, 29) and in *Usd al-Ghāba*, i, 343, we find a man فروة بن الشيطان, while in the Diwan of Tufail (ed. Krenkow, iii, 37), there is mention of a certain Shaitān b. al-Ḥakam.

[3] *Vide* the discussion in Robertson Smith, *Kinship*, 229 ff.

[4] *Vide* Robertson Smith in *Journal of Philology*, ix, 99 ff.; G. B. Gray, *Hebrew Proper Names*, p. 91, and Baudissin, *Studien zur semitischen Religionsgeschichte*, i, pp. 257–292.

[5] Goldziher, *Abhandlungen*, i, 10; van Vloten, *Feestebundel aan de Goeje*, 38 ff. Also Sprenger, *Leben*, ii, 242, n. 2. Wellhausen, however, *Reste*, 157, n., thinks that this has been substituted for some earlier name and is not itself an old Arabic name.

[6] *Vide* his essay "Dämonen, Geister und Zauber bei den alten Arabern" in *WZKM*, vii, particularly pp. 174–8, and see Goldziher, *Abhandlungen*, i, 6 ff.

old poetry, and would fit this early serpent connection, but the theological connotations of Shaiṭān as leader of the hosts of evil, is obviously derived from Muḥammad's Jewish or Christian environments. In the Rabbinic writings שָׂטָן is used in this sense, as are the Gk. Σατᾶν and the Syr. ܣܛܢܐ.[1] From the Syr. come the Arm. սատանայ,[2] and also the Phlv. ideogram שידא (*PPGl*, 209), the Shidān of the Paikuli fragment,[3] iii, 2, but it is from the Eth. ሰይጣን which occurs beside ሰይጣን for ὁ διάβολος, that many scholars have sought to derive the Ar. شيطان.[4] Whether this is so it is now perhaps impossible to determine, but we may take it as certain that the word was in use long before Muḥammad's day,[5] and he in his use of it was undoubtedly influenced by Christian, probably Abyssinian Christian, usage. (Fischer, *Glossar*, 165, thinks that the word is from שטן but influenced by the genuine Arabic شيطان meaning demon.)

شِيعَة (*Shī'a*).

vi, 65, 160 ; xv, 10 ; xix, 70 ; xxviii, 3, 14 ; xxx, 31 ; xxxiv, 54 ; xxxvii, 81 ; liv, 51.

Sect or party.

Both plurals شِيَع and أشياع are used in the Qur'ān.

The verb شاع in the sense of *to be published abroad*, occurs in xxiv, 18, and it is usual for the Muslim authorities to derive شيعة from this (cf. Rāghib, *Mufradāt*, 272). Schwally, *Idioticon*, 61, however, points out that in the meaning of *sect* the word has developed under

[1] סטנא is the form on the incantation bowls, cf. Montgomery, *Aramaic Incantation Texts*, Glossary, 296.

[2] Hubschmann, *Arm. Gramm.*, i, 316.

[3] Herzfeld, *Paikuli*, Glossary, p. 243. Of the same origin is also the Soghdian *s't'nh* (Henning, *Manichäisches Beitbuch*, 1937, p. 142).

[4] Nöldeke, *Neue Beiträge*, 47 ; Pautz, *Offenbarung*, 48 ; Ahrens, *Muhammed*, 92 ; Rudolph, *Abhängigkeit*, 34 ; Margoliouth, *ERE*, x, 540. Praetorius, *ZDMG*, lxi, 619–620, thinks the Eth. is derived from the Arabic, but see Noldeke, op. cit., against him.

[5] Wellhausen, *Reste*, 157, and see Horovitz, *KU*, 121.

Syrian Christian influence, Syr. ܦܠܓܐ being a *faction* as well as *group* (*agmen*, πλῆθος), *PSm*, 2576.

أَلصَّابِئُونَ (*Aṣ-Ṣābi'ūn*).

ii, 59 ; v, 73 ; xxii, 17.[1]

The Ṣābians.

Like the اهل الكتاب and the Magians, they represent a group specially honoured in the Qur'ān as الذين آمنوا, but whom they represent, is still an unsolved puzzle.

The exegetes had no idea what people was meant by الصابؤن, as is evident from the long list of conflicting opinions given by Ṭab. on ii, 59. They also differed as to its derivation, some taking it from صَبَا *to long for* (Shahrastānī, ed. Cureton, 203), and others from صَبَأَ, which they say means *to change one's religion* (Ṭab., loc. cit.).

Bell, *Origin*, 60, 148, is inclined to think that the word is just a play on the name of the Sabaean Christians of S. Arabia. He himself notes the difficulties of this theory, and though it has in its favour the fact that an-Nasafī on xxii, 17, calls the Ṣābians نوع من النصارى, the fact that Muḥammad himself was called a Ṣābī by his contemporaries,[2] seems to show that the word was used technically in his milieu, and is not a mere confusion with Sabaean. Grimme, *Mohammed*, 1904, p. 49, also looked to S. Arabia for the origin of the word, which he would relate to Eth. ጸበሐ, whose secondary meaning is *tributum pendere*, and which he would interpret as "Almosen spendend". This, however, is somewhat far-fetched.[3]

Wellhausen's theory *Reste*, 237, was that it was from Aram. צבא =צבע, and given to the sect or sects because of their baptismal

[1] Sprenger, *Leben*, ii, 184, thinks we should read صابيا in xix, 13, referring to John the Baptist.

[2] Bukhārī (ed. Krehl), i, 96, 97 ; ii, 387, 388 ; Ibn Hishām, 229 ; and the verse of Sarāqa in *Aghānī*, xv, 138.

[3] *Vide* Rudolph, *Abhängigkeit*, 74, n.

practices.[1] We find this צבא *to baptize* in Mandaean (Nöldeke, *Mand. Gramm*, 235), and as Brandt points out,[2] we find the root in the sect names Μασβωθαῖοι and Σεβουαῖοι. If, as Pedersen holds,[3] the Ṣābians are Gnostics, this derivation is probably as near as we are likely to attain.

صِبْغَة (*Ṣibgha*).

ii, 132.

Baptism.

The passage is Madinan and is a polemic against the Jews and Christians, so that صبغة would seem to be a reference to Christian baptism.[4]

صَبَغَ is probably *to dye*, and صِبْغ *dye, tincture* (cf. Syr. ܨܶܒܳܥܳܐ), occurs in xxiii, 20, meaning *juice*. It is possible that صبغ in all its meanings is a borrowed word, though in this case the غ would show that it must have been very early naturalized. In any case it is clear that the meaning *baptism* is due to Christian influence.

From ܨܒܥ = Aram. צבע *to dip*, it was an easy transition to *to baptize*, and particularly in the Christian-Palestinian dialect we get ܐܨܒܥ *to baptize*, ܐܨܛܒܥ *to be baptized*, ܡܨܒܥܘܬܐ *baptism*, ܡܨܒܥܢܐ *baptist* (Schulthess, *Lex*, 166; *PSm*, 3358). The Christian reference of صبغة is clear from Zam. on the passage, and the influence was probably Syriac.

صُحُف (*Ṣuḥuf*).

xx, 133; liii, 37; lxxiv, 52; lxxx, 13; lxxxi, 10; lxxxvii, 18, 19; xcviii, 2.

[1] Rudolph, op. cit., pp. 68, 69. Pautz, *Offenbarung*, 148, n., with less likelihood suggests the Syr. ܨܒܥ become ܨܒ̈ܥܝ.

[2] *Die jüdischen Baptismen*, 112 ff. See also Horovitz, *KU*, 121, 122.

[3] Browne, *Festschrift*, p. 383 ff. Torrey, *Foundation*, 3, assumes that the Ṣābi'ans were the Mandaeans, but this is questionable. Cf. Ahrens, *Muhammed*, 10.

[4] So Rudolph, *Abhängigkeit*, 75, and Lane, *Lex*, sub voc., though Ullmann, *Koran*, 14, would take it to refer to circumcision.

Plu. of صحيفة—a page of writing.

It is one of the technical terms connected with Muḥammad's conception of heavenly Books. All the passages save xcviii, 2, are early, and some of them very early.

Horovitz, *KU*, 69, is doubtless right in thinking that Muḥammad used it as a general term for such sacred writings as were known at least by hearsay to the Arabs, and as such it could be applied later to his own revelations. The word occurs not infrequently in the old poetry in the sense of pages of writing, e.g. in 'Antara, xxvii, 2 (Ahlwardt, *Divans*, p. 52)—

كوحى صحائف من عهد كسرى   فاهداها لاعجم طمطمى

" Like a message on pages from the time of Chrosroes, which I sent to a tongue-tied foreigner,"

or the verses in *Aghānī*, xx, 24—

كتاب فى الصحيفة من لقيط   الى من بالجزيرة من إياد

" A page of writing from Laqīṭ to whatever Iyādites are in al-Jazīrah." [1]

The philologers have no adequate explanation of the word from Arabic material, for صَحَّفَ is obviously denominative.[2] It is in S. Arabia that we find the origin of the word. Grimme, *ZA*, xxvi, 161, quotes 𐩮𐩢𐩰𐩩 with its plu. 𐩮𐩢𐩰 from the S. Arabian inscriptions,[3] and in Eth. ጸሐፈ *to write* is in very common use,[4] while መጽሐፍ meaning both *scriptura* and *liber* is clearly the source of the Ar. مصحف so commonly used in later times for the Qur'ān.[5] The use of the word in the early literature shows that it was a word already borrowed

[1] Also Mutalammis (ed. Vollers, *Beitr. Ass.*, v, 171), and further references by Goldziher in *ZDMG*, xlvi, 19. Nöldeke-Schwally, i, 11, notes that in the poetry it never means a collection of writings in a book, as Muhammad uses it.

[2] Fraenkel, *Fremdw*, 248.

[3] Glaser, 424, 8, 11; Halévy, 199, 8; and cf. Rossini, *Glossarium*, 223.

[4] Dillmann, *Lex*, 1266 ff. Pautz, *Offenbarung*, 123, n., is inclined to derive the Qur'ānic word from Ethiopic.

[5] Grohmann, *WZKM*, xxxii, 244. This was also in use in pre-Islamic Arabia as Andrae, *Ursprung*, 36, notes, and was borrowed by the Jews, cf. מצחף תורה (Nöldeke, *Neue Beiträge*, 50, n.). *Itqān*, 120, makes it clear that مصحف was recognized as Abyssinian in origin.

from S. Arabia in pre-Islamic times [1] and thus ready to Muḥammad's hand for his technical use of it in connection with sacred writings.

صَدَقَةٌ (*Ṣadaqa*).

ii, 192, 265, 266, 273, 277; iv, 114; ix, 58, 60, 80, 104, 105; lviii, 13, 14.

Alms, tithes.

The denominative verb تَصَدَّقَ *to give alms*, occurs in ii, 280; v, 49; xii, 88; أَصَّدَّقَ in iv, 94; ix, 76; lxiii, 10, and the participles مُصَدِّقٌ and مُتَصَدِّقٌ are used several times, e.g. ii, 38, 85; xxxiii, 35. These passages are all late, and the word is used only as a technical religious term, just like Heb. צדקה, Phon. צדק, Syr. ܙܕܩܬܐ. The Muslim authorities derive the word from صدق *to be sincere*, and say that *alms* are so called because they prove the sincerity of one's faith. The connection of the root with צדק is sound enough, but as a technical word for alms there can be no doubt that it came from a Jewish or Christian source. Hirschfeld, *Beiträge*, 89, argues for a Jewish origin,[2] which is very possible. The Syr. ܙܕܩܬܐ with ܙ for צ would seem fatal to a derivation from a Christian source, but in the Christian-Palestinian dialect we find ܨܕܩܬܐ translating ἐλεημοσύνη in common use in several forms,[3] which makes it at least possible that the source of the Arabic word is to be found there.

صِدِّيقٌ (*Ṣiddīq*).

iv, 71; xii, 46; xix, 42, 57; lvii, 18; and صِدِّيقَةٌ v, 79.

A person of integrity.

Obviously it may be taken as a genuine Arabic formation from صدق on the measure فِعِّيل, though this form is not very common.

[1] Fraenkel, in *Beitr. Ass.*, iii, 69; Nöldeke, *Neue Beiträge*, 50; Cheikho, *Naṣrāniya*, 181, 222; Horovitz, *KU*, 69; Zimmern, *Akkad. Fremdw*, 19.

[2] So Fraenkel, *Vocab*, 20; Sprenger, *Leben*, ii, 195 n.; Rudolph, *Abhängigkeit*, 61; Ahrens, *Muhammed*, 180; von Kremer, *Streifzüge*, p. ix.

[3] Schulthess, *Lex*, 167; Schwally, *Idioticon*, 79; and cf. Horovitz, *JPN*, 212.

As used in the Qur'ān, however, it seems to have a technical sense, being used in the sing. only of Biblical characters, and in the plu. as "the righteous", and for this reason it has been thought that we can detect the influence of the Heb.-Aram. צדיק. Thus Fleischer, *Kleinere Schriften*, ii, 594, says: "Das Wort ist dem heb.-aram. צדיק entlehnt, mit Verwandlung des Vocals der ersten Silbe in *i* nach dem bekannten reinarabischen اتباع."

In the O.T. צדיק means *just, righteous*, and is generally rendered by δίκαιος in the LXX. In the Rabbinic צדיקא the sense of piety becomes even more prominent and it is used in a technical sense for *the pious*, as in *Succa*, 45, b. It is precisely in this sense that Joseph, Abraham, and Idrīs are called صديق, and the Virgin Mary صديقة in the Qur'ān, and there can be little doubt that both the Arabic صديق and the Eth. ጻድቅ are of this Aram. origin.[1]

صِرَاطٌ (*Ṣirāṭ*).

Occurs some forty-five times, e.g. i, 5, 6; ii, 136, 209, etc.

A Way.

The word is used only in a religious sense, usually with the adj. مستقيم, and though frequently used by Muḥammad to indicate his own preaching, it is also used of the teaching of Moses (xxxvii, 118) and Jesus (iii, 44), and sometimes means the religious way of life in general (cf. vii, 15).

The early Muslim authorities knew not what to make of the word. They were not sure whether it was to be spelled صراط, سراط, or زراط,[2] and they were equally uncertain as to its gender, al-Akhfash

[1] Cf. Horovitz, *KU*, 49; Vacca, *EI*, iv, 402; Ahrens, *Christliches*, 19; Grimme, *ZA*, xxvi, 162, thought it was of S. Arabian origin, and this may be supported by the occurrence of ዕᎺ¶ = Ṣiddīq (?) as a proper name in the inscription, Glaser, 265 (= *CIS*, iv, No. 287), though the vocalization here may be Ṣādiq (Rossini, *Glossarium*, 222; cf. Ryckmans, *Noms propres*, i, 182, 269). The Phon. name Συδυκ may also represent צדיק (Harris, *Glossary*, 141).

[2] *Vide* Bagh. on i, 6, and Jawharī, sub voc.

propounding a theory that in the dialect of Ḥijāz it was fem. and in the dialect of Tamīm masc. Many of the early philologers recognized it as a foreign word, as we learn from as-Suyūṭī, *Itq*, 322; *Muzhir*, i, 130; *Mutaw*, 50. They said it was Greek, and are right in so far as it was from the Hellenized form of the Lat. *strata* that the word passed into Aram. and thence into Arabic.

The word was doubtless first introduced by the Roman administration into Syria and the surrounding territory, so that *strata* became *στράτα* (cf. Procopius, ii, 1), and thence Aram. אסטרטיא; איסרטיא; אסרטא; סרטיא[1]; Syr. ܐܣܛܪܛܐ.[2] From Aram. it was an early borrowing into Arabic, being found in the early poetry.[3]

صَرْحٌ (*Ṣarḥ*).

xxvii, 44; xxviii, 38; xl, 38.

Tower.

The Lexicographers were not very sure of its meaning. They generally take it to mean a *palace* or some magnificent building (Jawharī), or the name of a castle (*TA*, ii, 179), while some say it means *glass tiles*—بلاط من قوارير. All these explanations, however, seem to be drawn from the Qur'ānic material, and they do not explain how the word can be derived from صرح.

Nöldeke, *Neue Beiträge*, 51, pointed out that in all probability the word is from Eth. ጽርሕ *a room*, sometimes used for *templum*, sometimes for *palatium*, but as Dillmann, *Lex*, 1273, notes, always for *aedes altiores conspicuae*. This is a much likelier origin than the Aram. צריח, which, though in the Targum to Jud. ix, 49, it means *citadel* or *fortified place*, usually means a deep cavity in a rock, and is the equivalent of Ar. ضريح not of صرح.[4] It is doubtful if the word

[1] Cf. Krauss, *Griechische und lateinische Lehnwörter im Talmud*, ii, 82, 413. A parallel formation is סרדיוט (= סטרטיוט) = *στρατιώτης*.

[2] Of particular interest is the fact that in an eschatological sense it passed from Aramaic into Pahlavi as סלמן *srāt*. Cf. Bailey in *JRAS*, 1934, p. 505.

[3] Fraenkel, *Vocab*, 25; von Kremer, *Ideen*, 226, n.; Dvořák, *Fremdw*, 26, 31, 76; Vollers, *ZDMG*, l, 614; li, 314.

[4] Hoffmann, *ZA*, xi, 322. What Fraenkel, *Fremdw*, 237, means by צרחת I know not.

occurs in the genuine old poetry, but it is found in the S. Arabian inscriptions, where 𐩧𐩱𐩥𐩢, 𐩧𐩱𐩥𐩢 = aedificium elatum (Rossini, *Glossarium*, 225).

صَلَبَ (*Ṣalaba*).

iv, 156 ; v, 37 ; vii, 121 ; xii, 41 ; xx, 74 ; xxvi, 49.

To crucify.

The passages are all relatively late. Once it refers to the crucifixion of our Lord (iv, 156), once to the crucifixion of Joseph's prison companion (xii, 41), and in all the other passages to a form of punishment which Muḥammad seems to have considered was a favourite pastime of Pharaoh, but which in v, 37, he holds out as a threat against those who reject his mission.

The word cannot be explained from Arabic, as the verb is denominative from صليب. This صليب occurs in the old poetry, e.g. an-Nābigha, ii, 10 (Ahlwardt, *Divans*, p. 4), and 'Adī b. Zaid (*Aghānī*, ii, 24), etc., and is doubtless derived from Aram. צליבא; Syr. ܙܩܝܦܐ, as Fraenkel, *Fremdw*, 276, claims. The word is not original in Aram., however, and perhaps came originally from some Iranian source from a root represented by the Pers. چليپا (Vollers, *ZDMG*, l, 614). Mingana, *Syriac Influence*, 86, claims that it was from Syr. rather than from Jewish Aram. that the word came to Arabic, and as the Eth. ተሰቀለ seems to be of this origin,[1] it may be so.[2]

صَلَوَاتٌ (*Ṣalawāt*).

xxii, 41.

Places of worship.

Though the Commentators are not unanimous as to its meaning they are in general agreed that it means the synagogue of the Jews, and as such many of them admit that it is a borrowing from Heb. (Baiḍ. and Zam. on the passage[3]: al-Jawālīqī, *Mu'arrab*, 95; as-Suyūṭī,

[1] The form ሰቀለ is later and derived from the Arabic (Nöldeke, *Neue Beiträge*, 35).

[2] So Ahrens, *Christliches*, 40.

[3] That it was a borrowing is evident from the large crop of variant readings of the word noted by al-'Ukbarī, *Imlā'*, ii, 89.

Itq, 322; al-Khafājī, 123; as-Sijistānī, 201). This idea that it is Hebrew is derived, of course, from the notion that the word means synagogues. It could be from the Aram. צלותא which means *prayer*, but the theory of Ibn Jinnī in his *Muḥtasab*, quoted by as-Suyūṭī, *Mutaw*, 55, that it is Syriac, is much more likely,[1] for though ܨܠܘܬܐ means *prayer*, the commonly used ܒܝܬ ܨܠܘܬܐ means a place of prayer, i.e. προσευχή, which Rudolph, *Abhängigkeit*, 7, n.,[2] would take as the reference in the Qur'ānic passage. As we find 𐩮𐩡𐩥𐩩 = *chapel* in a S. Arabian inscription,[3] however, it is possible that the word first passed into S. Arabian and thence into the northern language.

صَلَّى (*Ṣallā*).

Of very frequent occurrence.

To pray.

Besides the verb we find in the Qur'ān صَلَوٰة *prayer*, مُصَلٍّ *one who prays*, and مُصَلًّى *place of prayer*. صَلَّى, however, is denominative from صَلَوٰة, as Sprenger, *Leben*, iii, 527, n. 2, had noted,[4] and صَلَوٰة itself seems to have been borrowed from an Aramaic source (Nöldeke, *Qorans*, 255, 281).

The origin, of course, is from צלותא = ܨܠܘܬܐ, as has been generally recognized,[5] for the Eth. ጸሎት is from the same source (Nöldeke, *Neue Beiträge*, 36). It may have been from Jewish Aramaic but more probably from Syr.,[6] for the common phrase اقام الصلاة, as Wensinck, *Joden*, 105, notes, is good Syriac. It was an early borrowing (Horovitz, *JPN*, 185), used in the early poets and thus quite familiar

[1] Fraenkel, *Vocab*, 21; Dvořák, *Fremdw*, 31; Schwally, *Idioticon*, 80, 125.

[2] See also Pautz, *Offenbarung*, 149.

[3] Hommel, *Südarab. Chrest.*, 125; Rossini, *Glossarium*, 224.

[4] The primary meaning of صلى is *to roast*, cf. Heb. צלה; Eth. ጸለወ. al-Khafājī, 124, seems to feel that صلى is a borrowed form.

[5] Fraenkel, *Vocab*, 21; Wensinck, *EI*, Art. "*Ṣalat*"; Bell, *Origin*, 51, 91, 142; Pautz, *Offenbarung*, 149; Rudolph, *Abhängigkeit*, 56; Grünbaum, *ZDMG*, xl, 275; Mittwoch, *Entstehungsgeschichte des islamischen Gebets*, pp. 6, 7 ff.; Zimmern, *Akkad. Fremdw*, 65; Ahrens, *Muhammed*, 117.

[6] Mingana, *Syriac Influence*, 86; Schwally, *Idioticon*, 80, 125.

in pre-Islamic days,[1] and the substantive 𐩭𐩬𐩯 *preces* is found in the S. Arabian inscriptions (Rossini, *Glossarium*, 224).

صَنَمٌ (*Ṣanam*).

vi, 74 ; vii, 134 ; xiv, 38 ; xxi, 58 ; xxvi, 71.

An idol.

Found only in the plu. أَصنام, and only in relatively late passages. It is curious that it occurs only in connection with the Abraham legend, save in one passage (vii, 134), where it refers to the Canaanites.

As we find 𐩮𐩬𐩣 in the S. Arabian inscriptions,[2] D. H. Müller, *WZKM*, i, 30, would regard صنم as a genuine Arabic word. It has, however, no explanation from Arabic material, and the philologers are driven to derive it from شمن meaning وثن (*LA*, xv, 241 ; al-Khafājī, 124).

It was doubtless an early borrowing from Aramaic. The root צלם appears to be common Semitic,[3] cf. Akk. *ṣalmu* [4] and Ar. صَلَمَ *to cut off*, so Heb. צלם ; Phon. צלם ; Aram. צלמא ; Syr. ܨܠܡܐ, an *image*, would doubtless mean something *cut out* of wood or stone. צלמא and צלמתא occur not infrequently in the Nabataean inscriptions (*RES*, ii, 467, 477 ; Cook, *Glossary*, 101),[5] and it was from some such Aram. form that the word came into use in N. Arabia,[6] giving us the צנמת we find in a Safaite inscription,[7] the صنم of the early Arabic poetry and of the Qur'ān, and perhaps a Nabataean צנם in an inscription from Madā'in Ṣāliḥ.[8]

[1] Nöldeke, *Neue Beiträge*, 29, and cf. Geyer, *Zwei Gedichte*, i, 203 = *Dīwān*, iv, 11.
[2] *CIS*, iv, No. ii, l. 4, and see Gildemeister, *ZDMG*, xxiv, 180 ; *RES*, ii, 485.
[3] But see Nöldeke, *ZDMG*, xl, 733.
[4] Zimmern, *Akkad. Fremdw*, 8.
[5] So the S. Arabian 𐩮𐩬𐩣 (Rossini, *Glossarium*, 224 ; *RES*, ii, 485).
[6] Fraenkel, *Fremdw*, 273 ; Pautz, *Offenbarung*, 175, n. 2 ; Robertson Smith, *Kinship*, 300.
[7] Halévy, in *JA*, viie série, xvii, 222.
[8] *RES*, ii, No. 1128.

صُوَاعٌ (*Ṣuwā'*).

xii, 72.

A drinking cup.

It occurs only in the Joseph story for the king's drinking cup which was put in Benjamin's sack.

The word was a puzzle to the exegetes and we find a fine crop of variant readings—صاع, صوع, صاغ, صوغ, or صَوَاع, besides the accepted صُوَاع. Either صاع or صوع would make it mean a measure for grain, and صاغ or صوغ would probably mean something fashioned or moulded, e.g. a gold ornament.

The Muslim authorities take the word as Arabic, but Nöldeke has shown that it is the Eth. ጽዋዕ, which is actually the word used of Pharaoh's cup in the Joseph story of Gen. xl [1] in the Ethiopic Bible.

صَوَامِعُ (*Ṣawāmi'*).

xxii, 41.

Plu. of صَوْمَعَةٌ a cloister.

The Commentators differ among themselves as to whether it stands for a Jewish, a Christian, or a Ṣābian place of worship. They agree, however, in deriving it from صمع (cf. Ibn Duraid, 166), and Fraenkel agrees,[2] thinking that originally it must have meant a high tapering building.[3] The difficulty of deriving it from صمع, however, is obvious, and al-Khafājī, 123, lists it as a borrowed word.

Its origin is apparently to be sought in S. Arabia, from the word that is behind the Eth. ጸማዕት a *hermit's cell* (Nöldeke, *Beiträge*,

[1] *Neue Beiträge*, 55.

[2] *Fremdw*, 269.

[3] It certainly has the meaning of *minaret* in such passages as *Aghānī*, xx, 85; *Amālī*, ii, 79; Jaḥīz, *Maḥāsīn*, 161, and Dozy, *Supplément*, i, 845. So the Judaeo-Tunisian צמעה means *campanile* (Nöldeke, *Neue Beiträge*, 52). Lammens, *ROC*, ix (1904), pp. 35, 3?, suggests that originally صومعة meant the *pillar* of a Stylite ascetic.

52),[1] though we have as yet no S. Arabian word with which to compare it.

صُورَةٌ (*Ṣūra*).

xl, 66 ; lxiv, 3 ; lxxxii, 8.

Form, picture.

We also find the denominative verb صَوَّرَ in iii, 4 ; vii, 10 ; xl, 66 ; lxiv, 3.

That the philologers had some difficulty with the word is evident from the Lexicons, cf. *LA*, vi, 143, 144. The word has no root in Arabic, for it does not seem possible to explain it from a √صور which means *to incline a thing towards* (cf. Heb. סור *to turn aside*, and the *sūru, to rebel* of the Amarna tablets).

Fraenkel, *Fremdw*, 272, suggests, therefore, that it is derived from the Syr. ܨܘܪܬܐ *form, image, figure*, from a root ܨܘܪ to *describe, picture, form* (cf. Heb. צור *to delineate*). In Aram. also צורא and צורתא mean *picture, form*, and in the S. Arabian inscriptions we find 𐩮𐩥𐩧 not infrequently with the meaning of *image*.[2] It is very probable that it was from S. Arabia that the word came into use in the North,[3] and doubtless at an early period, as it occurs in the early poetry.

صَوْمٌ (*Ṣaum*) and صِيَامٌ (*Ṣiyām*).

ii, 179, 183, 192 ; iv, 94 ; v, 91, 96 ; xix, 27 ; lviii, 5.

Fasting.

The verb occurs in ii, 180, 181, and the participle in xxxiii, 35, صام being obviously denominative from صوم.

It will be noticed that the passages are all late, and that the word is a technical religious term, which was doubtless borrowed from some outside source. That there were Jewish influences on the Qur'ānic

[1] Rudolph, *Abhängigkeit*, 7 n.

[2] *Vide* Hommel, *Chrestomath*, 125 ; Mordtmann, *Himyar. Insch.*, 14, 15 ; Rossini, *Glossarium*, 223.

[3] So Zimmern, *Akkad. Fremdw*, 27.

teaching about fasting has been pointed out by Wensinck, *Joden*, 120 ff.,[1] while Sprenger, *Leben*, iii, 55 ff., has emphasized the Christian influence thereon. In Nöldeke-Schwally, i, 179–180, attention is drawn to the similarity of the Qur'ānic teaching with fasting as practised among the Manichaeans, and Margoliouth, *Early Development*, 149, thinks its origin is to be sought in some system other than the Jewish or Christian, though doubtless influenced by both, so it is not easy to determine the origin of the word till we have ascertained the origin of the custom.

Fraenkel, *Vocab*, 20, would derive it from the Heb. צוֹם,[2] but it is more likely to have come from Aram. צוֹם, Syr. ܨܘܡܐ, which is also the source of the Eth. ጾም (Nöldeke, *Neue Beiträge*, 36), and the Arm. ծոմ.[3] The Syr. form is the nearer phonologically to the Arabic and may thus be the immediate source, as Mingana, *Syriac Influence*, 86, urges. The word would seem to have been in use in Arabia before Muḥammad's day,[4] but whether fasting was known in other Arab communities than those of the Jews and Christians is uncertain.[5]

طَاغُوت (*Ṭāghūt*).

ii, 257, 259 ; iv, 54, 63, 78 ; v, 65 ; xvi, 38 ; xxxix, 19.

Idolatry.

This curious word is used by Muḥammad to indicate an alternative to the worship of Allah, as Rāghib, *Mufradāt*, 307, recognizes. Men are warned to "serve Allah and avoid Ṭāghūt" (xvi, 38 ; xxxix, 19) ; those who disbelieve are said to fight in the way of Ṭāghūt and have Ṭāghūt as their patron (iv, 78 ; ii, 259) ; some seek oracles from Ṭāghūt (iv, 63), and the People of the Book are reproached because some of them, though they have a Revelation, yet believe in Ṭāghūt (iv, 54 ; v, 65).

It is thus clearly a technical religious term, but the Commentators know nothing certain about it. From Ṭab. and Bagh. on ii, 257, we

[1] Cf. Schwally, *Idioticon*, 74.

[2] Grünbaum, *ZDMG*, xl, 275, is uncertain whether from Heb. or Aram.; cf. also Pautz, *Offenbarung*, 150, n. 3.

[3] Hübschmann, *Arm. Gramm*, i, 306.

[4] Cheikho, *Naṣrāniya*, 179.

[5] Schwally, *Idioticon*, 74 n.: "Naturlich mussen auch die heidnischen Araber das Fasten als religiöse Übung gehabt haben, aber das vom Islam eingeführte Fasten empfanden sie als ein Novum."

learn that some thought it meant الشيطان, others الساحر or الكاهن, others أوثان or أصنام, and some thought it a name for al-Lāt and al-'Uzzā. The general opinion, however, is that it is a genuine Arabic word, a form فعلوت from طغى *to go beyond the limit* (*LA*, xix, 232; *TA*, x, 225, and Rāghib, op. cit.). This is plausible, but hardly satisfactory, and we learn from as-Suyūṭī, *Itq*, 322; *Mutaw*, 37, that some of the early authorities recognized it as a loan-word from Abyssinian.

Geiger, 56, sought its origin in the Rabbinic טעות *error* which is sometimes used for idols, as in the Jerusalem Talmud, *Sanh*, x, 28[d], אוי לכם ולטעותכם "woe to you and to your idols", and whose cognate טעותא is frequently used in the Targums for *idolatry*,[1] a meaning easily developed from the primary verbal meaning of טעא *to go astray* (cf. Heb. טעה; Syr. ܛܥܐ; Ar. طغى).

Geiger has had many followers in this theory of a Jewish origin for Ṭāghūt,[2] but others have thought a Christian origin more probable. Schwally, *Idioticon*, 38, points out that whereas in Edessene Syriac the common form is ܛܥܝܘܬܐ meaning *error*, yet in the Christian-Palestinian dialect we find the form ܛܥܘܬܐ,[3] which gives quite as close an equivalent as the Targumic טעותא. The closest parallel, however, is the Eth. ጣዖት from an unused verbal root ጠዐወ (the equivalent of טעה, طغى), which primitively means defection from the true religion, and then is used to name any superstitious beliefs, and also is a common word for idols, translating the εἴδωλα of both the LXX and N.T. It is probable, as Nöldeke, *Neue Beiträge*, 35, notes, that this word itself is ultimately derived from Aramaic, but we can be reasonably certain that as-Suyūṭī's authorities were right in giving the Arabic word an Abyssinian origin.[4]

[1] Geiger, 203, and see examples in Levy, *TW*, i, 312.

[2] Von Kremer, *Ideen*, 226, n.; Fraenkel, *Vocab*, 23; Pautz, *Offenbarung*, 175; Eickmann, *Angelologie*, 48; Margoliouth, *ERE*, vi, 249; Hirschfeld, *Judische Elemente*, 65.

[3] Schulthess, *Lex*, 76. Mingana, *Syriac Influence*, 85, also holds to a Syr. origin for the word.

[4] Nöldeke, op. cit., 48. It should be noted, however, that in the incantation texts טעותא means *false deity*, which is very close to the Qur'ānic usage. Cf. Montgomery, *Aramaic Incantation Texts*, p. 290.

طَالُوتُ (*Ṭālūt*).

ii, 248, 250.

Saul.

Some of the early authorities know that it was a foreign word. Baiḍ. tells us that it is اسم عبرى, and al-Jawālīqī, *Mu'arrab*, 103; al-Khafājī, 128, give it as non-Arabic.

The Heb. word is שאול,[1] and none of the Christian forms derived therefrom give us any parallel to طالوت. The philologers derive his name from طال to be tall, evidently influenced by the Biblical story, as we see from Bagh. on ii, 248. Geiger, 182, suggested that طالوت was a rhyming formation from طال to parallel جالوت. The word is not known earlier than the Qur'ān,[2] and would seem to be a formation of Muḥammad himself from שאול, a name which he may not have heard or remembered correctly, and formed probably under the influence of طال to rhyme with جالوت.[3]

طَبَعَ (*Ṭaba'a*).

iv, 154; vii, 98, 99; ix, 88, 94; x, 75; xvi, 110; xxx, 59; xl, 37; xlvii, 18; lxiii, 3.

To seal.

Only found in late Meccan and Madinan passages, and always in the technical religious sense of God "sealing up the hearts" of unbelievers.

The primitive meaning of the Semitic root seems to be *to sink in*, cf. Akk. *ṭēbū*, *to sink in*, *ṭabbī'u*, *diver*; Heb. טבע; Aram. טְבַע; Syr. ܛܒܰܥ, *to sink*; Eth. ጠምቀ, *to dip, to immerse*.[4] From this came

[1] This was known to the Commentators, e.g. ath-Tha'labī, *Qiṣaṣ*, 185, says that his name in Heb. is شاول بن قيس, which is a very fair representation of שאול בן קיש.

[2] The occurrence in Samau'al is obviously not genuine; cf. Nöldeke, *ZA*, xxvii, 178.

[3] Horovitz, *KU*, 123; *JPN*, 163.

[4] Maybe the Ar. طَبَع *rust* represents this primitive sense.

the more technical use for a die, e.g. Phon. טבע *coin* [1]; Akk. *ṭimbu'u, signet-ring* ; Heb. טַבַּעַת *signet* ; Syr. ܛܒܥܐ *seal* (*σφραγίς*) and *coin* (*νόμισμα*).

Fraenkel, *Fremdw*, 193, pointed out that in this sense of sealing the Arabic verb is denominative from طابع which is derived from the Syr. ܛܒܥܐ.[2] We actually find ܛܒܥ used in the sense of *obstupefecit* in Eph. Syr., ed. Overbeck, 95, l. 26—ܗܘܐ ܗܠܝܢ ܕܒܝܫ ܬܚܘܡܐ ܛܒܥܬܐ ܕܗܘܢܐ, and טבע occurs in the incantation texts (Montgomery, *Aramaic Incantation Texts*, Glossary, p. 105).

طَبَق (*Ṭabaq*).

lxvii, 3 ; lxxi, 14 ; lxxxiv, 19.

Stage or degree.

The form طِبَاق used in lxvii, 3; lxxi, 14, is really the plu. of طَبَقَة.

It is used only of the stages of the heavens, both in a physical and a spiritual sense, and for this reason, Zimmern, *Akkad. Fremdw*, 46, derives it directly from Mesopotamia, the Akk. *tubuqtu*, plu. *tubuqāti*, meaning *Welträume* (*wohl in 7 Stufen übereinander gedacht*).

طَهَرَ (*Ṭahara*).

Occurs very frequently, e.g. iii, 37 ; v, 45.

To make clean or pure.

The root itself is genuine Arabic, and may be compared with Aram. טְהַר *to be clean* ; טיהרא, Syr. ܛܗܪܐ *brightness* ; Heb. טָהַר *to be clean, pure* ; the S. Arabian 𐩷𐩠𐩧 in Hal, 682 (Rossini, *Glossarium*, 159), and the Ras Shamra טהר.

In its technical sense of " to make religiously pure ", however, there can be little doubt that it, like the Eth. አጥሀረ and ተጠሀረ (Nöldeke, *Neue Beiträge*, 36), has been influenced by Jewish usage. It will be remembered that טהר is used frequently in Leviticus

[1] In Tyrian circles as early as the third century B.C. Cf. Harris, *Glossary*, 105.

[2] As Fraenkel notes, the un-Arabic form طابع is itself sufficient evidence that it is a borrowed form.

for ceremonial cleanness, and particularly in Ezekiel for moral cleanliness. Similar is its use in the Rabbinic writings, and in late passages Muḥammad's use of the word is sometimes strikingly parallel to Rabbinic usage.

طُوبَى (*Ṭūbā*).

xiii, 28.

Good fortune, happiness.

The favourite theory among the philologers was that it came from طيب (Rāghib, *Mufradāt*, 312), though not all of them were happy with this solution as we see from Ṭab. on the passage, and both as-Suyūṭī, *Itq*, 322, and al-Jawālīqī, *Mu'arrab*, 103, quote authority for its being a foreign word.[1]

It is obviously the Syr. ܛܘܒܐ = *μακάριος* or *μακαρισμός*, as Fraenkel, *Vocab*, 24, saw,[2] which, of course, is connected with the common Semitic root טוב, which appears in Arabic as طيب [3] and S. Arabian as 𐩷𐩥𐩨.

طُورٌ (*Ṭūr*).

ii, 60, 87; iv, 153; xix, 53; xx, 82; xxiii, 20; xxviii, 29, 46; lii, 1; xcv, 2.

Mt. Sinai.

Twice it is expressly coupled with سيناء, and except in lii, 1, where it might mean *mountain* in general, it is used only in connection with the experiences of the Israelites at Sinai.[4]

It was early recognized by the philologers as a foreign word. al-Jawālīqī, *Mu'arrab*, 100; Ibn Qutaiba, *Adab al-Kātib*, 527; as-Suyūṭī, *Muzhir*, i, 130; and Baiḍ. on lii, 1, give it as a Syriac word, though others,

[1] They were uncertain, however, whether to regard it as Abyssinian or Indian—*Mutaw*, 39, 51.

[2] So Mingana, *Syriac Influence*, 86; Dvořák, *Fremdw*, 18.

[3] Lagarde, *Übersicht*, 26, 69.

[4] See Kunstlinger, "Ṭūr und Ğabal im Ḳurān," in *Rocznik Orjentalistyczny*, v (1927), pp. 58–67.

as we learn from as-Suyūṭī, *Itq*, 322, thought that it was a Nabataean word.

Heb. צור = πέτρα, from meaning a single rock or boulder, comes to have the sense of *cliff*, and Aram. טורא is a *mountain*. So in the Targums טורא דסיני is Mt. Sinai,[1] but the طور سينا of the Qur'ān is obviously the Syr. ܛܘܪ ܣܝܢܝ which occurs beside ܛܘܪܐ ܕܣܝܢܝ.[2]

طُوفَان (*Ṭūfān*).

vii, 130 ; xxix, 13.

The Deluge.

The Commentators did not know what to make of it. Ṭab. tells us that some took it to mean *water*, others *death*, others a *torrent of rain*, others a *great storm*,[3] and so on, and from Zam. we learn that yet others thought it meant *smallpox*, or the *rinderpest* or a *plague of boils*.

Fraenkel, *Vocab*, 22, recognized that it was the Rabbinic טופנא which is used, e.g., by Onkelos in Gen. vii, and which occurs in the Talmud in connection with Noah's story (*Sanh.* 96a). Fraenkel's theory has been generally accepted,[4] but we find טופאניא in Mandaean meaning *deluge* in general (Nöldeke, *Mand. Gramm.*, 22, 136, 309),[5] and Syr. ܛܘܦܢܐ is used of Noah's flood in Gen. vi, 17, and translates κατακλυσμός in the N.T., so that Mingana, *Syriac Influence*, 86, would derive the Arabic word from a Christian source.

The flood story was known before Muḥammad's time, and we find the word طوفان used in connection therewith in verses of al-A'shā and Umayya b. Abī-ṣ-Ṣalt,[6] but it is hardly possible to decide whether it came into Arabic from a Jewish or a Christian source.

[1] *Vide* Onkelos on Ex. xix, 18.

[2] Fraenkel, *Vocab*, 21 ; Mingana, *Syriac Influence*, 88 ; and see Horovitz, *JPN*, 170 ; *KU*, 123 ff. ; Guidi, *Della Sede*, 571.

[3] It can hardly be connected, however, with the Gk. τυφῶν.

[4] Hirschfeld, *Beiträge*, 45 ; Horovitz, *KU*, 23 ; Massignon, *Lexique*, 52 ; Wellhausen, *ZDMG*, lxvii, 633.

[5] Also on the incantation bowls, cf. Montgomery, *Aramaic Incantation Texts*, Glossary, p. 290.

[6] Al-A'shā in Geyer, *Zwei Gedichte*, i, 145 = *Dīwān*, xiii, 59 ; Umayya, xxvi, 1 ; xxx, 10 (ed. Schulthess).

طِينٌ (*Ṭīn*).

iii, 43; v, 110; vi, 2; vii, 11; xvii, 63; xxiii, 12; xxviii, 38; xxxii, 6; xxxvii, 11; xxxviii, 71, 77; li, 33.

Clay.

The Qur'ān uses it particularly for the clay out of which man was created.

Jawharī and others take it to be from طان, but this verb is clearly denominative, and Fraenkel, *Fremdw*, 8, is doubtless correct in thinking it a loan-word from N. Semitic.

We find טינא *clay* in Jewish Aram. but not commonly used. The Syr. ܛܝܢܐ was much more widely used. From some source in the Mesopotamian area the word passed into Iranian, where we find the Phlv. ideogram 𐭲𐭩𐭭𐭠 *tīna*, meaning *clay* or *mud* (*PPGl*, 219; Frahang, *Glossary*, p. 119), and it was probably from the same source that it came as an early borrowing into Arabic, where we find it used in a general sense in the old poetry, e.g. *Ḥamāsa*, 712, l. 14.

عَالَمٌ (*'Ālam*).

Of very frequent occurrence (but only in the plu. عَالَمِين).[1]

The world, the universe.

The form is not Arabic as Fraenkel, *Vocab*, 21, points out, and the attempts of the Muslim authorities to prove that it is genuine Arabic are not very successful.[2] Rāghib, *Mufradāt*, 349, quotes as parallels طَابَع and خَاتَم, but these are borrowings from ܛܒܥܐ and ܚܬܡܐ respectively (Fraenkel, *Fremdw*, 252 and 193). Another indication that the word is foreign is the plu. form عالمين (Fraenkel, *Vocab*, 21).

It is difficult, however, to decide whether the word was borrowed from Jewish or Christian sources.[3] Hirschfeld, *Beiträge*, 37, pleads for

[1] Fischer, *Glossar*, 86, shows that this plu. in the Qur'ān means "mankind".

[2] In S. Arabian, however, we have 𐩲𐩡𐩣 = *mundum* (Rossini, *Glossarium*, 207).

[3] That it was an early borrowing is clear from the fact that 𐩲𐩡𐩣𐩬 occurs in a monotheistic S. Arabian inscription published by Mordtmann and Müller in *WZKM*, x, 287; cf. p. 289 therein.

a Jewish origin,[1] and there is much to be said in favour of this. Heb. עולם means any duration of time, and in the Rabbinic writings it, like Aram. עָלְמָא, comes to mean *age* or *world*, as e.g. העולם הזה "this world" as contrasted with the next העולם הבא (Levy, iii, 655). Grünbaum also points out, *ZDMG*, xxxix, 571, that the common Qur'ānic رب العالمين is precisely the רבון העולמים of the Jewish liturgy. On the other hand, עלמא occurs in Palm. and עלם in Nab. inscriptions,[2] and the Syr. ܥܠܡܐ, which Fraenkel, *Vocab*, 21, suggested as its origin, means both αἰών and κόσμος, while the expression ܠܥܠܡܝܢ in the Christian-Palestinian dialect, is, as Schwally notes,[3] a curiously close parallel in form to the Qur'ānic للعالمين.

عَبْد (*'Abd*).

Of very frequent occurrence (also other forms, e.g. عبادة, etc.).

A worshipper.

The root is common Semitic, cf. Akk. *abdu*[4]; Heb. עבד; O.Aram. עבד; Syr. ܥܒܕܐ; Phon. עבד; Sab. 𐩲𐩨𐩵 (and perhaps Eth. ዐበመ, Dillmann, *Lex*, 988).

The question of its being a loan-word in Arabic depends on the more fundamental question of the meaning of the root. If its primitive meaning is *to worship*, then the word retains this primitive meaning in Arabic, and all the others are derived meanings. There is reason, however, to doubt whether *worship* is the primitive meaning. In the O.Aram. עבד means *to make* or *to do*, and the same meaning is very common in Jewish Aram. and Syr. In Heb. עָבַד is *to work*,[5] and so עֶבֶד primarily means worker, as Nöldeke has pointed out,[6] and the sense of *to serve* is derived from this.[7] With עבד meaning *to*

[1] So de Sacy, *JA*, 1829, p. 161 ff. Pautz, *Offenbarung*, 105, n. 5, and see Sacco, *Credenze*, 28; Ahrens, *Muhammed*, 41, 129; Horovitz, *JPN*, 215.

[2] It occurs with the meaning of *age* or *time* in the Zenjirli inscription.

[3] *Idioticon*, 67, 68 = εἰς τοὺς αἰῶνας.

[4] Zimmern, *Akkad. Fremdw*, 47.

[5] Notice particularly the Niph. נֶעֱבַד *to be tilled*, used of land.

[6] *ZDMG*, xl, 741. He compares the Eth. ገበረ *to work* and ገባር *a labourer*.

[7] Gerber, *Verba Denominativa*, p. 14.

P

serve, we get Heb. עֶבֶד ; Aram. עַבְדָּא ; Syr. ܥܒܕܐ ; Phon. עבד ; and Akk. *abdu*, all meaning *slave* or *vassal*, like the Ar. عَبْدٌ, Sab. 𐩲𐩨𐩵. From this it is a simple matter to see how with the developing cults עבד comes to be a *worshipper*, and عَبَدَ *to worship*, i.e. to serve God.

The inscriptions from N. Arabia contain numerous examples of עבד joined with the name of a divinity, e.g. עבדדושרא = عبد ذى شرى ; עבדמנת = عبد مناة ; עבדלת = عبد اللات ; עבדאלהא = عبد الله ; עבדאלעזא = عبد العزّى, to quote only from the Sinaitic inscriptions.[1] Also in the S. Arabian inscriptions we find 𐩲𐩨𐩵𐩲𐩻𐩩𐩧 'Abd 'Athtar ; 𐩲𐩨𐩵𐩫𐩡𐩡 'Abd Kallal ; 𐩲𐩨𐩵𐩦𐩣𐩪 'Abd Shams, etc.[2] It thus seems clear that the sense of *worship*, *worshipper* came to the Arabs from their neighbours in pre-Islamic times,[3] though it is a little doubtful whether we can be so definite as Fischer, *Glossar*, 77, in stating that it is from Jewish עבד.

عَبْقَرِىٌّ (*'Abqarī*).

lv, 76.

A kind of rich carpet.

It occurs only in an early Meccan Sūra in a passage describing the delights of Paradise.

The exegetes were quite at a loss to explain the word. Zam. says that it refers to عبقر, a town of the Jinn, which is the home of all wonderful things, and Ṭab., while telling us that عبقرىّ is the same as

[1] Cook, *Glossary*, 87, 88. For the Safaitic see עבדאם : עבדנר, etc., in Littmann, *Semitic Inscriptions*, 1904 ; Ryckmans, *Noms propres*, i, 155, 240, 241, and compare the Phon. examples in Harris' *Glossary*, 128, 129.

[2] *Vide* Pilter, *Index of South Arabian Names*, for references, and Rossini, *Glossarium*, 201.

[3] It was commonly used in this sense in the old poetry, see Cheikho, *Naṣrāniya*, 172. Ahrens, *Christliches*, 20, would derive عبادة directly from the עֲבֹדָה ; cf. Horovitz, *JPN*, 213.

زرابى or ديباج, states that the Arabs called every wonderful thing عبقرى.

It seems to be an Iranian word. Addai Sher, 114, suggests that it is the Pers. آبكار, i.e. آب كار, meaning "something splendid", from آب *splendour* and كار *something made*. That would be Phlv. سر *āb* = *lustre, splendour* [1] (cf. Skt. आभा) and وسد *kār* = *labour, affair* [2] from Av. وسد *kār* (cf. Skt. कार),[3] so Phlv. سروسد would mean a splendid or gorgeous piece of work. It must be admitted, however, that this derivation seems very artificial.

عَتِيق (*'Atīq*).

xxii, 30, 34.

Ancient.

It occurs only in a Madinan Sūra in a reference to the Ka'ba البيت العتيق.

The exegetes had some trouble with the word, though they usually try to derive it from عَتَقَ, whose meaning, as commonly used in the old poetry, is *to be free*. The verb occurs in Akk. *etēqu*; Heb. עתק meaning *to move, to advance*, but the sense of *to be old* seems purely an Aram. development, and occurs only as an Aramaism in Hebrew.[4]

Aram. עתיק, עתיקא; Syr. ܥܬܝܩܐ are quite commonly used, and עתק, in the sense of *old*, occurs in a Palm. inscription of A.D. 193,[5] but Vollers, *ZDMG*, xlv, 354; li, 315, claims that the root owes this meaning to the Lat. *antiquus*, in which case the word probably came early into Arabic from an Aramaic source.[6]

[1] *PPGl*, 87, and cf. Horn, *Grundriss*, § 3.

[2] West, *Glossary*, 194, and Horn, *Grundriss*, § 831.

[3] Bartholomae, *AIW*, 444 ff.

[4] *BDB*, 801.

[5] de Vogüé, *Inscriptions*, No. 6, l. 4, and cf. Lidzbarski, *Handbuch*, 348; Ryckmans, *Noms propres*, i, 172.

[6] It was used in the early poetry, e.g. Al-A'shā (Geyer, *Zwei Gedichte*, i, 18) and *Mufaḍḍaliyāt*, xxvi, 34.

عَدْنٌ (*'Adn*).

ix, 73; xiii, 23; xvi, 33; xviii, 30; xix, 62; xx, 78; xxxv, 30; xxxviii, 50; xl, 8; lxi, 12; xcviii, 7.

Eden.

It is always found in the combination جنات عدن as *Garden of Eden*, and always used eschatologically, never in the sense of the earthly home of Adam and Eve. It is not found in the earliest Sūras, and is commonest in quite late passages. Muḥammad apparently learned the phrase only in its later sense of *Paradise*, and in xxvi, 85, refers to it as جنة النعيم.

The general theory of the Muslim savants is that it is a genuine Arabic word from عَدَنَ *to abide* or *stay in a place* (*LA*, xvii, 150; *TA*, ix, 274), and Rāghib, *Mufradāt*, 328, says that عَدْنٌ means استقرار. Some, however, recognized it as a loan-word, as we learn from as-Suyūṭī, *Itq*, 323, though the authorities were divided as to whether it was Syriac or Greek.

Obviously جنات عدن represents the Heb. גַן עֵדֶן, and as עֵדֶן is properly *delight*, *pleasure* (the Gk. ἡδονή),[1] the جنة النعيم of xxvi, 85, is a very fair translation. The Arabic equivalent of עֵדֶן, however, is غَدَنَ, with its derivatives غَدَنٌ and غَدْنَةٌ *delicacy*, *softness*, which clearly disposes of the theory of the Lexicographers of a derivation from عدن.

Marracci, *Refutationes*, 315, claimed that the derivation of the Arabic word was directly from the Heb. and this has been accepted by many later writers,[2] though Geiger, 47, admits that it is only in the later Rabbinic writings that עֵדֶן means a heavenly abode. It is possible, however, that it came from the Syr. ܥܕܝ, which is used not

[1] Cf. עָדַן *to be soft*, and the Hiph. *to live delicately*, *voluptuously*. Sycz, *Eigennamen*, 14, however, wants to derive it from Babylonian *ēdinu* meaning *field* or *steppe*.

[2] De Sacy in *JA*, 1829, vol. iv, pp. 175, 176; Pautz, *Offenbarung*, 215 n.; Sacco, *Credenze*, 163.

only of the earthly Eden of Genesis but also of Paradise, and of that blessed state into which Christ brings men during their earthly sojournings.[1] It was from the Syr. that the Arm. ադեն[2] was derived, but one must admit with Horovitz, *Paradies*, 7, that the Syriac word was not so commonly used as the Rabbinic עדן, and the probabilities are thus in favour of a Jewish derivation.

عَرُوبٌ (*'Arūb*).

lvi, 36.

Pleasing.

The word is found only in an early Meccan passage describing the delights of Paradise, where the ever-virgin spouses are عُرُبًا أَتْرَابًا, which is said to mean that they will be well pleasing to their Lords and of equal age with them.

The difficulty, of course, is to derive it from the Ar. root عرب, which does not normally have any meaning which we can connect with عروب in this sense. For this reason Sprenger, *Leben*, ii, 508, n., suggested that it was to be explained from Heb. ערב, one of the meanings of which is *to be sweet, pleasing*, used, e.g., in Ez. xvi, 37; Cant. ii, 14, very much as in the Qur'ānic passage. So in the Targums עריב means *sweet, pleasing* (Levy, *TW*, ii, 240), but the word is not a common one, and it is not easy to suggest how it came to the Arabs. It is commonly used in the old poetry, which would point to an early borrowing.

عَزَّرَ (*'Azzara*).

v, 15; vii, 156; xlviii, 9.

To help.

It is used only in late passages in the technical sense of giving aid in religious matters.

Obviously it is not used in the normal sense of *to correct* or *punish*,

[1] *Vide* Andrae, *Ursprung*, 151.

[2] Hübschmann, *ZDMG*, xlvi, 231; *Arm. Gramm*, i, 300. In the old version of Genesis, however, the word used is Եդեմ, which is obviously from the Greek Ἐδέμ.

nor can it be a normal development of عَزَرَ *to reprove, blame.* The Lexicons are forced to illustrate this Qur'ānic use of the word from the Ḥadīth whose usage is obviously dependent on the Qur'ān itself (*LA*, vi, 237).

It thus seems probable that the verb is denominative, formed from a borrowed עֵזֶר or עֶזְרָה meaning *help, succour,* which would have come to Muḥammad from his contact with the Jewish communities.[1] As the Heb. and Phon. עזר; Aram. עדר; Syr. ܥܕܪ are cognate with the Ar. عَذَرَ *to aid,* it is possible to consider عزر as a by-form of عذر, just as עזר occurs, though infrequently, beside עדר in the Palm. inscriptions,[2] but the fact that it is عَزَّرَ and not عَزَرَ which means *to help* is against this, and in favour of its being a denominative.

عُزَيْر (*'Uzair*).

ix, 30.

Ezra.

The reference is to the Biblical Ezra,[3] and the name was recognized by the philologers as foreign. al-Jawālīqī, *Mu'arrab,* 105, for example, recognizes it as Hebrew.

The form of the name is difficult to explain. The Heb. is עֶזְרָא and none of the Christian forms taken from this help us to explain عُزَير. Finkel, *MW*, xvi, 306 suggests that it is a misreading for عزيز from Ps. ii, 7, but this does not seem possible. Majdī Bey in the *Bulletin de la Soc. Khédiviale de Géographie,* viie sér., No. 3 (1908), p. 8, claims that it represents *Osiris*, but this is absurd. Casanova, *JA*, ccv (1924), p. 360, would derive it from עזזאל or עזיאל, but all the probabilities are that it stands for עזרא, and the form may be due to Muḥammad himself not properly grasping the name,[4] or possibly

[1] So Horovitz, *JPN*, 214.

[2] Lidzbarski, *Handbuch*, 338.

[3] Baiḍ. on the passage tells us that the Jews repudiated with some asperity the statement of the Qur'ān that they called Ezra the Son of God.

[4] See also Horovitz, *KU*, 127, 167; *JPN*, 169; Künstlinger, *OLZ*, xxxv (1932), 381–3.

giving it deliberately the contemptuous diminutive form. A comparison with the Mandaean Elizar [1] is too remote to be fruitful.

عِفْرِيتٌ (*'Ifrīt*).

xxvii, 39.

Demon.

The philologers would derive it from عفر *to rub with dust*, and tell us that the word is applied to Jinn or to men as meaning one who rolls his adversary in the dust (cf. *LA*, vi, 263). That the philologers had difficulty with it is evident from the number of possible forms given by Ibn Khālawaih, 109.

Grimme, *ZA*, xxvi, 167, 168, suggests that the word was formed under S. Arabian influence, but there seems nothing in this, and Barth, *ZDMG*, xlviii. 17, would take it as a genuine Arabic word.[2] Hess, *ZS*, ii, 220, and Vollers, *ZDMG*, l, 646, however, have shown that it is Persian, derived from Phlv. [Pahlavi] *āfrītan* [3] (cf. Av. [Avestan] *āfrīnāṯ* [4]), which in Mod. Pers. is آفريد, the participle from آفريدن *to create*, Paz. *āfrīdan*, Phlv. [Pahlavi] (Shikand, *Glossary*, 226), and used like the Ar. مخلوق for *creature*.

عِلِّيُّونَ (*'Illīyūn*).

lxxxiii, 18, 19.

It is supposed to be the name of a place in the upper part of the heavens (or the name of the upper part of the heavens itself), where the Register of men's good actions is preserved. Some said it was the angel court (اسم ديوان الملائكة), *LA*, xix, 327 ; others that it means the *heights* (Ṭab. *in loco*), and others, arguing that كتاب مرقوم in v. 20 interprets 'Illiyūn, said it meant a *book* (Bagh).

[1] This Elizar appears as the chief of all priests ; cf. Lidzbarski, *Johannesbuch*, ii, 78 ff.

[2] *Vide* also his *Nominalbildung*, § 250.

[3] Horn, *Grundriss*, § 39, and cf. Vullers, *Lex*, i, 44.

[4] Reichelt, *Awestisches Elementarbuch*, Glossary, 428.

Fraenkel, *Vocab*, 23, was doubtless right in taking it to be the Heb. עֶלְיוֹן, which is used as an appellation of God among both Hebrews and Phœnicians,[1] and as meaning *higher* or *upper* is used of chambers of a house (Ez. xli, 7; xlii, 5), and in the Rabbinic writings refers to things heavenly as opposed to things earthly (Levy, *Wörterbuch*, iii, 653).[2]

Grimme, *ZA*, xxvi, 163, wants to connect it with Eth. ዐለየ, whose participle, he says, means *bunt gefärbte*, and would refer it to the spotted pages of the books. There is little doubt, however, that we must regard it as a borrowing from the Jews.

عِمَادٌ (*'Imād*).

xiii, 2; xxxi, 9; civ, 9 (sing. عَمَدٌ); lxxxix, 6.

A column or pole.

The word can hardly be derived from the Arabic verbal root عَمَدَ *to afflict*, and was apparently borrowed from the Aramaic.

Zimmern, *Akkad. Fremdw*, 31, goes back to an Akk. *imdu* meaning a *support* for a house or a wall, from a root *emēdu*, *'md*, *to stand*, which he would consider as having influenced the Canaanitish and Aramaean areas, whence we find Heb. עַמּוּד; Phon. עמד *pillar*, and Aram. עמודא; Palm. עמודא; Syr. ܥܡܘܕܐ *pillar*. If so it must also have influenced the S. Arabian area, for there we find Sab. 𐩲𐩣𐩵 (D. H. Müller, *Epigraphische Denkmäler aus Abessinien*, 80)[3] and Eth. ዐምድ, also meaning *pillar*.

From the Aramaic, according to this theory, would have come the Ar. عمود a *pillar*, and thence the denominative verb عَمَدَ *to prop*, from which the Qur'ānic عماد would have been derived. In this case it would have been an early borrowing.

[1] Hoffmann, *Phönizische Inschriften*, pp. 48, 50, and Philo Byblius in Eusebius, *Prep. Evang.*, i, 80 (ed. Gainsford), κατὰ τούτους γίνεταί τις Ἐλιοῦν καλούμενος Ὕψιστος.

[2] Noldeke, *Neue Beiträge*, 28, and Horovitz, *JPN*, 215, agree that the origin was Jewish.

[3] Cf. Rossini, *Glossarium*, 209; Ryckmans, *Noms propres*, i, 166.

عِمْرَان (*'Imrān*).

iii, 30, 31 ; lxvi, 12.

'Imrān, the father of Moses, Aaron, and Miriam.

In these passages we have the well-known confusion between Miriam the sister of Moses and Aaron, and Miriam the mother of our Lord, and in spite of the attempts at defence made by Gerock,[1] Sale,[2] and Weil,[3] we have no need to look elsewhere than the עַמְרָם of the O.T. for the ultimate source of the name, though the direct borrowing would seem to have been from the Syr. ܥܡܪܐܢ.

Sycz, *Eigennamen*, 60, would take it as a genuine Arabic name applied to עמרם because the name seems to be a formation from عمر, and used in pre-Islamic times. Ibn Duraid, *Ishtiqāq*, 314, tells us of an عمران among the Quḍā'a, and Ibn Qutaiba, *Ma'ārif*, 223, speaks of an عمران بن مخزوم at Mecca. D. H. Müller, *WZKM*, i, 25, says the name was known in S. Arabia, and evidence for its existence in N. Arabia is found in a Greek inscription from the Hauran given by Lidzbarski, *Ephemeris*, ii, 331, which reads Αὔθου Σαλέμου κὲ 'Εμράνου Βάσσου, as well as the Abū 'Imrān mentioned in Al-A'shā.[4] Horovitz, *KU*, 128, also quotes Littmann's unpublished second volume No. 270 for an occurrence of the name in the Safaite inscriptions (cf. Ryckmans, *Noms propres*, i, 167).

This, however, hardly affects the Qur'ānic name, for though we may agree that there was an early Arabic name of this form, it is surely clear, as both Lidzbarski and Horovitz note, that the Qur'ānic name came to Muḥammad from his Jewish or Christian sources, though in the form it takes he may have been influenced by the Arabic name (Horovitz, *JPN*, 159).

عَنْكَبُوت (*'Ankabūt*).

xxix, 40.

Spider.

[1] *Christologie*, pp. 22–8, followed by Sayous, *Jésus-Christ d'après Mahomet*, Paris, 1880, pp. 35, 36.

[2] *Koran*, p. 46, n. 3.

[3] *Muhammad der Prophet*, 1843, p. 195, n.

[4] *Dīwān* (ed. Geyer), xxvii, 18.

The ending ـوت would suggest that it is of Aram. origin (Geiger, 45), and this is confirmed by the fact that the Heb. is עַכָּבִישׁ, where the Heb. שׁ would lead us to expect a ش in Arabic, as e.g. פרעשׁ and برغوث ; שׁלג and ثلج, etc.

The form in the Targums is עַכָּבִיתָא or עַכּוּבִיתָא, as in קיין עכוביתא *spider's web*, and it was probably from some Aram. form that it entered Arabic.[1] The word occurs with *n* already in the N. Arabian inscriptions (Jaussen and Savignac, *Mission*, 25).[2]

عِيد (*'Īd*).

v, 114.

A festival.

This sole occurrence is in the latest Madinan Sūra in connection with Muḥammad's curious confusion on the Lord's supper.

The Lexicons try to derive it from عاد, though as we see from the discussion of al-Azharī in *LA*, iv, 314, they were somewhat in difficulties over it. Fraenkel, *Fremdw*, 276, pointed out that it has no derivation in Arabic, and it was doubtless borrowed from the Syr. ܥܐܕܐ,[3] though the root is common Semitic, and the Targumic עידא is not impossible as the source. It would have been an early borrowing, for already in the Minaean inscriptions 𐩲𐩺𐩵𐩱 means *festum instituit* (Rossini, *Glossarium*, 205).

عِيسَى (*'Īsā*).

ii, 81, 130, 254 ; iii, 40–8, 52, 78 ; iv, 156–169 ; v, 50, 82, 109–116 ; vi, 85 ; xix, 35 ; xxxiii, 7 ; xlii, 11 ; xliii, 63 ; lvii, 27 ; lxi, 6, 14.

Jesus.

The majority of these passages are late. The name is generally

[1] *Vide BDB*, 747.

[2] *Vide* Hess, *Die Entzifferung der thamudischen Inschriften*, No. 153.

[3] Cf. Cheikho, *Naṣrāniya*, 173 ; Fischer, *Glossar*, 90.

عيسى بن مريم, and is frequently accompanied by characteristic N.T. titles, e.g. المسيح ; كلمة الله ; روح الله.

Many Muslim authorities take the word as Arabic and derive it from عيس *to be a dingy white*, whence عَيَس a reddish whiteness (Lane, sub voc.), or from عَيْس meaning a *stallion's urine*; so Rāghib, *Mufradāt*, 359 (cf. *LA*, viii, 31). Zam. on iii, 40, however, dismisses these suggestions with some scorn,[1] and there were many who recognized it as a foreign word.[2] al-Jawālīqī, *Mu'arrab*, 105; al-Khafājī, 134, give it as such, and in *LA*, viii, 30 ff., we read that Sībawaih, Ibn Sīda, Jawharī, and az-Zajjāj classed it as معرب. Jawharī, *Ṣiḥāḥ*, sub voc., gives it as Syriac, but Baiḍ. on ii, 81, says it is Hebrew.

The name is still a puzzle to scholarship. Some have suggested that it is really Esau עֵשָׂו, and was learned by Muḥammad from Jews who called Jesus so out of hatred.[3] There is no evidence, however, that Jews ever referred to Jesus by this name. Others take it as a rhyming formation to correspond with موسى and يحي, on the analogy of Hārūn and Qārūn; Hārūt and Mārūt; Yājūj and Mājūj, etc. There may be some truth in this.[4] Derenbourg, *REJ*, xviii, 128, after pointing out how the Tetragrammaton יהוה in Gk. became ΠΙΠΙ, suggests that perhaps ישוע "lu à la manière occidentale" has produced عيسى, but this is hardly likely.

Fraenkel, *WZKM*, iv, 334, 335, suggests that the name عيسى may have been so formed from ܝܫܘܥ by Christians in Arabia before

[1] Baiḍ. follows Zam. in this. Zwemer, *Moslem Christ*, 34, has quite misunderstood Baiḍ. on this point. Baiḍ. does not argue for a derivation from أعيس, but definitely repudiates it. al-'Ukbarī, *Imlā'*, i, 164, says clearly لا يعرف له اشتقاق.

[2] See the discussion in Abū Ḥayyān, *Bahr*, i, 297.

[3] This was suggested by Roediger (Fraenkel, *WZKM*, iv, 334, n.) and by Landauer (Noldeke, *ZDMG*, xli, 720, n.), and is set forth again by Pautz, *Offenbarung*, 191. The case against it is elaborated by Derenbourg, *REJ*, xviii, 127, and Rudolph, *Abhängigkeit*, 66.

[4] This theory was elaborated by Lowenthal in 1861, cf. *MW*, i, 267–282, and Ahrens, *Christliches*, 25.

Muḥammad. It is not unusual to find Arabic using an initial ע in words borrowed from Aram.,[1] and the dropping of final ע is evidenced by the form *Yisho* of the Manichaean "köktürkish" fragments[2] from Turfan,[3] and the late Jewish ישו for ישוע (Levy, *Wörterbuch*, ii, 272). The form *'Īsa*, however, does not occur earlier than the Qur'ān,[4] whereas يسوع appears to have been used in personal names at an early period, cf. *Aghānī*, xx, 128.

Till further information comes to hand we shall have to content ourselves with regarding it as some form of "konsonanten permutation"[5] due, maybe, to Muḥammad himself, and perhaps influenced, as Horovitz, *KU*, 128, suggests, by Nestorian pronunciation.

فَاجِرٌ (*Fājir*).

lxxi, 28; plu. فَجَرَة, lxxx, 42, and فُجَّار, xxxviii, 27; lxxxii, 14; lxxxiii, 7.

Wicked.

With this must be taken the verb فَجَرَ *to act wickedly*, lxxv, 5, and فُجُور *wickedness*, xci, 8.

This set of words, as Ahrens, *Christliches*, 31, notes, has nothing to do with the root فَجَرَ *to break forth* or its derivatives. Rather we have here a development from a word borrowed from the Syr. ܦܓܪܐ which literally means a *body* or *corpse*, but from which were formed the technical words of Christian theology, ܦܓܪܢܐ *corporalis*, and ܦܓܪܢܘܬܐ *corporalitas*, referring to the sinful body, the *flesh* that wars against the spirit. Thus in 2 Pet. i, 13, ܒܦܓܪܐ ܗܢܐ = ἐν τούτῳ τῷ σκηνώματι, and in 1 Cor. iii, 3, ܦܓܪܢܐ = σωματικός, and in

[1] Examples in Vollers, *ZDMG*, xlv, 352.

[2] So sometimes in the Iranian and Soghdian Manichaean fragments, see Henning, *Manichaica*, ii, 70, and *Manichaisches Beichtbuch*, 142.

[3] Le Coq in *SBAW*, Berlin, 1909, p. 1053; cf. also the Arm. Յիսուս.

[4] But note the monastery in S. Syria, mentioned by Mingana, *Syriac Influence*, 84, which as early as A.D. 571 seems to have borne the name *'Isānīya*.

[5] Bittner, *WZKM*, xv, 395.

this technical sense it may very well have been in use among the Christian Arabs long before the time of Islam.

فَاطِرٌ (*Fāṭir*).

vi, 14 ; xii, 102 ; xiv, 11 ; xxxv, 1 ; xxxix, 47 ; xlii, 9.

Creator.

It occurs only in the stereotyped phrase فاطر السموات والارض.

The root فَطَرَ is *to cleave* or *split*, and from this we have several forms in the Qur'ān, viz. فُطُور a *fissure*, تَفَطَّرَ *to be rent asunder*, etc. On the other hand, فَطَرَ *to create* (cf. فِطْرَةٌ, xxx, 29), is a denominative from فَاطِر.

The primary sense is common Semitic, cf. Akk. *paṭāru*, *to cleave*, Heb. פטר, Phon. פטר *to remove*, Syr. ܦܛܪ *to release*, etc. The meaning of *to create*, however, is peculiar to Ethiopic, and as Nöldeke, *Neue Beiträge*, 49, shows, the Ar. فاطر is derived from ፈጠረ though Arabicized in its form.[1]

فَتْحٌ (*Fatḥ*).

xxvi, 118 ; xxxii, 28.

Judgment, decision.

The verb فَتَحَ *to open*, with its derivatives, is commonly used and is genuine Arabic, but in these two passages [2] where it has a peculiar technical meaning, Muḥammad seems to be using, as Horovitz, *KU*, 18, n., noted, an Eth. word ፍትሕ, which had become specialized in this sense and is used almost exclusively of legal affairs, e.g. ፈትሐ *to give judgment* ; ተፈትሐ *iudicari* ; ተፋትሐ *litigare* ; ፍትሕት *iudicium*,

[1] That the early authorities felt that the word was foreign is clear from the tradition about Ibn 'Abbās in *LA*, vi, 362, already referred to in our Introduction, p. 7.

[2] Horovitz would add cx, 1, اذا جاء نصر الله والفتح, but as this apparently refers to the conquest of Mecca (Noldeke-Schwally, i, 219), it would seem to mean *victory* rather than *judgment* in the technical legal sense of the other passages.

and ፍትሕ which is both *iudicium* and *sententia iudicis*. This sense had already become domiciled in S. Arabia, as we see from the use of ΨX◊ in the inscriptions (Rossini, *Glossarium*, 221).

فَخَّارٌ (*Fakhkhār*).

lv, 13.

Potter's clay.

The passage refers to the creation of man, and that it means *earthenware* is the general consensus of the authorities (cf. as-Sijistānī, 245; Rāghib, *Mufradāt*, 380).

It is obvious that it cannot be derived from the verbal root فخر,[1] and Fraenkel, *Vocab*, 22, compared it with ܦܚܪܐ an earthenware pot, which occurs as a loan-word in the Jewish פחרא.[2] The Syr. ܦܚܪܐ [3] is a word in fairly common use and translates κεραμεύς (cf. ܕܦܚܪܐ ܐܪܥܐ = γῆ κεραμική), and there can be little doubt that it is the origin of the Arabic word,[4] though Horovitz, *JPN*, 216, withholds judgment as to whether it is of Jewish or Christian origin.

فُرَاتٌ (*Furāt*).

xxv, 55; xxxv, 13; lxxvii, 27.

Sweet river water.

The passages are all Meccan and refer to the sweet river water as opposed to the salt water of the sea, and in the two latter passages the reference is apparently to some cosmological myth.

In any case the word فُرَاتٌ is derived from the river Euphrates (Horovitz, *KU*, 130), which from the Sumerian *Pura-nun*, "great water," appears in Akk. as *Purattu*, or *Purāt*,[5] and in O.Pers. as *Ufrātu*,[6]

[1] Noldeke, *Mand. Gramm.*, 120, n. 2.
[2] Fraenkel, *Fremdw*, 70; but cf. פֶּחָר in Dan. ii, 41.
[3] This itself may be of Akk. origin, see Zimmern, *Akkad. Fremdw*, 26.
[4] Nöldeke, *Neue Beiträge*, 45, n. 2; Vollers, *ZDMG*, li, 324; Fraenkel, *Fremdw*, 257.
[5] Delitzsch, *Paradies*, 169 ff.
[6] Spiegel, *Die altpersischen Keilinschriften*, p. 211, and cf. Meillet, *Grammaire du vieux Perse*, p. 164.

whence the Gk. Ἐυφράτης. From the Akk. come the Heb. פרת and Syr. ܦܪܬ, whence in all probability the Ar. فُرَات, if indeed this was not an early borrowing from Mesopotamia.

فِرْدَوْس (*Firdaws*).

xviii, 107; xxiii, 11.

Paradise.

The authorities are agreed that it means a garden—بستان (Jawharī, *Ṣiḥāḥ*, i, 467; *LA*, viii, 43), but they differed considerably as to what sort of a garden it means.[1] There are also divers opinions as to its precise location and significance as referring to the celestial Paradise.

It was early recognized as foreign (Siddiqi, *Studien*, 13, and note Fraenkel's remark, *Fremdw*, 149), though some claimed that it was genuine Arabic derived from فَرْدَسَة meaning *width* or *amplitude*.[2]

Some said it was Nabataean,[3] where the reference is possibly to the פרדס of late Jewish legend. 'Ikrima held that it was Ethiopic,[4] and many said it was Syriac,[5] but the favourite theory among the philologers was that it was of Greek origin. as-Suyūṭī, *Itq*, 323; *Muzhir*, i, 130, 134, gives this as the prevalent theory, it is given by al-Jawālīqī, 110; ath-Tha'ālibī, *Fiqh*, 318; and al-Khafājī, 148, and we learn from the Lexicons (cf. *LA*, viii, 44) that it was supported by such authorities as az-Zajjāj, Mujāhid, Ibn Sīda, and al-Kalbī.

Obviously فردوس represents the Gk. παράδεισος, and on the ground of the plu. فراديس G. Hoffmann[6] would derive it directly from the Greek. It seems, however, merely a coincidence that this

[1] Lane, *Lex*, 2365; and Ṭab. on xviii, 107.

[2] *Vide* Qāmūs, sub voc.; *LA*, viii, 44; *TA*, iv, 205. This was the theory of al-Farrā' and it was supposed to be supported by the fact that it occurs as a name for Damascus. The verse of Jarir quoted in Bekrī, *Mu'jam*, p. 368, is post-Islamic, however, and doubtless influenced by the Qur'ān.

[3] as-Suddī in al-Jawālīqī, *Mu'arrab*, 110.

[4] Bagh. on xviii, 107.

[5] Qāmūs, sub voc. *TA*, iv, 105, and al-Jawālīqī.

[6] *ZDMG*, xxxii, 761, n.; Lagarde, *GA*, 76 and 210; Pautz, *Offenbarung*, 215, n.; but see A. Müller in Bezzenberger's *Beiträge*, 280, n.

plu. form (which is not uncommon in borrowed words, e.g. صناديق ; تلاميذ ; خنازير, etc.), is so close in sound to the Greek word, and it is unlikely that it came directly into Arabic from Greek.

The original word is Iranian, the Av. 𐬞𐬀𐬌𐬭𐬌𐬛𐬀𐬉𐬰𐬀 *pairidaēza*, which in the plu. means a " circular enclosure ".[1] Xenophon introduced the word into Greek, and uses it of the parks and gardens of the Persian Kings,[2] e.g. *Anab*, I, ii, 7, etc. After this date it is used fairly frequently, and in the LXX is sometimes used to translate גן or גן עדן. But it was also borrowed into other languages.[3] In late Akk. we find *pardisu*,[4] and in Heb. פרדס a *park* or *garden*, also in Aram. the פרדיסא of the Targums, and Syr. ܦܪܕܝܣܐ commonly mean *garden* and are of Iranian origin,[5] like the Arm. պարտէզ.[6]

Tisdall, *Sources*, 126, thought that فردوس was borrowed from late Heb., but in the sense of *Paradise* it is very rarely used in Heb.[7] Its origin is almost certainly Christian, and probably Syriac, for ܦܪܕܝܣܐ was very commonly used for the abode of the Blessed, and could easily have been learned by the Arabs from the Aram. speaking Christians of Mesopotamia or N. Arabia.[8] Vollers, *ZDMG*, l, 646, suggests that possibly the plu. form فراديس was the form that was borrowed, and فردوس later formed from this.

It was a pre-Islamic borrowing, and possibly occurs in the Thamudic inscriptions.[9]

[1] Bartholomae, *AIW*, 865; Haug, *Parsis*, 5. It survives in Mod. Pers. پاليز *garden* (Horn, *Grundriss*, § 279), and Kurdish پريز *garden* (cf. Justi, *Die kurd. Spiranten*, 29).

[2] This makes it the more strange that Liddell and Scott should have considered the word Semitic.

[3] Telegdi, in *JA*, ccxxvi (1935), p. 250.

[4] *ZA*, vi, 290. On the suggested Semitic origin of the Avestic word, see Delitzsch, *Paradies*, 95, 96, and Nöldeke thereon in *ZDMG*, xxxvi, 182.

[5] The Syr. ܦܪܕܝܣܢܐ, besides Arm. պարտիզպան and Pers. پاليزبان for *gardener*, is conclusive evidence of the Iranian origin, بان, being the Phlv. 𐭯𐭠𐭭𐭪 *pānak*, a *protector*, or *keeper* (Horn, *Grundriss*, § 176; Nyberg, *Glossar*, 169).

[6] Hübschmann, *Arm. Gramm.*, i, 229; Lagarde, *Armenische Studien*, § 1878.

[7] As Horovitz, *Paradies*, 7, notes. Cf. also Schaeder in *Der Islam*, xiii, 326.

[8] Horovitz, *Paradies*, 7; Grünbaum, *ZDMG*, xxxix, 581; Geiger, 48; Fraenkel, *Vocab*, 25; Sacco, *Credenze*, 163, n.

[9] פרדס, cf. Littmann, *Entzifferung*, 43.

فِرْعَوْن (*Fir'aun*).

Occurs some seventy-four times, e.g. ii, 46.

Pharaoh.

The Commentators tell us that Fir'aun was the title of the kings of the Amalekites,[1] just as Chosroes and Cæsar were titles of the kings of Persia and Roum (Ṭab. and Baiḍ. on ii, 46). It was thus recognized as a foreign word taken over into Arabic (Sībawaih in Siddiqi, *Studien*, 20, and al-Jawālīqī, *Mu'arrab*, 112).

Hirschfeld, *New Researches*, 13, thinks that it came to Arabic from Hebrew, the form being due to a misreading of פרעה as פרעון, but there is no need to descend to such subtleties when we note that the Christian forms give us the final ن. In Gk. it is Φαραῶν, in Syr. ܦܪܥܘܢ, and in Eth. ፈርዖን. The probabilities are that it was borrowed from Syriac (Mingana, *Syriac Influence*, 81; Sprenger, *Leben*, i, 66; Horovitz, *JPN*, 169).

There does not seem to be any well authenticated example of the word in pre-Islamic times, for the oft quoted examples from Zuhair and Umayya are spurious.[2] Sprenger has noticed the curious fact that the name does not occur in the Sūra of Joseph where we should naturally expect it, which may indicate that the name was not known to Muḥammad at the time that story was composed, or may be was not used in the sources from which he got the material for the story.

فُرْقَان (*Furqān*).

ii, 50, 181; iii, 2; viii, 29, 42; xxi, 49; xxv, 1.

Discrimination.

In all the passages save viii, 42, it is used as though it means some sort of a Scripture sent from God. Thus "we gave to Moses and Aaron the Furqān and an illumination" (xxi, 49), and "We gave to Moses the Book and the Furqān" (ii, 50), where it would seem to

[1] As Noldeke showed in his essay *Über die Amalekiter*, Gottingen, 1864, this name is used by Arabic writers in a very loose way to cover all sorts of peoples of the Near East of whose racial affinities they had no exact knowledge. The term is used indifferently for Philistines, Canaanites, and Egyptians, and Bagh. in his note on ii, 46, tells us that Pharaoh was the ruler of the Amalekite Copts!

[2] Horovitz, *KU*, 130, however, would defend the genuineness of one passage in Umayya.

be the equivalent of Taurah. In iii, 2, it is associated with the Taurah and the Injīl, and xxv, 1, and ii, 181, make it practically the equivalent of the Qur'ān, while in viii, 29, we read, "if ye believe God, he will grant you a Furqān and forgive your evil deeds." In viii, 42, however, where the reference is to the Battle of Badr, "the day of the Furqān, the day when the two hosts met," the meaning seems something quite different.

The form of the word would suggest that it was genuine Arabic, a form فُعلان from فَرَق, and thus it is taken by the Muslim authorities. Ṭab. on ii, 50, says that Scripture is called Furqān because God فرق به بين الحق والباطل, and as referring to Badr it means the day when God discriminated (فرق) between the good party and the evil (Rāghib, *Mufradāt*, 385). In this latter case it is tempting to think of Jewish influence, for in the account of Saul's victory over the Ammonites in 1 Sam. xi, 13, where the Heb. text reads היום עשה יהוה תשועה בישראל, in the Targum it reads יומא דין עבד יהוה פורקנא בישראל, where יום פורקנא is exactly يوم الفرقان.[1]

The philologers, however, are not unanimous as to its meaning. Some took it to mean نصر ; Baiḍ. on xxi, 49, tells us that some said it meant فلق البحر, and Zam. on viii, 29, collects a number of other meanings. This uncertainty and confusion is difficult to explain if we are dealing with a genuine Arabic word, and is sufficient of itself to suggest that it is a borrowed term.[2]

Arguing from the fact that in the majority of cases it is connected with Scriptures, Hirschfeld, *New Researches*, 68, would derive it from פְּרָקִים, one of the technical terms for the divisions of the

[1] Lidzbarski, *ZS*, i, 92, notes an even closer verbal correspondence with Is. xlix, 8, where for וביום ישועה עזרתיך the Pesh. has ܘܒܝܘܡܐ ܕܦܘܪܩܢܐ ܥܕܪܬܟ.

[2] This is strengthened by the fact that there are apparently no examples of its use earlier than the Qur'ān. Fleischer, *Kleinere Schriften*, ii, 125 ff., who opposed the theory that it is a foreign word, is compelled to admit that it was probably a coining of Muḥammad himself. See Ahrens, *Christliches*, 31, 32.

text of the Hebrew Scriptures.[1] This, however, is rather difficult, and Margoliouth, *Mohammed*, 145 (but see *ERE*, ix, 481 ; x, 538), while inclining to the explanation from פרקים, refers it, not to the sections of the Pentateuch, but to a book of Sayings of the Jewish Fathers, which Muḥammad heard of from the Jews, and which he may have thought of as similar to the Taurah and the Injīl. This theory is more probable than that of Hirschfeld, and has in its favour the fact that resemblances have been noted between phrases and ideas in the Qur'ān and the well-known פרקי אבות.[2] It also, however, has its difficulties, and in any case does not explain the use of the word in viii, 42.

Linguistically there is a closer equivalence in the Aram. פרקן, פורקן *deliverance* or *redemption*, and Geiger, 56 ff.,[3] suggested this as the source of the Arabic word. He would see the primary meaning in viii, 29—" He will grant you *redemption* and forgive your evil deeds," where the Targumic פורקנא would fit exactly (cf. Ps. iii, 9, etc.). Nowhere, however, is פורפנא used of revelation, and Geiger is forced to explain فرقان in the other passages, by assuming that Muḥammad looked upon revelation as a means of deliverance from error.

Geiger's explanation has commended itself to many scholars,[4] but Fraenkel, *Vocab*, 23, in mentioning Geiger's theory, suggested the possibility of a derivation from Syr. ܦܘܪܩܢܐ, a suggestion which has been very fruitfully explored by later scholars.[5] Not only is ܦܘܪܩܢܐ the common word for *salvation* in the Peshitta and the ecclesiastical writers (*PSm*, 3295), but it is the normal form in the Christian-Palestinian dialect, and has passed into the religious vocabulary of Eth. as ፍርቃን (Nöldeke-Schwally, i, 34) and Armenian as փուրկան.[6] It is of much wider use than the Rabbinic

[1] So Grimme, *Mohammed*, ii, 73, thinks it means sections of a heavenly book and compares the Rabbinic פֶּרֶק, פִּרְקָא ; but see Rudolph, *Abhängigkeit*, 39.

[2] Rudolph, *Abhängigkeit*, 11 ; Hirschfeld, *Beiträge*, 58.

[3] So Torrey, *Foundation*, 48.

[4] Ullmann, *Der Koran* (Bielefeld, 1872), p. 5 ; von Kremer, *Ideen*, 225 ; Sprenger, *Leben*, ii, 337 ff. ; Pautz, *Offenbarung*, 81.

[5] Schwally, *ZDMG*, lii, 135 ; Knieschke, *Erlösungslehre des Koran* (Berlin, 1910), p. 11 ff. See also Wellhausen, *ZDMG*, lxvii, 633 ; Massignon, *Lexique*, 52 ; Mingana, *Syriac Influence*, 85.

[6] Merx, *Chrestomathia Targumica*, 264 ; Hübschmann, *ZDMG*, xlvi, 267 ; *Arm. Gramm.*, i, 318.

פורקנא, but as little does it refer to revelation, so even if we agree that the borrowing was from Syr. we still have the problem of the double, perhaps triple, meaning of the word in the Qur'ān.

Sprenger thought we might explain this by assuming the influence of the Ar. root فرق on the borrowed word.[1] Schwally, however, has suggested that this is not necessary, as the word might well have had this double sense before Muḥammad's time, under the influence of Christian or Jewish Messianic thought,[2] and Lidzbarski, *ZS*, i, 91, points out that in Gnostic circles " Erlösung und Heil besonders durch Offenbarung vermittelt werden ".[3] There is the difficulty, however, that there seems to be no evidence of the use of the word in Arabic earlier than the Qur'ān, and Bell, *Origin*, 118 ff., rightly insists that we must associate the use of the word for revelation with Muḥammad himself. He links up the use of the word in the Qur'ān with the story of Moses, and thinks that as in the story of Moses the deliverance was associated with the giving of the Law, so Muḥammad conceived of his Furqān as associated with the revelation of the Qur'ān. Wensinck, *EI*, ii, 120, would also attribute the use of the word in the sense of revelation to Muḥammad himself, but he thinks we have two distinct words used in the Qur'ān, one the Syr. ܦܘܪܩܢܐ meaning *salvation* or *deliverance*, and the other a genuine Arabic word meaning *distinction*, which Muḥammad used for *revelation* as that which makes a distinction between the true and the false.[4] Finally, Horovitz, *KU*, 77, would make a sort of combination of all these theories, taking the word as of Syriac origin, but influenced by the root فرق and also by the Heb. פרקים (cf. also *JPN*, 216–18).

In any case it seems clear that فرقان is a word that Muḥammad himself borrowed to use as a technical term, and to whose meaning

[1] *Leben*, ii, 339, " Wenn Mohammed Forkan auch aus dem Aramäischen entnommen hat, so schwebte ihm doch die arabische Etymologie vor." See also Rudolph, *Abhängigkeit*, 39; Bell, *Origin*, 118; Noldeke, *Sketches*, 38.

[2] Noldeke-Schwally, i, 34: " in erster Linie und am wahrscheinlichsten unter Christen, in zweiter Linie in messianisch gerichteten judischen Kreisen."

[3] He refers, for examples, to Liechtenhan's *Die Offenbarung im Gnosticismus*, p. 123 ff.; but as Rudolph, *Abhangigkeit*, 92, points out, this idea is not confined to Gnostic circles.

[4] Wensinck seems to have been unduly influenced by the theories of the native Commentators.

he gave his own interpretation. The source of the borrowing was doubtless the vocabulary of the Aramaic-speaking Christians, whether or not the word was also influenced by Judaism.

فَلَق (*Falaq*).

vi, 95, 96; xxvi, 63; cxiii, 1.

To split or cleave.

Three forms occur in the Qur'ān: (i) فالق, *he who causes to break forth*, vi, 95, 96; (ii) إِنفَلَق *to be split open*, xxvi, 63; (iii) فَلَق the *dawn*, cxiii, 1.

Zimmern, *Akkad. Fremdw*, 12, notes that the Arabic verb is denominative, and would derive it from an Aramaic source. The Akk. *palāqu*, *to slay* or *kill*, is a denominative from *pilaqqu*, a *hatchet* which itself may be derived from the Sumerian *balag*. From this Akk. *pilaqqu* were derived on the one hand the Syr. ܦܠܩܐ and Mand. פילקא, both meaning *hatchet*, and on the other hand the Skt. परशु *hatchet*[1]; Gk. πέλεκυς, *axe*.[2]

Syr. ܦܠܩܐ is used to translate the Heb. כַּשִּׁיל in Ps. lxxiv, 6, and would probably have been the origin of the form that was first borrowed and from which all the others have been developed.[3]

فُلْك (*Fulk*).

Occurs some twenty-three times, cf. vii, 62.

Ship.

It is used of shipping in general (xxx, 45; xlv, 11), of Noah's Ark (vii, 62; x, 74), and of the ship from which Jonah was cast (xxxvii, 140).

The root فَلَك means *to have rounded breasts* (Lane, *Lex*, 2443),

[1] For परशु see Delitzsch, *Prolegomena*, 147, and Ipsen in *Indog. Forschungen*, xli, 177 (Alt-Sumerisch-akkadische Lehnwörter im Indogermanischen).

[2] For πέλεκυς see *ZDMG*, ix, 874; Kretschmer, *Einleitung*, 105 ff.; Levy, *Fremdwörter*, 178.

[3] In S. Arabian, however, we find 𐩰𐩡𐩤 (Rossini, *Glossarium*, 218), though this may have come from the Aramaic.

and from the same primitive Semitic root we get Akk. *pilakku*; Heb. פֶּלֶךְ; Ar. فَلْكَة, all meaning the whirl of a spindle, and by another line of derivation Ar. فَلَك; Eth. ፈለክ for the celestial hemisphere. So the philologers as a rule endeavour to derive فُلْك from this root, imagining it is so named from its rounded shape.[1]

The philologers, however, were somewhat troubled by the fact that it could be masc., fem., and plu., without change of form (*LA*, xii, 367), and there can be little doubt that the word is a borrowing. Vollers, *ZDMG*, l, 620; li, 300, claims that it is the Gk. ἐφόλκιον, which usually means a small boat towed after a ship,[2] but from the *Periplus Maris Erythraei*, § 16,[3] we gather that as used around the Red Sea it must have meant a vessel of considerable size. The borrowing was probably direct from the Greek, though there is a possibility that it came through an Aram. medium.[4]

فِيل (*Fīl*).

cv, 1.

Elephant.

The only occurrence of the word is in an early Sūra mentioning the Abyssinian campaign under Abraha against Mecca. Abraha's army was known as جيش الفيل, because for the first time in Arab experience, African elephants had been used in an attack. Muḥammad was doubtless using a well-known term when he referred to Abraha's army as أصحاب الفيل.

The word seems to be of Iranian origin.[5] In Phlv. we find پیل, پیل[6];

[1] Rāghib, *Mufradāt*, 393, however, reverses this position, and thinks the celestial sphere was called فلك because it was like a boat.

[2] *Vide* Athenaeus, 208 F.

[3] In C. Muller, *Geographi Graeci Minores*, i, 271.

[4] Fraenkel, *Fremdw*, 212. Halévy, *ZA*, ii, 401, denies the derivation from ἐφόλκιον, claiming that in that case the Arabic word would have been فلق.

[5] Hommel, *Säugethiere*, 24.

[6] *PPGl*, 187; West, *Glossary*, 112; *Shikand*, Glossary, 264; Nyberg, *Glossar*, 186, whence in Mod. Pers. it is پیل.

Paz. *pīl*, representing an old Iranian form which was borrowed on the one hand into Skt. पीलु [1] and Arm. փիղ,[2] and on the other into Akk. *pīru*, *pīlu* [3]; Aram. פִּילָא ; Syr. ܦܝܠܐ.

Some of the philologers endeavoured to find an Arabic derivation for the word,[4] but it is fairly clear that it was a borrowing either directly from Middle Persian, or through the Aram. (Horovitz, *KU*, 98). It occurs in the old poetry and therefore must have been an early borrowing.

Rossini, *JA*, xie sér., vol. xviii, 31, after pointing out the difficulty of believing that elephants could have made the journey between Yemen and Mecca, thinks that oral tradition among the Arabs confused the expedition of Abraha with an earlier one under the chieftain Afilas whose name ΑΦΙΛΑC occurs on coins of the end of the third century A.D. as an Ethiopian conqueror of S. Arabia. On this theory الفيل in the Qur'ān would be a corrupted representation of أفيل.

قَارُونُ (*Qārūn*).

xxviii, 76, 79 ; xxix, 38 ; xl, 25.

Korah.

As Geiger, 155, has shown, the Qur'ānic account of Korah is based on the Rabbinic legends, and we might assume that the word is derived from the Heb. קֹרַח. The dropping of the final guttural, however, makes this a little difficult. The final guttural, as a matter of fact, is missing in the Gk. Κορέ and Eth. ቆሬ, but neither of these help us with the Arabic form. Hirschfeld, *New Researches*, 13, n., made the suggestion that قارون is due to a misreading of קרח as קרון, a mistake which is very possible in Hebrew script. It is fairly certain, however, that Muḥammad's information came from oral sources, and it is difficult to believe that anyone sufficiently acquainted with Heb. or Aram. to be able to read him the story would have made such

[1] Vox apud Indos barbara—Vullers, *Lex*, i, 402, as against Hommel, 324 ff., and see Monier Williams, *Sanskrit Dictionary*, p. 630.

[2] Hübschmann, *Arm. Gramm.*, i, 255.

[3] Vollers, *ZDMG*, l, 652 ; Zimmern, *Akkad. Fremdw*, 50, thinks the Aram. and Heb. forms were derived from the Akkad.

[4] e.g. Sībawaih in *Ṣiḥāḥ*, sub voc.

a blunder. There is a Mandaean form כרון[1] (Lidzbarski, *Ginza*, Göttingen, 1925, p. 157), but there can be no certainty that this is connected with قارون, and if it is it was probably influenced by the Qur'ānic form. Thus it seems best to look on it as a rhyming formation to parallel هارون (Sycz, *Eigennamen*, 43; Horovitz, *KU*, 131; *JPN*, 163), though whether from the Heb. קרח or from a Christian form without the guttural, it is impossible to say.[2]

قُدُسٌ (*Qudus*).

ii, 81, 254; v, 109; xvi, 104.
Purity, sanctity.

We also find القدّوس an epithet for God, lix, 23; lxii, 1; قدّس *to bless, sanctify*, ii, 28; مُقدّس and مُقدّسة *holy, sacred*, v, 24; xx, 12; lxxix, 16.

The root is common Semitic and would seem to have meant primitively *to withdraw, separate*,[3] and some of the philologers would derive the meaning of the Qur'ānic words from this sense (cf. Baiḍ. on ii, 28). It has long been recognized, however, that as a technical religious term, this sense is a N. Semitic development, and occurs only as a borrowed sense of the root in S. Semitic.[4] Thus Eth. ቀደሰ in the sense of *holy* (i.e. ቅዱስ) is a borrowing from Aram., as Nöldeke, *Neue Beiträge*, 35, shows, and there can be little doubt that Fraenkel, *Vocab*, 20; *Fremdw*, 57, is correct in tracing the Arabic word to a similar source. Hirschfeld, *Beiträge*, 39 ff., thinks the Arabic use developed under Jewish influence, but the Qur'ānic use is more satisfactorily explained from Christian Aram.,[5] particularly the روح القدس from ܪܘܚܐ ܕܩܘܕܫܐ; while the form قُدُّوس may have come from the Eth. ቅዱስ (Horovitz, *JPN*, 218).[6]

[1] Brandt, *Mandäische Schriften*, 149, suggested the equivalence with قارون.

[2] The foreign origin of the word was recognized by some of the Muslim authorities, cf. Sībawaih in Siddiqi, 20.

[3] Baudissin, *Studien*, ii, 19 ff., and Robertson Smith, *Religion of the Semites*, 150.

[4] Which is fatal to Grimme's theory of S. Arab. origin, *ZA*, xxvi, 166.

[5] Fraenkel, *Vocab*, 24; Pautz, *Offenbarung*, 36; Mingana, *Syriac Influence*, 85, 86.

[6] The קדוש = the Holy One, of the incantation texts, however, should be noted. Cf. Montgomery, *Aramaic Incantation Texts*, Glossary, p. 300.

قُرْآن (*Qur'ān*).

Occurs some seventy times, e.g. ii, 181 ; v, 101 ; vi, 19.

A reading from Scripture.

The root קרא in the sense of *proclaim, call, recite,* does not occur in Akkadian nor in S. Semitic as represented by the S. Arabian and Ethiopic, which leads one to suspect that قَرَأَ is a borrowing from the Canaanite-Aramaic area.[1] The root is found in Heb. and Phon. but it is most widely used in the Aram. dialects, being found both in the O.Aram. and the Egyptian Aram., and in the Nab. and Palmy. inscriptions, as well as in Jewish Aram. and Syriac.

The verb قَرَأَ is used fairly often in the Qur'ān, and with four exceptions, always in reference to Muḥammad's own revelation. Of these exceptions in two cases (x, 94 ; xvii, 95), it is used of other Scriptures, and in two cases (xvii, 73 ; lxix, 19), of the Books of Fate men will have given them on the Day of Judgment. Thus it is clear that the word is used technically in connection with Heavenly Books.[2] The sense of قَرَأَ also is *recite* or *proclaim*, that of *read* only came later.[3]

The usual theory is that قرآن is a verbal noun from this قَرَأَ. It is not found earlier than the Qur'ān, so the earlier group of Western scholars was inclined to think that Muḥammad himself formed the word from the borrowed root.[4] There is some difficulty about this, however. In the first place the form is curious, and some of the early philologers, such as Qatāda and Abū 'Ubaida derived it from قَرَنَ *to bring together*, basing their argument on lxxv, 17.[5] Others, as-Suyūṭī tells us, were unsatisfied with both these derivations, and said it had no root, being a special name for the Arab's Holy Book, like Taurah

[1] Noldeke-Schwally, i, 33 ; Wellhausen, *ZDMG*, lxvii, 634 ; Fischer, *Glossar*, 104 b.

[2] Noldeke-Schwally, i, 82 : "Vielmehr wird قرأ im Qorane überall vom murmelnden oder leiernden Hersagen heiliger Texte gebraucht."

[3] *Vide* Hurgronje, *RHR*, xxx, 62, 155 ; Dyroff, in *MVAG*, xxii, 178 ff. ; Noldeke-Schwally, i, 81 ; and Pedersen, *Der Islam*, v, 113.

[4] Von Kremer, *Ideen*, 224, 225.

[5] Jawharī, sub voc. ; as-Suyūṭī, *Itq*, 118, 119.

for the Jews or Injīl for the Christians.[1] It thus looks as though the word is not native, but an importation into the language.

Marracci, 53, looked for a Jewish origin, suggesting that it was formed under the influence of the Heb. מִקְרָא in its late sense of *reading*, as in Neh. viii, 8, and frequently in the Rabbinic writings. Geiger, 59, supports this view, and Nöldeke in 1860, though inclining to the view that it was a formation from قرأ, yet thought that it was influenced by the use of מקרא.[2] The tendency of more recent scholarship, however, has been to derive it from the Syr. ܩܪܝܢܐ which means "the Reading" in the special sense of Scripture lesson. In Syriac writings it is used in the titles for the Church lessons, and the Lectionary itself is called ܟܬܒܐ ܕܩܪܝܢܐ. This is precisely the sense we need to illustrate the Qur'ānic usage of the word for portions of Scripture, so there can be little doubt that the word came to Muḥammad from Christian sources.[3]

قُرْبَان (*Qurbān*).

iii, 179 ; v, 30.[4]

A sacrifice, or gift offered to God.

Both passages have reference to O.T. events, the former to the contest between Elijah and the priests of Baal, and the latter to the offerings of Cain and Abel. Both passages are Madinan.

The Muslim authorities take the word as genuine Arabic, a form فعلان from قرب *to draw near* (Rāghib, *Mufradāt*, 408). Undoubtedly it is derived from a root קרב *to draw near, approach*, but in the sense of *oblation* it is an Aramaic development, and borrowed thence into the other languages. In O.Aram. we find קרבן in this sense, and the Targumic קרבנא, Syr. ܩܘܪܒܢܐ are of very

[1] as-Suyūṭī, *Itq*, 118, and *LA*, i, 124. Note also that Ibn Kathīr read قرأن not قرآن.

[2] Torrey, *Foundation*, 48, suggests a Jewish קֶרְאָן, but such a form is hypothetical.

[3] Horovitz, *Der Islam*, xiii, 66 ff., and *KU*, 74 ; Buhl, *EI*, ii, 1063 ; Wellhausen, *ZDMG*, lxvii, 634 ; Noldeke-Schwally, i, 33, 34 ; Mingana, *Syriac Influence*, 88 ; Massignon, *Lexique*, 52 ; Ahrens, *Muhammed*, 133.

[4] In xlvi, 27, it means "favourites of a Prince" and not *sacrifice*.

common use. From the Aram. it was borrowed into Eth. as ቍርባን (Nöldeke, *Neue Beiträge*, 37), and the 𐩤𐩧𐩨𐩬 of the S. Arabian inscriptions is doubtless of the same origin.[1]

Hirschfeld, *Beiträge*, 88, would derive the Arabic word from the Hebrew,[2] but Sprenger, *Leben*, i, 108, had already indicated that it was more likely from the Aram. and the probabilities seem to point to its being from the Syriac.[3] It must have been an early borrowing as it occurs in the early literature.

قِرْطَاسٌ (*Qirṭās*).

vi, 7, 91.

Parchment, or papyrus.[4]

In both passages the reference is to the material on which the Divine revelations were written down.

The Muslim authorities make little effort to explain the word. Some recognized it as a foreign word,[5] a fact which indeed is apparent from the uncertainty that existed as to its spelling.[6] It was evidently an early borrowing, for it occurs in the old poetry, and probably came to the Arabs from their more cultured Northern neighbours. Von Kremer suggested that it was from the Gk. χάρτη,[7] but Sachau[8] and Fraenkel[9] are nearer the mark in thinking that χάρτης is the form behind قرطاس, especially as this form is found also in the Arm. քարտէս,[10] and the Aram. קרטיסא.[11]

It is not likely that the word came directly from the Greek, and Fraenkel, *Fremdw*, 245, thought that it came through the Aram. קרטיסא[12] meaning a *paper* or *document*, as in Levit. Rabba, § 34.

[1] *ZDMG*, xxx, 672; Rossini, *Glossarium*, 234. The verb 𐩤𐩧𐩨 means to approach a woman sexually.

[2] So Fraenkel, *Vocab*, 20. Ahrens, *Christliches*, 32, favours a Jewish origin.

[3] Schwally, *Idioticon*, 84; Mingana, *Syriac Influence*, 85; Wensinck, *EI*, ii, 1129. See Cheikho, *Naṣrāniya*, 209, for early examples of the use of the word.

[4] Mingana, *Woodbrooke Studies*, ii, 21.

[5] al-Jawālīqī, *Mu'arrab*, 125; as-Suyūṭī, *Itq*, 323; al-Khafājī, 159.

[6] *LA*, viii, 54, notes قَرْطاس ; قِرْطس ; قُرْطس ; قُرطاس and قِرطاس.

[7] *Kulturgeschichte des Orients*, ii, 305.

[8] Notes to the *Mu'arrab*, p. 57.

[9] *Fremdw*, 245, cf. also Vollers, *ZDMG*, l, 617, 624; li, 301.

[10] Hubschmann, *ZDMG*, xlvi, 253; Brockelmann, *ZDMG*, xlvii, 11.

[11] Krauss, *Griechische Lehnwörter*, ii, 567 (also כרטיסא, ibid., ii, 297).

[12] In *Vocab*, 17, he suggests כרטיסא, on which see Levy, *Wörterbuch*, ii, 398.

Mingana, *Syriac Influence*, 89, prefers to derive it through the Syr. ܩܪܛܝܣܐ, which occurs beside ܩܪܛܝܣܐ, the source of the Eth. ክርጣስ. It is really impossible to decide, though the fact that Ṭarafa in his *Mu'allaqa*, l. 31, seems to look on قرطاس as something peculiarly Syrian, may count in favour of Mingana's claim.

قَرْيَة (*Qarya*).

Occurs some fifty-seven times both in sing. and plu. forms.

A village.

In Heb. קריה is a poetical synonym for עיר a *town* or *city*, and it is a question whether it and the related קֶרֶת ; Phon. קרת (cf. *Carthage*) ; Ras Shamra קר, קרת ; and Moab. קר (*Mesha Inscription*, 11, 12, 24) are not really related to the Heb. עיר and derived from the Sumerian *uru*, a *state*. In any case the Heb. קריה is parallel with the Syr. ܩܪܝܬܐ a *town* or *village*, and from the Syriac came the Arabic قرية, as Zimmern, *Akk. Fremdw*, 9, notes. (Cf. Nöldeke, *Beiträge*, 61 ff., and *Neue Beiträge*, 131.)

قُرَيْش (*Quraish*).

cvi, 1.

Quraish.

The philologers differ considerably among themselves over the origin of the name of this tribe. The popular etymology was that they were so called from their trading and profiting—من التجارة والتقريش (cf. Zam. on the verse and Ibn Hishām, 60). Others derived it from a verb تقرّش *to gather together*, holding that they were so called from their gathering or assembling at Mecca (cf. *LA*, viii, 226 ; Yāqūt, *Mu'jam*, iv, 79). Another theory derived the name from a tribal ancestor, Quraish b. Makhlad, but as it does not explain this name it does not help us much.[1]

[1] From a statement in the *Chronicles of Mecca*, ii, 133 (ed. Wüstenfeld), we would gather that some thought the name was formed quite arbitrarily from three letters of the alphabet.

The most satisfactory theory is that which derives the word from قِرْش a *shark*,[1] cf. Zam. on the verse and *LA*, viii, 226. This is scoffed at by Yāqūt, but is accepted by aṭ-Ṭabarī and al-Damīrī,[2] and it may well have been a totemistic tribal name. Nöldeke, *Beiträge*, 87, accepts this قِرْش theory, and links the word with the Aram. כרשא, which occurs in the Talmud, *Baba bathra*, 74[a], for a kind of fish, which Lewysohn thinks means the *sun-fish*,[3] and would derive from the Pers. خورشيد. It is true that Pers. خُورِس means "something eatable", but خورشيد is from the Av. 𐬓𐬁𐬭𐬆-𐬑𐬱𐬀𐬉𐬙𐬆𐬨 *hvārə-xšaetəm*, meaning *sol-splendidus*,[4] and has apparently nothing to do with fish of any kind. Nöldeke suggests with much more probability that it is a shortened form of the Gk. καρχαρίας,[5] a word which is used for a kind of small shark with pointed teeth, and which Nicander the Colophonian [6] said was used also for a lamia or a squill.

قِسْط (*Qist*).

iii, 16, 20; iv, 126, 134; v, 11, 46; vi, 153; vii, 28; x, 4, 48, 55; xi, 86; xxi, 48; lv, 8; lvii, 25.

Justice, equity.

It would seem on the surface to be a derivative from قَسَطَ which occurs in iv, 3; lx, 8; xlix, 9, and of which other derivatives are found in ii, 282; xxxiii, 5; lxxii, 14, 15. This قسط, however, may be a denominative and as-Suyūṭī, *Itq*, 323; *Mutaw*, 49, tells us

[1] Or *sword-fish* (Margoliouth, *Mohammed*, 9). Ibn Faqīh (ed. de Goeje, p. 290) describes it as سمكة اعظم من التنين.

[2] Tabarī, *Annales*, i, 1104; Damīrī, *Ḥayawān*, ii, 291 ff.; *vide* also *Khizana*, i, 98.

[3] *Zoologie der Talmud*, Frankfurt, 1858, p. 271. This is accepted by Levy, *Wörterbuch*, ii, 416, and Goldschmidt, *Der Babylonische Talmud*, vi, 1136; though Jastrow, *Dict. Talmud*, i, 667, gives it as meaning probably the shark.

[4] Bartholomae, *AIW*, 1848; cf. Yasht, x, 118; v, 90.

[5] Cf. also Hess in *ZS*, ii, 220.

[6] In his Book on Dialects quoted by Athenaeus, vii, 76.

that some early authorities thought قِسْط was a borrowing from Greek.[1]

The root קשט is widely used in Aramaic but occurs elsewhere apparently as a loan-word. Thus קשוט ; קושטא, like Syr. ܩܘܫܛܐ, means *truth, right*[2]; Mand. קשט is *to be true*, and Palm. קשט *to succeed*, while in the Christian-Palestinian dialect we find ܩܫܛܐ *true*.[3] The Heb. קֹשֶׁט is an Aramaizing, as Toy pointed out in his Commentary on Proverbs, and Fraenkel is doubtless correct in taking the Ar. قِسْط as also of Aram., probably of Christian Aram. origin.[4]

قِسْطَاس (*Qisṭās*).

xvii, 37 ; xxvi, 182.

A balance.

There was practical agreement among the early authorities that the word means primarily a *balance*, and then metaphorically *justice* (cf. Rāghib, *Mufradāt*, 413 ; *LA*, viii, 59). It was also very generally recognized as a loan-word. Some considered it as a genuine Arabic word, a variant of قسط,[5] but the weight of the authorities as we see from as-Suyūṭī, *Itq*, 323 ; *Muzhir*, i, 130 ; al-Jawālīqī, *Mu'arrab*, 114 ; ath-Tha'ālabī, *Fiqh*, 318, and as-Sijistānī, 257, was in favour of its being taken as a borrowing from Greek.[6] Its foreign nature is indeed indicated by the variety of spellings we find.[7]

It was evidently an early borrowing, for it occurs in verses of

[1] This may be a reminiscence of the Lat. *iusticia*, though Sprenger, *Leben*, ii, 219, thinks that it may be the Lat. *sextarius*.

[2] Notice also the כושטא = honesty (with כ), of the incantation texts ; cf. Montgomery, *Aramaic Incantation Texts*, Glossary, p. 292.

[3] Schwally, *Idioticon*, 86 ; Schulthess, *Lex*, 185.

[4] *Fremdw*, 205 ; Noldeke, *SBAW*, Berlin (1882), liv, 5, thinks the noun is an Arabicizing of ܩܘܣܛܐ, but Dvořák, *Fremdw*, 76, 78, would regard it as an Arabic word taken as foreign through its similarity in sound with قسطاس.

[5] See Zam. on xxvi, 182, and the remarks in *TA*, iv, 218.

[6] See also as-Suyūṭī, *Muzhir*, i, 137 ; Ibn Qutaiba (*Adab al-Kātib*), 527 ; al-Khafājī, 156 ; as-Suyūṭī, *Mutaw*, 49.

[7] al-Jawālīqī notes قُسطاس ; قِسْطاس ; قُسطار ; to which we may add from *TA*. قُصطاس and قِصْطاس.

'Adī b. Zaid, an-Nābigha,[1] and others. The origin of the word, however, is not easy to settle. Sachau in his notes to the *Mu'arrab*, p. 51, quotes Fleischer as suggesting that it goes back to the Lat. *constans* as used of the *libra*.[2] Fraenkel, *Fremdw*, 282, suggests a hypothetical *κούστως as a possible origin, and in *WZKM*, vi, 261, would interpret it from ζυγοστασία. Vullers, *Lex*, ii, 725, thought that it was probably a mangling of the Gk. ζεῦγος a *yoke*, and Dvořák, *Fremdw*, 77 ff., would derive it from ξέστης from the Lat. *sextarius* used as a measure of fluid and dry materials.

All these suggestions seem to be under the influence of the theory of the philologers that the word is of Greek origin. It would seem much more hopeful to start from the Aram. קסטא ; קיסטא ; קוסטא meaning *measure*, or the Syr. ܩܣܛܐ. The final *s* here, however, presents a difficulty, and Vollers, *ZDMG*, l, 633,[3] suggests that it is from the Gk. δικαστής a *judge*, which in Syr. is ܕܝܩܣܛܣ (*BB*, in *PSm*, 891), and with the ܕ taken as the genitive particle, would give us ܩܣܛܣ. This, influenced by the similar ܕܩܣܛܐ also = δικαστής, would give us قسطاس. This is very ingenious and may be true, but Mingana, *Syriac Influence*, 89, thinks it simpler to take it from ܩܣܛܐ representing ξέστης in some form in which the final ܣ had survived.

قِسِّيسُون (*Qissīsūn*).

v, 85.

Priests.

From the passage it is clear that it refers to Christian teachers, and though one would not care to press the point, its occurrence alongside رهبان may indicate that it referred to the ordinary clergy as distinct from the monks.

It was generally considered by the philologers as a genuine Arabic

[1] Fraenkel, *WZKM*, vi, 258, however, thinks the verse attributed to an-Nābigha is under Qur'ānic influence.

[2] On which see Fraenkel, *Fremdw*, 198. It was rejected by Noldeke, but defended by Ginzburg in *Zapiski*, viii, 145 ff.

[3] See also l, 620; li, 301, 323.

word[1] derived from قَسَّ *to seek after* or *pursue* a thing, so that a قسيس is so called " because he follows the Book and its precepts ", as-Sijistānī, 259. Obviously the word is the Syr. ܩܫܝܫܐ=πρεσβύτερος, as has been generally recognized by Western scholars.[2] This word could hardly fail to be known to any Arab tribes which came into contact with the Christians of the North and East, and as a matter of fact both forms of the word were borrowed into Arabic, ܩܫܐ (cf. Aram. קשׁא) as قس, and ܩܫܝܫܐ as قسيس, while the Ḥadīth لا يغير قسيس من قسيسية shows that they were not unacquainted with the abstract noun ܩܫܝܫܘܬܐ.

We meet with the word in the early poetry,[3] which shows it must have been an early borrowing, and as a matter of fact it occurs as a borrowing both in Eth. ቀሲስ,[4] and in the S. Arabian inscriptions (e.g. Glaser, 618, 67 — [illegible]),[5] on the ground of which Grimme, *ZA*, xxvi, 162, would take the word to be from a S. Arabian source, though with little likelihood.

قَصْرٌ (*Qaṣr*).

vii, 72 ; xxii, 44 ; xxv, 11 ; lxxvii, 32.

A castle.

The word has no verbal root in Arabic, and was noted by Guidi, *Della Sede*, 579, as a borrowing. Fraenkel, *Vocab*, 14, is doubtless correct in deriving it from Lat. *castrum*, through Gk. κάστρον and Aram. קצרא.[6] The word occurs not infrequently in the early poetry, and is probably to be considered as one of the words which came into Syria and Palestine with the Roman armies of occupation.[7]

[1] But see al-Jawālīqī, *Mu'arrab*, 39.

[2] Geiger, 51 ; Fleischer, *Kleinere Schriften*, ii, 118 ; Freytag, *Lex*, sub voc. ; Fraenkel, *Vocab*, 24 ; *Fremdw*, 275 ; Rudolph, *Abhangigkeit*, 7 ; Horovitz, *KU*, 64 ; Mingana, *Syriac Influence*, 85.

[3] Cf. *Aghānī*, xiii, 47, 170 ; xvi, 45.

[4] Noldeke, *Neue Beiträge*, 37 ; Pautz, *Offenbarung*, 136, n.

[5] Cf. on it Praetorius in *ZDMG*, liii, 21 ; Rossini, *Glossarium*, 233.

[6] That קצרא as used in the Mishnah and Jerusalem Talmud is but a form of קסטרא, which like ܩܣܛܪܐ was derived directly from κάστρον, has been shown by Nöldeke, *ZDMG*, xxix, 423 ; cf. also Guidi, op. cit., and Krauss, *Griechische Lehnwörter*, ii, 562.

[7] Fraenkel, *Fremdw*, 234 ; Vollers, *ZDMG*, l, 614 ; li, 316.

قِطّ (*Qiṭṭ*).

xxxviii, 15.

A judge's sentence.

In general the opinion of the Commentators is that قِطّ means some sort of writing (cf. Bagh. *in loco*, and Rāghib, *Mufradāt*, 417). Some, however, recognized it as a foreign word, for as-Suyūṭī, *Itq*, 323, quotes authority for its meaning *book* in Nabataean.

Halévy suggested that it was to be derived from Akk. *kithu*, but this is hardly likely. Fraenkel, *Fremdw*, 249, agrees with as-Suyūṭī's authorities in taking it as a loan-word from Aramaic.[1] In the Mishnah גט means an official document, though later it was specialized in the meaning of "bill of divorce". So גִּט and גִּיטָא both mean *writing* and *document*, and Levy, *Wörterbuch*, i, 322, suggests they may be originally from Gk. χάρτης. Syr. ܓܛܐ became specialized in the meaning of *haereditas*, and is not so likely an origin. If a borrowing, it must have been early, for several examples occur in the old poetry.[2]

قَطِرَانٌ (*Qaṭirān*).

xiv, 51.

Pitch.

This curious word occurs only in a passage descriptive of the torments of the wicked on the Last Day, where the pronunciation of the Readers varied between قَطِرَان ; قَطْرَان ; and قِطْرَان. This last reading is supported by the early poetry and is doubtless the most primitive.[3]

Zam. tells us that it was an exudation from the Ubhal tree used for smearing mangy camels, but from the discussion in *LA*, vi, 417, we learn that the philologers were somewhat embarrassed over the word, and we have an interesting tradition that Ibn 'Abbās knew not

[1] The ultimate origin is apparently the Sumerian *gida*, whence comes Akk. *gittu*, and the Aram. forms, cf. Zimmern, *Akkad. Fremdw*, 19.

[2] Cf. the verse of Al-A'shā in Jawharī, s.v. قطط (where Cheikho, *Naṣrāniya*, 222, thinks that by قط al-A'shā means the Gospel); and Mutalammis in Yāqūt, *Mu'jam*, iv, 228.

[3] *Vide* Ṭab. on the verse.

what to make of it, and wanted to read قِطْرٍ آنٍ,[1] which would make it mean "red-hot brass", and link it with the قِطْر of xviii, 95, and xxxiv, 11.

The truth seems to be that it is the Aram. עִטְרָן ; Syr. ܥܛܪܢܐ meaning *pitch*, which though not a very common word is an early one. Some confusion of ע and ק must have occurred when the word was borrowed, but it is interesting that the primitive form قِطْرَان of the poets preserved exactly the vowelling of the Aram.[2]

قُفْل (*Qufl*).

xlvii, 26.

A lock.

Only in the plu. أَقْفَال, where al-Jawālīqī, *Mu'arrab*, 125, says it is a borrowing from Persian.[3]

The verb قَفَلَ is denominative[4] and the word cannot be derived from an Arabic root. It is probably the Aram. קופלא a *fetter*, or Syr. ܩܘܦܠܐ, which translates the Gk. κλεῖθρον, and would have been an early borrowing.[5]

قَلَم (*Qalam*).

iii, 39 ; xxxi, 26 ; lxviii, 1 ; xcvi, 4.

Pen, or the reed from which pens were made.

It means a *pen* in all the passages save iii, 39, where it refers to the reeds which were cast to decide who should have care of the maiden Maryam, and where the أَقْلَام, of course, stands for the ῥάβδοι of the *Protev. Jacobi*, ix.[6]

[1] Baiḍ. gives this as the reading of Ya'qūb.
[2] Cf. Fraenkel, *Fremdw*, 150 ; Zimmern, *Akkad. Fremdw*, 60.
[3] So as-Suyūṭī, *Itq*, 323. al-Jawālīqī is probably referring to the Pers. كوپال.
[4] Fraenkel, *Fremdw*, 16 ; Zimmern, *Akkad. Fremdw*, 35, gives it from the Aramaic.
[5] Cf. Krauss, *Griechische Lehnwörter*, ii, 517, and *ZDMG*, xxvii, 623.
[6] In Tischendorf, *Evangelia Apocrypha*, 1876, p. 18.

The native authorities take the word from قَلَمَ *to cut* (cf. *LA*, xv, 392), but this is only folk-etymology, for the word is the Gk. κάλαμος a *reed* and then a *pen*,[1] though coming through some Semitic form. κάλαμος was borrowed into Aram., where we find קולמוס, Syr. ܩܠܡܐ, but it was from the Eth. ቀለም, as Nöldeke, *Neue Beiträge*, 50, has shown, that the word came into Arabic. It was an early borrowing, for it is found both in the old poetry and in the S. Arabian inscriptions (Rossini, *Glossarium*, 232, for 𐩤𐩡𐩣 as *calamus odoratus*).

قَمِيص (*Qamīṣ*).

xii, 18–28, 93.

Shirt.

It is curious that the word occurs only in the Joseph story.

The authorities usually take it as an Arabic word, though as-Suyūṭī, *Muzhir*, i, 135, quotes al-Aṣma'ī to the effect that some held it was of Persian origin.

It is clear that it cannot have an Arabic derivation, and the underlying word is doubtless the Gk. καμίσιον. This καμίσιον has been taken as a borrowing from Semitic, but, as Boissacq, 403, shows in his note on κάμμαρος, it is genuine Indo-European. The Gk. καμίσιον passed into Syr. as ܩܡܝܣܐ,[2] and into Eth. as ቀሚስ, which is used in *Josippon*, 343, for a *tunic* or *shirt*, and is in all probability the source of the Arabic word.[3] It must have been an early borrowing for we find it not infrequently in the old poetry.

قِنْطَار (*Qinṭār*).

iii, 12, 68; iv, 24.

Qinṭār—a measure.

It was recognized by the philologers as of foreign origin, and though some, like Sībawaih, held to an Arabic origin, Abū 'Ubaida (*LA*, vi,

[1] κάλαμος is a good Indo-European word, as is evident from the Skt. कलम; Norse *halmr*; Slav. *slama*; cf. Boissacq, 397.

[2] See Fraenkel, *Fremdw*, 45.

[3] Vollers, *ZDMG*, li, 311, thinks that the Arabic came from the Lat. *camisia*, but this is hardly likely.

432) expressly states that the Arabs did not know the meaning of the word.[1] Some said it was a Berber word (as-Suyūṭī, *Itq*, 323), others that it was Syriac (as-Suddī in *Mukhaṣṣaṣ*, xii, 266), but the majority were in favour of its being Greek (ath-Tha'ālibī, *Fiqh*, 318; as-Suyūṭī, *Muzhir*, i, 134).

Undoubtedly it is the Gk. κεντηνάριον, which represents the Lat. *centenarium*, and passed into Aram. as קנטינר, Syr. ܩܢܛܝܢܪܐ.[2] It was from the Aram., as Fraenkel, *Vocab*, 13; *Fremdw*, 203, shows, that the word came into Arabic, and in all probability from the shortened Syr. form ܩܢܛܪܐ.[3]

قِيَامَة (*Qiyāma*).

Occurs some seventy times, cf. ii, 79.

Resurrection.

It occurs only in the expression يوم القيامة, which is a technical eschatological term for the Last Day.

The Muslim authorities naturally relate it to the root قام to *stand* or *rise*, but it has been pointed out many times, that as an eschatological term it has been borrowed from Christian Aramaic.[4] In the Edessene Syriac we find ܩܝܡܐ commonly used, but it is in the Christian-Palestinian dialect, where it translates ἀνάστασις (Schwally, *Idioticon*, 82), that we find ܩܝܡܬܐ, which provides us with exactly the form we want.

قَيُّوم (*Qayyūm*).

ii, 256; iii, 1; xx, 110.

Self-subsisting.

It occurs only in the phrase الحى القيّوم used of Allah.

[1] This is evident from the variety of opinions on its meaning collected by Ibn Sīda in the *Mukhaṣṣaṣ*, xii, 266, and Ibn al-Athīr in *Nihāya*, iii, 313.

[2] Krauss, *Griechische Lehnwörter*, ii, 553. It was from this form that the Arm. կենդինար was derived (Hübschmann, *Arm. Gramm*, i, 356).

[3] Mingana, *Syriac Influence*, 89; Vollers, *ZDMG*, li, 316.

[4] Cf. Pautz, *Offenbarung*, 165, n. 1; Mingana, op. cit., 85. Horovitz, *JPN*, 186, notes that the phrase is not Jewish.

The Commentators are unanimous that the meaning is القائم الدائم (Ṭab., Baiḍ., and as-Sijistānī, 250), but they were in difficulties over the form, and there are variants قيام, قيم, and قائم. Their trouble in explaining the form is well illustrated by al-'Ukbarī, *Imlā'*, i, 70, for the only possibility is to take it as on the measure فيعول, and we have reason to suspect all words of this form. It is not strange, therefore, in spite of its obvious connection with قام, to find that some of the authorities took it as a word borrowed from the Syriac.[1]

Hirschfeld, *Beiträge*, 38, would derive it from Hebrew, and certainly קים is used in connection with חי in Jewish texts of the oldest period,[2] but ܩܝܘܡܐ is also commonly used in the same sense and we cannot absolutely rule out a Syriac origin for the word.

كَأْسٌ (*Ka's*).

xxxvii, 44; lii, 23; lvi, 18; lxxvi, 5, 17; lxxviii, 34.

Cup.

It is found only in early passages in descriptions of the pleasures of Paradise.

This is not a S. Semitic word, as it is entirely lacking in Eth. and without a root and of uncertain plu. in Arabic. There can thus be little doubt of its Aram. origin.[3]

The Heb. word is כוס, while in the Ras Shamra texts we have כס, and in Aram. כוסא, כסא, and כוזא (cf. Ar. كُوزٌ), and Syr. ܟܣܐ.[4] As the Syr. ܟܣܐ seems to be the source of the Pers.

[1] as-Suyūṭī, *Itq*, 324; *Mutaw*, 54.

[2] Fraenkel, *Vocab*, 23; Noldeke-Schwally, i, 184, n.; and see Sprenger, *Leben*, ii, 204, n. It is noteworthy that the best attested variant reading قيّام agrees closely in form with קַיָּם. See also Horovitz, *JPN*, 219, who, as a matter of fact, would derive the word حي also from the Jewish חי.

[3] Fraenkel, *Fremdw*, 171; Zimmern, *Akkad. Fremdw*, 34. D. H. Müller, however, *WZKM*, i, 27, thinks that the medial Hamza proves it to be genuine Arabic.

[4] Cf. also the כס of the Elephantine papyri (Cowley, *Aramaic Papyri*, No. 61).

كاسه [1] we may take it as most probable that the Arabic also was borrowed at an early period [2] from the same source.

كَافُورٌ (*Kāfūr*).

lxxvi, 5.

Camphor.

The verse is an early one descriptive of the joys of Paradise, where the Commentators were uncertain whether كافور was the name of the fountain from which the Blessed drink, or the material used to temper the drink (cf. Ṭab. and Baiḍ. on the verse).

It is usually taken as an Arabic word (*LA*, vi, 465), but the variety of spellings—كافور, قافور, قَفُور, and قفّور—would suggest otherwise, and several of the early authorities noted it as a loan-word from Persian.[3]

The ultimate source is probably to be found in the Muṇḍa dialects of India, whence it passed into Dravidian, e.g. Tamil கற்பூரம், Malayalam കർപ്പൂരം, and into Skt., cf. कर्पूर.[4] It passed also into Iranian, where we find Phlv. kāpūr,[5] which gives the Mod. Pers. كافور, and Arm. քափուր,[6] and into Aram. where we find Syr. ܟܦܘܪܐ [7] and Mand. גופארא.[8] It is very probable that the Syriac like the Gk. καφουρά is from the Iranian, and Addai Sher, 136, would make the Arabic also a borrowing from the Persians. The probabilities are, however, that it, like the Eth. ከፉር, is to be taken as derived from the Syriac.[9] We find the

[1] Addai Sher, 131. The Persian Lexicons take this to be the source of the Arabic word, cf. Vullers, *Lex*, ii, 769, كاس معرب كاسه است.

[2] It occurs in the early poets, e.g. Al-A'shā and 'Alqama.

[3] as-Suyūṭī, *Itq*, 324; al-Jawālīqī, *Mu'arrab*, 129; al-Khafājī, 170; ath-Tha'ālibī, *Fiqh*, 318.

[4] For further examples see Laufer, *Sino Iranica*, 591.

[5] Justi, *Glossary to Bundahesh*, 201. The Persian Lexicons, e.g. *BQ*, 691, note that camphor came to them from India.

[6] Hübschmann, *Arm. Gramm.*, i, 257.

[7] Also ܩܦܘܪܐ, ܟܦܘܪ, and ܩܦܘܪܐ, *PSm*, 3688, 3689.

[8] Nöldeke, *Mand. Gramm.*, 112.

[9] Fraenkel, *Vocab*, 11; *Fremdw*, 147.

word in the early poetry (e.g. in al-A'shā),[1] but the story told by Balādhurī (ed. de Goeje, 264), that the Arab soldiers who conquered Madā'in found stores of camphor there and took it for salt, would seem to show that the article was not widely known in Arabia.

كَاهِنٌ (*Kāhin*).

lii, 29; lxix, 42.

A soothsayer.

It occurs only in the early Meccan period and in a depreciatory sense, for Muḥammad rejects with some asperity the idea that in giving forth his revelations he was on a level with the كَهَنَة. This shows that the word was pre-Islamic, and it seems that the Arabic كاهن was the equivalent of the Gk. μάντις or the Lat. *vates*, i.e. he was a *Seer* rather than a *Prophet*.[2]

The Muslim authorities naturally take it from كهن, but this verb seems denominative. The Heb. word is כֹּהֵן and means *priest*, as in Phon. and in the Ras Shamra tablets, and from the Heb. came the Aram. כהנא; Syr. ܟܘܗܢܐ.[3] That the Arabic word also was borrowed directly from the Hebrew is not likely. Pautz, *Offenbarung*, 175, n. 2, has a theory that it came by way of the Eth. ካህን, but like this word itself, and the Arm. քահանայ,[4] it is more likely to have come from the Aram.[5] As a matter of fact it occurs not infrequently in the Sinaitic inscriptions from N. Arabia,[6] where we find כהנא and the fem. כהנתא,[7] and actually in No. 550 כהן עזיא, i.e. the priest of al-'Uzzā, so that as Nöldeke, *Neue Beiträge*, 36, n., insists, we have clear evidence that it came into use in N. Arabia from some Aram. source long before Islam.

The analogy of the inscriptions would lead us to conclude that

[1] Geyer, *Zwei Gedichte*, i, 61.

[2] *LA*, xvii, 244; Wellhausen, *Reste*, 134; Goldziher, *Abhandlungen*, i, 18 ff., 107 ff.; Sprenger, *Leben*, i, 255.

[3] G. B. Gray, *Sacrifice in the Old Testament*, p. 183.

[4] Hübschmann, *Arm. Gramm.*, i, 318; *ZDMG*, xlvi, 252.

[5] Cheikho, *Naṣrāniya*, 200; Mingana, *Syriac Influence*, 85.

[6] Euting, *Sinäitische Inschriften*, Nos. 550, 249, 348, and 223.

[7] Cf. also the Safaite כהנת (Ryckmans, *Noms propres*, i, 113)

the primitive sense in Arábic was *priest*, and that of *soothsayer* a later development, in spite of Fischer's claim that *soothsayer* is the original sense.[1]

كِبْرِيَاء (*Kibriyā'*).

x, 79; xlv, 36.

Glory.

It is connected in form but not in meaning with the Arabic root كبر.

The root is common Semitic, cf. Akk. *kabāru*, to *become great*, Heb. כבר (in Hiph.) *to make many*; Aram. כְּבַר; Syr. ܟܒܰܪ; Eth. ከበረ *to honour*, and cf. Sab. 𐩫𐩨𐩧 *large* and *Prince* (Hommel, *Südarab. Chrest*, 127; Rossini, *Glossarium*, 167).

The usual theory is that the Qur'ānic word is a development from the Ar. كبر *to become great, magnificent*, but as it was in Eth. that the root developed prominently the meaning of *gloriosum, illustrum esse*, we may perhaps see in the Eth. ክብር commonly used as meaning *gloria, honor* (= δόξα), and then *magnificentia, splendor* (Dillmann, *Lex*, 846), the source of the word (cf. Ahrens, *Christliches*, 23; *Muhammad*, 78).

كَتَبَ (*Kataba*).

Of frequent occurrence.

To write.

Besides the verb we should note the derived forms in the Qur'ān—كتاب a *book, writing* (plu. كُتُب), كَاتِب *one who writes*, مَكْتُوب *written*, إِكْتَتَبَ *to cause to be written*, and كَاتَبَ *to write a contract of manumission*.

The word appears to be a N. Semitic development and found only as a borrowed term in S. Semitic. Heb. כָּתַב; Aram. כְּתַב;

[1] *EI*, sub voc. Fischer also claims that the word is Arabic and not a borrowed term, as does Nielsen in *HAA*, i, 245.

Syr. ܟܬܒ ; Nab. כתב, and Phon. כתב all mean *to write*, and with them Buhl compares Ar. كتب *to draw or sew together*.[1]

The borrowing was doubtless from Aram.,[2] and Fraenkel, *Fremdw*, 249, thinks that the borrowed word was كتاب, which like Eth. መጽሐፍ came from Aram. כתבא ; Syr. ܟܬܒܐ, and that then the verb and other forms developed from this. The borrowing may have taken place at al-Ḥīra, whence the art of writing spread among the Arabs,[3] but as both nominal and verbal forms are common in Nabataean (cf. *RES*, ii, 464 ; iii, 443), it may have been an early borrowing from N. Arabia.

كُرْسِيّ (*Kursiy*).

ii, 256 ; xxxviii, 33.

Throne.

It has no verbal root, though some have endeavoured to connect it with كرس (cf. Rāghib, *Mufradāt*, 441), a connection which is hardly possible.

Fraenkel, *Vocab*, 22, noted that it was a borrowing from the Aramaic. In the Zenjirli inscription we find כרסא,[4] which is connected with Akk. *kussū*, Heb. כִּסֵּא, and Ras Shamra כסא, but the commoner form is כורסיא,[5] Syr. ܟܘܪܣܝܐ or ܟܪܣܝܐ. This gives us precisely the form we want, but whether the word was from Jewish sources as Hirschfeld, *Beiträge*, 88, claims, or from Christian as Schwally, *ZDMG*, liii, 197, holds, it is quite impossible to decide.[6]

[1] *Vide* Fleischer in *ZDMG*, xxvii, 427, n. From this we have كتيبة *squadron*.

[2] *BDB*, 507 ; D. H. Müller, *WZKM*, i, 29 ; Horovitz, *KU*, 67 ; Fischer, *Glossar*, 112 ; Künstlinger in *Rocznik Orjentalistyczny*, iv, 238 ff.

[3] *Vide* Krenkow in *EI*, ii, 1044.

[4] D. H. Muller, *Inschriften von Sendschirli*, 58, 44 ; cf. Cook, *Glossary*, 66.

[5] Found also on incantation bowls ; cf. Montgomery, *Aramaic Incantation Texts*, Glossary, p. 292.

[6] Cf. Nöldeke, *Mand. Gramm.*, 128 ; Rudolph, *Abhängigkeit*, 12. The word comes ultimately from the Sumerian *guza*, whence Akk. *kussu* ; Zimmern, *Akkad. Fremdw*, 8.

كَفَرَ (*Kafara*).

Used very frequently.

To deny the grace or existence of God: then—to be an unbeliever.

In its various forms it is of common use in the Qur'ān, and the root is undoubtedly Arabic, but as a technical religious term it has been influenced by outside usage.

The primitive sense of كفر *to cover or conceal*, corresponds with the Aram. כפר; Syr. ܟܦܪ, and a derivative from this primitive sense occurs in the Qur'ān, lvii, 19, in the word كُفَّار *husbandmen*, i.e. "they who cover the seed". The form كَفَرَ, however, corresponds with the Heb. כִּפֶּר, Aram. כַּפֵּר, and means *to cover* in the sense of *atone*.[1] In this sense it is used with عن, and as-Suyūṭī, *Itq*, 324; *Mutaw*, 56, tells us that some early authorities noted this كفر عن as derived from Hebrew or Nabataean. The commoner use, however, is with ب, in the sense of to deny the existence or goodness of God, and this use with ب is characteristic of Syriac. The form كافر an *unbeliever* and كُفر *unbelief*, may indeed be independent borrowings from the Heb. כֹּפֶר, Syr. ܟܦܘܪܐ and ܟܦܘܪܘܬܐ (Ahrens, *Christliches*, 41), though a כפר as a proper name seems to occur in the Thamudic inscriptions (Ryckmans, *Noms propres*, i, 115). The form كفارة may, however, be a direct borrowing from the Jews, cf. Horovitz, *JPN*, 220.

Hirschfeld, *Beiträge*, 90; Horovitz, *KU*, 59, and Torrey, *Foundation*, 48, 144, would have the dominant influence on the Arabic in this connection from the Jewish community, and Pautz, *Offenbarung*, 159, n.; Mingana, *Syriac Influence*, 86, stand for a Christian source. Again it is really impossible to decide (cf. Ahrens, *Christliches*, 21).

[1] The S. Arabian 𐩫𐩰𐩧 seems also to have this meaning; cf. Rossini, *Glossarium*, 170.

كَنْزٌ (*Kanz*).

xi, 15 ; xviii, 81 ; xxv, 9 ; xxvi, 58 ; xxviii, 76.

Treasure.

The denominative verb كَنَزَ *to treasure up* is also found in ix, 34, 35.

Some of the Muslim authorities take it as genuine Arabic and derive it from كَنَزَ, but it was well known to the early philologers that it was a foreign word and it is noted as such by al-Jawālīqī, *Mu'arrab*, 133 ; ath-Tha'ālibī, *Fiqh*, 317 ; al-Khafājī, 170, all of whom give it as Persian كنج, meaning, of course, گنج, which *BQ*, 797, defines as زر و گوهری که در زیر زمین دفن کنند.

That it was originally Iranian is certain. Paz. *ganz* ; Phlv. *ganj* means *treasury*,[1] and the word has been widely borrowed, cf. Skt. गञ्ज ; Arm. գանձ [2] ; Baluchi, *ganj* ; Gk. γάζα ; Sogd. *γnz*, and in the Semitic family, cf. גנזי המלך of Esth. iii, 9 ; Aram. גנזא, גניזה, and גזא [3] : Syr. ܓܙܐ, and Mand. גינזא,[4] all meaning *treasury*. The direct borrowing of all these from Middle Persian seems clear from the fact that the Phlv. *ganjāβar* [5] for the *treasurer* is also common to them all, cf. Skt. गञ्जवर ; Arm. գանձաւոր (Gk. γαζοφύλαξ) ; Heb. גזבר ; Syr. ܓܙܒܪܐ, ܓܝܙܒܪܐ, and Aram. גזברא (cf. Telegdi in *JA*, ccxxvi (1935), p. 237 ; Henning in *BSOS*, ix, 83).

It is most probable that the word came direct from Middle Persian into Arabic,[6] though ز for might point to Aram. influence on the word. The word must have been borrowed long before Muḥammad's time, though it occurs but rarely in the old poetry.

[1] West, *Glossary*, 274 ; *PPGl*, 112 ; Nyberg, *Glossar*, 77 ; Herzfeld, *Paikuli*, Glossary, 159. Lagarde, *Arm. Stud*, § 453, thinks that it is an old Median word which passed later into Iranian and thence to India ; cf. also his *GA*, 27.

[2] Hubschmann, *Arm. Gramm*, i, 126.

[3] Levy, *Worterbuch*, i, 316, however, thinks that גניזה and גזא are from גנז *to hide*.

[4] Nöldeke, *Mand. Gramm*, 51.

[5] *PPGl*, 119 ; Frahang, *Glossary*, 79. It is the Pers. گنجور, and Paz. *ganzubar* (Shikand, *Glossary*, 245). Compare also Phlv. *ganjēnak* = barn or storehouse (Šāyast, *Glossary*, 161).

[6] Vollers, *ZDMG*, l, 613, 647.

كُوبٌ (*Kūb*).

xliii, 71 ; lvi, 18 ; lxxvi, 15 ; lxxxviii, 14.

A goblet.

It occurs only in early Sūras in descriptions of the pleasures of Paradise, and was recognized by some of the early authorities as a Nabataean word (cf. as-Suyūṭī, *Itq*, 319; *Mutaw*, 60).[1] Some, of course, endeavoured to derive it from كاب, but this verb is obviously denominative (*TA*, i, 464 ; *LA*, ii, 225).

The word is commonly used in the early poetry, cf. ʿAdī b. Zaid, al-Aʿshā (Geyer, *Zwei Gedichte*, i, 56 = *Dīwān*, ii, 21), ʿAbda b. aṭ-Ṭabīb,[2] etc., and seems to have been an early loan-word from Aram., as Horovitz, *Paradies*, 11, has noted, though Aram. כובא ; Syr. ܟܘܒܐ both seem to be from the Byzantine κοῦπα (Lat. *cupa*, cf. Fraenkel, *Vocab*, 25), from the older Gk. κύμβη.[3]

كَيْلٌ (*Kail*).

vi, 153 ; vii, 83 ; xii, 59, 65, 88 ; xvii, 37 ; xxvi, 181.

A measure.

The philologers insist that it means a measure of food-stuffs (Rāghib, *Mufradāt*, 460), but in the Qur'ān it is used in a quite general sense.

Fraenkel, *Fremdw*, 204, pointed out that it is the Syr. ܟܝܠܐ, which, like the Aram. כיילא, means *measure*. כיילא is seldom used, but ܟܝܠܐ is of very common use and has many derivatives, and was borrowed into Iranian,[4] so that it was the Syriac word that would have passed at an early date into Arabic.

لَاتَ (*Lāta*).

xxxviii, 2.

There was not.

[1] *Vide* also Sprenger, *Leben*, ii, 507, n.

[2] In *Mufaddaliyāt* (ed. Lyall), xxvi, 76.

[3] Levy, *Fremdw*, 151, points out a very probable Semitic origin for κύμβη in the sense of *ship*, but in that under discussion the borrowing seems to be the other way, for as Boissacq, sub voc., points out, it is a true Indo-European word. Vollers, *ZDMG*, li, 316, would derive كوب from the Italian, but see Nallino therein, p. 534.

[4] Cf. Nöldeke, *GGA*, 1868, ii, 44.

The philologers were in some straits to explain the word as can be seen by consulting the two columns which Lane, *Lex*, 2683, devotes to a summary of their opinions. The three commonest theories were (i) that it was لا with the meaning of ليس, to which a fem. ت has been added[1]; (ii) that it was the negative لا with a fem. ending[2]; (iii) that it was another way of writing ليس.[3] Some tried to overcome the difficulty by reading لا تحين instead of لات حين, and some, as we learn from as-Suyūṭī, *Itq*, 275; *Mutaw*, 54, admitted that it was a loan-word of Syriac origin.

Aram. לית and Syr. ܠܝܬ, contracted from לא אית and represented by the Ar. ليس, are of very common use, and from some Aram. source the word was borrowed as an ideogram into Middle Persian where we find לוית *lōīt*,[4] which was also commonly used and gave rise to לויתיה *lōītīh*, meaning *non-existence, unreality*.[5] It was thus probably borrowed at an early date into Arabic,[6] though, as it occurs in the early poetry,[7] Barth has argued that it is genuine Arabic.[8]

لَوْحٌ (*Lauḥ*).

vii, 142, 149, 153; liv, 13; lxxxv, 22.

A board or plank.

There are two distinct uses of the word in the Qur'ān. In liv, 13, it is used for the planks of Noah's ark, and elsewhere for tablets of revelation, in Sūra, vii, for the tablets of Moses, and in lxxxv, 32, for the heavenly archetype of the Qur'ān.

[1] This was the opinion of Sībawaih and Khalīl given by Zam. on the verse.

[2] So al-Akhfash in Zam.

[3] See Ṭab. on the verse, and *LA*, ii, 391. Bagh. says that it was Yemenite.

[4] West, *Glossary*, 141; *PPGl*, 149.

[5] West, *Glossary*, 142.

[6] Mingana, *Syriac Influence*, 93.

[7] Geyer, *Zwei Gedichte*, i, 18 = *Dīwān*, i, 3, and see examples in *ZDMG*, lxvii, 494, and Reckendorf, *Syntax*.

[8] *ZDMG*, lxvii, 494 ff.; lxviii, 362, 363, and see Bergsträsser, *Negationen im Kur'ān*.

In the related languages we find both these meanings. The Heb. לוח means both the planks of a ship (as in Ez. xxvii, 5), and the stone tablets of the Ten Commandments (Ex. xxiv, 12). Similarly, Aram. לוחא can mean a *table* for food, or, as constantly in the Targums, the *tablets* of the Covenant, so Syr. ܠܘܚܐ is used of a wooden board, e.g. the τίτλος affixed to the Cross, and for the *tablets* of the Covenant. Also the Eth. ሰሌዳ, though not a common word, is used for the broken boards on which Paul and his companions escaped from shipwreck in Acts xxvii, 44 (ed. Rom.), and also for writing tablets of wood, metal, or stone.

In the early Arabic poetry we find the word used only in the sense of plank, cf. Ṭarafa iv, 12; Imru'ul-Qais, x, 13, and Zuhair, i, 23 (in Ahlwardt's *Divans*),[1] and the Lexicons take this as the primitive meaning. The word may be a loan-word in both senses, but even if a case could be made out for its being a genuine Arabic word in the sense of *plank*, there can be no doubt that as used for the Tables of Revelation it is a borrowing from the older faiths. Hirschfeld, *Beiträge*, 36, would have it derived from the Hebrew, but Horovitz, *KU*, 66; *JPN*, 220, 221, is more likely to be correct [2] in considering it as from the Aram., though whether from Jewish or Christian sources it is difficult to say.

If we can trust the genuineness of a verse of Sarāqa b. 'Auf in *Aghānī*, xv, 138, which refers to Muḥammad's revelations as أَلْوَاح, we may judge that the word was used in this technical sense among Muḥammad's contemporaries.

لُوط (*Lūṭ*).

Occurs some twenty-seven times, cf. vi, 86.

Lot.

Always the Biblical Lot, whose name some of the authorities derive from لاط (cf. Rāghib, *Mufradāt*, 472; ath-Tha'labī, *Qiṣaṣ*, 72), but which Jawharī recognizes as a foreign name.[3]

[1] Cf. also ash-Shammākh, xvii, 13, in Geyer, *Zwei Gedichte*, i, 136.
[2] *Vide* also Fraenkel, *Vocab*, 21; Cheikho, *Naṣrāniya*, 221.
[3] So al-Jawālīqī, *Mu'arrab*, 134; al-Khafājī, 175.

The name is apparently unknown in pre-Islamic literature, though it must have been known to the circle of Muḥammad's audience.[1] From its form one would conclude that it came from the Syr. ܠܘܛ rather than the Heb. לוט,[2] a conclusion that is strengthened by the Christian colouring of the Lot story.[3]

مَآئِدَة (*Mā'ida*).

v, 112, 114.

Table.

A late word found only in a late Madinan verse, where the reference is to a table which Jesus brought down for His disciples.

The Muslim authorities take it to be a form فَاعِلَة from مَادَ (cf. *LA*, iv, 420), though the improbability of their explanations is obvious. It has been demonstrated several times that the passage v, 112–15 is a confusion of the Gospel story of the feeding of the multitude with that of the Lord's Supper.[4] Fraenkel, *Vocab*, 24,[5] pointed out that in all probability the word is the Eth. ማእድ፡, which among the Abyssinian Christians is used almost technically for the *Lord's Table*, e.g. ማእድ፡ እግዚአብሔር, while Nöldeke's examination of the word in *Neue Beiträge*, 54, has practically put the matter beyond doubt.[6]

Addai Sher, 148, however, has argued in favour of its being taken as a Persian word. Relying on the fact that مائدة is said by the Lexicons to mean *food* as well as *table*, he wishes to derive it from Pers. مَيْدَه, meaning *farina triticea*.[7] Praetorius also, who in *ZDMG*, lxi, 622 ff., endeavours to prove that Eth. ማእድ፡ and the Amh. ማድ፡ are taken from Arabic, takes مائدة back to Pers. ميز[8] (earlier pro-

[1] Horovitz, *KU*, 136.

[2] But see Sycz, *Eigennamen*, 37.

[3] *Vide* Künstlinger, "Christliche Herkunft der Ḳuranischen Lōtlegende," in *Rocznik Orjentalistyczny* (1931), vii, 281–295.

[4] Nöldeke, *ZDMG*, xii, 700; Bell, *Origin*, 136.

[5] *Vide* also his *Fremdw*, 83, and Jacob, *Beduinenleben*, 235.

[6] *Vide* also Wellhausen, *Reste*, 232, n.; Pautz, *Offenbarung*, 255, n.; Vollers, *ZDMG*, li, 294; Cheikho, *Naṣrāniya*, 210.

[7] Vullers, *Lex*, ii, 1252.

[8] Vullers, *Lex*, ii, 1254.

nounced *māz*), through forms ميذ, ميد, and ميّده. Now there is a Phlv. word [illegible] *myazd*,[1] meaning a sacred repast of the Parsis, of which the people partake at certain festivals after the recitation of prayers and benedictions for the consecration of the bread, fruit, and wine used therein. It seems, however, very difficult to derive مائدة from this, and still more difficult from the forms proposed by Praetorius. Nöldeke rightly objects that the forms *mīz* and *māz* which Praetorius quotes from the Mehrī and 'Umanī dialects in favour of his theory, are hardly to the point, for these dialects are full of Persian elements of late importation. Praetorius has given no real explanation of the change of *z* to *d*, whereas on the other side may be quoted the Bilin *mīd* and the Beja *mēs* which are correct formations from a stem giving ማእድ in Eth., and thus argue for its originality in that stock.

مَاعُونٌ (*Mā'ūn*).

cvii, 7.

Help.

This curious word occurs only in an early Meccan Sūra, though v, 7, is possibly Madinan (cf. Nöldeke-Schwally, i, 93), and the Commentators could make nothing of it. The usual theory is that it is a form فاعول from مَعَنَ, though some derived it from عَانَ.

Nöldeke, *Neue Beiträge*, 28, shows that it cannot be explained from Arabic material,[2] and that we must look for its origin to some foreign source. Geiger, 58,[3] would derive it from Heb. מעון a *refuge*, which is possible but not without its difficulties. Rhodokanakis, *WZKM*, xxv, p. 67, agrees that it is from Hebrew but coming under the influence of معونة (cf. Aram. מאונא; Syr. ܡܥܘܢܐ), developed the meaning of *benefit*, *help*.[4]

[1] West, *Glossary*, 222.

[2] Fleischer, *Kleinere Schriften*, ii, 128 ff., would have it a genuine Arabic word, but as Noldeke says: "aus dem Arabischen lässt sie sich nicht erklären, wie denn schon die Form auf ein Fremdwort deutet."

[3] So von Kremer, *Ideen*, 226. The word is used by al-A'sha, and Horovitz, *JPN*, 221 ff., thinks Muḥammad may have learned the word from this poet.

[4] So Torrey, *Foundation*, 51.

مَالِكٌ (*Mālik*).

xliii, 77.

Mālik is the angel who has charge over Hell.

The native authorities derived the name from مَلَكَ to *possess, rule over*. This root may have influenced the form, but the source is doubtless the Biblical *Moloch*. The Heb. form is מֹלֶךְ, and it may possibly have come direct from Heb.,[1] but the Syr. ܡܠܟܡ (*PSm*, 1989) is much more likely.

مَثَانِى (*Mathānī*).

xv, 87 ; xxxix, 24.

The word evidently refers to Revelation, for xv, 87, reads: " We have given thee the seven *Mathānī* and the wondrous Qur'ān," while in xxxix, 24, we read: " God has sent down the best of accounts, in agreement with itself, a *Mathānī*, whereat the skins of those who fear their Lord do creep."

aṭ-Ṭabarī's account makes it clear that the exegetes did not understand the meaning of the word. All Muslim explanations go back to some development of the root ثَنَى, but their extreme artificiality creates a suspicion that the word is a borrowed technical term.

Geiger, 58, thought that it was an attempt to reproduce the Hebrew משנה, the collection of oral Tradition which took its place with the Jews beside the Torah. This explanation has been accepted by many later writers,[2] but how are we to explain the *seven* associated with the word ? Sprenger, *Leben*, i, 462 ff.,[3] thought that Muḥammad was here referring to " die sieben Straflegenden ", which fits very well with the statement in xxxix, 24, but, as Horovitz, *KU*, 26 (cf. *JPN*, 194, 195), points out, it rests on no basis of actual use of the word in any such sense. Nöldeke, *Neue Beiträge*, 26, makes an improvement on Geiger's theory by suggesting that the derivation was from Aram. מתניתא,[4]

[1] Tisdall, *Sources*, 123.

[2] Cf. von Kremer, *Ideen*, 226, 300 ; Pautz, *Offenbarung*, 87, n. ; Mingana, *Syriac Influence*, 87.

[3] D. H. Müller, in his *Propheten*, i, 43, 46, n. 2, also propounds this theory, and Rhodokanakis, *WZKM*, xxv, 66, says that Müller arrived at the conclusion independently of Sprenger. It has been accepted by Grimme, *Mohammed*, ii, 77.

[4] Nöldeke-Schwally, i, 114 ; Margoliouth, *ERE*, x, 538.

which has the same meaning as משנה, but is much nearer the Arabic. The puzzle of what Muḥammad meant by the *seven*, however, still remains.[1]

مِثْقَال (*Mithqāl*).

iv, 44 ; x, 62 ; xxi, 48 ; xxxi, 15 ; xxxiv, 3, 21 ; xcix, 7, 8.

A measure of weight—a mithqāl.

Naturally the Muslim authorities take it to be a form مِفْعَال from ثَقَلَ *to weigh* (cf. Baiḍ. on iv, 44, and *LA*, xiii, 91), but as Fraenkel, *Fremdw*, 202, notes, the primitive meaning of ثَقَلَ is *to be hard*, and the word مِثْقَال seems to be from Syr. ܡܬܩܠܐ[2] ; Aram. מתקלא, the equivalents of the Heb. משקל.[3] It occurs in the old poetry, however, and thus would have been an early borrowing.

مَثَل (*Mathal*).

Of frequent occurrence, cf. ii, 210 ; iii, 113 ; vii, 175.

Parable.

The root is common Semitic, and genuine Arabic forms such as مِثْل *likeness, similitude* ; تَمَثَّلَ *to seem like*, etc., are used in the Qur'ān. The forms مَثَل and its plu. أَمْثَال, however, where the meaning is that of the O.T. משל or N.T. παραβολή, which the Peshitta renders by ܡܬܠܐ, would seem to have come under the influence of Syriac usage.[4]

Hirschfeld, *New Researches*, 83 ff., would trace the influence to Jewish sources, but Mingana, *Syriac Influence*, 85, is probably right in thinking that it was Christian Aramaic.[5]

[1] Casanova, *Mohammed et la fin du monde*, 37, thinks that in xv, 87, it does not refer to the Qur'ān, but means *benefits*, as though derived from ثَنَى *to double*. Mainz in *Der Islam*, xxiii, 300, suggests the Syriac root ܣܒܥܐ + ܬܢܐ = *satietas, abundantia*. See also Künstlinger in *OLZ*, 1937, 596 ff.

[2] Whence also the Arm. մթքալ, though this may be a late borrowing from Arabic. Cf. Hübschmann, *Arm. Gramm.*, i, 271.

[3] Zimmern, *Akkad. Fremdw.*, 23, suggests an ultimate Mesopotamian origin.

[4] Note al-Khafājī, 192.

[5] On the whole question of the Qur'ānic Mathal, see Buhl in *Acta Or.*, ii, 1–11.

أَلْمَجُوسُ (*Al-Majūs*).

xxii, 17.

The Magians, or Zoroastrians.

They are mentioned in a late Madinan verse along with Jews, Christians, and Ṣābians.

The early authorities know that the sun-worshippers are meant, and it was early recognized that it was a foreign word.[1] Ibn Sīda and others derived the word from منج said to mean قصير and كوش said to mean الاذن, and tell us that it referred to a man منج كوش, so called because of the smallness of his ears, who was the first to preach the Magian faith.[2] Others, however, knew that it was derived from the Iranian *Magush* (*LA*, viii, 99).

It is clearly the O.Pers. *Magush*,[3] with the acc. form of which, *magum*, we can compare the Av. 𐬨𐬀𐬖𐬀𐬎𐬎 *magav* or 𐬨𐬋𐬖𐬎 *moγu*,[4] and Phlv. [Pahlavi] *maγōī*.[5] From Av. 𐬨𐬋𐬖𐬎 come the Arm. մոգ,[6] and Heb. מָג, as well as the Mod. Pers. مغ.[7] In Phlv. we also find a form [Pahlavi] *magōšīā*,[8] derived directly from the O.Pers., and this appears in the Aram. אמגושא, Gk. *μάγος*,[9] Syr. ܡܓܘܫܐ, and the מגוש of the Aramaic of the Behistun inscription.[10]

Lagarde, *GA*, 159, would derive مجوس from the Gk. *μάγος*, and

[1] al-Jawālīqī, *Mu'arrab*, 141; as-Suyūṭī, *Itq*, 324; *Mutaw*, 47; al-Khafājī, 182.

[2] *TA*, iv, 245; *LA*, viii, 99.

[3] *Vide* Meillet, *Grammaire Du Vieux Perse*, p. 148; and note Haug, *Parsis*, 169.

[4] Bartholomae, *AIW*, 1111; Horn, *Grundriss*, 221; Frahang, *Glossary*, 94; Herzfeld, *Paikuli*, Glossary, 213.

[5] West, *Glossary*, 223; *PPGl*, 152 and [Pahlavi], 160; Frahang, *Glossary*, 114. See also *ZDMG*, xliv, 671, for its occurrence on a Sasanian gem.

[6] Hübschmann, *Arm. Gramm.*, i, 195.

[7] Vullers, *Lex*, ii, 1197; *BQ*, 863.

[8] *PPGl*, 152; Frahang, *Glossary*, p. 113. In the Assyrian transcription of the Behistun inscription it is written *magushu*. Note also the *magūstān* = priestly order. *Paikuli*, Glossary, 214.

[9] There is an alternative theory that the Greek is a sing. formed from *Μάγοι*, the name of an ancient Median tribe, but we find *Μαγουσαῖοι* in Eusebius.

[10] Cowley, *Aramaic Papyri*, p. 254.

though Vollers, *ZDMG*, li, 303, follows him in this there is little to be said in its favour. The word was well known in pre-Islamic days and occurs in the old poetry,[1] and so may quite well have come direct from Middle Persian, though it is also a possibility that it may have come through the Syr. ܡܟܘܟܐ.[2]

مَدْيَن (*Madyan*).

vii, 83; ix, 71; xi, 85, 98; xx, 42; xxii, 43; xxviii, 21, 22, 45; xxix, 35.

Midian.

The references are all to the stories of Moses and Shu'aib, and the place is clearly the Biblical מִדְיָן, but derived through a Christian channel. (Nöldeke, *Ency. Bibl.*, iii, 3081.)

Some of the early authorities endeavoured to derive it from مَدَنَ (*LA*, xvii, 289), but al-Jawālīqī, *Mu'arrab*, 143, is inclined to take it as a foreign borrowing.

The presumption is that it came to Arabic through the Syr. ܡܕܝܢ.[3]

مَدِينَة (*Madīna*).

vii, 108, 120; ix, 102, 121; xii, 30; xv, 67; xviii, 18, 81; xxvi, 35, 53; xxvii, 49; xxviii, 14, 17, 19; xxxiii, 60; xxxvi, 19; lxiii, 8.

A city.

The popular derivation among the Lexicons is that it is a form فَعِيلَة from مَدَنَ *to settle*, though others considered that it was from دَانَ to *possess* (*LA*, xvii, 288, 289). The great argument in favour of a derivation from مَدَنَ is the plu. مُدُن beside مَدَائِن, for, said the philologers (cf. Ibn Barī in *LA*), how could it have such a plu. form if the ن were not part of the root?

[1] *Vide* Horovitz, *KU*, 137.

[2] Mingana, *Syriac Influence*, 95; Ahrens, *Muhammad*, 9.

[3] See the discussion in Horovitz, *KU*, 138; *JPN*, 153, 154, where he would draw a distinction between the Madyan of the early Sūras of the Qur'ān where it means Midian, and the Madyan of later passages where it refers to the Arabian Madyan opposite the Sinai peninsula, the Μοδιάνα of Ptolemy.

The truth is that it is from a root related to دَانَ, but is not an Arabic formation at all, being like the Heb. מדינה, a borrowing from the Aram. מדינתא, Syr. ܡܕܝܢܬܐ.[1] Aram. מדינתא means a *province* and then a *city*,[2] and Syr. ܡܕܝܢܬܐ is *city*.[3] From Aram. it was borrowed into Middle Persian where we find the ideogram [Pahlavi] *madīna*, meaning a large fortified city (*PPGl*, 150).

مَرْجَان (*Marjān*).

lv, 22, 58.

Small pearls.

The word occurs only in a description of Paradise, and was early recognized as borrowed from Persia,[4] but it is certain that it did not come directly from Iranian into Arabic.[5]

We find in Phlv. [Pahlavi] *murvārīt*,[6] a *pearl* used, e.g. in the *Gosht-i-Fryānō*, ii, 13, in describing the crowns presented to the daughters of Spitama after death. From Middle Persian the word was borrowed widely, e.g. Gk. μαργαρίτης[7]; Aram. מרגניתא; Syr. ܡܪܓܢܝܬܐ, and from some Aram. form[8] it came into Arabic. It would have come at an early date for it is used in the old poetry and was doubtless well known in the pre-Islamic period.

مُرْسَى (*Mursā*).

xi, 43.

Harbour, haven.

[1] Fraenkel, *Fremdw*, 280; Horovitz, *KU*, 137.

[2] It has this meaning in Arabic as early as the Nemāra inscription; cf. *RES*, i, No. 483.

[3] There is some discussion of the meaning of the word by Torrey in *JAOS*, xliii, 230 ff.

[4] al-Jawālīqī, *Mu'arrab*, 144; as-Suyūṭī, *Itq*, 324; *Muḥīt*, sub voc., and see Sachau's note to the *Mu'arrab*, p. 65.

[5] In spite of Addai Sher, 144, and his attempted derivation from مر+جان.

[6] West, *Glossary*, 213; *Šāyast*, Glossary, 163; cf. Horn, *Grundriss*, 218, n.

[7] Also μαργαρίς—ίδος, from which comes the Arm. մարգարիտ and the European forms.

[8] Fraenkel, *Fremdw*, 59. The Mand. מארגאניאתא would also seem to be from the same source, *vide* Nöldeke, *Mundart*, 53; Mingana, *Syriac Influence*, 90; Vollers, *ZDMG*, l, 611; li, 303.

With this meaning it is used only in the Noah story, though the same word occurs in vii, 186; lxxix, 42, meaning *fixed time*. In this latter sense it is obviously from رسا, and the philologers want to derive the مُرْسَى of xi, 43, from this same root.[1]

It seems, however, that we have here a loan-word from Eth. መርሶ a *haven* (Nöldeke, *Neue Beiträge*, 61; Bell, *Origin*, 29).

مَرْيَمُ (*Maryam*).

Occurs some thirty-four times, cf. ii, 81.

The name refers always to the mother of Jesus, though in xix, 29; iii, 31; lxvi, 12, she is confused with Miriam, the sister of Moses and Aaron (*infra*, p. 217).

Some of the philologers took the name to be Arabic, a form مفعل from رام, meaning *to depart from a place*.[2] Some, however, noted it as a foreign word,[3] and Baiḍ. on iii, 31, goes as far as to say that it is Hebrew. Undoubtedly it does go back to the Heb. מִרְיָם, but the vowelling of the Arabic مَرْيَمُ would point to its having come from a Christian source rather than directly from the Hebrew. The Gk. Μαρίαμ; Syr. ܡܰܪܝܰܡ; Eth. ማርያም are equally possible sources, but the probabilities are in favour of its having come from the Syriac.[4]

There seems no evidence for the occurrence of this form in pre-Islamic times,[5] though the form مارية, the name of the Coptic slave girl sent from Egypt to Muḥammad,[6] is found in a verse of al-Ḥārith b. Ḥilliza, iii, 10 (ed. Krenkow, Beirut, 1922).

[1] There was some uncertainty over the reading in this passage, see Zam. and Ṭab. thereon, and *LA*, xix, 35, 36.

[2] Jawharī, sub voc., *LA*, xv, 152.

[3] al-Jawālīqī, *Mu'arrab*, 140; *TA*, viii, 132; al-Khafājī, 183.

[4] Mingana, *Syriac Influence*, 82.

[5] See the discussion in Horovitz, *KU*, 138–140; *JPN*, 154.

[6] Ibn Hishām, 121; *Usd al-Ghāba*, v, 543, 544, and see Caetani, *Annali*, iii, 828.

مِزَاجٌ (*Mizāj*).

lxxvi, 5, 17; lxxxiii, 27.

Tempering.

Both passages refer to the tempering of the drink of the blessed in Paradise.

The Muslim authorities take it from مَزَجَ *to mix*, but Fraenkel, *Fremdwörter*, 172, points out that مِزَاج is not an Arabic formation, but is the Syr. ܡܙܓܐ *potus mixtus*, which later became technically used for the eucharistic cup of mixed water and wine. In fact the Syr. ܡܙܓ (cf. Heb. מָזַג; Aram. מְזַג), while used for mixing in general, became specialized for the mixing of drinks. There can thus be little doubt that it was borrowed in pre-Islamic times as a drinking term.[1] See also under امشاج (*infra*, p. 70).

مَسْجِدٌ (*Masjid*).

Occurs some twenty-eight times, e.g. ii, 139, 144, 145, 187, 192, etc.

A place of worship.

As we have already seen (*infra*, p. 163), the verb سجد in the technical sense of *worship* has been influenced by Aramaic usage. The form مسجد seems not to have been a formation from this in Arabic, but to have been an independent borrowing from the North.

Nöldeke, *ERE*, i, 666, 667, has drawn attention to this fact of the Aramaic origin of the word. In the Nabataean inscriptions we find מסגדא not infrequently meaning "place of worship",[2] as for example in an inscription from Bosra (de Vogüé), p. 106[3]: דה מסגדא דיעבד תימו בר ולד־אל־בעל "This is the place of worship which Taimu, son of Walid el-Ba'al built." The Syr. ܡܣܓܕܐ, however, seems to be a late borrowing from the Arabic, but we find מסגדא in the Elephantine papyri.[4]

[1] Horovitz, *Paradies*, 11; Geyer, *Zwei Gedichte*, i, 87 ff.; Zimmern, *Akkad. Fremdw.*, 40.

[2] Cook, *Glossary*, 75; Duval in *JA*, viii[e] Ser., vol. xv, 482.

[3] *ZDMG*, xxii, 268.

[4] Cowley, *Aramaic Papyri*, p. 148.

In the Qur'ān it is used of the fane at Qubā' (ix, 109), of the Temple at Jerusalem (xvii, 1), of the Church built over the Seven Sleepers (xviii, 20), and other places of worship, so that it is clear that for Muḥammad it meant any place of worship. In the same general sense it is used in the pre-Islamic poetry,[1] and so must have come at an early date from the more settled communities in the North.[2]

مِسْكٌ (*Misk*).

lxxxiii, 26.

Musk.

This sole occurrence is in an early Meccan description of Paradise.

The word was widely used among the Arabs in the pre-Islamic period [3] and was quite commonly recognized as a loan-word from the Persian.[4]

The Phlv. [Pahlavi] *mushk* [5] seems to have come ultimately from the Skt. मुष्क,[6] but it was from the Iranian, not the Indian form, that were borrowed the Arm. մուշկ [7]; Gk. μόσχος: Aram. מושק; Syr. ܡܘܫܟܐ; Eth. ምስክ. It is more likely to have come direct from Middle Persian into Arabic [8] than through the Syriac, as Mingana, *Syriac Influence*, 88, claims.

مِسْكِين (*Miskīn*).

Of very frequent occurrence, e.g. ii, 77, 172; ix, 60.

Poor.

Note therefrom the formation مَسْكَنَة *poverty, indigence*, ii, 58; iii, 108.

Fraenkel, *Vocab*, 24, pointed out that the Arabic word is from the Syr. ܡܣܟܝܢܐ, though this comes itself ultimately from Akkadian. The *muškēnu* of the Cuneiform inscriptions was interpreted by Littmann

[1] Horovitz, *KU*, 140.

[2] Schwally, *ZDMG*, lii, 134; Lammens, *Sanctuaires*, passim; Von Kremer, *Streifzuge*, ix, n.

[3] Siddiqi, *Studien*, 85; Geyer, *Zwei Gedichte*, i, 90 ff.: ii, 79.

[4] al-Jawālīqī, *Mu'arrab*, 143; ath-Tha'ālibī, *Fiqh*, 318; as-Suyūṭī, *Itq*, 324; *Muzhir*, i, 136; al-Khafājī, 182; *LA*, xii, 376.

[5] Justi, Glossary to the *Bundahesh*, p. 241.

[6] Vullers, *Lex*, ii, 1185.

[7] Hübschmann, *Arm. Gramm*, i, 196.

[8] Vollers, *ZDMG*, l, 649, 652.

in *ZA*, xvii, 262 ff., as *leper*, but Combe, *Babyloniaca*, iii, 73, 74, showed that it meant the humble classes,[1] and so *poor*. It passed into Heb. as מִסְכֵּן, מִסְכֵּין meaning *poor*, and into Aram. מִסְכֵּינָא; Syr. ܡܣܟܢܐ with the same meaning, and it was from Aram. that the Ar. مسكين and Eth. ምስኪን were derived.[2]

مَسِيح (*Masīḥ*).

iii, 40; iv, 156, 169, 170; v, 19, 76, 79; ix, 30, 31.

Messiah (ὁ Μεσσίας).

It is used only as a title of Jesus, and only in late passages when Muḥammad's knowledge of the teachings of the People of the Book is much advanced.

The Muslim authorities usually take it as an Arabic word from مَسَحَ *to wipe* (Ṭab. on iii, 20). Others said it was from مَسَحَ *to smear* or *anoint* (Rāghib, *Mufradāt*, 484), others derived it from ساح *to travel* (*LA*, iii, 431), and some, like Zam. and Baiḍ., rejected these theories and admitted that it was a borrowed word.

Those Muslim philologers who noted it as foreign, claimed that it was Hebrew, and this has been accepted by many Western scholars,[3] though such a derivation is extremely unlikely. Hirschfeld, *Beiträge*, 89, would derive it from Aram. מְשִׁיחָא, which is possible, though as it is used in early Arabic particularly with regard to Jesus, we are safer in holding with Fraenkel, *Vocab*, 24,[4] that it is from Syr. ܡܫܝܚܐ especially as this is the source of the Arm. Մեսիայ[5]; Eth. መሲሕ[6]; the Manichaean *mšiχa* of the "köktürkisch" fragments[7]; the Pazend

[1] Johns, *Schweich Lectures*, 1912, p. 8, would derive it from *kanu* "to bow down", so that originally it would mean *suppliant*. See, however, Zimmern, *Akkad. Fremdw*, 47.

[2] Noldeke, *Neue Beiträge*, 45. Note also the Phon. מסכן (Harris, *Glossary*, 120).

[3] Sayous, *Jesus Christ d'après Mahomet* (Paris, 1880), p. 21; Pautz, *Offenbarung*, 193, n. 3.

[4] So Lagarde, *Übersicht*, 94; Margoliouth, *Chrestomathia Baidawiana*, 163; Cheikho, *Naṣrāniya*, 186; Mingana, *Syriac Influence*, 85.

[5] This, however, may be direct from the Greek; cf. Hübschmann, *Arm. Gramm*, i, 364.

[6] Nöldeke, *Neue Beiträge*, 34.

[7] Le Coq in *SBAW*, Berlin, 1909, p. 1204; Salemann, *Manichaeische Studien*, i, 97.

mashyâê; Phlv. [Pahlavi script] (Shikand, *Glossary*, 258), and the Manichaean Soghdian *mšyh'* (Henning, *Manichäisches Beichtbuch*, 142).

The word was well known in both N. and S. Arabia in pre-Islamic times.[1]

مِشْكَاةٌ (*Mishkāt*).

xxiv, 35.

A niche in a wall.

The word was early recognized as foreign (Siddiqi, 13). as-Suyūṭī, *Itq*, 324, gives it as Abyssinian on the authority of Mujāhid,[2] and al-Jawālīqī, *Mu'arrab*, 135,[3] and al-Kindī, *Risāla*, 85, both know that it is an Abyssinian borrowing. Some, of course, sought to interpret it as an Arabic word from شكا (*LA*, xix, 171, quoting Ibn Jinnī), but their difficulties with the word make it obvious that it is a loan-word.

The philologers were correct in their ascription of its origin, for it is the Eth. መስኮት (መሥኮት), which is an early word formed from ሰከወ (cf. סכא, ܣܟܐ), and quite commonly used.[4]

مِصْرُ (*Miṣr*).

ii, 58; x, 87; xii, 21, 100; xliii, 50.

Egypt.

It occurs only in connection with the stories of Moses and Joseph.

The fact that it is treated as a diptote in the Qur'ān would seem to indicate that it was a foreign name, and this was recognized by some of the exegetes, as we learn from Baiḍ. on ii, 58, who derives it from مصرائيم, which obviously is intended to represent the Heb. מצרים.

The Eth. ምስር = Minaean 𐩣𐩮𐩧[5] is the only form without the final ending, and so S. Arabia was doubtless the source of the Qur'ānic form (but see Zimmern, *Akkad. Fremdw*, 91).

[1] Horovitz, *KU*, 129, 130; Ryckmans, *Noms propres*, i, 19; Rossini, *Glossarium*, 179.

[2] See also *Mutaw*, 41; *Muzhir*, i, 130, for other authorities.

[3] Who quotes from Ibn Qutaiba, *vide Adab al-Kātib*, p. 527, and al-Anbarī, *Kitāb al-Aḍdād*, p. 272.

[4] Noldeke, *Neue Beiträge*, 51; Vollers, *ZDMG*, li, 293.

[5] *Vide* Ryckmans, *Noms propres*, i, 348; Rossini, *Glossarium*, 180.

مُصَوِّر (*Muṣawwir*).

lix, 24.

One who fashions.

It is one of the names of God, and its form is undoubtedly Arabic. Lidzbarski, *SBAW*, Berlin, 1916, p. 1218, however, claims that in this technical sense it is a formation from the borrowed Aram. צַיָּר,[1] which frequently occurs in the Rabbinic writings as a name of God, and is also found in the Palm. inscriptions in the combination עבד ציּרא (Lidzbarski, *Ephemeris*, ii, 269).

مَعِين (*Ma'īn*).

xxiii, 52; xxxvii, 44; lvi, 18; lxvii, 30.

A fountain, or clear flowing water.

It occurs only in early and middle Meccan passages.

The philologers were uncertain whether it was a form فعيل from معن *to flow*, or connected with ماعون, or from عان, so called because of its clearness—cf. Zam. on xxiii, 52, and *LA*, xvii, 179, 298.

The word עין, for a spring of water, is of course common Semitic, but Fraenkel, *Fremdw*, 281, noted that the Qur'ānic معين is the Heb. מעין, Syr. ܡܥܝܢܐ = πηγή, commonly used for *spring* or a *bubbling fountain*. From one of these sources, probably from the Syriac, it came into Arabic.

مِقْلاد (*Miqlād*).

xxxix, 63; xlii, 10.

Key.

Only in the plural form مَقَاليد in the phrase "His are the keys of heaven and earth", where the use of مفاتيح in the similar phrase in vi, 59, proves that it means *keys*, though in these two passages many of the Commentators want it to mean خزائن *storehouses*.[2]

[1] *Vide* also Hirschfeld, *Beiträge*, 87.

[2] Rāghib, *Mufradāt*, 422, and Baiḍ. on vi, 59.

It was early recognized as a foreign word, and said by the philologers to be of Persian origin.[1] The Pers. كليد to which they refer it is itself a borrowing from the Gk. κλείς, κλεῖδα (Vullers, *Lex*, ii, 876), which was also borrowed into Aram. אקלידא; Syr. ܩܠܝܕܐ, ܡܩܠܝܕܐ or ܐܩܠܝܕܐ. In spite of Dvořák's vigorous defence of the theory that it passed directly from Persian into Arabic,[2] we are fairly safe in concluding that the Ar. أقليد is from the Syr. ܐܩܠܝܕܐ,[3] and the form مقلاد formed therefrom on the analogy of مفتاح, etc.[4]

مِلَّة (*Milla*).

ii, 114, 124, 129; iii, 89; iv, 124; vi, 162; vii, 86, 87; xii, 37, 38; xiv, 16; xvi, 124; xviii, 19; xxii, 77; xxxviii, 6.

Religion, sect.

It is most commonly found in the phrase ملّة ابراهيم, but is used for the faith of Jews and Christians (e.g. ii, 114), and for the old heathen beliefs (e.g. xii, 37; xiv, 16).[5] The Muslim authorities take it as an Arabic word but have some difficulty in explaining it.[6]

It has long been recognized as one of those religious terms for which Muḥammad was indebted to the older religions. Sprenger held that it was an Aramaic word which the Jews brought with them to the Ḥijāz, and Hirschfeld, *Beiträge*, 44, agrees,[7] as does Torrey, *Foundation*, 48. The Aram. מלא, like the late Heb. מלה, means *word*, but could be used figuratively for the religious beliefs of a person. The Syr. ܡܠܐ, ܡܠܬܐ, however, is a more likely source, for besides meaning *word*,

[1] al-Jawālīqī, *Mu'arrab*, 139; as-Suyūṭī, *Itq*, 324; *Mutaw*, 46; al-Khafājī, 181.

[2] *Fremdw*, 79 ff.; *Muhīt*, sub voc., wants to derive it directly from Greek.

[3] Fraenkel, *Fremdw*, 15, 16; Mingana, *Syriac Influence*, 88.

[4] Fraenkel, *Fremdw*, 16, thinks that a form with מ may have been known in the Aramaic from which the Arabic word was borrowed.

[5] Rāghib, *Mufradāt*, 488, says that ملّة can only be used for a religion that was proclaimed by a Prophet. Cf. *LA*, xiv, 154.

[6] See Sprenger, *Leben*, ii, 276, n.

[7] In his *New Researches*, 16, Hirschfeld suggests that in Muḥammad's mind מלה = מלא may have been somewhat confused with מילה *circumcision*, so that מלא representing the doctrine of Abraham, and מילה representing the outward sign of the Abrahamic covenant, being confused together, produced ملّة as the دين of Abraham. This seems, however, a little far-fetched.

ῥῆμα, it is also used to translate λόγος, and is used technically for religion.[1] It is possible, as Horovitz, *KU*, 62, 63, suggests, that the meaning was also influenced by the sense of *way*, which may be derived from the Arabic root itself (cf. Ahrens, *Christliches*, 33).

There seems to be no evidence for the use of مِلَّة in its Qur'ānic sense in the pre-Islamic period,[2] so it may have been a borrowing of Muḥammad himself, but doubtless was intelligible to his audiences who were more or less acquainted with Jews and Christians.

مَلَكٌ (*Malak*).

Of very frequent occurrence. Cf. ii, 28.

Angel.

It also occurs in the form مَلْأَكٌ, with the plu. مَلَائِكَة.

The Muslim authorities are unanimous in taking it as Arabic, though they dispute among themselves whether it should be derived from مَلَكَ or أَلَكَ (Rāghib, *Mufradāt*, 19, 490; *LA*, xii, 274, and Ṭab. on ii, 28).

There can be little doubt, however, that the source of the word is the Eth. መልአክ with its characteristic plu. መላእክት,[3] which is the common Eth. word for ἄγγελος, whether in the sense of *angelus* or *nuntius*, and thus corresponds exactly with Heb. מלאך; Phon. מלאך; Syr. ܡܠܐܟܐ.[4] It is very possible, however, that Jewish influences also have been at work on the word, for Hirschfeld, *Beiträge*, 46, points out the close correspondence of such phrases as ملك الموت (xxxii, 11) with מלאך המות,[5] and ملك الملك (iii, 25) with מלכא מלך מלכיא. The word would seem to have been borrowed

[1] Nöldeke, *Neue Beiträge*, 25, 26; *Sketches*, 38; Vollers, *ZDMG*, li, 293, 325; Nöldeke-Schwally, i, 20, 146.

[2] Nöldeke-Schwally, i, 146, n., but see Horovitz, *KU*, 62.

[3] Nöldeke, *Neue Beiträge*, 34; Hirschfeld, *Beiträge*, 45; Bell, *Origin*, 52; Dvořák, *Fremdw*, 64; Rhodokanakis, *WZKM*, xxv, 71; Ahrens, *Muhammad*, 92; Pautz, *Offenbarung*, 69; but see Bittner, *WZKM*, xv, 395.

[4] Mingana, *Syriac Influence*, 85, would derive the Arabic from this Syriac form; cf. also Fischer, *Glossar*, 118.

[5] So Geiger, 60; but we find this also in Eth., cf. መልአክ ፡ ሞት.

into Arabic long before the time of Muḥammad, for the Qur'ān assumes that Arabian audiences are well acquainted with angels and their powers,[1] and the form, indeed, occurs in the N. Arabian inscriptions.[2]

مَلِكٌ (*Malik*).

xii, 72, 76, etc.

A king.

With this must be taken مَالِكٌ in the sense of *Lord*, مَلِيكٌ a *monarch* (liv, 55), and مُلْكٌ *dominion, kingdom.*

The primitive root مَلَكَ *to possess*, with its derivatives, is common Semitic, and the Muslim savants naturally take the sense of *king*, *kingdom*, etc., to be derived from this.

Zimmern, *Akkad. Fremdw*, 7, however, has pointed out that this technical sense of *kingship* first developed in Akkadian, and then was taken over into the Hebrew, Phœnician, and Aramaic dialects, and also into S. Semitic in the Sab. 𐩣𐩡𐩫 and Ar. مَلِكٌ. It may also have been from Mesopotamia that it passed into Middle Persian as 𐭬𐭫𐭪𐭠 (Frahang, *Glossary*, 116; Herzfeld, *Paikuli*, Glossary, 216).

مَلَكُوتٌ (*Malakūt*).

vi, 75; vii, 184; xxiii, 90; xxxvi, 83.

Kingdom, dominion.

The usual theory of the Muslim philologers is that it is an Arabic word from the root مَلَكَ *to possess*, though they are a little hazy as to the explanation of the final ت.[3] Some of them, as we learn from as-Suyūṭī, *Itq*, 324, recognized that it was foreign and derived it from Nabataean.

The وت ending is almost conclusive evidence of its being from

[1] Sprenger, *Leben*, ii, 18; Eickmann, *Angelologie*, 12; Bell, *Origin*, 52.

[2] Huber, *Journal d'un Voyage en Arabie*, Paris, 1891, No. 89, l. 13.

[3] Rāghib, *Mufradāt*, 489. It is noteworthy that there was a variant reading ملكوث.

Aramaic.[1] Geiger, 60, and Tisdall, *Sources*, 126,[2] would take it from Heb. מלכות, which is commonly used in the Rabbinic writings, but the Aram. מלכותא ; Syr. ܡܠܟܘܬܐ are more likely, as Fraenkel, *Vocab*, 22, noted,[3] since these have the double sense of *βασιλεία* and *ἡγεμονία* precisely as in the Qur'ān, and moreover an Aramaic form was the source of both the Eth. መለኮት (Nöldeke, *Neue Beiträge*, 33) and the Phlv. ideogram malkōtā (*PPGl*, 153; Frahang, *Glossary*, p. 116).

Mingana, *Syriac Influence*, 85, would specify a Syriac origin for the word, but it is impossible to decide, though in some respects the Aramaic מלכותא seems to offer closer parallels than the Syr. ܡܠܟܘܬܐ. Ahrens, *Muhammad*, 78, points out that Muḥammad had not grasped the idea of the *βασιλεία τῶν οὐρανῶν*, and treats the word as meaning rather "Herrschaft über den Himmel", i.e. somewhat in the sense of مُلْك.[4]

مَنّ (*Manna*).

ii, 54; vii, 160; xx, 82.

Manna.

The Commentators have little idea what is meant. They identify it with ترنجبين, the Persian manna, or صمغ, a gum found on trees whose taste is like honey, or الخبز الرقاق thin bread, or عسل honey, or شراب a syrup, etc. As a rule they take it to be derived from مَنّ to *benefit*, and say that it was so called because it was sent as provision to the Children of Israel (*LA*, xvii, 306).

The word is used only in connection with the quails, so there can be no doubt that the word came to Muḥammad along with سلوى when he learned the Biblical story. The Hebrew word is מָן which is the source of the Gk. *μάννα* and Syr. ܡܢܐ. The Christian forms are

[1] Geiger, 44; Sprenger, *Leben*, ii, 257, n.

[2] So von Kremer, *Ideen*, 226; Sacco, *Credenze*, 51.

[3] Dvořák, *Fremdw*, 31; Massignon, *Lexique technique*, 52; Horovitz, *JPN*, 222.

[4] Cf. the מלכותא of the incantation texts; Montgomery, *Aramaic Incantation Texts*, Glossary, p. 294.

obviously much nearer to the Arabic than the Hebrew, and as we have already seen that the probabilities are that سلوى came from the Syriac, we may conclude that منّ is from the same source,[1] especially as the Syriac is the source of the Arm. մանանայ.[2]

Apparently there is no evidence of pre-Islamic use of the word,[3] though the story may well have been familiar to Muḥammad's audience.

مُنَافِقُونَ (*Munāfiqūn*).

Occurs some thirty-three times in both masc. and fem. forms.

Hypocrites.

Naturally the Lexicons seek to derive it from نفق with the meaning of نفذ, so that the *Munāfiqūn* are those who have departed from the law (Rāghib, *Mufradāt*, 522).

The word, however, has long been recognized as a borrowing from Ethiopic.[4] The form ኅፈቀ (ነፈቀ) has the meaning *hypocritam agere*, which نفق has not originally in Arabic, such a form as نافق, e.g. in نافق فى الدين, being late, if not as Nöldeke, *Neue Beiträge*, 48, thinks, a direct borrowing from ኅፈቀ. The form መናፍቅ = αἱρετικός is of frequent occurrence in the *Didascalia*,[5] and is clearly the source of مُنَافِق, which possibly was borrowed by Muḥammad himself, as there appears no trace of the word in this technical sense in the early literature.[6]

[1] Fraenkel, *Vocab*, 21; Mingana, *Syriac Influence*, 86; Horovitz, *KU*, 17; *JPN*, 222.

[2] Hübschmann, *Arm. Gramm*, i, 310.

[3] The Commentaries and Lexicons quote a verse from Al-A'shā, but as Lyall remarks in his notes to the *Mufaḍḍaliyāt*, p. 709, it does not occur in the poem as quoted by aṭ-Ṭabarī, *Annales*, i, 987 ff., nor in the *Diwān*, and so is rightly judged by Horovitz, op. cit., as an interpolation based on the Qur'ān.

[4] Wellhausen, *Reste*, 232; Nöldeke, *Neue Beiträge*, 48, 49; Ahrens, *Muhammad*, 165.

[5] Dillmann, *Lex*, 712.

[6] Nöldeke-Schwally, i, 88, n. 5; Ahrens, *Christliches*, 41.

مَنْفُوش (*Manfūsh*).

ci, 4.

Teased or carded (as wool).

Zimmern, *Akkad. Fremdw*, 28, takes the Akk. *napāšu, to card* or *tease* wool, as the origin of the Aram. נפס, *to tease wool*, from which came the Ar. نفش. Cf. also Haupt, in *Beit. Ass*, v, 471, n.

مِنْهَاج (*Minhāj*).

v, 52.

Pathway.

Only in a late Madinan verse where the reference is to a "rule of faith" and a "way of life", as was clearly seen by the Commentators. The philologers naturally took it to be a normal formation from نهج, and this is possible; but Hirschfeld, *Beiträge*, 89, has pointed out (cf. also Horovitz, *JPN*, 225), that in its technical religious sense it corresponds precisely with the Rabbinic מנהגא used for religious custom or way of life, and suggests that as used in the Qur'ān, it is a borrowing from the Jews. Schwally, *ZDMG*, liii, 197–8, agrees, and we may admit that there seems at least to be Jewish influence on the use of the word.

مُهَيْمِن (*Muhaimin*).

v, 52; lix, 23.

That which preserves anything safe.

In v, 52, it is used of that which preserves Scripture safe from alteration, and in lix, 23, as a title of Allah, the Preserver. There is a variant reading مُهَيْمَن in both passages.

The philologers take it as genuine Arabic, but as Nöldeke, *Neue Beiträge*, 27, points out, we can hardly get the meaning we want from the verb همن. Fraenkel, *Vocab*, 23, noted that it was a borrowing from the Aram. מהימנא or Syr. ܡܗܝܡܢܐ.[1] It is difficult to

[1] So Nöldeke, *Neue Beiträge*, 27; Hirschfeld, *Beiträge*, 87; Horovitz, *JPN*, 225.

decide whether it came from Jewish or Christian sources, but the parallels with Syriac are closer.[1]

مَوَاخِرُ (*Mawākhir*).

xvi, 14 ; xxxv, 13.

Plu. of مَاخِرَةٌ, that which ploughs the waves with a clashing noise, i.e. a ship.

Zimmern, *Akkad. Fremdw*, 45, suggests that it was derived from Akk. *elippu māḫirtu*, a ship making its way out into a storm. If this is so it would have been an early borrowing direct from Mesopotamia.

مُؤْتَفِكَةٌ (*Mu'tafika*).

ix, 71 ; liii, 54 ; lxix, 9.

That which is overthrown or turned upside down.

All three passages refer to the destruction of Sodom and Gomorrah.

The Muslim authorities take it from أَفَكَ as we see from Rāghib, *Mufradāt*, 18, and the word certainly is Arabic in its form. Sprenger, *Leben*, i, 492, however, claimed that this particular formation is due to the Rabbinic הפך used in the story of Sodom and Gomorrah. This theory is a little difficult, but has been accepted by Hirschfeld, *Beiträge*, 37, and Horovitz, *KU*, 13, 14 ; *JPN*, 187, and Ahrens, *Christliches*, 41, agree.

مُوسَى (*Mūsā*).

Of very frequent occurrence, e.g. ii, 51, 57 ; xi, 20.

Moses.

It was very commonly recognized as a foreign name,[2] the usual theory being that it was from an original form موشا, which some say

[1] So Nöldeke, op. cit., and Mingana, *Syriac Influence*, 88.

[2] al-Jawālīqī, *Mu'arrab*, 135 ; al-Khafājī, 182 ; Bagh. on ii, 48, and even Rāghib, *Mufradāt*, 484.

means *water* and *trees* in Hebrew,[1] and others in Coptic,[2] this name being given to Moses because of the place from which he was taken.

It is possible that the name came direct from the Heb. מֹשֶׁה, or as Derenbourg in *REJ*, xviii, 127, suggests, through a form מוסי used among the Arabian Jews. It is much more likely, however, that it came to the Arabs through the Syr. ܡܘܫܐ[3] or the Eth. ሙሴ, especially as it was from the Syr. that the Pazend *Mushâê*, Phlv. [illegible] and Arm. Մուշէ were borrowed.

There appears to be no well-attested example of the use of the word earlier than the Qur'ān,[4] so that it may have been an importation of Muḥammad himself, though doubtless well enough known to his audience from their contacts with Jews and Christians.

ميكَالَ (*Mīkāl*).

ii, 92.

Michael.

As an angel he is mentioned with Gabriel in a passage where the Commentators claim that the two are contrasted, Gabriel as the opponent of the Jews and Michael as their protector. He thus occupies in the Qur'ān the place given him in Dan. x, 13, 21, etc., as the Patron of Israel.

The early authorities were a little uncertain as to the spelling of the word, and al-Jawālīqī, 143, notes the forms ميكائيل ; ميكال ; ميكايل ; ميكئل ; and ميكعل. This would suggest that it was a foreign word, and it is given as such by Ibn Qutaiba, *Adab al-Kātib*, 78, and al-Jawālīqī, op. cit.

The word may have come directly from מיכאל, or more likely from the Syr. ܡܝܟܐܝܠ or ܡܝܟܝܠ, as it was from Syriac that the form

[1] Rāghib gives the form as مشوحا.

[2] So Ṭab. on ii, 48; ath-Tha'labī, *Qiṣaṣ*, 118, who tell us that in Coptic *mu* means *water* and *sha* means *trees*. This obviously rests on the Jewish theory given in Josephus, *Antiq*, II, ix, 6: τὸ γὰρ ὕδωρ μῶ οἱ Αἰγύπτιοι καλοῦσιν, ὑσῆς δὲ τοὺς ἐξ ὕδατος σωθέντας, which fairly well represents the Coptic ⲙⲱⲟⲩ *water* and ⲟⲩϫⲉ *rescued*.

[3] Cf. the form מושא on a Christian incantation bowl from Nippūr (Montgomery, *Aramaic Incantation Texts*, p. 231).

[4] So Horovitz, *KU*, 143; *JPN*, 156.

in the Persian Manichaean fragments from Turfan was derived.[1] It is difficult to say how well the name was known in pre-Islamic times.[2]

نَبِيّ (*Nabīy*).

Of very frequent occurrence, e.g. ii, 247 ; iii, 61 ; viii, 65.

Prophet.

Usually the word is taken to be from نَبَأَ *to bring news* (as-Sijistānī, 312), though some thought it was from a meaning of that root *to be high*.[3]

Fraenkel, *Vocab*, 20, pointed out that the plu. نبيّون, beside the more usual أنبياء, would suggest that the word was a foreign borrowing, and that it was taken from the older religions has been generally accepted by modern scholarship.[4] Sprenger, *Leben*, ii, 251, would derive it from the Heb. נָבִיא, and this view has commended itself to many scholars.[5] There are serious objections to it, however, on the ground of form, and as Wright has pointed out,[6] it is the Aram. נְבִיָּא, which by the dropping of the sign for emphatic state, gives us the form we need. Thus there can be little doubt that نبي, like Eth. ነቢይ (Nöldeke, *Neue Beiträge*, 34), is from the Aram.,[7] and probably from Jewish Aram. rather than from Syr. ܢܒܝܐ. It was seemingly known to the Arabs long before Muḥammad's day,[8] and occurs, probably of Mani himself, in the Manichaean fragments (Salemann, *Manichaeische Studien*, i, 97).

[1] Muller in *SBAW*, Berlin, 1904, p. 351 ; Salemann, *Manichaeische Studien*, i, 95.

[2] Cf. Horovitz, *KU*, 143, and Rhodokanakis, *WZKM*, xvii. 282.

[3] Ibn Duraid, *Ishtiqāq*, 273 ; and see Fraenkel, *Fremdw*, 232, n.

[4] Margoliouth, *Schweich Lectures*, 22, however, thinks that the Hebrew is to be explained from the Arabic, and Casanova, *Mohammed et la Fin du Monde*, 39, n., argues that نبي is a proper derivation from نبا, which is absurd, though Fischer, *Glossar*, 131, thinks that this root had an influence on the word. So Ahrens, *Muhammad*, 128.

[5] Von Kremer, *Ideen*, 224 ; Hirschfeld, *Beiträge*, 42 ; Rudolph, *Abhängigkeit*, 45 ; Grimme, *Mohammed*, ii, 75, n. 2 ; Sacco, *Credenze*, 116.

[6] *Comparative Grammar*, 46.

[7] So Guidi, *Della Sede*, 599 ; Horovitz, *KU*, 47 ; *JPN*, 223, seems doubtful whether Heb. or Aram.

[8] Hirschfeld, *Beiträge*, 42.

نُبُوَّة (*Nabūwwa*).

iii, 73 ; vi, 89 ; xxix, 26 ; xlv, 15 ; lvii, 26.

Prophecy.

The word occurs only in late Meccan passages (but see Ahrens, *Christliches*, 34), and always in connection with the mention of the previous Scriptures with which the Arabs were acquainted. It is thus clearly a technical word, and though it may be a genuine development from نبى, there is some suspicion that it is a direct borrowing from the Jews.

In late Heb. נבואה is used for *prophecy* (cf. Neh. vi, 12, and 2 Chron. xv, 8), and in one interesting passage (2 Chron. ix, 29) it means a prophetic document. In Jewish Aram. נבואתא also means *prophecy*, but apparently does not have the meaning of " prophetic document ",[1] nor is the Syr. ܢܒܝܘܬܐ so near to the Arabic as the Hebrew, which would seem to leave us with the conclusion that it was the Hebrew word which gave rise to the Arabic, or at least influenced the development of the form (Horovitz, *JPN*, 224).

نُحَاسٌ (*Nuḥās*).

lv, 35.

Brass.

We find the word only in an early Meccan Sūra in a description of future punishment.

There was considerable uncertainty as to the reading of the word, for we find different authorities supporting نِحَاس ; نُحُس ; and نَحُسٌ,[2] and even those who accepted the usual نُحَاس were not certain whether it meant *smoke* or *brass*. The philologers also had some difficulty in finding a derivation for the word, and we learn from *LA*, viii, 112, that Ibn Duraid said, " it is genuinely Arabic but I know not its root."

[1] Horovitz, *KU*, 73, says it does, and refers to Bacher's *Die exegetische Terminologie der jüdischen Traditionsliteratur*, ii, 123, but Bacher gives this meaning of " prophetischer Abschnitt " only for נבואה, and does not quote any example of it for נבותא.

[2] *Vide* Zam. on the passage.

It is, as Fraenkel, *Fremdw*, 152, pointed out, a borrowing, and means *brass*. In Heb. נְחֹשֶׁת and נְחוּשָׁה occur not infrequently meaning *copper* or *bronze*, and נחשת with a similar meaning occurs in the Phon. inscriptions.[1] So the Aram. נְחָשָׁא of the Targums[2]; Syr. ܢܚܫܐ, and Palmy. נחשא[3] are commonly used, and likewise the Eth. ናሕስ *aes, cuprum*, which one would judge from Dillmann, *Lex*, 633, to be a late word, but which occurs in the old Eth. inscriptions.[4] It is possible also that the old Egyptian *ṯḥś.t* (for *copper*),[5] which is apparently a loan-word in Egyptian, may be of the same origin.

Apparently the word has no origin in Semitic,[6] and so one may judge that it is a borrowing from the pre-Semitic stratum of language. The Arabic word may thus have come directly from this source, but in view of the difficulties the philologers had with the word, we should judge that it was rather a borrowing from the Aramaic.

نَذْر (*Nadhr*).

ii, 273; lxxvi, 7; plu. نُذُور xxii, 30.

A vow.

With this is to be taken the denominative verb نَذَرَ ii, 273; iii, 31; xix, 27.

This group of words has nothing to do with the forms of نَذَرَ *to warn*, so commonly used in the Qur'ān, and which are genuine Arabic.

In the sense of *vow* it is a borrowing from the Judæo-Christian circle[7]; cf. Heb. נֵדֶר; Phon. נדר; Syr. ܢܕܪܐ, all from a root נדר which is a parallel form to נזר, *to dedicate, consecrate* (cf. Akk. *nazāru, curse*), and Sab. ןዘ𐩬 (Hommel, *Südarab. Chrest*, 128).[8] It must have been an early borrowing.

[1] Lidzbarski, *Handbuch*, 322; Harris, *Glossary*, 123.
[2] And the נחש of the Elephantine papyri (Cowley, *Aramaic Papyri*, p. 299).
[3] Cf. de Vogüé, *Inscriptions*, No. xi, l. 4, and in the Fiscal inscription, *ZDMG*, xlii, 383; cf. also נחש in the *Nērab* inscription in Lidzbarski, *Handbuch*, 445.
[4] D. H. Müller, *Epigraphische Denkmäler aus Abessinien*, 1894, p. 52.
[5] W. M. Müller, *Asien und Europa*, 1893, p. 127. See Erman-Grapow, v, 396.
[6] Levy, *Wörterbuch*, iii, 374, suggests a derivation from غس *to be hard*, but this is hardly likely.
[7] Ahrens, *Christliches*, 34.
[8] See also Rossini, *Glossarium*, 184.

نُسْخَةٌ (*Nuskha*).

vii, 153.

A copy, or exemplar.

The word occurs only in a late Sūra in reference to the Tables of Stone given to Moses, but the verb formed from it—استنسخ, is used in an earlier passage, xlv, 28, though again the reference is to a heavenly book.

The Muslim authorities take the word as a form فُعْلة with the meaning of مفعولة from نسخ in the sense *to copy*, and some (cf. *LA*, iv, 28) would make *copy* the primitive meaning of the root. A comparison with the cognate languages, however, shows that *copy* is a secondary meaning of the root, cf. Akk. *nusḫu* = *extract*, and Syr. ܢܣܚ *to copy*, beside Akk. *nasāḫu*, Heb. נָסַח ; O.Aram. נסח and the Targumic נְסַח, where the original sense is clearly to *remove, tear away* (*evellere*), which original meaning is found in the Qur'ān in ii, 100 ; xxii, 51, where the word is used, as Hirschfeld, *Beiträge*, 36, points out, precisely as נסח is in Deut. xxviii, 63 ; Ezr. vi, 11.

Hoffmann, *ZDMG*, xxxii, 760, suggested that the Arabic word was from Aram. נוסחא, but this is used only in late Rabbinic writings and gained the technical sense of "variant reading", e.g. נוסחא אחרינא. Again in Syr. the only form is ܢܘܣܚܐ, which is also late (*PSm*, 2400), and as Lagarde, *GA*, 196, points out,[1] comes from the Iranian, where Phlv. ܢܣܟ, *nask*[2]; Av. [Avestan] *naska* means a book of the Avesta. The Iranian word, however, as Spiegel showed in his *Studien über das Zendavesta*,[3] cannot be explained from Indo-European material, and like the Arm. նիշ[4] is in all probability an ancient borrowing from some Semitic source in Mesopotamia.

It is, of course, possible that it came to Arabic also from Mesopotamia, but we find נסחת in a Nabataean inscription from

[1] Also Vollers, *ZDMG*, l, 649.

[2] *PPGl*, 165, 166 ; Šāyast, *Glossary*, 163 ; West, *Glossary*, 243 ; Haug, *Parsis*, 181.

[3] *ZDMG*, ix, 191, and *JA* for 1846.

[4] Hübschmann, *Arm. Gramm*, i, 204, however, compares նիշ with the Syr. ܢܝܫܐ, though deriving both from an Iranian original. See Lagarde, *GA*, 66, and Zimmern, *Akkad. Fremdw*, 13, who relates it to the Akk. *nišu*. Arm. նուսխայ, however, is a late borrowing from Arabic ; see *ZDMG*, xlvi, 264.

N. Arabia of A.D. 31,[1] where it has precisely this meaning of *copy* which we find for the Akk. *nusḫu*, and it was doubtless from this technical use of the word in N. Arabia that the word came into use in Arabic (Zimmern, *Akkad. Fremdw*, 29).

نَصَارَى (*Naṣārā*).

ii, 59, 105, 107, 114, 129, 134 ; iii, 60 ; v, 17, 21, 56, 73, 85 ; ix, 30 ; xxii, 17.

Christians.

This name occurs only in Madinan passages, and except for iii, 50, only in the plu. form.

It is taken by the Muslim authorities as a genuine Arabic formation from نصر, derived either from the name of the village ناصرة,[2] which was the native village of Jesus, or from انصار *helpers*, the name of the Disciples (cf. Sūra, iii, 45).[3]

Sūra, v, 85, would seem conclusive evidence that the word was in use in pre-Islamic times, and indeed the word occurs not uncommonly in the early poetry. The question of the origin of the name, however, is exceedingly difficult to solve.

The Talmudic name for Christians was נוֹצְרִים, a name derived probably from the town of Nazareth, though some would derive it from the name of the sect of Νασαραῖοι.[4] It is possible that the Arabs learned this word from the Jews, though as the Jews used it more or less as a term of contempt this is hardly likely. Also we find the Mandaeans calling themselves נאצוראיא,[5] which may be from the Ναζωραῖοι of the N.T., though, as it is difficult to imagine the Mandaeans wanting to be known as Christians,[6] it may be that this

[1] *CIS*, ii, 209, l. 9 ; Lidzbarski, *Handbuch*, 453 ; Euting, *Nab. Inschr.*, No. 12 ; Cook, *Glossary*, 82, and cf. Horovitz, *JPN*, 224.

[2] Yāqūt, *Mu'jam*, iv, 729 ; Rāghib, *Mufradāt*, 514 ; ath-Tha'labī, *Qiṣaṣ*, 272.

[3] The Commentaries on ii, 59. See Hirschfeld, *Beitrage*, 17, and Sprenger, *Leben*, ii, 533.

[4] Krauss in *JE*, ix, 194.

[5] Lidzbarski, *Mandäische Liturgien*, xvi ff. ; Brandt, *ERE*, viii, 384.

[6] Lidzbarski, *ZS*, i, 233 ; Noldeke, *ZA*, xxxiii, 74, says : " aber wie die Mandäer zu dem Namen *Nasoraye* gekommen sind, bleibt doch dunkel." Pallis, *Mandaean Studies*, 1926, p. 161, suggests that the Mand. נאצוראיא is simply the Arabic نصارى, which name was assumed by the Mandaeans in Islamic times to escape Muslim persecution, and this is very likely the truth.

also represents the Νασαραῖοι of Epiphanius and Jerome,[1] who were a Judæo-Christian sect related to the Elkesites, and the name may have come to the Arabs from this source.[2]

The most probable origin, however, is the Syr. ܢܨܪܝܐ which represents the Ναζωραῖοι of Acts xxiv, 5, and was a commonly used designation of Christians who lived under Persian suzerainty.[3] As it was from this area that the old Arm. Նածրացի was borrowed,[4] the case is very strong for the Ar. نصارى having come from the same source.

نَمَارِقُ (*Namāriq*).

lxxxviii, 15.

Cushions.

Only in an early Sūra in a description of the delights of Paradise.

al-Kindī, *Risāla*, 85, noted it as a loan-word from Persian,[5] though it is not given as such by al-Jawālīqī or as-Suyūṭī. It occurs not infrequently in the early poetry for the cushion on a camel's back, and must have been an early borrowing.

Lagarde, *Symmicta*, i, 60,[6] pointed out that it is from the Iranian *namr* meaning *soft*. In the old Iranian we find *namrā*,[7] which gives Av. 𐬥𐬀𐬨𐬭𐬀 *namra* (Bartholomae, *AIW*, 1042, cf. Skt. नम्र), and Phlv. [Pahlavi] *narm* (West, *Glossary*, 240; Salemann, *Manichaeische Studien*, i, 101), and from some Middle Persian form *namr* + the suffix [Pahlavi] *ak*, it passed both into Aram. נמרקין and Ar. نمرق, for which a plu. نمارق was then formed.

[1] Epiphanius, *Panarion*, xxix, and Jerome, *Comment. on Matt.* xii.

[2] Bell, *Origin*, 149; Margoliouth, *ERE*, x, 540, thinks it was Heb.

[3] Horovitz, *KU*, 145, 146. See also Mingana, *Syriac Influence*, 96; Fischer, *Glossar*, 135.

[4] Hübschmann, *ZDMG*, xlvi, 245; *Arm. Gramm.*, i, 312.

[5] See also Sprenger, *Leben*, ii, 504, n.

[6] Followed by Fraenkel, *Vocab*, 8.

[7] This form occurs in *nemr* in the Zaza dialect to-day (Horn, *Grundriss*, No. 1028).

نُوحٌ (*Nūḥ*).

Occurs some fifty-three times, e.g. iii, 30 ; iv, 161 ; xi, 34.

Noah.

Some of the Muslim authorities would derive the name from نَاحَ to *wail*,[1] though as al-Jawālīqī, *Mu'arrab*, 144, shows, it was commonly recognized as of non-Arabic origin.[2]

The story of Noah was well known in pre-Islamic days, and was often referred to by the poets, though as a personal name it apparently was not used among the Arabs before Islam.[3]

The form of the Ar. نوح is in favour of its having come from the Syr. ܢܘܚ rather than directly from the Heb. נֹחַ.[4]

نُونٌ (*Nūn*).

xxi, 87.

Fish.

Only in the title ذو النون given to Jonah, so that it is the equivalent of صاحب الحوت in lxviii, 48, whence came the theory النون الحوت العظيم (Rāghib, *Mufradāt*, 531 ; *LA*, xvii, 320).

It is a N. Semitic word, cf. Akk. *nunu* ; Aram. נוּנָא ; Syr. ܢܘܢܐ, and Phon. and late Heb. נון. Guidi, *Della Sede*, 591, recognized that it was a loan-word in Arabic, and there can be little doubt that it was from the Syriac that it entered Arabic, though as the word is used in the early poetry it must have been an early borrowing.[5]

هَارُوتُ وَمَارُوتُ (*Hārūt wa Mārūt*).

ii, 96.

Hārūt and Mārūt are the two fallen angels at Babylon who teach men Magic.

[1] *Vide* Goldziher, *ZDMG*, xxiv, 209.

[2] *Vide* also Jawharī, s.v. لوط.

[3] Horovitz, *KU*, 146.

[4] Margoliouth, *ERE*, x, 540 ; Mingana, *Syriac Influence*, 82.

[5] It possibly occurs as a proper name in the Safaite inscriptions ; cf. Ryckmans, *Noms propres*, i, 138.

The philologers recognized the names as non-Arabic, as is clear from al-Jawālīqī, *Mu'arrab*, 140.[1]

Lagarde, *GA*, 15 and 169, identified them with the Haurvatāt and Amərətāt of the Avesta,[2] who were known in later Persia as Khurdād and Murdād,[3] and from being nature spirits became names of archangels and were revered by the ancient Armenians as gods.

This identification has been generally accepted,[4] though Nestle, *ZDMG*, lv, 692, wants to compare them with Khillīt and Millīt,[5] and Halévy, *JA*, ixe ser., vol. xix, 148 ff., claims that Mārūt is the Ἀρμαρος of Enoch vi, 7, which he thinks in the original text may have read הרמרות. This, however, is unlikely in itself and is practically put out of the question by the fact that the better reading in that passage of Enoch is Φαρμαρός. It is curious, however, that in the Slavonic Enoch (xxxiii, 11, B), we find appearing the two angel names Orioch and Marioch.[6]

Margoliouth, *ERE*, viii, 252, thought that the form of the names pointed to an Aramaic origin and would look on them as Aramaic personifications of mischief and rebellion, and Wensinck, *EI*, ii, 273, notes that ܡܪܘܬܐ is a common Syriac word for power or dominion, so it may be that there has been Aramaic influence on the transmission of the names to Muḥammad.

هٰرُون (*Hārūn*).

Occurs some twenty times, e.g. ii, 249; iv, 161; xxxvii, 114.

Aaron.

[1] *Vide* Sachau's notes, p. 63, and al-Khafājī, 183.

[2] It had been earlier recognized; cf. Boetticher, *Horae aramaicae*, Berlin, 1847 p. 9, and Littmann says that Andreas independently of Lagarde had come to the same conclusion. On the spirits see Darmesteter, *Haurvatad et Ameretad*, 1875.

[3] On this form of the name see Marquart, *Untersuchungen zur Geschichte von Eran*, ii, 214, n. 6.

[4] Littmann in *Andreas Festschrift*, 84; Tisdall, *Sources*, 99; Rudolph, *Abhängigkeit*, 67, 75; Fr. Müller, in *WZKM*, viii, 278. Marquart, *Untersuchungen zur Geschichte von Eran*, Philol. Suppl. x, i, 1905, p. 214, n. 6, suggests Phlv. [Pahlavi] *harōt*, and [Pahlavi] *amurt*, which he would derive from O.Pers. *haruvatāh* and *amrtatāh*. See Herzfeld, *Paikuli*, Glossary, 144.

[5] Burton, *Nights*, x, 130, claimed these as Zoroastrian, but Bergmann, *MGWJ*, xlvi, 531, compared them with the Talmudic חילק ובילק. Horovitz, *KU*, 148, rightly insists that they could have had no influence on the Qur'ānic forms.

[6] See Littmann, op. cit., 83; Horovitz, *KU*, 147; *JPN*, 164, 165.

It always refers to the O.T. Aaron, though in xix, 29, where Muḥammad makes his well-known confusion between Miriam the sister of Moses and Mary the mother of Jesus, the exegetes endeavour to show that some other Aaron is meant.

The name was commonly recognized as foreign (*LA*, xvii, 326; al-Jawālīqī, *Mu'arrab*, 151; *TA*, ix, 367), but its origin is not at once apparent. The Hebrew form is אַהֲרֹן, which by interchange of the first and second letters, would give us هارون, as some have suggested.[1] This interchange, however, is not necessary to explain it, for in the Christian-Palestinian dialect we find that the usual ܐܗܪܘܢ has become ܗܪܘܢ by dropping the lightly pronounced initial ܐ,[2] and it was doubtless from this source that the word came into Arabic. It seems to have been known and used by the Arabs long before Islam.[3]

هَامَانُ (*Hāmān*).

xxviii, 5, 7, 38; xxix, 38; xl, 25, 38.

Haman.

In the Qur'ān, instead of being concerned in the story of Esther, he figures as a dignitary at the court of Pharaoh in Egypt during the time of Moses.

Many of the early authorities recognized it as a foreign name (al-Jawālīqī, *Mu'arrab*, 153; al-Khafājī, 207). There was an attempt by some of the exegetes to make out that this هَامَان was a different person from the Haman of the Esther story, whom they call هيمون, as Geiger, 156, notes. There is no doubt, however, that by هامان is meant the הָמָן of Esth. iii,[4] and we may find the source of the confusion in xxix, 38; xl, 25, where he is associated with Korah, for in Rabbinic legends Haman and Korah were bracketed together.

The probabilities are that the word came to the Arabs from Jewish sources.

[1] Sycz, *Eigennamen*, 43; but see Horovitz, *JPN*, 161.

[2] Schulthess, *Lex*, 3, and cf. the *Palestinian Syriac Lectionary*, p. 51.

[3] Horovitz, *KU*, 149; *JPN*, 162.

[4] Sycz, *Eigennamen*, 41; Horovitz, *KU*, 149; Eisenberg, *EI*, ii, 245.

هَاوِيَة (*Hāwiya*).

ci, 6.

The verse is early Meccan, and *Hāwiya* is apparently one of the names of Hell.

The passage reads: "and as for him whose balances are light—*Hāwiya* is his mother. And who shall teach you what that is? It is a raging fire."

The common explanation is that هاوية is إسم النار, but this obviously depends on the نار حامية at the end of the verse, and makes the أمّ difficult,[1] so some Commentators said that أمّ in this passage means *skull* and that هاوية is the participle of هوى *to fall*, the verse meaning that he was to be cast into the abyss (Zam. and ar-Rāzī in loc.).[2] Others, however, insisted that أمّ must have its natural sense of *mother*, and هاوية must mean *childless*, as in the old poetry هوت أمّه means "his mother is bereft of him" (Ṭab. and *LA*, xx, 250).

Sprenger, *Leben*, ii, 503, claims that this latter was the only natural explanation of the word, and Fischer in the *Nöldeke Festschrift*, i, 33 ff., makes an elaborate defence of it.[3] If this is correct, then the two later clauses are meaningless, and Fischer takes them as a later interpolation by someone who had no clue to the meaning.[4] This is a tempting solution, but a little difficult, as the concluding clauses are quite characteristic, and as Torrey points out (*Browne Festschrift*, 467), the curious lengthened form of the pron. in هيه which is paralleled by such forms as كتابيه and سلطانيه in lxix, is unlikely to have been the work of a later interpolator.

[1] The usual way out is to make أمّه mean مأواه; cf. Shaikh Zade's super-commentary to Baiḍ. in loc.

[2] *BDB*, 217, equate هاوية meaning *pit of hell* with הַוָּה a *chasm*; cf. Syr. ܗܘܬܐ a *gulf* or *chasm*.

[3] His arguments have been accepted by Goldziher, *Vorlesungen*, 33, and Casanova, *Mohammed et la Fin du Monde*, 153.

[4] He thinks that the نار حاوية was borrowed from lxxxviii, 4.

Torrey's own suggestion is that it is the Heb. הֹוָה *disaster*, occurring in Is. xlvii, 11, and Ez. vii, 26. Torrey thinks that this word would have been very frequently on the lips of the Jews whom Muḥammad met, "every educated Jew had it at his tongue's end. The whole splendid passage in Isaiah may well have been recited to Muḥammad many times, with appropriate paraphrase or comment in his own tongue, for his edification. The few hell-fire passages in the Hebrew Scriptures must have been of especial interest to him, and it would be strange if some teacher had not been found to gratify him in this respect"—p. 471.

There are objections, however, to this theory. Neither of the O.T. passages mentioned above, though they do prophesy destruction, can strictly be called "hell-fire" passages, and the word neither in the Bible nor in the Rabbinic writings seems to have any connection with "hell-fire", as the Qur'ān certainly thinks it has, if we are to admit the authenticity of the whole passage. Moreover this Sūra is very early, much earlier than the time when he had much contact with the Jews, even if we could admit that the word was as constantly on Jewish lips as Torrey supposes. It would seem rather to have been one of those strange words picked up by Muḥammad in his contact with foreigners in Mecca in his early years, and thus more likely of Christian than of Jewish origin. One might venture a suggestion that it is connected with the Eth. ሐወየ,[1] which in the form ሕዋዩ means the fiery red glow of the evening sky (cf. Matt. xvi, 2), and as ሐዉ means *fire* or *burning coal*. This at least gives us the connection with نارحامية, and the change of guttural is not difficult in Ethiopic where such changes are common.

وَثَن (*Wathn*).

xxii, 31; xxix, 16, 24.

An idol.

Used only in the plu. أَوثان, and only in fairly late passages.

The word 𐩥𐩻𐩬 occurs in the S. Arabian inscriptions,[2] and as this corresponds with the Eth. ወቲን (plu. አውታን)[3] meaning *idol*,

[1] Mainz in *Der Islam*, xxiii, 300, suggests (ܘܬܡܣܟܐ?) ܗܘܢܐ.

[2] *JA*, vii^e ser., vol. xix, p. 374; Rossini, *Glossarium*, 142.

[3] Cheikho, *Naṣrāniya*, 206, wrongly gives this as ወሐን.

we may agree with Fraenkel, *Fremdw*, 273, that the word came from S. Arabia. Margoliouth, *ERE*, vi, 249, however, thinks that it is perhaps connected with the Heb. ישן *old*, which may have been used as a term of abuse.

وَرْدَةٌ (*Warda*).

lv, 37.

Rose.

The passage is eschatological and وردة means *rose-red*, referring to the colour of the sky, a meaning derived, of course, from the original sense of *rose*.

It was very commonly recognized that it was a loan-word,[1] though it is curious that the philologers make no suggestion as to its origin, for it is obviously a borrowing from Persia. The primitive Indo-European root **urdho* means a *spiny tree*, from which comes the Gk. ῥόδον = Ϝρόδον, and the Av. [Avestan script] *varəδa* (Bartholomae, *AIW*, 1369), whence Arm. վարդ *rose*,[2] and Phlv. [Pahlavi script] *varta* (*PPGl*, 228).[3] From the Iranian it was borrowed into Semitic,[4] where we find Aram. ורדא, Syr. ܘܪܕܐ,[5] and from the Aram., as Fraenkel, *Vocab*, 11, noted, it passed into Arabic. As a proper name Οὐάρδα, Οὐάρδης is found in the N. Arabian inscriptions.[6]

وَزِيرٌ (*Wazīr*).

xx, 30; xxv, 37.

A minister, counsellor.

Both passages refer to Aaron being given to Moses as his *Wazīr*, where the reference is obviously to Ex. iv, 16.

[1] as-Suyūṭī, *Itq*, 325; *Muzhir*, i, 137; al-Jawālīqī, *Mu'arrab*, 151; *TA*, ii, 531.

[2] Hubschmann, *Arm. Gramm*, i, 244. So Sogd. *wrd* (Henning, *Manichäisches Beichtbuch*, 1937, p. 137) and Parthian *w'r* (Henning, *BSOS*, ix. 88).

[3] Though some suspect the Phlv. form of being a reborrowing from Semitic, *vide* Horn, *Grundriss*, 207; Frahang. *Glossary*, 77. Mod. Pers. borrowed back ورد from Arabic in Islamic times.

[4] Cf. Telegdi in *JA*, ccxxvi (1935), p. 241.

[5] Cf. also the Mand. ואורדא, Noldeke, *Mand. Gramm.*, 56, and cf. Zimmern, *Akkad. Fremdw.*, 55, for an even earlier borrowing.

[6] Wuthnow, *Die semitischen Menschennamen in griechischen Inschriften und Papyri des vorderen Orients*, 1930, p. 92; Ryckmans, *Noms propres*, i, 81.

The usual explanation of the word is that it is a form فعيل from وزر to *bear* or *carry*, and thus means one who carries the burdens of the Prince (cf. Rāghib, *Mufradāt*, 542). Lagarde, *Übersicht*, 177, n., however, pointed out that it is an Iranian word, and in his *Arm. Stud*, § 2155, he derives it from the Phlv. [Pahlavi script] *vičir*, which originally meant a *decree, mandate, command*, but which later, as in the *Dinkard*, came to mean *judge* or *magistrate*.[1] This word, of course, is good Iranian, being from the Av. [Avestan script] *vīčira* meaning *deciding*,[2] which was borrowed into Arm. as [Armenian script],[3] and is related to the form behind the Mod. Pers. وچر or وجر *judge*[4]; گزير or *prefect*,[5] and وزير, which is generally regarded as a loan-word from Arabic but which Bartholomae, *AIW*, 1438, rightly takes as a genuine derivative from the older Iranian word.

The borrowing was doubtless direct from the Middle Persian, for the Syr. ܘܙܝܪܐ seems to be late and a borrowing from Arabic (*PSm*, 1061).

يَاجُوجُ وَ مَاجُوجُ (*Yājūj wa Mājūj*).

xviii, 93; xxi, 96.

Gog and Magog.

Both passages are reflections of Syriac legends concerning Alexander the Great.

It was recognized very commonly that the names were non-Arabic (cf. al-Jawālīqī, *Mu'arrab*, 140, 156; al-Khafājī, 215; *LA*, iii, 28), and there was some doubt as to whether they should be read with Hamza or without.

The names were apparently well known in pre-Islamic Arabia, and we find references to them in the early poetry, where the statements about them would indicate that knowledge of them came to Arabia

[1] West, *Glossary*, 237. It was a fairly common word, and enters into a number of compounds; cf. Nyberg, *Glossar*, 242.

[2] Bartholomae, *AIW*, 1438; Reichelt, *Awestisches Elementarbuch*, 490.

[3] Hübschmann, *Arm. Gramm*, i, 248; Spiegel, *Huzvâresh Grammatik*, Wien, 1856, p. 188.

[4] Vullers, *Lex*, ii, 1411.

[5] Vullers, *Lex*, ii, 1000; Horn, *Grundriss*, 242; Hübschmann, *Pers. Studien*, 94.

from Christian eschatological writings.[1] The names, of course, were originally Heb. גוג and מגוג, which in Syr. are ܓܘܓ and ܡܓܘܓ. In the Syriac Alexander legend ܓܘܓ is generally spelled ܐܓܘܓ,[2] which is a variant reading of the word in the Qur'ān (Nöldeke, *Qorans*, 270). The Mandaean demons Hag and Mag, which Horovitz, *JPN*,163, quotes, are more likely to be derived from the Qur'ān than the Qur'ānic names from them.[3]

يَاقُوت (*Yāqūt*).

lv, 58.

Ruby.

It was very generally recognized as a loan-word from Persian.[4] Some Western scholars such as Freytag [5] have accepted this at face value, but the matter is not so simple, for the Modern Pers. ياقوت is from the Arabic (Vullers, *Lex*, ii, 1507), and the alternative form ياكند, like the Arm. յակունդ, is from the Syr. ܝܩܘܢܕܐ.[6]

The ultimate source of the word is the Gk. ὑάκινθος, used as a flower name as early as the Iliad,[7] and which passed into the Semitic languages, cf. Aram. יקינטון [8]; Syr. ܝܩܝܢܬܐ, and into Arm. as յակինթ.[9] It was from Syr. ܝܩܝܢܬܐ that the word passed into Eth. as ያክንት,[10] and with dropping of the weak נ into Arabic.[11]

It occurs in the old poetry (cf. Geyer, *Zwei Gedichte*, i, 119), and thus must have been an early borrowing.

[1] Noldeke, *Alexanderroman, passim*; Mingana, *Syriac Influence*, 95; Geiger, 74, however, would derive the names from Rabbinic legend. See Horovitz, *KU*, 150.

[2] Cf. Budge's edition of the metrical discourse of Jacob of Serug in *ZA*, vi, 357 ff.

[3] See on them Lidzbarski, *Ginza*, p. 154; Brandt, *Mandäische Schriften*, p. 144.

[4] al-Jawālīqī, *Mu'arrab*, 156; ath-Tha'ālibī, *Fiqh*, 317; as-Suyūṭī, *Itq*, 325; *Mutaw*, 47, 48; al-Khafājī, 216; *TA*, i, 598.

[5] *Lexicon*, sub voc.

[6] Noldeke in Bessenberger's *Beiträge*, iv, 63; Brockelmann, *ZDMG*, xlvii, 7.

[7] Il, xiv, 348. Boissacq, 996, points out that the word is pre-Hellenic.

[8] For other forms see Krauss, *Griechische Lehnwörter*, ii, 212.

[9] Hübschmann, *Arm. Gramm*, i, 366.

[10] Nöldeke, *Neue Beiträge*, 40.

[11] Fraenkel, *Vocab*, 6; *Fremdw*, 61; Mingana, *Syriac Influence*, 90; Vollers, *ZDMG*, li, 305. Note also Parthian *y'kwnd* (Henning, *BSOS*, ix, 89).

يَحْيَى (*Yaḥyā*).

iii, 34 ; vi, 85 ; xix, 7, 13 ; xxi, 90.

John the Baptist.

Usually the Muslim authorities derive the name from the Arabic verb of similar form, and say that John was so called because of his quickening virtue, either in quickening the barrenness of his mother, or in quickening the faith of his people.[1] Some felt that they were committed to an Arabic origin of the name by Sūra xix, 8—لَمْ نَجْعَلْ لَهُ مِن قَبْلُ سَمِيًّا, which, however, as Marracci pointed out,[2] is merely a misunderstanding of Lk. i, 61, and there were some (e.g. Baiḍ. on iii, 34, and xix, 8)[3] who knew and admitted that it was a foreign name.

We may be sure that the name came into Arabic from some Christian or Christianized source.

Sprenger, *Leben*, ii, 335, thought that perhaps it might have come from the Ṣābians, for in the Mandaean books we find the name in the form יאהיא (Lidzbarski, *Johannesbuch*, ii, 73), but the probability is that this form is due to Islamic influence.[4]

A more subtle theory is that it is a misreading for يُحَنَّى which would be derived from the Syr. ܝܘܚܢܢ.[5] The primitive script had no vowel points, and يحى might have been read يُحَنَّى as easily as يَحْيَى.[6] This solution has much in its favour, and might be accepted were it not for the fact that we have epigraphical evidence from N. Arabia that in pre-Islamic times Christians in that area were using a form יחיא, probably derived from the Syriac.[7] Jaussen and Savignac found this

[1] Ṭab. on iii, 34, and ath-Thaʿlabī, *Qiṣaṣ*, 262.

[2] *Refutationes*, 435. So Sayous, 27, n.; Palmer, *Qoran*, ii, 27, n.; Pautz, *Offenbarung*, 254.

[3] So al-Khafājī, 215 ; al-ʿUkbarī, *Imlā'*, i, 88. Zam. halts between two opinions.

[4] Nöldeke, *ZA*, xxx, 159.

[5] Nöldeke noted that יוחנן, from which ܝܘܚܢܢ was formed, can occur in a hypochoristic form יוחאי, and as a matter of fact יוחאי or יוחי does occur in late Jewish names, and Fraenkel, *WZKM*, iv, 337, and Grimme, *Mohammed*, ii, 96, n. 8, have thought that يحيى could be derived from this. Barth, *Der Islam*, vi, 126, n., and Mingana, *Syriac Influence*, 84, have rightly insisted, however, that the name is of Christian not Jewish origin.

[6] Barth, op. cit.; Casanova, *JA*, 1924, p. 357; Margoliouth, *ERE*, x, 547; Cheikho, *Naṣrāniya*, 189; Torrey, *Foundation*, pp. 50, 51.

[7] But see Lidzbarski, *Johannesbuch*, ii, 73, and Rhodokanakis, *WZKM*, xvii, 283.

form יהודא in a graffito at Al-'Alā,[1] and it is possibly found again in another inscription from the same area.[2] It would thus seem that Muḥammad was using a form of the name already naturalized among the northern Arabs, though there appears to be no trace of the name in the early literature.

يَعْقُوب (*Ya'qūb*).

ii, 126–134 ; iii, 78 ; iv, 161 ; vi, 84 ; xi, 74 ; xii, 6, 38, 68 ; xix, 6, 50 ; xxi, 72 ; xxix, 26 ; xxxviii, 45.

Jacob.

He is never mentioned save in connection with some other member of the Patriarchal group.

There were some who considered it as Arabic derived from عقب, but in general it was recognized as a foreign word, cf. al-Jawālīqī, 155 ; Zam. on xix, 57 ; Baiḍ. on ii, 29 ; as-Suyūṭī, *Muzhir*, i, 138, 140 ; al-Khafājī, 215. Apparently it was known among the Arabs in pre-Islamic days.[3]

It may have come from the Heb. יעקב, though the fact that Muḥammad has got his relationship somewhat mixed [4] might argue that he got the name from Christian sources, probably from the Syr. ܝܥܩܘܒ,[5] which was the source of the name in the Manichaean fragments (Salemann, *Manichaeische Studien*, i, 86).

يَغُوث (*Yaghūth*).

lxxi, 23.

Yaghuth.

It is said to have been an idol in the form of a lion, worshipped among the people of Jurash and the Banū Madhḥij.[6] It would thus

[1] *Mission archéologique*, ii, 228. For the form יהוד see Euting, *Sin. Inschr.*, No. 585 ; *CIS*, ii, 1026.

[2] Lidzbarski, *Ephemeris*, iii, 296, and cf. Horovitz, *KU*, 151, for an inscription from Harrān. It is possible that a Jewish form יהוי occurs in the Elephantine papyri (cf. Cowley, *Aramaic Papyri*, No. 81, l. 28), but the reading is not sure.

[3] Cheikho, *Naṣrāniya*, 234 ; Horovitz, *KU*, 153. Horovitz plays with the idea that it may have been a genuine old Arab name. Cf. *JPN*, 152.

[4] xi, 74, on which see Hurgronje, *Verspreide Geschriften*, i, 24.

[5] Mingana, *Syriac Influence*, 82.

[6] Ibn al-Kalbī, *Kitāb al-Aṣnām*, p. 10 ; Wellhausen, *Reste*, 19 ff. ; Ryckmans, *Noms propres*, i, 16.

appear to be of S. Arabian origin, and this is confirmed by the fact that we find תם־יעת in the Thamudic inscriptions,[1] and Ἰαοῦθος in Safaite [2] and Thamudic.[3]

The name would seem to mean *helper* (Yâqūt, *Mu'jam*, iv, 1022), and the S. Arabian 𐩶𐩥𐩻 means to *help* (cf. Ar. غاث ; Heb. עוש ; Rossini, *Glossarium*, 215).

يَقْطِين (*Yaqṭīn*).

xxxvii, 146.

A gourd.

The word occurs in the Jonah story for the gourd tree which Allah caused to grow up over the Prophet. The reference is obviously to the Biblical story in Jonah iv, 6–11, and يقطين seems to be an attempt to reproduce the קִיקָיוֹן of the Hebrew story.[4] The word was apparently heard during an oral recitation of the story, and then reproduced from memory in this garbled form.

يَقِين (*Yaqīn*).

iv, 156; xv, 99; xxvii, 22; lvi, 95; lxix, 51; lxxiv, 48; cii, 5, 7.

Certain.

The simple verb يَقِنَ does not occur in the Qur'ān, but we find أَيْقَنَ ii, 3; v, 55, etc.; إِسْتَيْقَنَ xxvii, 14; lxxiv, 31, and the participles موقن and مستيقن, besides يقين.

At first sight it seems clearly to be a borrowing, for there is no Semitic √ יקן, and yet we find both يقين and the verbal forms therefrom used in the oldest poetry, so it must have come into the language

[1] D. H. Müller, *Epigraphische Denkmäler aus Arabien*, p. 19; Littmann, *Entzifferung*, 27, 32. It is possible that we have a parallel to the name in the Edomitish proper name יְעוּשׁ in Gen. xxxvi, 18.

[2] Dussaud et Macler, *Voyage archéol. au Safâ*, p. 77; Wuthnow, *Die semitischen Menschennamen*, p. 56.

[3] Ryckmans, *Noms propres*, i, 174; Hess, *Entzifferung*, Nos. 46, 67.

[4] So Torrey, *Foundation*, 52.

at an early date. The prevalent theory is that it is derived from Gk. εἰκών through the Aramaic.[1] εἰκών means *image, likeness, similitude*, and from εἰκόνα were borrowed the Aram. יקונא[2]; Syr. ܨܘܪܬܐ meaning *image, picture.* From ܨܘܪܬܐ was formed a verb ܢܩܫ to *depict, describe*, whence ܡܨܘܪܢܐ and ܡܨܘܪܢܝܐ mean *characteristic.* From some dialectal form of ܨܘܪܬܐ the word must have passed into Arabic.

يَمّ (*Yamm*).

vii, 132; xx, 39, 81, 97; xxviii, 6, 40; li, 40.

Sea, flood, river.

It is used only in the Moses story, and refers sometimes to the Nile, sometimes to the sea. It was early recognized as foreign (Siddiqi, *Studien*, 13),[3] though the early authorities were uncertain of its origin. al-Jawālīqī, *Mu'arrab*, 156, says it is Syriac, which was also the opinion of Ibn Qutaiba,[4] according to as-Suyūṭī, *Itq*, 326. as-Suyūṭī, however, also tells us that Ibn al-Jawzī said it was Hebrew and Shaidala that it was Coptic.[5]

It apparently came to Arabic from Syriac ܝܡܐ, as Fraenkel, *Vocab*, 21, saw,[6] though it may possibly have come into Arabic from some primitive non-Semitic source. The word clearly is not Semitic, for Heb. יָם; Phon. ים; Aram. ימא; and Ras Shamra ים cannot be explained from Semitic material, and the word is a loan-word in Egyptian *jm*; Coptic ⲓⲁⲙ, ⲓⲟⲙ, or ⲉⲓⲟⲙ, and in Akk. *iamu*. As the word occurs in the old poetry and was an early borrowing we cannot be absolutely sure that it was not primitive, having come into Arabic, as into the other Semitic languages, from some autochthonous source.

يَهُود (*Yahūd*).

ii, 107, 114; iii, 60; v, 21, 56, 69, 85; ix, 30.

The Jews.

[1] Fraenkel, *Fremdw*, 273; Vollers, *ZDMG*, l, 617; li, 305, who depend, however, on a suggestion of Noldeke.

[2] Beside the much more common איקונין from εἰκόνιον.

[3] Cf. as-Suyūṭī, *Muzhir*, i, 130, and *LA*, xvi, 134.

[4] *Adab al-Kātib*, 527.

[5] *Mutaw*, 55, 57.

[6] So Fraenkel, *Fremdw*, 231, quoting Nöldeke, and cf. Guidi, *Delle Sede*, 573.

We also find the form هود in ii, 105, 129, 134, and the denominative verb هاد, ii, 59; iv, 48, etc.

The philologers recognized it as a foreign word, though they were uncertain whether to derive it from Hebrew[1] or Persian.[2] It is curious that anyone should have sought for a Persian origin, and yet Addai Sher, 158, accepts the theory, claiming that هاد, يهود, هَوْدًا, with the meaning of رجع الى الحق is from the Pers. هوده. It is true that in *Šāyast-ne-šāyast*, vi, 7, we find Phlv. [Pahlavi] *Yahūt*,[3] and in Avestic the form [Avestan] *Yahūd*, but these, like the *čaχūd* of the Christian Soghdian texts (cf. Jansen's "Wörterverzeichnis" to F. W. K. Müller's *Soghdische Texte*, p. 93), are obviously derived from the Aramaic.

Hirschfeld, *New Researches*, 27, thinks that Muḥammad's use of the verb هاد shows that he got the word from Jewish Aramaic sources,[4] and not understanding it perfectly, gave it an Arabic etymology by connecting it with the root هاد to *repent*, which is the reason for the form هود beside يهود. The fatal objection to this theory, however, is that we find the form يهودى in the old poetry,[5] so that it would have been well known in Arabia before Muḥammad's day. Horovitz points out that in the Qur'ān يهود always means the Jews of Muḥammad's day, the Jews of antiquity being referred to as Banū Isrāīl.

The word 𐩺𐩠𐩵 occurs in the S. Arabian inscriptions (Glaser, 394/5),[6] and Grimme, *ZA*, xxvi, 161, suggests that it came to the Ḥijāz from the South, which is very possible, though the ultimate origin, of course, will be the Jewish יהודי.

[1] al-Jawālīqī, *Mu'arrab*, 157; as-Suyūṭī, *Itq*, 326; al-Khafājī, 216.

[2] as-Suyūṭī, *Mutaw*, 47.

[3] Salemann, *Manichaeische Studien*, i, 87, and the Paz. *Zuhud* in Shikand, *Glossary*. Cf. also Henning, *Manichaica*, iii, 66.

[4] So also p. 104; *Beiträge*, 15 ff.; Pautz, *Offenbarung*, 121; Grünbaum, *ZDMG*, xl, 285; Horovitz, *KU*, 154; Geiger, 113.

[5] Imru'l-Qais, xl, 7 (Ahlwardt, *Divans*, p. 141), and see Margoliouth, *Schweich Lectures*, 79.

[6] See Ryckmans, *Noms propres*, i, 231, 299.

يُوسُفُ (*Yūsuf*).

Occurs twenty-two times in Sūra xii, elsewhere only in vi, 84, and xl, 36.

Joseph.

The early authorities differed as to whether it was an Arabic word derived from أَسِفَ or a borrowing from Hebrew (ath-Tha'labī, *Qiṣaṣ*, 75). Zam. on xii, 4, in his usual vigorous style combats the theory of an Arabic origin, and al-Jawālīqī, *Mu'arrab*, 155, also notes it as foreign.[1]

Geiger, 141, and Sycz, *Eigennamen*, 26, 27, would take it as a direct borrowing from the Heb. יוֹסֵף, but the Syr. ܝܘܣܦ or Eth. ዮሴፍ might equally well have been the source. Grimme, *ZA*, xxvi, 166, on the ground that in N. Arabia we should expect a form *Yūsif* rather than *Yūsuf*, would have the name derived from S. Arabia. If the Muslim legends about Dhū Nawās can be trusted, the name يوسف would have been known in S. Arabia, for they tell us that his name was يوسف بن شرحبيل. The name, however, appears to have been known also in the N., for we find a Yūsuf b. 'Abdallah b. Salām in *Usd al Ghāba*, v, 132.[2] One suspects that the name came from Jewish sources rather than Christian.

يُونُسُ (*Yūnus*).

iv, 161 ; vi, 86 ; x, 98 ; xxxvii, 139.

Jonah.

He is also referred to as صاحب الحوت in lxviii, 48, and as ذو النون in xxi, 87.

Some early authorities endeavoured to derive it from آنس, but Zam. on xii, 4, vigorously combats the view that the variant readings يُونَس and يُونِس given by Jawharī, s.v. أنس, provide any ground for such a derivation, and al-Jawālīqī, *Mu'arrab*, 155 ; al-Khafājī, 215, give it as foreign.

[1] So al-Khafājī, 215, and see Sprenger, *Leben*, ii, 336.

[2] Horovitz, *KU*, 154.

The form of the word is conclusive evidence that it came to Muḥammad from Christian sources.[1] The Heb. יונה becomes Ἰωνᾶς in the LXX and N.T., and Sprenger would derive the Arabic form directly from the Greek.[2] This is hardly likely, however, from what we know of the passage of Biblical names into Arabic, and as a matter of fact we find the final س both in the Eth. ዮናስ and in the Christian-Palestinian ܝܘܢܣ,[3] which occurs regularly for the Edessene ܝܘܢܐ or ܝܘܢܢ. Grimme, *ZA*, xxvi, 166, thinks that in N. Arabia we would expect a form *Yūnas* and that *Yūnus* is due to S. Arabian influence, but there is as little to this as to his similar theory of *Yūsif* and *Yūsuf*. The fact that the Arm. Յովնան is from Syr.,[4] though from the classical dialect, would lead us to conclude that the Qur'ānic form also came from Syriac.

The name was possibly known among the pre-Islamic Arabs, though the examples collected from the literature are doubtful.[5]

[1] This is admitted even by Hirschfeld, *Beiträge*, 56. See also Sycz, *Eigennamen*, 48; Horovitz, *KU*, 155; Mingana, *Syriac Influence*, 83; Rudolph, *Abhängigkeit*, 47.

[2] *Leben*, ii, 32, and Margoliouth, *ERE*, x, 540.

[3] Schulthess, *Lex*, 82; *Christ. Palast. Fragments* (1905), p. 122.

[4] Hübschmann, *Arm. Gramm.*, i, 295.

[5] Passages in Cheikho, *Naṣrānīya*, 234, 275, 276; and see Horovitz, *KU*, 155; *JPN*, 170.

ADDENDA

p. 32, line 3.—Unless the Nabataean اريا is intended to represent the Aram. אריא; Syr. ܐܪܝܐ (cf. Heb. ארי : אריה : Eth. አርዮ).

p. 94, line 8.—Akk. *u-dun-tum.* Rather *atūnu* from Sumerian *udūna*: cf. Brockelmann, *Lexicon Syriacum*, 55 b.

p. 121, line 7.—It is possible that the Heb. חותם, Aram. חתמא, ܚܬܡܐ are borrowed words, and an Egyptian origin has been suggested (*ZDMG*, xliv, 685; xlvi, 117).

p. 123, line 5.—ܓܢܘܐ. *PSm.* 751 gives this as the form in Mandaean: the normal Syriac form is ܓܘܐ (*PSm.* 696).

p. 179, line 9.—מַגָּל. The *nūn* must have been pronounced originally in this word, as it is from נגל. See on it Fraenkel, *Fremdw.* 133.

p. 186, n. 1.—Both the noun and the verb are found in this technical sense in the old poetry: cf. al-A'shā, *Dīwān* (ed. Geyer), lxvi, 9.

INDICES

Phoenician

Ras Shamra

Moabitish

Aramaic

Syriac

Mandæan

Nabatæan

Palmyrene

Safaite

Thamudic

S. Arabian

Ethiopic

Baluchi

Old Persian

Avestic

Pazand

Pahlavi

Parthian

Persian

Armenian

Greek

Soghdian

Ossetian

Kurdish

Turfan

Old Turkish

Latin

Afghan

Turkish

Turki

Norse

Slavonic

Edomitish